VBScript &ActiveX
WIZARDRY

VBScript & ActiveX WIZARDRY

Scott Palmer

CORIOLIS GROUP BOOKS

PUBLISHER	KEITH WEISKAMP
PROJECT EDITOR	RON PRONK
COVER DESIGN	ANTHONY STOCK
COVER ARTIST	GARY SMITH
INTERIOR DESIGN	MICHELLE STROUP
PRODUCTION	ROB MAUHAR
PROOFREADER	GWEN HENSON
INDEXER	DIANE GREEN COOK

The Coriolis Group
7339 E. Acoma Drive, Suite 7
Scottsdale, AZ 85260
Phone: (602) 483-0192
Fax: (602) 483-0193
Web address: www.coriolis.com

1-57610-052-9 : $39.99

Printed in the United States of America

10 9 8 7 6 5 4 3 2 1

Dedicated to Beth Demain—a true friend.
I'm lucky to know her.

Acknowledgments

Though my name is on the cover, *VBScript And ActiveX Wizardry* was very much a team effort. First and foremost, I'd like to thank Project Editor Ron Pronk for his help, encouragement, and sage counsel. I'm also grateful to Keith Weiskamp, president of The Coriolis Group, for giving me the opportunity to write this book. Jeff Duntemann, vice president of The Coriolis Group, remains one of my literary inspirations, if a computer book can in any sense be considered "literary."

I'd also like to thank Rob Mauhar, who did the layout; Gwen Hensen, who proofread the pages; Diane Cook, who prepared the index; and Tony Stock, who—as always—created a dazzling cover design.

No acknowledgments page would be complete without thanks to my agent, Connie Clausen, who is at once my business associate, tutor, friend, and taskmaster.

As always, my family and friends were a great help and patiently endured the inevitable tribulations of a book project.

CONTENTS

Chapter x Client-Side Data Validation 199

Chapter xi An ActiveX Miscellany 241

Chapter xii Images, Video, And Sound 265

Chapter xiii A VBScript And ActiveX FAQ 279

Chapter xiv   A Wizardly Web Game   285

Chapter xv   Writing CGI Programs With Visual Basic   321

INTRODUCTION

In the beginning, there was HTML. No, that's not quite right.

In the beginning—at least, in the beginning of the Internet—there was an almost impossibly confusing melange of protocols, each with its own commands and picky little syntax rules. You used different commands to use FTP, Gopher, mail, news, and all the other things people were trying to do over the Internet. Heaven help you if you misplaced a comma or used the wrong kind of quote mark in a command line. Even for Internet junkies, it could be frustrating.

Then came HTML, and with HTML came the Web. The bizarre jungle of Internet commands and protocols suddenly had a friendly, graphical face. Users no longer needed to remember the syntax for dozens of different commands. And with the advent of Web search engines, users no longer needed to remember complex Internet addresses for all their favorite sites.

But even HTML had its shortcomings. Yes, it created an Internet environment—the World Wide Web—that was vastly easier to use than before. What it didn't do, however, was let you create Web pages that were truly "active" on their own. About the most a Web page could do was to display simple text and graphics, play a sound, or send some data to a Web server for processing. It couldn't process data or respond to user events by itself.

It's only in the last year that the situation has changed. Java and JavaScript enabled Web page creators to bundle new, more active features into their HTML documents. Both offer new power—but at a price. The price is that you have to learn a subset of the C++ programming language, which is more difficult and more work than many people want.

Enter Microsoft. With its new Visual Basic Script language, it combines the Web page scripting power of JavaScript with the ease and familiarity of Visual Basic—the easiest and most popular programming language in the world. With

ActiveX controls, it allows you to use the same technology for Web and non-Web programs. And with the ActiveX Control Pad, it lets you create visual Web page layouts that include ActiveX controls and Visual Basic Script code.

That's where you come in. And that's where this book can help you.

Why This Book Is For You

This book is your guide to learning Visual Basic Script (VBScript) and how it works with ActiveX controls. Complete with tips and little-known techniques, it teaches you:

☆   How to embed VBScript code in your Web pages

☆   How to write code in the VBScript language

☆   How to avoid the pitfalls of VBScript programming

☆   How to use ActiveX controls with VBScript

☆   How to create ActiveX Web page layouts with the ActiveX Control Pad

☆   How to use the most important ActiveX controls with VBScript

☆   How to make VBScript work together with CGI programs on a Web server

☆   How to create Web server CGI programs in Visual Basic

☆   How to move non-Web Visual Basic programs to the Web with VBScript

Because VBScript is a subset of Microsoft's Visual Basic, we assume that you've already had some exposure to Visual Basic itself. If you need to learn the basics of Visual Basic, check out *The Visual Basic Programming EXplorer* by Peter Aitken (Coriolis Group Books, 1996).

How To Use This Book

There are two ways you can use this book. First, if you're completely new to VBScript, you can read it "front to back" for a tutorial that will cover all the important aspects of creating Web programs in Visual Basic Script. Second, if you're already using VBScript, you can dip into it here and there, picking up tricks and techniques as you need them.

The best way to *learn* VBScript with this book is to examine the program code and follow the detailed explanations of how it works—then try the techniques on your own. As for ActiveX layouts, we've included the HTML code to show you how the ActiveX object tags work together with VBScript. If you want to use the ActiveX layouts from the book, the best way is simply to get them from the appropriate chapter directory on the book's accompanying CD-ROM. Typing in the code by hand is a tremendous waste of time. To create a new ActiveX layout, of course, the best way is to use the ActiveX Control Pad, which you can download from Microsoft's Web site at **www.microsoft.com/intdev/**.

A Note About ActiveX Layouts

There's one important note about the code printed in this book. When you create a Web page that uses an ActiveX layout, you're actually creating *two* HTML documents: first, the ActiveX layout itself, and second, a Web page document that contains the layout.

This second document "contains" the ActiveX layout by including an **<object>** tag for Microsoft's HTML Layout control, which is an ActiveX control itself. And if the ActiveX layout isn't in the same directory as the containing HTML file, the **<object>** tag for the HTML Layout control has to include the disk directory path of the ActiveX layout.

As a result, one or two of the code listings in this book might not work "as is" because their HTML Layout control **<object>** tags refer to specific directories on *my* hard disk. All the VBScript code, HTML code, and ActiveX layouts have been tested with the final release of Internet Explorer, so if something doesn't work, simply use the ActiveX Control Pad to "reinstall" the ActiveX layout's **<object>** tag in the containing HTML document. When you set up your own Web pages with ActiveX layouts on your Web site, you'll do the same thing to adjust the directory paths.

So let's get started! VBScript is powerful, fun, and easy to use. In no time, you'll be creating Web pages that talk to the user, display video, take orders for products...or just play some cool games. The only limit is your imagination.

1

WHAT IS
VISUAL BASIC
SCRIPT?

Visual Basic Script isn't
exactly Visual Basic,
but it's pretty close.
And once you know
how it differs, you can
use it to make your
Web pages jump!

If you've only been following the news casually—glancing at *InfoWorld* while shaving your cat, or catching Microsoft sound bites during the hockey play-offs—you might think that Visual Basic Script (VBScript, for short) is a visual development environment much like Visual Basic itself. In that environment, you'd develop your Web pages by the following process:

1. Draw the Web page on your PC screen, using visual tools provided with the VBScript product.
2. Using the mouse, position controls from a toolbox on the Web page. The toolbox would be just like the one provided with Visual Basic, except that the controls would be designed for Web pages instead of regular PC programs.
3. Write Visual Basic "engine code" that interacts with the controls, getting data from the user, doing calculations, and returning results—whether as more data or as multimedia events such as graphics, animation, and sound.

That's a pretty reasonable guess, and as Meatloaf once said, "two out of three ain't bad." But it's a little off the mark. You do use controls, and you do write code. After that, the similarity to Visual Basic gets a little tricky.

What VBScript Is—And Isn't

The process of developing a Web page with VBScript is significantly different from that of developing a program with Visual Basic. To develop a program with Visual Basic, you need know only Visual Basic itself. That's because you do everything inside the Visual Basic development environment.

VBScript, however, isn't a user product like Visual Basic. Instead, it's an interpreter that can be incorporated into a Web browser. A Web browser equipped with the interpreter can run VBScript mini-programs that are embedded in Web pages. Microsoft's Internet Explorer 3.0 includes a VBScript interpreter, and Microsoft—intent on winning people away from JavaScript, a rival Web page scripting language that's already entrenched—is making it easy for other Web browsers to use VBScript, too.

If VBScript isn't a development environment, then what is it? That's already implied: It's a language for writing mini-programs that you embed in your Web pages. It's a lot like a stripped-down version of regular Visual Basic. Variables are declared in the same way, the same control structures are used (**if...endif, select** case, and so on), and you write subs and functions in pretty much the same way. If you already know Visual Basic, then writing VBScript code will be instantly familiar. The two things that won't be familiar from Visual Basic are:

☆ The way you create Web pages

☆ The way you insert controls such as buttons and text boxes into those pages

Because VBScript is just a scripting language, it won't by itself suffice to create any Web pages. You need two other elements: HTML and ActiveX controls.

Where to learn more about Visual Basic.
This book teaches you about VBScript, not about Visual Basic proper. If you need a quick, fun introduction to Visual Basic programming, check out The Visual Basic 4 Programming Explorer (Coriolis, 1995). For more advanced Visual Basic techniques—including some that are similar to wizardly tricks we'll do in this book—check out The Visual Basic 4 Multimedia Adventure Set (Coriolis, 1995).

Using HTML With VBScript

Love it or hate it, HTML is the language you'll use to create your Web pages. When you need to put explanatory text in one location, radio buttons in another, a list box, image file, and command buttons elsewhere on your Web page, you'll use HTML to do it. Unlike Visual Basic, VBScript doesn't do any of that for you.

At the same time, you should realize that in laying out your Web page with HTML, you aren't doing anything all that different from what you'd do in Visual Basic. It's just more bother because there's no visual draw-the-interface tool to help you along. If you've ever loaded a Visual Basic form file into a text editor, you saw the same kind of fiddly stuff that you write in HTML—just in Visual Basic. Figure 1.1 shows an example of a Visual Basic form, while Listing 1.1 shows you a bit of the code that Visual Basic generates behind the scenes to create that form.

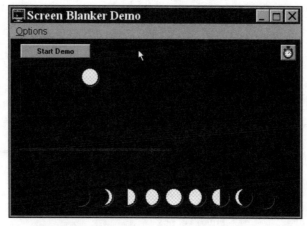

Figure 1.1 A form in Visual Basic.

Listing 1.1 Part of the code that creates the form in Figure 1.1.

```
Begin VB.Form DemoForm
    BackColor      =    &H00000000&
    Caption        =    "Screen Blanker Demo"
    ClientHeight   =    4425
    ClientLeft     =    960
    ClientTop      =    1965
    ClientWidth    =    7470
    BeginProperty Font
        name           =    "MS Sans Serif"
        charset        =    1
        weight         =    700
        size           =    8.25
        underline      =    0    'False
        italic         =    0    'False
        strikethrough  =    0    'False
    EndProperty
    ForeColor      =    &H00000000&
    Height         =    5115
    Icon           =    "BLANKER.frx":0000
    Left           =    900
    LinkMode       =    1    'Source
    LinkTopic      =    "Form1"
    ScaleHeight    =    4425
    ScaleWidth     =    7470
    Top            =    1335
    Width          =    7590

    Begin VB.Timer Timer1
        Interval       =    1
        Left           =    6960
        Top            =    120
    End
```

```
Begin VB.CommandButton cmdStartStop
    BackColor       =    &H00000000&
    Caption         =    "Start Demo"
    Default         =    -1   'True
    Height          =    390
    Left            =    240
    TabIndex        =    0
    Top             =    120
    Width           =    1830
End

Begin VB.PictureBox picBall
    AutoSize        =    -1   'True
    BackColor       =    &H00000000&
    BorderStyle     =    0    'None
    ForeColor       =    &H00FFFFFF&
    Height          =    480
    Left            =    1800
    Picture         =    "BLANKER.frx":030A
    ScaleHeight     =    480
    ScaleWidth      =    480
    TabIndex        =    1
    Top             =    720
    Visible         =    0      'False
    Width           =    480
End
```

Just as in an HTML file, the code in Listing 1.1 first sets up the form (page) itself, including the title. Then, it sets about defining various controls and where they will be placed on the form.

HTML And VBScript: A Simple Example

To see the continuity between Visual Basic proper and VBScript with HTML, let's look at a couple of examples. At this point, don't worry too much about the details of the code. We'll go into all that later on in the book. Here, just start to get a feeling for how VBScript fits into HTML code.

The first example we'll look at is a generic "Hello, world" script. Yes, I know: snooze city. I've spiced it up a little, if you want to call it that, by using a little dialect from the wonderful novel *Christy*, by Catherine Marshall. Instead of saying "hello," this script will "swap howdys" with the user of the Web page. The HTML document that includes the script is shown in Listing 1.2. The Web page it generates (in Microsoft's Internet Explorer 3.0) is shown in Figure 1.2, and the message box displayed by the script is shown in Figure 1.3.

Listing 1.2   A simple HTML document with a VBScript script.

```
<html>
<head>
<title>How VBScript Fits Into an HTML Document</title>
</head>

<body>
<font size=5>

<center>
<h1>Using VBScript in an HTML document</h1>
</center>
<p>
<p>In HTML, you define the Web page, including any controls
that the page should contain. Then, in VBScript, you can
define how those controls should respond to various events.</p>
<p>In this case, you use HTML to define a button. Then, you
use VBScript to tell Internet Explorer how it should react
when the user clicks the button: It should display a message
box saying "Hello, VBScript wizard-to-be!"</p>
<br><br>
<center>
<input type=button value="Swap Howdys" name="Btn_HelloWorld">
</center>

<script language="vbscript">
<!--
'
' Notice that comments inside the script
' use Visual Basic comment notation instead
' of HTML comment notation.
'
    Sub Btn_HelloWorld_OnClick
        MsgBox "Hello, VBScript wizard-to-be!",0,"VBScript Example"
    End Sub
-->
</script>
</body>
</html>
```

Listing 1.2 and the Web page it generates are still pretty simple stuff. As I said before, we'll get into the details of how to write VBScript code in the chapters that follow. But for now, just look at how the VBScript code fits into the HTML document. First, we've got all the usual HTML tags—beginning the document, doing a little formatting, and displaying a button.

Once that's out of the way, we see our first bit of VBScript. We use the HTML script tag to indicate the beginning of the script and the language it will use. Then, inside HTML comment tags, we insert the script code itself.

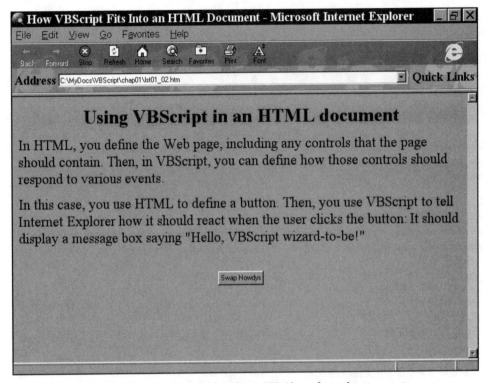

Figure 1.2 The Web page created by the HTML code in Listing 1.2.

 Always put your script inside HTML comment tags.
It bears repeating: Always put your VBScript code inside HTML comment tags. That way, browsers that do not support VBScript as a scripting language will simply ignore it. Otherwise, such a non-VBScript browser will most likely display the code on the Web page, as some non-JavaScript browsers do even now.

Figure 1.3 The message box displayed by the VBScript code in Listing 1.2.

Inside the HTML comment tags, we're in the VBScript world, so regular Visual Basic comment syntax applies: When you start a line with an apostrophe or the word **rem**, the line is ignored by the VBScript interpreter. And because it's already inside the HTML comment tags, it's also ignored by the Web browser.

In this particular script, all we've done is to define an event procedure for the input button specified in the HTML code. When the user clicks on the button, the code inside the event procedure will be executed.

The event procedure is the only thing in this particular script, so after that, we close the script with a closing HTML comment tag, then the script-ending tag **</script>**. Presto! We're done.

HTML And VBScript: A More Interesting Example

Perhaps we can at least make the Web page do something a little more interesting. Instead of simply saying a generic "howdy," let's make it prompt the user for his or her name, then incorporate that name into the "howdy" greeting. That sounds a little more like a real program. Listing 1.3 shows the HTML document with embedded VBScript code to do just that. Figure 1.4 shows the Web page created by the code in Listing 1.3.

Listing 1.3   Prompting the user for his/her name.

```
<html>
<head>
<title>How VBScript Fits Into an HTML Document</title>
</head>

<body>
<font size=5>

<center>
<h1>A Little More You Can Do with VBScript</h1>
</center>
<p>
<p>This shows a little more of what you can do with VBScript.
In Listing 1.2, clicking the button just gave a generic Hello
message. In this listing, the user enters his/her name, then
the VBScript mini-program assigns the name text to a variable
and uses the name in the Hello message!</p>
<p>Sure, it's not rocket science--yet--but it gives you a
taste of what's to come: Web pages that interact with the user
in ways previously undreamt of!</p>
```

```
<p>
<p>
<p>
<center>
<br><br>
<p>Enter your first name:</p>
<input type=text value="" align=left name="TB_UserName">
<p>
<input type=button value="Swap Howdys" name="Btn_HelloWorld">
</center>

<script language="VBScript">
<!--
'
' Notice that comments inside the script
' use Visual Basic comment notation instead
' of HTML comment notation.
'
     dim UserName ' declare variable to hold user's name

     Sub Btn_HelloWorld_OnClick
          UserName = TB_UserName.value
          MsgBox "Howdy, " & Username & "!",0,"VBScript Example"
     End Sub
-->
</script>
</body>
</html>
```

This Web page is a little more fun than the generic "howdy" page. It contains a text box in which the user can enter his or her name. Once the name is entered, clicking on the command button activates the *HelloWorld_OnClick* event procedure.

If you look at the VBScript code, you'll see that just above the event procedure, we declared (**dim**ensioned) a variable to hold the name from the text box created by the HTML code. The idea of using a **dim** statement to declare a variable is familiar to all Visual Basic programmers. What's less familiar is that, unlike Visual Basic, VBScript has only one data type: the all-purpose **variant** data type that can handle anything you throw at it. That's why the **dim** statement doesn't declare the variable *as* any particular data type.

Once the variable is declared, the rest is easy. When the user clicks on the button control, its **OnClick** event fires, causing the event procedure to execute. Inside the event procedure, VBScript assigns the text control's **value** property to the **UserName** variable. Then, it uses the VBScript **MsgBox** statement to display the "howdy" message and glom it together with the **UserName** variable. The result is shown in Figure 1.5.

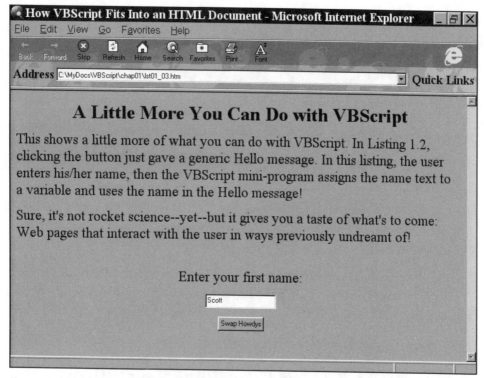

Figure 1.4   The Web page created by the HTML code in Listing 1.3.

The rest of the listing proceeds exactly as before. The end-of-comment mark terminates the comment containing the VBScript code, the **</script>** tag formally ends the script, and the **</body>** and **</html>** tags terminate the document body and the HTML document, respectively.

HTML And VBScript: The Bottom Line

The bottom line is this: *You must know HTML if you're going to use Visual Basic Script.* In order to work, your VBScript mini-programs will need to be in an HTML document that includes appropriate ActiveX controls or other kinds of

Figure 1.5   The message box displayed by the VBScript code in Listing 1.3, assuming that your name is "Scott."

applets. If you have no HTML, you have no Web page. If you have no Web page, VBScript can't do a thing.

Note: If you're new to Web page development, you might be confused by the word *script*. Very often, you'll hear people talk about *CGI scripts*. Those are programs on a Web server that can create new Web pages in response to user input. CGI scripts can be written in a variety of languages, including Visual Basic, as we'll see later in this book. However, CGI scripts are a completely different kind of script from those you'll be creating with VBScript. Don't confuse the two.

If you need to get up to speed on HTML, there are several excellent books on the subject. One of the best is *NetScape 2 and HTML Wizardry* (Coriolis, 1996). Another is *Serving the Web* (Coriolis, 1996), which also contains a superb explanation of CGI scripts.

Although Microsoft stays pretty close to the HTML standard, Microsoft's Internet Explorer has its own set of HTML extensions. You can find out about Explorer's HTML extensions at Microsoft's Web site, http://www.microsoft.com.

If you really, really don't want to mess with HTML…

If you really, really don't want to mess with HTML, there is an alternative. Microsoft's "Front Page" Web design package allows you to visually lay out your Web pages, much as you'd lay out a form in Visual Basic. It's fast, easy, and powerful. It's also pretty expensive—at this writing, $140—but well worth the money. If you're a little less HTML-phobic, an excellent and much cheaper alternative (around $50) is Sausage Software's "HotDog" Web editor, deservedly one of the most popular Web page editors in the world.

Apart from the fact that Front Page includes a standalone Web server so that you can test entire networks of Web pages, the main difference between Front Page and HotDog is that Front Page insulates you almost completely from the HTML code: Everything is visual. HotDog, on the other hand, sports toolbar buttons that insert HTML tags for you, making it unnecessary for you to type them or remember their exact syntax. Neither can do anything for you that you can't do on your own, but they both make your life as a Web author much easier.

VBScript And ActiveX Controls

If VBScript is just a language, and includes neither a development environment nor controls like those in Visual Basic, then where do you get the controls to use with your VBScript mini-programs?

The answer is that you use ActiveX controls. "ActiveX" is just Microsoft's new name for Internet-ready OCX controls. Some controls are included with Internet Explorer itself, as follows:

☆ **Intrinsic.** These are controls such as command buttons, list boxes, radio buttons, check boxes, and text boxes.

☆ **Chart.** This is a versatile control that lets you create line graphs, bar charts, area charts, and many other types of chart.

☆ **Label.** This is a clickable text label that can display text at any angle.

☆ **New item.** This is a time-sensitive label that marks a particular line of your Web page as "New!" and then, obligingly, disappears on a date you specify.

☆ **Preloader.** This downloads the contents of a Web address and lets you speed up certain types of page and image display.

☆ **Timer.** This is very much like the Timer control used in Visual Basic. It fires an event at intervals you specify, causing an event procedure to execute.

☆ **ActiveVRML.** This can be used to display interactive 3D animations.

Other ActiveX controls are available from Microsoft and third-party vendors. You insert an ActiveX control by using the HTML **<object>** tag, then call it in your VBScript code in much the same way as you saw in Listings 1.2 and 1.3. You'll see many examples of how to use ActiveX controls as you progress through this book.

Where To From Here?

In the chapters that follow, you'll learn all about VBScript and what you can do with it—from the basic stuff to the truly wizardly! So if you need to review HTML or Visual Basic, go to the restroom, or get a snack, do it now: It's going to be a fast ride.

11

YOUR FIRST
VBSCRIPT
PROGRAM

Ready to get down and dirty? More fun than a Jello jump, safer than dissing your mother-in-law, VBScript lets you power up Web pages with surprising ease. In this chapter, you'll create programs that show you all the basics.

In the previous chapter, we were looking at the "big picture." There were a couple of short VBScript programs, but they weren't explained in any detail. Now, we'll walk you through those programs so that you can see how they're put together and start creating your own.

Of course, this is a "Wizardry" book, even if we're in the beginning stages of working with VBScript. Therefore, later in the chapter, you'll get some simple wizardry about how to incorporate ActiveX controls into your Web pages and use them in your VBScript code. You'll be amazed by how easy it is.

The "Hello" Program

In Chapter 1, we started off with a version of the "Hello, World" program that has been in almost every programming book ever written. There's a reason, other than lack of imagination, why this example is so popular: it illustrates all the essential jobs a program has to do, but has no extraneous features to complicate things. For your convenience, it's reproduced in Listing 2.1. The resulting Web page is shown in Figure 2.1.

Listing 2.1   A simple HTML document with a VBScript script.

```
<html>
<head>
<title>How VBScript Fits Into an HTML Document</title>
</head>

<body>
<font size=5>

<center>
<h1>Using VBScript in an HTML document</h1>
</center>
<p>
<p>In HTML, you define the Web page, including any controls
that the page should contain. Then, in VBScript, you can
define how those controls should respond to various events.</p>
<p>In this case, you use HTML to define a button. Then, you
use VBScript to tell Internet Explorer how it should react
when the user clicks the button: it should display a message
box saying "Hello, VBScript wizard-to-be!"</p>
<br><br>
<center>
<input type=button value="Swap Howdys" name="Btn_HelloWorld">
</center>
```

```
<script language="vbscript">
<!--
'
' Notice that comments inside the script
' use Visual Basic comment notation instead
' of HTML comment notation.
'
    Sub Btn_HelloWorld_OnClick
        MsgBox "Hello, VBScript wizard-to-be!",0,"VBScript Example"
    End Sub
-->
</script>
</body>
</html>
```

In this case, of course, it's a little more complicated than most "Hello" examples because it has got all that HTML code in it, too. But it's still an excellent way to see the main features of a VBScript program. Let's examine the listing one feature at a time. We won't rehearse the intricacies of the HTML code except where they're relevant to VBScript.

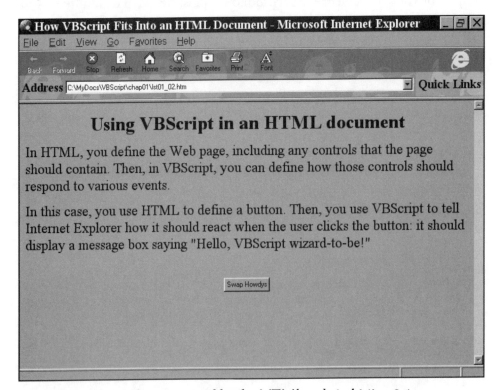

Figure 2.1　The Web page created by the HTML code in Listing 2.1.

The <Script> Tag

The first thing to notice is that the whole section of VBScript code is surrounded by the HTML tags that mark the beginning and end of a script. **<script>** marks the beginning, and (as you might expect) **</script>** marks the end.

Don't forget the </script> tag!
If you can load your HTML document into your Web browser, but nothing much seems to happen—not even an error message—then make sure that you've remembered to end the script with a **</script>** tag. Failure to do so will lead to unpredictable consequences, but one possible result is that you see a blank Web page with absolutely nothing going on.

The Comment Delimiters

Inside the **<script>** .. **</script>** tags, you can also see that the entire script is enclosed inside HTML comment marks, as shown in the code snippet below.

```
<!--
   Sub Btn_HelloWorld_OnClick
       MsgBox "Hello, VBScript wizard-to-be!",0,"VBScript Example"
   End Sub
-->
```

The reason for enclosing the script inside comment marks is that some Web browsers don't yet support Visual Basic Script. When someone uses one of those browsers to load your Web page, the comment marks will keep the VBScript code from displaying on the page as normal text.

A few browsers don't recognize multiline comments.
The HTML comment marks themselves have been around for a while, but until the development of the HTML 3.0 standard, they could only be used for single-line comments—not

for multiline comments like a section of VBScript code. As a result, a few older browsers might not support multiline comments, and there's just no way to keep these browsers from displaying your VBScript code as regular text.

Program Comments In VBScript

Inside the script, you're no longer in HTML: you're in VBScript country now, pardner. As a result, you can use regular Visual Basic comment marks. There are two comment marks in Visual Basic, and both apply to single lines: unlike C, C++, Pascal, and HTML(!), Visual Basic and VBScript don't yet support multi-line comments.

Both comment marks are placed to the left of the comment. Another way of looking at the situation is that the VBScript interpreter will ignore anything on a line that is to the *right* of a comment mark. Acceptable VBScript comment marks are the apostrophe (') and the word **rem**, for "remark."

THE APOSTROPHE

You can place this at the beginning of a line, as in Listing 2.1, or in the middle of a line, to the right of some code. Often, you might use an apostrophe "in the middle" to explain a particular code line. Here's an example of each.

```
' The apostrophe at the beginning of the line.
MsgBox "Blah blah blah."  ' This starts in the middle.
```

THE WORD REM

Like the apostrophe, you can place this anywhere on a line. There's just one difference: if you put the **rem** comment mark in the middle of a line, it must be preceded by a colon. That tells the compiler that a **rem** comment is coming. Here's an example of each.

```
rem The remark at the beginning of the line.
MsgBox "Blah blah blah."  : rem This starts in the middle.
```

Note that Visual Basic and VBScript are generally not case-sensitive, so they treat **rem**, **REM**, **rEm**, and other upper/lower case variations as the same word.

A Sub Procedure

The word **sub** in VBScript refers to "subroutine," and is synonymous with "procedure." A sub (or procedure) is a named block of code that does something. And if you're not quite sure what *that* is, well, it's a bunch of code lines that you refer to by a single name, such as *Btn_HelloWorld_OnClick*. In Listing 2.1, you used a very simple sub:

```
Sub Btn_HelloWorld_OnClick
    MsgBox "Hello, VBScript wizard-to-be!",0,"VBScript Example"
End Sub
```

This is a block of code (three lines of VBScript) with a name (*Btn_HelloWorld_OnClick*) that does something (displays a message box on the user's PC screen). In this case, the name of the sub also tells you when it's activated: whenever the user clicks on the button with the name *Btn_HelloWorld*.

Note that there are basically two kinds of subs: ones that you write yourself, and ones that come built into VBScript (or Visual Basic). *Btn_HelloWorld_OnClick* is the kind of sub that you write yourself. But **MsgBox** is also a sub: it's one of the subs that is predefined in VBScript. Predefined subs are often called *statements*.

The MsgBox Statement

The **MsgBox** statement, as its name implies, simply displays a message box on the user's screen, as shown in Figure 2.2. Its code line, however, is just a little cluttered:

```
MsgBox "Hello, VBScript wizard-to-be!",0,"VBScript Example"
```

To display a message box, you first use the VBScript keyword **MsgBox**. Capitalization generally doesn't matter in VBScript, so **MsgBox** works just the same as **MsgBox** or **MsgBox**. Then, you can include several "parameters"—*i.e.,* values that you pass to the sub:

☆ A text string for the prompt to be displayed in the message box. Here, it's "Hello, VBScript wizard-to-be!"

Figure 2.2　The message box displayed by the Hello program in Listing 2.1.

☆ A number (or expression) indicating which buttons should be displayed in the message box, such as OK, Yes, No, and Cancel. If you don't specify a number, you need to include two commas to indicate that this parameter is left blank. In that case, VBScript assumes that the number is zero. However, each different kind of button (OK, Yes, Cancel, etc.) returns a different integer value to tell the program which button the user clicked. With the program in Listing 2.1, we haven't set up any way to catch the value, so there's not much point in fiddling with different buttons. We'll see how to do that later in the book.

☆ A text string for the title of the message box. In this case, it's "VBScript Example."

There are a couple of other optional parameters (helpfile and context), but they're less commonly used, so don't worry about them right now.

The parameters *must* be separated by commas. If you don't want to include a parameter, there are two possible cases.

☆ If you're omitting a parameter that would be the last one in the parameter list—i.e., you aren't including any more parameters to the right of it—then you can just omit the parameter and that's all you have to do.

☆ If you're omitting a parameter that *isn't* the last parameter in the list—i.e., you're including parameters that come after it—then you should put two commas to mark where you *would* have put the parameter you're omitting. This tells VBScript that you're leaving out that parameter. If we'd wanted to omit the button parameter in the message box code line (which we could have done, since it defaults to zero, anyway), it would have looked like the code line below.

```
MsgBox "Hello, VBScript wizard-to-be!",,"VBScript Example"
```

Different kinds of message boxes.

To avoid confusion, you should be aware (at least in the back of your mind) that there are two versions of MsgBox: the sub version, which you've just seen in action, and the function version, which you haven't seen yet. We'll explain functions a little later in the chapter. But if you see a MsgBox statement that looks a little odd, chances are it's the MsgBox function instead of the sub.

Adding A Variable To The Hello Program

And now for something that's not *completely* different, but different enough to have a point. In the second version of our Hello program, we prompted the user for his/her name and then displayed the name in the message box. That required a couple of new tricks that you'll use again and again in your VBScript programming. For your convenience, Listing 2.2 reproduces the code for the Web page with the modified Hello program.

Listing 2.2 Prompting the user for his/her name.

```
<html>
<head>
<title>How VBScript Fits Into an HTML Document</title>
</head>

<body>
<font size=5>

<center>
<h1>A Little More You Can Do with VBScript</h1>
</center>
<p>
<p>This shows a little more of what you can do with VBScript.
In Listing 2.1, clicking the button just gave a generic Hello
message. In this listing, the user enters his/her name, then
the VBScript mini-program assigns the name text to a variable
and uses the name in the Hello message!</p>
<p>Sure, it's not rocket science--yet--but it gives you a
taste of what's to come: Web pages that interact with the user
in ways previously undreamt of!</p>
<p>
<p>
<p>
<center>
<br><br>
<p>Enter your first name:</p>
<input type=text value="" align=left name="TB_UserName">
<p>
<input type=button value="Swap Howdys" name="Btn_HelloWorld">
</center>

<script language="VBScript">
<!--
'
' Notice that comments inside the script
' use Visual Basic comment notation instead
```

```
' of HTML comment notation.
'
    dim UserName ' declare variable to hold user's name

    Sub Btn_HelloWorld_OnClick
        UserName = TB_UserName.value
        MsgBox "Howdy, " & Username & "!",0,"VBScript Example"
    End Sub
-->
</script>
</body>
</html>
```

The differences between this and Listing 2.1 are small but significant. First, in the HTML code, we provide a text box where the user can type his/her name. Second, in the VBScript code, we define and use a variable to hold the name. Third, we use the ampersand (&) to string together the user's name and some other text in the message box. Let's look at each of these changes in turn.

Adding A Text Box

We won't spend too much time on this, inasmuch as it's HTML rather than VBScript per se. The relevant HTML code is shown in the code snippet below.

```
<center>
<br><br>
<p>Enter your first name:</p>
<input type=text value="" align=left name="TB_UserName">
<p>
<input type=button value="Swap Howdys" name="Btn_HelloWorld">
</center>
```

After inserting a couple of line breaks to separate the text box from what's above it, we first put in a text prompt that tells the user what the text box is for: "Enter your first name." Then, we use the HTML **<input>** tag to insert the text box, setting the type to **text** (hence, it's a text box), the initial value to "" (blank), and the name to **TB_UserName** (for text box—user name). That's pretty much it.

Declaring A Variable

If you've done programming before, the concept of a variable will be familiar. What do you do when somebody hands you a rock, but you need to keep your hands free so you can do other things? Very simple: You find someplace to put the rock, such as a pocket or a little box. A variable is just like a little box where you can store things until you need them. In a computer program, those things are *values*—text strings, numbers, and so on.

With most programming languages—including "regular" Visual Basic—you need to use a different type of variable for each different type of value. If you create two text variables and store numbers in them, you can't then do arithmetic with the numbers. To do that, you need to create number-type variables and store the numbers in *them,* not in text-type variables.

In VBScript, however, you don't have to worry about that. You'll still deal with numbers, text, and other types of values, but to VBScript, they'll all be treated as a single type: the *variant* type. This is an all-purpose data type that VBScript inherits from Visual Basic: You can stick any kind of value in it and, on demand, convert it into the type you need. For practical purposes, you might even think of VBScript as considering all your variables to be text until and unless you tell it otherwise.

In Listing 2.2, we declare a variable by using the VBScript **dim** (for "dimension") statement.

```
dim UserName ' declare variable to hold user's name
```

To declare a variable, you simply use a **dim** statement, then the name of the variable. From that point on, whenever you need to refer to a value that's stored in the variable, you'll use the variable's name. Here, it's **UserName**. Remember, by the way, that VBScript generally doesn't pay any attention to capitalization: **UserName**, **USERNAME**, and **userNaMe** would all be treated as the same word.

A One-Line Comment Example

This code line also shows a typical use of a VBScript comment. After the **dim** statement, there's an apostrophe (comment mark) and a short explanation of what the code line does. This comment was included as an example. Normally, if the purpose of a code line is blindingly obvious, you don't need to write a comment explaining it.

Assigning A Value To The Variable

Once you've declared the variable in Listing 2.2, the next step is to give it a value. Assume that the user of your Web page has now typed his/her name into the text box, and clicked on the button. This fires the button's **OnClick** event, which in turn activates the **Btn_HelloWorld_OnClick** sub, shown in the code snippet below.

```
Sub Btn_HelloWorld_OnClick
    UserName = TB_UserName.value
    MsgBox "Howdy, " & Username & "!",0,"VBScript Example"
End Sub
```

Assigning a value to a variable is pretty simple stuff. You just construct a statement using the VBScript *assignment operator,* which is the equal sign (=). On the left side of the assignment operator, you put the name of the variable to which you'd like to assign a value. On the right side of the assignment operator, you put the value you'd like to assign. In this example, it's the value property of a text box, but it could be other things:

```
UserName = "Jim"                       ' assigns a text value
UserName = "Alicia" & "Silverstone"    ' joins two text values and assigns them
UserName = (5 + 3) - (87.75)           ' does arithmetic and assigns the result
UserName = AnotherVariableName         ' assigns the value in another variable
```

Remember that *UserName* is a variant type variable, so it can hold different types of values, even if some of them would be absurd or pointless in this case.

Using The Variable With The Message Box

The final step is to use the variable's value as part of the text in the message box. To do this, you use the ampersand to "concatenate" (glom together) the variable with the other text that will display in the message box, as shown in the code line below.

```
MsgBox "Howdy, " & Username & "!",0,"VBScript Example"
```

Remember that the first parameter after **MsgBox** is a text string for the text that will display in the message box. This doesn't need to be a "single" text string: You can use the ampersand to glom together several pieces of text into one big text string. That's what we've done in the above code line. The result is shown in Figure 2.3.

Figure 2.3   *The message box shows the glommed-together text.*

Using ActiveX Controls:
A Preview

In much the same manner as in Chapter 1, where we simply looked at an example to get a feel for it, but deferred a full explanation for later in the book, let's close this chapter with a look at how you'll use ActiveX controls in your VBScript programs.

You've probably heard the term "ActiveX" but aren't sure what it means. Well, join the club: Most of the world, including the techno-billionaires at Microsoft, is still trying to pin down exactly what it means. The short version, however, is this: An ActiveX control is a mini-mini-program that you can insert into a Web page and use in VBScript. It's like the command buttons, radio buttons, and list boxes you use in all your regular programs—in fact, those are some ActiveX controls you can use with VBScript!

In this example, we'll insert two ActiveX controls in an HTML document and use them in a VBScript program. The code is shown in Listing 2.3. The result is shown in Figure 2.4.

Listing 2.3   Using VBScript subs with ActiveX controls.

```
<HTML>
<HEAD>
<TITLE> A Slightly Hotter VBScript Example</TITLE>
</HEAD>
<BODY leftmargin=10 topmargin=30 bgcolor="white">

<OBJECT
    classid="clsid:99B42120-6EC7-11CF-A6C7-00AA00A47DD2"
        CODEBASE="c:\windows\system\ielabel.ocx"
    id=label1
    width=300
    height=100
    align=left
>
<param name="alignment" value="4" >
<param name="caption" value="0">
<param name="FontName" value="Arial">
<param name="FontSize" value="36">
</OBJECT>

<OBJECT
    ID=timer1
```

```
        CLASSID="CLSID:59CCB4A0-727D-11CF-AC36-00AA00A47DD2"
        codebase="c:\windows\system\ietimer.ocx"
        WIDTH=80
        HEIGHT=30 >
        <param name="Interval" value="1000">
        <param name="Enabled" value="False">
</OBJECT>

<br><br><br><br><br>
<FORM>
<input type=button value="Toggle the timer" align=middle name="Btn_Timer">
</FORM>

<script language="VBS">
<!--
    dim ClickNum

    sub timer1_timer
        ClickNum = ClickNum + 1
        label1.caption = ClickNum
    end sub

    sub Btn_Timer_OnClick
        ClickNum = 0
        label1.caption = ClickNum
        timer1.enabled = not timer1.enabled
    end sub
-->
</script>

</BODY>
</HTML>
```

What Happens Inside The ActiveX Example

We'll go into the full details of using ActiveX controls in Chapter 6. For now, however, let's take a look at the main features of Listing 2.3. It has two ActiveX controls: a label control, and a timer control.

The label control is inserted by using the HTML **<object>** tag, as shown in the code snippet below.

```
<OBJECT
    classid="clsid:99B42120-6EC7-11CF-A6C7-00AA00A47DD2"
        CODEBASE="c:\windows\system\ielabel.ocx"
    id=label1
    width=300
    height=100
    align=left
```

```
>
<param name="alignment" value="4" >
<param name="caption" value="0">
<param name="FontName" value="Arial">
<param name="FontSize" value="36">
</OBJECT>
```

Don't worry about the details, but notice a few things. First, when it's needed, the **codebase** line tells the Web browser the name of the ActiveX control and where to find it. Here, that's in the \Windows\System directory of my PC, but in a "live" Web site, it might be a URL address. Second, the **id** line specifies the name by which we'll refer to this control. Third, the **width, height,** and **align** lines specify the size and alignment of the label control on the Web page. Finally, four parameter lines specify various starting values for the control, such as the number it displays (0) when the user first loads the Web page.

The ActiveX timer control is inserted in the HTML document in exactly the same way, as shown in the code snippet below.

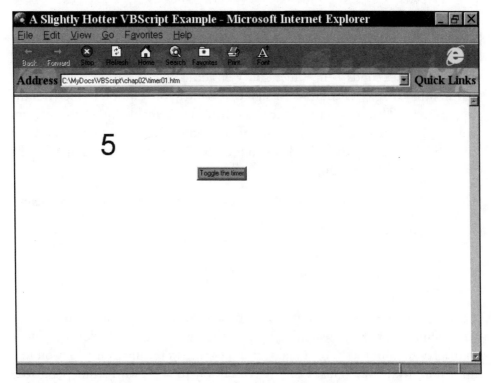

Figure 2.4 VBScript causes the ActiveX timer to update the text label.

```
<OBJECT
    ID=timer1
    CLASSID="CLSID:59CCB4A0-727D-11CF-AC36-00AA00A47DD2"
    codebase="c:\windows\system\ietimer.ocx"
    WIDTH=80
    HEIGHT=30 >
    <param name="Interval" value="1000">
    <param name="Enabled" value="False">
</OBJECT>
```

Pay attention, however, to the different parameters. For a timer, the "interval" specifies the number of milliseconds (thousandths of a second) between clicks of the timer. Each time the timer clicks, a timer event fires, and VBScript executes the **sub** procedure for the timer. And the "enabled" value specifies whether the timer is turned on or off. When it's off, it doesn't click. To get it to click, you must reset the enabled value to **true**.

Look at the **sub** procedure for the timer, shown in the code snippet below.

```
sub timer1_timer
    ClickNum = ClickNum + 1
    label1.caption = ClickNum
end sub
```

On each click of the timer—that's every second, since the interval was specified as 1,000 milliseconds—the timer sub will add 1 to the current value of the **ClickNum** variable. Then, it will assign that value to the caption property of the label control. This means that as long as the timer is enabled, the label control will display numbers in sequence, one after another: 1, 2, 3, 4, and so on. Each time the timer clicks, the sub adds 1 to the **ClickNum** variable and updates the caption of the label control.

Now, look at the code for the button control, shown in the code snippet below.

```
sub Btn_Timer_OnClick
    ClickNum = 0
    label1.caption = ClickNum
    timer1.enabled = not timer1.enabled
end sub
```

Each time the user clicks on the button, it does three things. First, it sets the value of **ClickNum** back to zero. Second, it updates the label control's caption, causing it to display the number zero. Finally, it either turns the timer on (if it's off) or turns it off (if it's on). This is a fairly typical way to work with a timer control.

Watch out for ENDIF.

If you've already done some programming in "regular" Visual Basic, you might have acquired the habit of terminating a multi-line **if** statement with the single word **endif**. However, you might not have paid attention to the fact that the Visual Basic development environment automatically parses that into **end if**. If you're writing a VBScript in a text editor or HTML editor and you type **endif** at the end of a multi-line **if** statement, it won't be changed to **end if**, and the VBScript interpreter will flag it as an error.

Adding A Function To The ActiveX Example

The previous example introduced you to ActiveX controls and gave you yet another chance to see VBScript sub procedures in action. But there's another kind of VBScript routine that's just as useful as subs, but significantly different: the *function*. Functions are like subs in that:

☆ They're named blocks of code.

☆ They can accept values and variables as parameters.

☆ They can have local variables declared inside them.

☆ They do processing and then pass control back to wherever they got it from in the first place.

☆ Some of them are already built into VBScript, but you can create your own for specialized jobs.

The main difference between functions and subs is their purpose: in a nutshell, subs *do program tasks* and functions *return values*. If you only use subs and ignore functions, you've lost much of the power of VBScript.

Let's modify the example in Listing 2.3 so that it uses a function in addition to the two subs. The function we'll create, admittedly, has no real purpose other than to show how functions work: It will check to see if the "click number" of the timer is greater than 9.

If the click number is greater than 9, then the sub for the timer event will start adding 5 instead of 1 to the **ClickNum** variable. As a result, the Web page label showing the click number will first increase by 1 on each click: 1, 2, 3, 4, and so on, until it gets to 10. Then, it will start increasing by 5 on each click: 15, 20, 25, and so on, until the user turns off the timer. The code is shown in Listing 2.4.

Listing 2.4   Adding a function to the ActiveX example.

```
<HTML>
<HEAD>
<TITLE> A VBScript Example Using Both Subs and Functions</TITLE>
</HEAD>
<BODY leftmargin=10 topmargin=30 bgcolor="white">

<OBJECT
    classid="clsid:99B42120-6EC7-11CF-A6C7-00AA00A47DD2"
        CODEBASE="c:\windows\system\ielabel.ocx"
    id=label1
    width=300
    height=100
    align=left
>
<param name="alignment" value="4" >
<param name="caption" value="0">
<param name="FontName" value="Arial">
<param name="FontSize" value="36">
</OBJECT>

<OBJECT
    ID=timer1
    CLASSID="CLSID:59CCB4A0-727D-11CF-AC36-00AA00A47DD2"
    codebase="c:\windows\system\ietimer.ocx"
    WIDTH=80
    HEIGHT=30 >
    <param name="Interval" value="1000">
    <param name="Enabled" value="False">
</OBJECT>

<br><br><br><br><br>
<FORM>
<input type=button value="Toggle the timer"
        align=middle name="Btn_Timer">
</FORM>

<script language="VBS">
<!--
    dim ClickNum

    function IsMoreThan9(TheNum)
        if TheNum > 9 then
            IsMoreThan9 = true
```

```
        else
            IsMoreThan9 = false
        end if
    end function

    sub timer1_timer
        if IsMoreThan9(ClickNum) then
            ClickNum = ClickNum + 5
        else
            ClickNum = ClickNum + 1
        end if
        label1.caption = ClickNum
    end sub

    sub Btn_Timer_OnClick
        ClickNum = 0
        label1.caption = ClickNum
        timer1.enabled = not timer1.enabled
    end sub

-->
</script>
</BODY>
</HTML>
```

This listing differs from the previous listing in two ways: First, we've added a function called **IsMoreThan9**(). Second, we've incorporated that function into the body of the timer event sub. Let's see how each of these changes works. The new function is shown in the following code snippet.

```
function IsMoreThan9(TheNum)
    if TheNum > 9 then
        IsMoreThan9 = true
    else
        IsMoreThan9 = false
    end if
end function
```

If you have any programming experience, this is pretty simple stuff. The function takes a single parameter, **TheNum**: The parameter is how we get the **ClickNum** variable inside the function. It's kind of a specialized doorway. Inside the function, an **if…else** statement checks to see if **TheNum** (the *nom de voyage* under which **ClickNum** is known inside the sub) is greater than 9. If it is, the **if** statement assigns the value **true** to the function. If any part of the program looks at the function, it will now see only the value **true** where the function is supposed to be.

On the other hand, if **TheNum** is less than or equal to 9, the **else** clause kicks in, and sets the function to a value of **false**. And if any part of the program looks at the function, it will see only the value **false**.

Now, let's see how the function is incorporated into the event sub for the timer. The code is shown in the following snippet.

```
sub timer1_timer
    if IsMoreThan9(ClickNum) then
        ClickNum = ClickNum + 5
    else
        ClickNum = ClickNum + 1
    end if
    label1.caption = ClickNum
end sub
```

Notice that although there were several lines of code *inside* the **IsMoreThan9()** function, the actual *use* of the function is baby simple. In the timer event code, the **if** clause passes a value to the **IsMoreThan9()** function—*i.e.,* the **ClickNum** variable. The function, using its internal code, looks at this value and determines if it's more than nine. If it's more than 9, the function tells the timer sub, "Yes, this value sure is more than nine"—in other words, it returns a value of **true** in the **if** clause.

We'll cover **if** clauses in more detail later in the book, but it should be obvious what's going on here. If **ClickNum**'s current value is more than 9—that is, if **IsMoreThan9()** returns a value of **true**—then the timer event adds 5 to the **ClickNum** variable. If **ClickNum** isn't over 9, and **IsMoreThan9()** returns a value of **false**, then we drop down to the **else** clause, and the timer event adds only 1 to the **ClickNum** variable.

Finally, as before, the timer event sub assigns the current value of **ClickNum** to the label control's caption property. This causes the current value of **ClickNum** to display on the Web page, making it look as if the page is counting 1-2-3... then 10-15-20... and so on.

Well, that's your introduction to ActiveX, subs, and functions. Try experimenting with these listings yourself. Change the interval property of the timer control and other initial values. Try creating a function that tests **ClickNum** in a different way.

Once you've played with them a little, you'll have a head start on understanding and using not only ActiveX controls, but VBScript subs and functions.

III

Data, Variables, And Constants

In this chapter, you'll learn about some building blocks of a VBScript program: data, variables, and constants. Armed with that knowledge, you can start creating your own VBScript programs right away!

N ow that you've seen a few simple examples of how VBScript works in practice, it's time to buckle down and learn at least the basics of the language.

Yes, it's true: Writing real programs is a lot more fun, just as chatting up French actress Charlotte Gainsbourg ("*Bonsoir, mademoiselle, vous être tres belle*") is a lot more fun than memorizing the forms of French words. In both cases, however, a little preliminary study is essential. Without it, you might write a VBScript program that doesn't work, or tell Ms. Gainsbourg that she's *beau* instead of *belle* and get your face slapped for using the masculine form of the adjective.

Let's start with a simple concept—*data*—and see where it leads us.

Data In Visual Basic Script

Data is, well, simply information. Your name is an item of data (a "datum"); so are your phone number, your street address, your age, and your weight—although those last two items might be considered *private* data.

One of the main occupations of any computer program in any language is to get data from someplace, massage it, and then hand it back to someone. Visual Basic Script programs are no exception. Let's go back to the version of the "Howdy" program that, in Chapter 2, got the user's name and then displayed it in a message box. For your convenience, the program code is reproduced in Listing 3.1. You've already seen the HTML code that surrounds the VBScript code, so we won't bore you with it again.

Listing 3.1   An example of using data in VBScript.

```
<script language="VBScript">
<!--
    dim UserName ' declare variable to hold user's name

    Sub Btn_HelloWorld_OnClick
        UserName = TB_UserName.value
        MsgBox "Howdy, " & Username & "!",0,"VBScript Example"
    End Sub
-->
</script>
```

The Web page containing this VBScript code displayed a text box named **TB_UserName** in which the user could type his/her name. The name, of course, is data. But once we've got the name from the user, we need someplace to put it so that our VBScript program can refer to it as needed.

That "place" is provided by a *variable,* which is essentially just a little box where VBScript can store data until it's needed by the program. Once you've "declared" the variable by using the **dim** statement—more about that in a moment—you can put things in it. Normally, a variable can only hold one thing at a time, but there are exceptions. If the program needs to look at the data, it just uses the variable's name, which is also the name of the data it contains.

In concept, that's really all there is to it. As usual, however, there's more of the story waiting to be told.

Data Types

Items of data represent aspects of the real world, and just like the real world, data comes in different types. In the real world, there are animals, vegetables, and minerals; uptunes and ballads; PCs and Macintoshes; Democrats and Republicans. In the computer world, there are whole numbers, decimal numbers, text strings, true/false values, and lots of other types of data.

The reason for having different types of things—whether it's in the real world or in a computer program—is for efficiency. Once we know what type of thing we're dealing with, we have a fair idea of how to deal with it. If someone hands us a rock, we know that we don't have to experiment to find out if it's good to eat; if someone hands us a cupcake, we know immediately that it *is* good to eat (even if it's not good *for* us). Similarly, if a computer program knows that something is a text string, it won't bother trying to add it as if it were a number.

When you declare a variable (or constant) in a computer program, you normally have to specify what data type it's supposed to be. For example, you might declare different types of variables as shown in the following code lines.

```
dim UserName as String
dim Weight as Integer
dim Price as Currency
dim NumberOfStars as Long
```

Visual Basic Script (and Visual Basic itself) simplify the situation considerably by having an all-purpose data type called the **variant** type. A variant-type variable can hold any type of data. That's why, in Listing 3.1, it wasn't necessary to specify a data type for the **UserName** variable. All we had to do was declare it:

```
dim UserName
```

Now, Visual Basic proper has the variant data type *in addition to* several other official data types. VBScript, however, has *only* the variant type as an official data type. If the data in a variable looks like it's a number, VBScript treats it as a number; if it looks like text, VBScript treats it as text. Listing 3.2 shows a simple example of using different kinds of data and putting them in variant-type variables. Figure 3.1 shows the Web page created by the HTML code in Listing 3.2.

Listing 3.2   The variant type automatically handles different kinds of data.

```
<HTML>
<HEAD>
<TITLE>Using the Variant Data Type</TITLE>
</HEAD>
<BODY>
<H1>Playing With Variant-Type Variables</H1>
<font size=4>
<p>In this Web page, you'll see how VBScript can treat
different types of data, even though all are stored in
variables of a single type: VBScript's all-purpose
"variant" type.</p>
<pre>
The values of the variables are as follows:
          Num1            15
          Num2            28.5
          Name1           "Jim"
          Name2           "Smith"
To see VBScript handles these different types, click on the
buttons below.
</pre>
<br>
<FORM>
<INPUT TYPE="button" name="Btn_AddNums"
          value="Add Num1 to Num2"><br><br>
<INPUT TYPE="button" name="Btn_ConcatNames"
          value="Concatenate Name1 and Name2"><br><br>
<INPUT TYPE="button" name="Btn_AddNameNum"
          value="Add Name1 to Num2">
</FORM>

<script language="vbs">

<!--
' declare variables to hold numbers
dim Num1, Num2

' declare variables to hold text
dim Name1, Name2
```

```
'assign values to the variables
Num1 = 15
Num2 = 27.8

Name1 = "Jim"
Name2 = "Smith"

sub Btn_AddNums_OnClick()
    dim total
    total = Num1 + Num2
    MsgBox "The total is " _
        & total & ".",,"Numbers added!"
end sub

sub Btn_ConcatNames_OnClick()
    dim fullname
    fullname = Name1 & " " & Name2
    MsgBox "The person's full name is " _
        fs& fullname & ".",,"Name assembled!"
end sub

sub Btn_AddNameNum_OnClick()
    dim NameNum
    NameNum = Name1 + Num2
    MsgBox "The sum is " _
        & NameNum & ".",,"What happened?"
end sub
-->
</script>

</BODY>
</HTML>
```

Inside The Data Types Program

The program in Listing 3.2 performs some fairly simple—but revealing—tasks. As you can see, the HTML code sets up three command buttons. When each one is clicked, it tells VBScript to carry out the corresponding **OnClick** sub, as defined in the script code.

The script code itself uses **dim** statements to declare four variables, *all* of the variant data type. The two variables which are meant to hold numbers are named **Num1** and **Num2**, while the two variables meant to hold text strings are named **Name1** and **Name2**. Naturally, VBScript attaches no significance to those variable names: We could quite easily use **Num1** to hold a text value or **Name2** to hold a number.

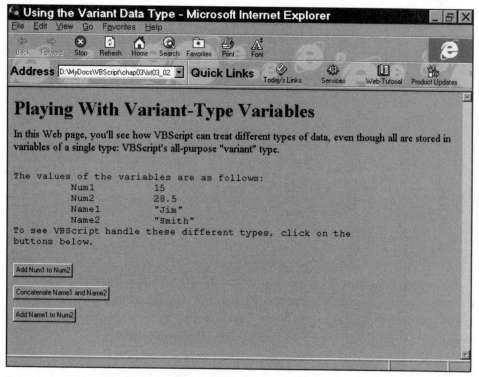

Figure 3.1   The Web page created by Listing 3.2.

Declaring multiple variables in one statement.

Notice that Listing 3.2 declares the Num1 and Num2 variables with a single **dim** statement, and uses another single **dim** statement to declare the Name1 and Name2 variables. This is a trick from Visual Basic: If several variables are of the same type, you can declare them all in one **dim** statement, as long as you separate the variable names by inserting commas between them.

In this case, of course, all the variables are of the same type—variant—so it really wasn't necessary to declare the Num and Name variables in separate **dim** statements. There are only two good reasons to do so. First, it makes the code easier to understand, because variables meant to hold different types of

values are declared separately. Second, it just feels more comfortable for an old Visual Basic programmer who's used to doing things that way.

Once the variables are declared ("**dim**ensioned"), the script loads values into
them. One of the variables gets a whole number, another gets a decimal number,
and two get text strings, as shown in the following code snippet.

```
Num1 = 15
Num2 = 27.8

Name1 = "Jim"
Name2 = "Smith"
```

Now, part of our purpose here is to prove that VBScript *really does* automatically
decide what type of data a variable contains. If VBScript knows that **Num1** and
Num2 contain numbers, while **Name1** and **Name2** contain text, then we should
be able to do arithmetic with one and string concatenation (or "glomming," to
use the technical term) with the other. Let's see if it works.

The *OnClick* event code for the first button attempts to add *Num1* to *Num2,* as
shown in the following code snippet.

```
sub Btn_AddNums_OnClick()
    dim total
    total = Num1 + Num2
    MsgBox "The total is " _
        & total & ".",,"Numbers added!"
end sub
```

First, inside the **sub**, we declare the "local" variable **total** to hold the total of the
two numbers. As a local variable, it can only be seen and used by code inside the
sub where it's declared. Then, we add the values of **Num1** and **Num2**: This is
the part that will only work if VBScript knows that the values are numbers.
Finally, we assign the sum to the **total** variable and use **total** in a message box
statement to display the result. The process succeeds, as shown in Figure 3.2.

Likewise, the **OnClick** event code for the second button attempts to concatenate the two text values "Jim" and "Smith," which have been assigned to the

Figure 3.2 VBScript adds two variables containing numbers.

Name1 and **Name2** variables. It uses the same method as the previous sub, as shown in the following code snippet.

```
sub Btn_ConcatNames_OnClick()
    dim fullname
    fullname = Name1 & " " & Name2
    MsgBox "The person's full name is " _
        & fullname & ".",,"Name assembled!"
end sub
```

As before, the process works like a charm. The result is shown in Figure 3.3.

Finally, the event code for the third button tries to do something which should be impossible—that is, if VBScript really *does* keep track of the data types stored in variant-type variables. It tries to add the text stored in **Name1** to the number stored in **Num2**, as shown in the following code snippet.

```
sub Btn_AddNameNum_OnClick()
    dim NameNum
    NameNum = Name1 + Num2
    MsgBox "The sum is " _
        & NameNum & ".",,"What happened?"
end sub
```

Will it succeed? Not on your life. The result is shown in Figure 3.4. VBScript really does keep track of the data type of values stored in variant-type variables.

One point should be mentioned before we move on. In this example, we've assigned values to variables by using what are called "literal" values—e.g., numbers and text strings, as shown in the following code snippet.

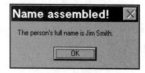

Figure 3.3 VBScript concatenates two text strings.

Figure 3.4   VBScript flags an error when the code tries to add text to a number.

```
Num1 = 15
Num2 = 27.8

Name1 = "Jim"
Name2 = "Smith"
```

That's only one way to assign values to variables. The other very common way to assign values to variables is to assign the value of one variable to another variable, as shown in the following code snippet.

```
Num1 = Num2
Num2 = Name1

Name1 = Name2
Name2 = Num1
```

Here, the first statement takes whatever value is in **Num2** and copies it into **Num1**. The value in **Num2** is left undisturbed by this process. Likewise, the second statement copies the current value of **Name1** into **Num2**, and so on. If we had started out with the values assigned in the previous code snippet, here's how the variables would have ended up:

- ☆ **Num1** now has the value 27.8.
- ☆ **Num2** now has the value "Jim."
- ☆ **Name1** now has the value "Smith."
- ☆ **Name2** now has the value 27.8 (because we changed the value of **Num1** in the first line of code).

MAKING THE CODE MORE EFFICIENT

For now, at least, nobody is going to accuse VBScript of being a speed demon. However, there's one thing we can do to make the program in Listing 3.2 run just a bit faster. Notice that in each **OnClick** sub, Listing 3.2 declares a separate variable to hold the result of the addition or concatenation, as shown in the following code snippet.

```
sub Btn_ConcatNames_OnClick()
    dim fullname
    fullname = Name1 & " " & Name2
    MsgBox "The person's full name is " _
        & fullname & ".",,"Name assembled!"
end sub
```

Now, this has the advantage of being a simple and straightforward way to handle the situation. You need to display the full name, so you create a variable to hold it. However, declaring the **fullname** variable and loading it with a value takes two lines of VBScript code that we really don't need. And each of those lines requires a small but finite amount of time to execute. The routine will run a little faster if we can get rid of them.

Fortunately, it's pretty easy, and if you're already a veteran programmer, you guessed the answer as soon as we asked the question. It's shown in the following code snippet.

```
sub Btn_ConcatNames_OnClick()
    MsgBox "The person's full name is " _
        & Name1 & " " & Name2 _
        & ".",,"Name assembled!"
end sub
```

All we had to do was drop the extra variable and concatenate the first and last names in the **MsgBox** statement itself—thus saving two steps and a couple of milliseconds.

You might be tempted to try the same thing with the routine that adds two numbers, shown in the following code snippet.

```
sub Btn_AddNums_OnClick()
    MsgBox "The total is " _
        Num1 + Num2 & total & _
        ".",,"Numbers added!"
end sub
```

Unfortunately, that requires more than just concatenating two text strings. It requires doing arithmetic, and the **MsgBox** statement isn't quite that smart. For dealing with numbers, you'll still need the extra two program statements.

VBScript "Data Subtypes"

Even though Visual Basic Script has only the variant type as an official data type, other types are "snuck in" as *subtypes* of the variant type. It's these subtypes that VBScript uses when it automatically determines the data type of the value in a variable. The data subtypes are shown in Table 3.1.

Table 3.1   Data subtypes in VBScript.

Subtype	Explanation
Empty	No value has been put in the variable. If you're treating the variable as a number type, then the empty value is 0 (zero). For a text type variable, it's an empty string ("").
Null	A value has been assigned to the variable, but it's an empty value. The variable contains no data.
Boolean	A true or false value.
Byte	An integer in the range 0 to 255.
Integer	An integer in the range -32,768 to +32,767.
Long	An integer in the range -2,147,483,648 to +2,147,483,647.
Single	A single-precision floating point (decimal) number in a range so vast that it's almost meaningless.
Double	A double-precision floating point (decimal) number in a range even vaster than the single subtype.
Date	A number that represents a date between January 1, 100 and December 31, 9999.
String	A text string of up to two billion characters in length, limited only by your hardware.
Object	An OLE automation object for running other programs inside VBScript.
Error	An error number for catching program malfunctions.

Declaring Variables

Declaring variables in VBScript is a fairly simple affair, but there are a few things you need to know.

First, in VBScript (and Visual Basic), there are two ways to declare a variable: *explicitly* and *implicitly.* You declare a variable explicitly when you name it in a **dim** statement, as we've seen many times already.

```
dim TheNum
```

But you can also declare a variable implicitly, simply by using a new variable name in your VBScript code. The following code lines give a couple of examples.

```
EinNummer = 15
MeinName = "Scott"
```

Those two code lines implicitly declare the variables *EinNummer* and *MeinName,* even if they're not set up with **dim** statements anywhere else in the code.

Using Option Explicit

There's a way to make VBScript reject any implicit variable declarations and require that all variables be "officially" declared through **dim** statements. That way is to put the code **option explicit** as the very first line in your Visual Basic script, as shown in the following code snippet.

```
<script language="vbs">
<!--
option explicit
```

When you include this line at the top of your code, VBScript won't allow any implicit variable declarations. If you have a VBScript program of more than half a page, it's a very good idea to include **option explicit** as a safeguard.

Now, you might be a little puzzled. If you don't want any implicit variable declarations, why not just refrain from making any? The answer is that if you make an implicit variable declaration *on purpose,* it's not very likely to cause problems—although it might.

You don't need **option explicit** to keep yourself from deliberately making implicit variable declarations. You do, however, need it to keep yourself from *accidentally* making implicit declarations. That's where problems usually arise. Suppose that your finger slips on the keyboard and you type a variable name incorrectly in an assignment statement. Presto! You've just created a new variable, assigned a value to it, and *failed* to assign a value to the variable to which you *thought* you were assigning a value. Your program will malfunction because it expects to get the original variable with a certain value. When you look at the code, 9 times out of 10, you'll miss the typo in the variable name.

The bottom line is that accidental implicit declarations can cause program bugs that are maddeningly hard to identify. **Option explicit** protects you from those bugs.

Declaring Constants

Program constants are useful because they give you easy-to-remember words that stand for particular values. For instance, you might use the constant *max_balance* to stand for the maximum allowable account balance for your Web customers.

Besides being easy to remember, constants give you a way to make "global" changes in your program without having to comb through your code. Suppose that you used a literal value for the maximum balance, such as 1000. If you wanted to increase the maximum balance to 1500, you would have to look through your code, find every occurrence of 1000, and change all of them to 1500—unless, of course, a particular occurrence of 1000 stood for something else, such as a particular customer's *actual* account balance.

If you used a constant, however, you need only change the value of the constant. Then, every place in your code where the constant is used, the value changes automatically.

VBScript, as a stripped-down version of Visual Basic, doesn't have any built-in support for creating constants. To create a constant, you simply declare a global variable—outside any sub or function, and at the top of your Visual Basic script. Then, you assign it a value. That's it, as shown in the following code snippet.

```
dim Max_Balance
Max_Balance = 1000
```

You do need to be a little extra careful, because even though you're using the name as a constant, it's still a variable. Its value could be changed by an errant line of code. But that is the only drawback of VBScript's approach to declaring constants.

Naming Variables And Other Program Elements

When you name variables, you must follow the same rules that apply to naming anything else in your VBScript program. Upper and lower case are not significant, so the variable names *SlotNum, SLOTNUM,* and *SloTnuM* are all treated as the same. In VBScript, a variable name:

☆ Must begin with a letter

☆ Can't contain a period

☆ Can't exceed 255 characters in length

☆ Must be unique within its scope

All those requirements should be pretty clear, except for the last one—"unique within its scope." Scope is explained in the next section.

Table 3.2 shows a few examples of legal and illegal variable names.

Scope Of Variables And Constants

In the discussion of Listing 3.2, one issue came up that shouldn't be passed over: the issue of *scope.* In a computer program, all identifiers—that is, names for things in the program—have a particular scope. The scope of an identifier is the part of the program in which it can be seen and used. If it can't be seen and used in a particular part of the program, an identifier is said to be "out of scope."

A variable declared *inside* a sub or function can't be seen or used by any code outside the sub or function. When we declared a **total** variable inside the **OnClick** sub for one of the buttons, it could not be seen anywhere outside the sub.

Variable Name	Legal?	Explanation
MyNum	Yes	Starts with a letter, contains no periods, not too long
2LiveCrew	No	Doesn't start with a letter; no talent
Doo.Be.Doo.Be	No	Contains periods and gratuitous Sinatra reference
Eeee_yaaaah	Yes	Underscore character is legal; accidentally dropped a Chevy on my foot

Table 3.2 Some examples of legal and illegal variable names.

That means we could use the same variable name anywhere outside the sub, and VBScript would have no chance of getting confused. Inside the sub, it would know that **total** always refers to the local variable declared inside the sub; outside the sub, **total** would refer to whichever variable named **total** had been declared in that part of the program.

Discussions of scope can get messy, so let's boil it down to a few rules of thumb:

- ☆ A variable (or constant) declared inside a sub or function can only be seen inside that sub or function.
- ☆ A variable (or constant) declared outside of any sub or function can be seen by any code anywhere in the program, as long as the code comes *after* the declaration in the program listing. In other words, you can't use a variable or constant before it's been declared.
- ☆ If a variable (or constant) will only be used inside one sub or function, then it should be declared as a local variable inside that sub or function. Otherwise—if it must be used by more than one part of the program—a variable (or constant) should be declared at the top of your Visual Basic script as a "global" program element.

Declaring And Using Arrays

In addition to the simple data types already discussed, VBScript lets you define and use complex data types called *arrays*. The best way to think of an array is as a sort of "rack" having a predetermined number of slots that can hold data items, as shown in Figure 3.5.

In the figure, you can see how arrays differ from normal variables. A normal variable holds just one value, such as "Kelly" or 3.14159. An array can hold multiple values of the same type, such as "Jim," "Cindy," "Brando," and "Brenda," which are all Walshes, I mean, text strings.

In an array, each slot has a number, and the first slot gets the number 0 (zero). To refer to a particular slot in the array, you just use the name of the array, then the slot number in parentheses.

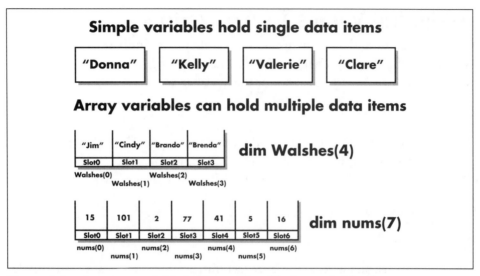

Figure 3.5 An array variable is like a rack with slots to hold values.

Don't forget that the first slot is number zero.
Don't forget that the first slot in a VBScript array is numbered zero—not 1. That means if you want to go from the beginning to the end of a 10-slot array (called "traversing" the array), you start at slot 0 and finish at slot 9, not at slot 10. Regular Visual Basic lets you number the first slot 1 instead of 0, but VBScript doesn't.

To declare an array variable, you simply use a normal **dim** statement. After the variable name, however, you add a left parenthesis, the number of slots you want in the array, and a right parenthesis, as shown in the following code line.

```
dim NumArray(10)
```

The parentheses and number mark the variable as being an array. Once you've declared the array, you can refer to individual array slots just as if they were "standalone" variables. To refer to an array slot—or to the value it contains— you simply use the name of the array with the desired slot number in parentheses. In Figure 3.5, for instance, **Walshes(2)** is the third slot in the first array and has a value of "Brando," while **nums(6)** is the seventh slot in the second array and has a value of 16.

Assigning Values To Array Slots

You assign values to slots in an array just as if they were individual variables, by using the VBScript assignment operator. The following code line, for example, assigns the value "Andrea" to slot 3 of the **Walshes** array.

```
Walshes(3) = "Andrea"
```

One advantage of arrays is that if you want to assign values that bear some relation to each other, you can often use a VBScript **for...next** loop (covered in Chapter 4) to do so. This is shown in the following code snippet.

```
for loopcounter = 0 to 6
    nums(loopcounter) = 0
next
```

Such loops are usually used to initialize (set initial values for) arrays, particularly when the initial values are null, such as 0 (for arrays of numbers) or "" (for arrays of text strings).

Once an array's slots are loaded with values, you can use any one of those values simply by using the name of the array with the appropriate slot number. For example, the following code line shows how you might use the value in slot 0 of Figure 3.5's **Walshes** array.

```
MsgBox "The father of Brandon & Brenda is " & Walshes(0) & "."
```

Last but not least, you can *change* the value in an array slot in exactly the same way as you'd change the value of any other variable. Just use the array slot on the left side of an assignment statement. If the current value of **Walshes(0)** is "Jim," you could change it as shown in the following code line.

```
Walshes(0) = "Larry Mollin"
```

No "record" type in VBScript.
If you're a Visual Basic programmer who likes to use the **type...end type** construct to declare data types that correspond to Pascal **records** and C **structs**, you're in for a mild disappointment. Visual Basic Script doesn't have the **type...end type** construct, and you cannot create those data types in VBScript.

A Simple Array Demonstration

Let's conclude this chapter with a look at how you might load and use a simple array in VBScript. Listing 3.3 shows how you would declare an array, set its initial values, and then access those values to display them in a message box. Figure 3.6 shows the Web page created by the code in Listing 3.3.

Listing 3.3   A simple array demonstration.

```
<HTML>
<HEAD>
<TITLE>A Simple Array Demonstration</TITLE>
</HEAD>
<BODY>
<H1>Displaying the value in an array slot</H1>
<P>This program will demonstrate how an array is
initialized, how values are put into array slots, and
how you can get at those values to view or change
them.</p>
<center>
<FORM>
<br><br>
<INPUT NAME="Btn_SetupArray"
    TYPE="BUTTON"
    value="Set initial values for the array">
    <br><br><br>

<INPUT NAME="Btn_DisplayVal"
    TYPE="BUTTON"
    value="Display value in slot">
</center>
</FORM>

<script language="VBS">
<!--
Option Explicit
dim AnArray(10)
dim SlotNum

sub Btn_SetupArray_OnClick()
    dim loopcounter

    for loopcounter = 0 to 9
        AnArray(loopcounter) = _
            (loopcounter * 2)
    next
    slotnum = 0
end sub
```

```
sub Btn_DisplayVal_OnClick()
    MsgBox "The value in slot number " _
        & SlotNum & " is " & AnArray(SlotNum) _
        & ".",,"Array Demo"
    if slotnum < 9 then
        slotnum = slotnum + 1
    else
        slotnum = 0
    end if
end sub

-->
</script>

</BODY>
</HTML>
```

Inside The Array Code

Let's see how the code in Listing 3.3 uses the array techniques we've discussed. By now, the HTML techniques should be familiar: We set up two buttons on

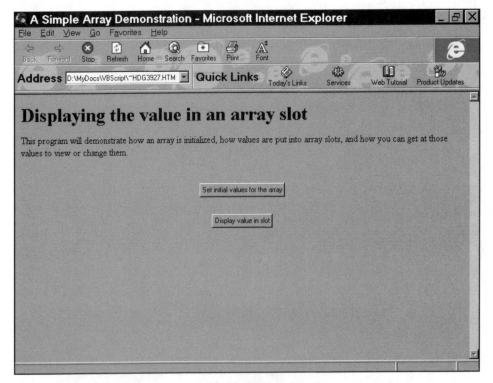

Figure 3.6   The Web page created by Listing 3.3.

the Web page, one initializes the array and the other displays the value in a given array slot.

At the top of the script, we put **Option Explicit** as a safeguard (though it's not really needed in a program this size). Then, as shown in the following code snippet, we declare two global variables, which have to be global because they're used by more than one sub.

```
<script language="VBS">
<!--
Option Explicit
dim AnArray(10)
dim SlotNum
```

One of the global variables, of course, is our array. It has 10 slots, numbered from 0 to 9. The second global variable, **SlotNum**, will help us keep track of which array slot we're using at the moment.

The first sub is the **OnClick** event procedure for the button that initializes the array, shown in the following code snippet.

```
sub Btn_SetupArray_OnClick()
    dim loopcounter

    for loopcounter = 0 to 9
        AnArray(loopcounter) = _
            (loopcounter * 2)
    next
    slotnum = 0
end sub
```

It first declares a local **loopcounter** variable to use with the **for...next** loop that will actually insert values into the array slots. The **loopcounter** variable is declared locally inside this sub, instead of as a global variable, because it's used *only* inside this sub.

The loop to load values into the array slots is a standard **for...next** loop. On the first pass through the loop, the value of **loopcounter** is 0, so **AnArray(loopcounter)** refers to the first slot in the array. As you can see, the assignment statement—here, split with the VBScript line continuation character (_) to stay within the book's page margins—assigns the value **loopcounter * 2** (the value of loopcounter times 2) to the current array slot. At the **next** line, the value of **loopcounter** gets increased by 1, and we go back to the top of the **for...next** loop to run through it again.

The whole process continues until the value of *loopcounter* gets to 9. At that point, we run through the loop a final time, assigning the value *18* to the array slot *AnArray(9)*. Then we drop out of the loop and move to the code line below the **next** statement. The value of the *SlotNum* variable is set to zero, and we're ready to display values in the array slots.

To display the values in the array slots, we move on to the *OnClick* event procedure for the *Btn_DisplayValue* button. This is shown in the following code snippet.

```
sub Btn_DisplayVal_OnClick()
    MsgBox "The value in slot number " _
        & SlotNum & " is " & AnArray(SlotNum) _
        & ".",,"Array Demo"
    if slotnum < 9 then
        slotnum = slotnum + 1
    else
        slotnum = 0
    end if
end sub
```

Once again, VBScript line continuation characters have been used here to keep the code lines within the page margins of the book: You don't need to use them in your own code.

The first part of the sub is a simple **MsgBox** statement. It displays the text "The value in slot number" and concatenates that text with:

☆ The **SlotNum** variable, meaning that the current value of *SlotNum* will be displayed in the message box

☆ The **AnArray(SlotNum)** array slot, meaning that whatever value is in that array slot will be displayed in the message box

After the **MsgBox** statement, we get to an interesting little construct called an **if...else** statement that will be explained fully in Chapter 4. Here, however, what it does is pretty simple:

☆ If the current value of **SlotNum** is less than 9, the first part of the **if** statement adds 1 to the value of **SlotNum**. This means that the next time the user clicks the button, the message box will display the value of the *next* array slot.

☆ If the current value of **SlotNum** is not less than 9, the second part of the **if** statement (the **else** clause) sets the value of **SlotNum** back to 0. This means that the next time the user clicks the button, the message box will again display the value in the first array slot, and the cycle can start over again.

And that's pretty much it! Experiment with your own data, variables, and constants so that you get a feel for how they work. In Chapter 4, we'll take an in-depth look at the different kinds of statements you can use in VBScript, as well as the expressions and operators that make those statements work.

IV

OPERATORS AND EXPRESSIONS

Data and variables are the building blocks of a VBScript program: Operators and expressions are the glue that holds them together. In this chapter, you'll learn how to use VBScript operators to create expressions that use your data and variables.

Depending on your personal proclivities, the word "operator" might suggest different things to you. If you're a "Saturday Night Live" fan, it might call up an image of Lily Tomlin doing her character as the prissy telephone operator. If you're a political animal, it might make you think of Hillary Clinton.

But if you're a programmer, operators mean something else entirely. If data and variables are the bricks of a VBScript program, operators are the mortar that binds them together into expressions—and expressions are the control switches that the program uses to decide what it should do or how it should display information. With operators and expressions, you're on your way to performing truly wizardly tricks with VBScript and ActiveX technology.

What Are Operators?

Operators aren't anything exotic: You use them every day. If you say, "I'll go to the store or shave the cat," you've just used **or**, which is a VBScript logical operator. If you add up your grocery bill, calculate the sales tax, and then add up the total, you've used two more VBScript operators: addition (+) and real-number division (/), which are—you guessed it—arithmetic operators. And if you say something really strange, like, "If my purse matches my shoes, then I have a color-coordinated outfit," you've used two more VBScript operators: equality (=), which is a relational operator, and implication (**imp**), which is another logical operator.

Operators apply to *terms,* which are also sometimes called *arguments.* For example, consider this use of the addition operator.

```
a + b
```

In this example, the operator is + (addition), while the terms are *a* and *b.* The whole thing, operator plus terms, is an *expression.* And terms don't have to be simple: A term can be an expression itself, as in the following example.

```
((a + b) / c) + d
```

Here, the first term is the expression *((a + b) / c)*—that is, the sum of *a* and *b,* divided by *c.* The second term is *d.* And the operator, again, is +. As before, the whole thing forms an expression. The situation is illustrated in Figure 4.1.

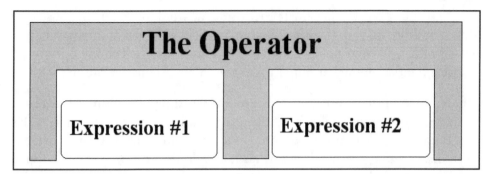

Figure 4.1   How an operator works with terms.

Most operators are *binary*, which means that they take two terms. The negation operator, however, only takes one term. It's called a *monadic* operator, and it reverses the value of the term to which it's applied. The negation operator is explained later in this chapter.

Expressions Have Values

Just like individual variables, constants, and literal values, expressions have values. If you took algebra, it's easy for you to see that if you plug in certain values for *a, b, c,* and *d,* then *((a + b) / c) + d* will have a specific value that depends on them. That example, of course, is familiar, but non-arithmetic expressions have values, too. Consider the following logical expression:

```
It is raining imp The streets are wet.
```

This uses the implication operator **imp** to make what amounts to a causal statement: *if* it's raining, *then* the streets are wet. And this whole statement is an expression with a value, just as much as *a + b* is an expression with a value. The only difference is that *a + b* is an arithmetic expression using an arithmetic operator, and it will have an arithmetic value.

The expression *It is raining* **imp** *The streets are wet* is a logical expression and will have a logical value of **true** (which in VBScript is -1) or **false** (which in VBScript is 0). And just as you determine the value of *a + b* by looking at the values of its terms, so you look at the truth-values of *It is raining* and *The streets are wet* to determine if the whole expression is true or false. In the particular case of logical implication—don't worry, we'll come back to it later in the chapter—the whole expression is true unless the antecedent (*It is raining*) is true while the consequent (*The streets are wet*) is false.

But that's all abstract discussion. Let's talk about the specific operators and how they're used to create expressions. As you work through several examples, you'll get a better understanding of both individual operators and the concept of operators in general.

Arithmetic Operators

Arithmetic operators, unsurprisingly, are those used with arithmetical and algebraic expressions in VBScript. The arithmetic operators are summarized in Table 4.1.

Let's see how the more important arithmetic operators are applied in VBScript programs.

Addition, Subtraction, And Multiplication

Our first example is a simple one: just add some numbers. As usual, it's a little more complicated to do it in a Web page than it is just to use your fingers. Listing 4.1 shows how the VBScript code is set up in the HTML document. Figure 4.2 shows the Web page created by the code.

Table 4.1   Arithmetic operators in VBScript.

Operator	Meaning	Example
+	Addition	a + b
-	Subtraction	a - b
*	Multiplication	a * b
/	Division	a / b
\	Integer Division	a \ b (always yields an integer result, discarding any decimal part)
mod	Modulus	a mod b gives the integer remainder from dividing a by b
–	Arithmetical Negation	–a reverses the sign of a
^	Exponentiation	a^b is a raised to the power of b
&	Concatenation	"The " & "Cat" equals "The Cat". Not really an arithmetic operator, but shoved into that category because it doesn't fit anywhere else.

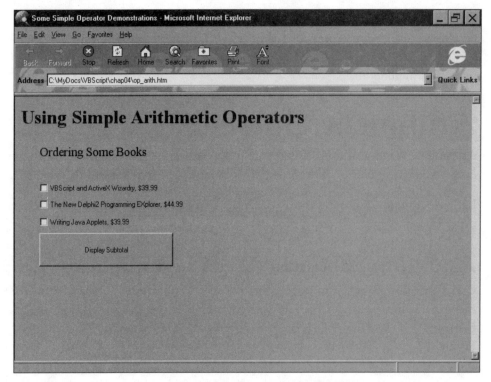

Figure 4.2   The Web page created by the code in Listing 4.1.

Listing 4.1   Using the addition operator in VBScript.

```
<HTML>
<HEAD>
<TITLE>Some Simple Operator Demonstrations</TITLE>
</HEAD>
<BODY>
<H1>Using Simple Arithmetic Operators</H1>
<pre>
    <OBJECT ID="Label1"
    CLASSID="CLSID:978C9E23-D4B0-11CE-BF2D-00AA003F40D0"
    STYLE="TOP:17pt;LEFT:116pt;WIDTH:239pt;
    HEIGHT:41pt;ZINDEX:0;">
        <PARAM NAME="Caption" VALUE="Ordering Some Books">
        <PARAM NAME="Size" VALUE="8431;1446">
        <PARAM NAME="FontName" VALUE="Times New Roman">
        <PARAM NAME="FontHeight" VALUE="320">
        <PARAM NAME="FontCharSet" VALUE="0">
        <PARAM NAME="FontPitchAndFamily" VALUE="2">
        <PARAM NAME="FontWeight" VALUE="0">
    </OBJECT>
```

```
<OBJECT ID="CB_VBS"
CLASSID="CLSID:8BD21D40-EC42-11CE-9E0D-00AA006002F3"
STYLE="TOP:74pt;LEFT:116pt;WIDTH:263pt;
HEIGHT:17pt;TABINDEX:1;ZINDEX:1;">
   <PARAM NAME="BackColor" VALUE="-2147483633">
   <PARAM NAME="ForeColor" VALUE="-2147483630">
   <PARAM NAME="DisplayStyle" VALUE="4">
   <PARAM NAME="Size" VALUE="9287;600">
   <PARAM NAME="Value" VALUE="False">
   <PARAM NAME="Caption"
     VALUE="VBScript and ActiveX Wizardry, $39.99">
   <PARAM NAME="FontCharSet" VALUE="0">
   <PARAM NAME="FontPitchAndFamily" VALUE="2">
   <PARAM NAME="FontWeight" VALUE="0">
</OBJECT>

<OBJECT ID="CB_Delphi2"
CLASSID="CLSID:8BD21D40-EC42-11CE-9E0D-00AA006002F3"
STYLE="TOP:107pt;LEFT:116pt;WIDTH:262pt;
   HEIGHT:17pt;TABINDEX:2;ZINDEX:2;">
   <PARAM NAME="BackColor" VALUE="-2147483633">
   <PARAM NAME="ForeColor" VALUE="-2147483630">
   <PARAM NAME="DisplayStyle" VALUE="4">
   <PARAM NAME="Size" VALUE="9234;600">
   <PARAM NAME="Value" VALUE="False">
   <PARAM NAME="Caption"
     VALUE="The New Delphi2 Programming EXplorer, $44.99">
   <PARAM NAME="FontCharSet" VALUE="0">
   <PARAM NAME="FontPitchAndFamily" VALUE="2">
   <PARAM NAME="FontWeight" VALUE="0">
</OBJECT>

<OBJECT ID="CB_JavaApp"
CLASSID="CLSID:8BD21D40-EC42-11CE-9E0D-00AA006002F3"
STYLE="TOP:140pt;LEFT:116pt;WIDTH:261pt;
   HEIGHT:21pt;TABINDEX:3;ZINDEX:3;">
   <PARAM NAME="BackColor" VALUE="-2147483633">
   <PARAM NAME="ForeColor" VALUE="-2147483630">
   <PARAM NAME="DisplayStyle" VALUE="4">
   <PARAM NAME="Size" VALUE="9208;741">
   <PARAM NAME="Value" VALUE="False">
   <PARAM NAME="Caption"
     VALUE="Writing Java Applets, $39.99">
   <PARAM NAME="FontCharSet" VALUE="0">
   <PARAM NAME="FontPitchAndFamily" VALUE="2">
   <PARAM NAME="FontWeight" VALUE="0">
</OBJECT>
<OBJECT ID="Cmd_Subtotal"
CLASSID="CLSID:D7053240-CE69-11CD-A777-00DD01143C57"
STYLE="TOP:182pt;LEFT:140pt;WIDTH:173pt;
   HEIGHT:41pt;TABINDEX:4;ZINDEX:4;">
```

```
    <PARAM NAME="Caption" VALUE="Display Subtotal">
    <PARAM NAME="Size" VALUE="6103;1446">
    <PARAM NAME="FontCharSet" VALUE="0">
    <PARAM NAME="FontPitchAndFamily" VALUE="2">
    <PARAM NAME="ParagraphAlign" VALUE="3">
    <PARAM NAME="FontWeight" VALUE="0">
</OBJECT>

</pre>

<script language="VBS">
<!--

dim subtotal

sub Cmd_Subtotal_Click
    subtotal = 0.0
    if CB_VBS then subtotal = subtotal + 39.99
    if CB_Delphi2 then subtotal = subtotal + 44.99
    if CB_JavaApp then subtotal = subtotal + 39.99

    MsgBox "The subtotal is currently $" & subtotal & ".",, _
        "Subtotal calculated."

end sub

-->
</script>
</BODY>
</HTML>
```

Notice that as you progress toward true VBScript wizardry, we're getting a little fancier in the code listings. In previous chapters, we've generally used HTML form controls to get input from the user. Here, we switch to an all-ActiveX lineup. In an HTML "layout"—a super-advanced, brand-new HTML feature—you can position ActiveX controls any way you like on a Web document. Later in the book, we'll cover HTML layouts, as well as Microsoft's HTML Layout control and new ActiveX Control Pad. But for the moment, let's see how simple arithmetic operators are used here. We'll also get just a taste of how some ActiveX controls are used with VBScript.

How to create layouts with ActiveX controls.

If you want to start creating layouts with ActiveX controls right away, the best thing you can do is go to **http://**

www.microsoft.com/intdev/ and download the latest version of the ActiveX Control Pad. It lets you visually lay out a Web page with ActiveX controls, and automatically generates the correct <object> tags for the controls, just like the ones you see in Listing 4.1.

As you can see in Figure 4.2, Listing 4.1 sets up a Web page with three check boxes and a command button—all ActiveX controls. Each check box corresponds to a particular book that someone might order from the Coriolis Group. When the user clicks the command button, the VBScript code determines which check boxes are checked. For each checked check box, the script adds the appropriate amount of money to the subtotal, using the addition operator. When the user clicks the command button, the click event code fires, displaying the message box shown in Figure 4.3.

HOW ACTIVEX CONTROLS ARE USED IN LISTING 4.1

There are a couple of interesting things to notice about this code. First, observe that when you're creating a click event sub for an ActiveX command button instead of an HTML form button, you name the sub **Click** instead of **OnClick**, as in the following code line.

```
sub Cmd_Subtotal_Click
```

Each kind of ActiveX control, just like a regular Visual Basic control, has certain associated properties and events. The name of the click event for an ActiveX command button is, well, **Click**.

Second, Listing 4.1 uses the properties of the check box controls to determine when to add to the subtotal variable. Observe how the values of the check boxes are used in the sub, as shown in the following code snippet.

Figure 4.3 The message box displayed by Listing 4.1.

```
if CB_VBS then subtotal = subtotal + 39.99
if CB_Delphi2 then subtotal = subtotal + 44.99
if CB_JavaApp then subtotal = subtotal + 39.99
```

If a check box is checked, then its *value* property is set to **true**. If its value is **true**, then when you put the control's name in the antecedent of an **if** statement, it causes the **if** statement to fire off, executing whatever instruction is in the **then** clause. If the check box isn't checked, then its value property is set to **false**, so the **if** statement doesn't fire.

There are two other ways we might have written those lines, but the way we did it is the most economical. The most obvious alternative is shown in the following code snippet.

```
if CB_VBS.value then subtotal = subtotal + 39.99
if CB_Delphi2.value then subtotal = subtotal + 44.99
if CB_JavaApp.value then subtotal = subtotal + 39.99
```

This approach uses basically the same logic, but it uses more words to accomplish the same result. It wastes words because it ignores one of the most useful features of ActiveX controls: Each type of ActiveX control has a **default** property. If you don't specify a property, and simply give the name of the control, then VBScript assumes you are talking about the control's default property. In the case of a check box control, the default property is—you guessed it—the "checked" status of the check box. Thus, in Listing 4.1, it was unnecessary to refer to the value property of each check box control: Leave out any mention of a property, and VBScript automatically uses the value property.

An even less economical way of writing the code is to write things like **if CB_VBS.value = true**, but that should be pretty clear from the foregoing discussion.

Subtraction works just like addition, except that it's, well, subtraction. If that's not crystal clear, you have a bright future calculating the government's budget deficit. Multiplication (*), which uses the asterisk character, also works the same as in first-grade arithmetic.

Division

Division gets its own section because VBScript gives it a couple of interesting wrinkles. To be more specific, there are two kinds of division in VBScript: regular division and *integer* division. These two kinds of division are illustrated in Listing 4.2. The Web page created by Listing 4.2 is shown in Figure 4.4.

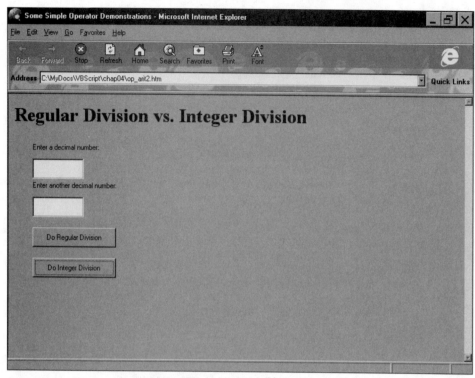

Figure 4.4 The Web page created by Listing 4.2.

Listing 4.2 Using VBScript's two kinds of division.

```
<HTML>
<HEAD>
<TITLE>Some Simple Operator Demonstrations</TITLE>
</HEAD>
<BODY>
<H1>Regular Division vs. Integer Division</H1>
<pre>
    <OBJECT ID="Label2"
    CLASSID="CLSID:978C9E23-D4B0-11CE-BF2D-00AA003F40D0"
    STYLE="TOP:66pt;LEFT:116pt;WIDTH:91pt;
    HEIGHT:17pt;ZINDEX:1;">
        <PARAM NAME="Caption" VALUE="Enter a decimal number:">
        <PARAM NAME="Size" VALUE="3201;582">
        <PARAM NAME="FontCharSet" VALUE="0">
        <PARAM NAME="FontPitchAndFamily" VALUE="2">
        <PARAM NAME="FontWeight" VALUE="0">
    </OBJECT>
    <OBJECT ID="TB_Num1"
    CLASSID="CLSID:8BD21D10-EC42-11CE-9E0D-00AA006002F3"
    STYLE="TOP:83pt;LEFT:116pt;WIDTH:66pt;
    HEIGHT:25pt;TABINDEX:3;ZINDEX:3;">
```

```
        <PARAM NAME="VariousPropertyBits" VALUE="746604571">
        <PARAM NAME="Size" VALUE="2328;873">
        <PARAM NAME="FontCharSet" VALUE="0">
        <PARAM NAME="FontPitchAndFamily" VALUE="2">
        <PARAM NAME="FontWeight" VALUE="0">
    </OBJECT>
    <OBJECT ID="Label3"
     CLASSID="CLSID:978C9E23-D4B0-11CE-BF2D-00AA003F40D0"
     STYLE="TOP:124pt;LEFT:116pt;WIDTH:116pt;HEIGHT:17pt;ZINDEX:2;">
        <PARAM NAME="Caption" VALUE="Enter another decimal number:">
        <PARAM NAME="Size" VALUE="4074;583">
        <PARAM NAME="FontCharSet" VALUE="0">
        <PARAM NAME="FontPitchAndFamily" VALUE="2">
        <PARAM NAME="FontWeight" VALUE="0">
    </OBJECT>
    <OBJECT ID="TB_Num2"
     CLASSID="CLSID:8BD21D10-EC42-11CE-9E0D-00AA006002F3"
     STYLE="TOP:149pt;LEFT:116pt;WIDTH:66pt;
     HEIGHT:25pt;TABINDEX:4;ZINDEX:4;">
        <PARAM NAME="VariousPropertyBits" VALUE="746604571">
        <PARAM NAME="Size" VALUE="2328;873">
        <PARAM NAME="FontCharSet" VALUE="0">
        <PARAM NAME="FontPitchAndFamily" VALUE="2">
        <PARAM NAME="FontWeight" VALUE="0">
    </OBJECT><br>
    <OBJECT ID="Cmd_RegularDiv"
     CLASSID="CLSID:D7053240-CE69-11CD-A777-00DD01143C57"
     STYLE="TOP:190pt;LEFT:116pt;WIDTH:107pt;
     HEIGHT:24pt;TABINDEX:5;ZINDEX:5;">
        <PARAM NAME="Caption" VALUE="Do Regular Division">
        <PARAM NAME="Size" VALUE="3783;846">
        <PARAM NAME="FontCharSet" VALUE="0">
        <PARAM NAME="FontPitchAndFamily" VALUE="2">
        <PARAM NAME="ParagraphAlign" VALUE="3">
        <PARAM NAME="FontWeight" VALUE="0">
    </OBJECT><br>
    <OBJECT ID="Cmd_IntegerDiv"
     CLASSID="CLSID:D7053240-CE69-11CD-A777-00DD01143C57"
     STYLE="TOP:231pt;LEFT:116pt;WIDTH:107pt;
     HEIGHT:24pt;TABINDEX:6;ZINDEX:6;">
        <PARAM NAME="Caption" VALUE="Do Integer Division">
        <PARAM NAME="Size" VALUE="3783;846">
        <PARAM NAME="FontCharSet" VALUE="0">
        <PARAM NAME="FontPitchAndFamily" VALUE="2">
        <PARAM NAME="ParagraphAlign" VALUE="3">
        <PARAM NAME="FontWeight" VALUE="0">
    </OBJECT>
</pre>

<script language="VBS">
```

```
<!--

dim num1, num2, result

sub Cmd_RegularDiv_Click
    num1 = TB_Num1.text
    num2 = TB_Num2.text

    result = num1 / num2
    MsgBox "With regular division, the result of " & _
    "dividing the first number by the second is " _
     & result & ".",,"Regular Division"
end sub

sub Cmd_IntegerDiv_Click

    num1 = TB_Num1.text
    num2 = TB_Num2.text

    result = num1 \ num2
    MsgBox "With integer division, the result of " & _
        "dividing the first number by the second is " _
        & result & ".",,"Integer Division"

end sub

-->
</script>
</BODY>
</HTML>
```

As before, this is pretty simple stuff in principle, but it helps to see an example. It sets up a Web page with two text boxes where you can enter two decimal numbers—that is, numbers with a nonzero part to the right of the decimal point. When the user clicks either of the command buttons, the first number is divided by the second.

There is, however, a big difference between the results of clicking the different buttons. If the user clicks the first button, the click event sub uses regular division (/), as shown in the following code snippet. If the user entered 5.7 for the first number and 2.1 for the second number, the program would display the message box shown in Figure 4.5.

```
num1 = TB_Num1.text
num2 = TB_Num2.text

result = num1 / num2
```

Figure 4.5   The message box displayed by the "regular division" button.

You can see that the result is 2.7 followed by a long string of decimal digits. This is quite different from the result you get with integer division. If the user clicks that button instead—with the same numbers entered in the text boxes—he/she gets the result shown in Figure 4.6.

As you can see, integer division rounds off the result to the nearest whole number, which in this case, is 3.

Modulus

The modulus (**mod**) operator gives the remainder from an integer division. For example, if you divide 5 by 14, don't do any rounding (unlike VBScript's integer division), and insist on an integer result, then the answer is 0—because 14 doesn't evenly go into 5 at all. The remainder is 5, so *5 mod 14* is 5.

Unless you've used the **mod** operator at some point in your own programming, the most obvious question is, "What the heck is it good for?" Odd as it might seem, the **mod** operator is very useful in controlling processes that cycle over and over. Consider *X mod 12:* Some of its possible values are shown in Table 4.2.

If that series of numbers reminds you of anything, it should: Our system of clock time in North America is **mod** 12. The table also illustrates that when you set up a **mod** cycle, you often need to treat even multiples of the **mod** number as a special case. In our system of clock time, the 12th and 24th hours are twelve o'clock, not zero o'clock.

At any rate, the **mod** operator is particularly useful when you want certain events to

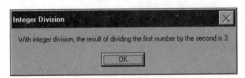

Figure 4.6   The message box displayed by the "integer division" button.

Table 4.2 Some possible values of X mod 12.

Value of X	Number of times 12 evenly divides X	Remainder (Value of X mod 12)
1	0	1
2	0	2
3	0	3
4	0	4
5	0	5
6	0	6
7	0	7
8	0	8
9	0	9
10	0	10
11	0	11
12	1	0
13	1	1
14	1	2
15	1	3
16	1	4
17	1	5
18	1	6
19	1	7
20	1	8
21	1	9
22	1	10
23	1	11
24	2	0

recur at specified intervals. Because the numbers in a **mod** cycle begin at zero, cycle to one less than the **mod** number, then start at zero again, it's a very predictable way to make events repeat. Listing 4.3 shows a simplified example of using the **mod** operator: not industrial strength, but adequate to show you how it's used. Figure 4.7 shows the Web page created by the code in Listing 4.3.

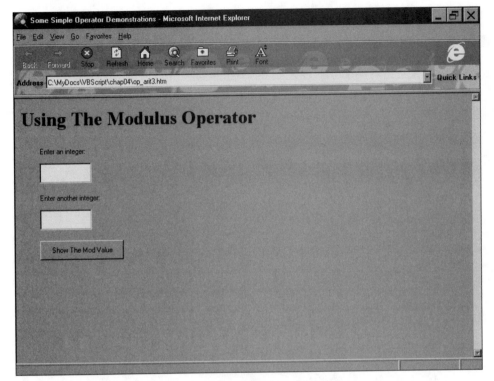

Figure 4.7   A Web page to demonstrate the **mod** operator.

Listing 4.3   VBScript code using the **mod** operator.

```
<HTML>
<HEAD>
<TITLE>Some Simple Operator Demonstrations</TITLE>
</HEAD>
<BODY>
<H1>Using The Modulus Operator</H1>
<pre>
    <OBJECT ID="Label2"
     CLASSID="CLSID:978C9E23-D4B0-11CE-BF2D-00AA003F40D0"
     STYLE="TOP:66pt;LEFT:116pt;WIDTH:300pt;
     HEIGHT:17pt;ZINDEX:1;">
        <PARAM NAME="Caption" VALUE="Enter an integer:">
        <PARAM NAME="Size" VALUE="3201;582">
        <PARAM NAME="FontCharSet" VALUE="0">
        <PARAM NAME="FontPitchAndFamily" VALUE="2">
        <PARAM NAME="FontWeight" VALUE="0">
    </OBJECT>
    <OBJECT ID="TB_Num1"
     CLASSID="CLSID:8BD21D10-EC42-11CE-9E0D-00AA006002F3"
     STYLE="TOP:83pt;LEFT:116pt;WIDTH:66pt;
```

```
      HEIGHT:25pt;TABINDEX:3;ZINDEX:3;">
         <PARAM NAME="VariousPropertyBits" VALUE="746604571">
         <PARAM NAME="Size" VALUE="2328;873">
         <PARAM NAME="FontCharSet" VALUE="0">
         <PARAM NAME="FontPitchAndFamily" VALUE="2">
         <PARAM NAME="FontWeight" VALUE="0">
      </OBJECT><br>
      <OBJECT ID="Label3"
       CLASSID="CLSID:978C9E23-D4B0-11CE-BF2D-00AA003F40D0"
       STYLE="TOP:124pt;LEFT:116pt;WIDTH:300pt;HEIGHT:17pt;ZINDEX:2;">
         <PARAM NAME="Caption" VALUE="Enter another integer:">
         <PARAM NAME="Size" VALUE="4074;583">
         <PARAM NAME="FontCharSet" VALUE="0">
         <PARAM NAME="FontPitchAndFamily" VALUE="2">
         <PARAM NAME="FontWeight" VALUE="0">
      </OBJECT>
      <OBJECT ID="TB_Num2"
       CLASSID="CLSID:8BD21D10-EC42-11CE-9E0D-00AA006002F3"
       STYLE="TOP:149pt;LEFT:116pt;WIDTH:66pt;
       HEIGHT:25pt;TABINDEX:4;ZINDEX:4;">
         <PARAM NAME="VariousPropertyBits" VALUE="746604571">
         <PARAM NAME="Size" VALUE="2328;873">
         <PARAM NAME="FontCharSet" VALUE="0">
         <PARAM NAME="FontPitchAndFamily" VALUE="2">
         <PARAM NAME="FontWeight" VALUE="0">
      </OBJECT><br>
      <OBJECT ID="Cmd_ShowMod"
       CLASSID="CLSID:D7053240-CE69-11CD-A777-00DD01143C57"
       STYLE="TOP:190pt;LEFT:116pt;WIDTH:107pt;
       HEIGHT:24pt;TABINDEX:5;ZINDEX:5;">
         <PARAM NAME="Caption" VALUE="Show The Mod Value">
         <PARAM NAME="Size" VALUE="3783;846">
         <PARAM NAME="FontCharSet" VALUE="0">
         <PARAM NAME="FontPitchAndFamily" VALUE="2">
         <PARAM NAME="ParagraphAlign" VALUE="3">
         <PARAM NAME="FontWeight" VALUE="0">
      </OBJECT><br>
</pre>

<script language="VBS">
<!--

dim num1, num2, result

sub Cmd_ShowMod_Click
    num1 = TB_Num1.text
    num2 = TB_Num2.text

    result = num1 mod num2
    MsgBox "The first number mod the second number is " & _
```

```
         result & ".",,"The Modulus Operator"
end sub

-->
</script>
</BODY>
</HTML>
```

The operation of the program is fairly simple. The user of the Web page enters a whole number in each text box. When he/she clicks on the command button, the **Click** event code assigns the number in each text box to a corresponding variable in the VBScript program. (Remember that VBScript looks at data and automatically decides what type it's likely to be. In this case, it looks at the "text" in the text boxes and decides that it's probably numeric.)

The sub then uses the **mod** operator with the two numbers, assigning the result to the variable *result*. A message box displays the result. That's all there is to it.

As for the other arithmetic operators—negation, exponentiation, and concatenation—their application is obvious, so we won't waste time on them here.

Logical Operators

Logical operators are the next group we'll look at. Logical operators work with terms that are true (-1) or false (0). They are summarized in Table 4.3.

In the following examples, we'll look at the logical operators one at a time. However, you should keep in mind that you can *combine* expressions with logical operators any way you like, as long as you follow the syntactical rules of VBScript. The following code snippet shows a few examples.

Table 4.3   Logical operators in VBScript.

Operator	Meaning	Example
not	Logical Negation	not(a = b)
or	Logical Disjunction	(a = b) or (c < d)
and	Logical Conjunction	(a = b) and (c < d)
xor	Logical Exclusion (a.k.a. "exclusive **or**")	(a = b) xor (c < d)
eqv	Logical Equivalence	(a = b) eqv (c < d)
imp	Logical Implication	(a = b) imp (c < d)

```
(a and b) or c
not a and not b and c
a or (not b and c)
not a or b and a imp b
```

That last line, by the way, is what's known as a *tautology:* an expression that will always be true. The reason is that *not a or b* is logically equivalent to *a imp b:* Whenever one is true, so is the other, and whenever one is false, so is the other.

Logical Negation

Logical negation is the simplest logical operator. Unlike most operators, it takes only one term. And like much political rhetoric, it reverses the truth-value of terms to which it's applied, turning false values into true and true into false. The "truth table" for negation is shown in Table 4.4.

Truth-tables are easy to read. Row one of Table 4.4 says is that if an expression *p* is true, then *not p* is false, while row two says that if an expression *p* is false, then *not p* is true. Row three says that if *p* has no truth value (*i.e.,* it has a null value), then applying the negation operator has no effect.

Logical Disjunction

Disjunction is just a big word that means "or." A disjunction expression is true if at least one of its terms is true. Although disjunctions will usually have only two terms, they can have more than that: *a or b or c or d...* and so on. The truth table for disjunction is shown in Table 4.5.

What you can tell from this truth table is that there's only one case in which the expression *p or q* is false: when *p* and *q* are *both* false. In all other cases where both *p* and *q* have values, the disjunctive expression is true. If *p* or *q* has a null value, it gets a little messy, but the big rule still applies: If at least one of its terms

Table 4.4 The truth table for logical negation.

p	not p
true	false
false	true
null	null

Table 4.5 The truth table for logical disjunction.

p	q	p or q
true	true	true
true	false	true
false	true	true
false	false	false

is true, then a disjunctive expression is true. If none of its terms is true, but one of its terms is null, then the expression as a whole takes a value of null.

Listing 4.4 shows VBScript code that puts the disjunction operator to work. Figure 4.8 shows the Web page created by the code.

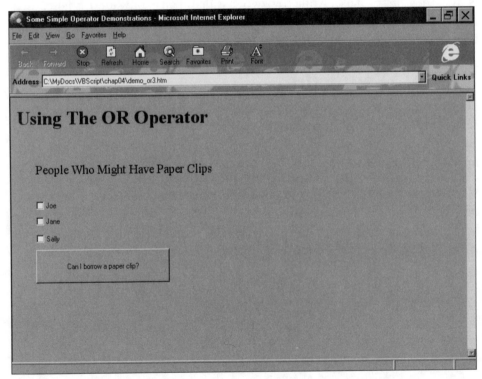

Figure 4.8 A Web page that uses disjunction.

Listing 4.4 An example of logical disjunction in VBScript.

```
<HTML>
<HEAD>
<TITLE>Some Simple Operator Demonstrations</TITLE>
</HEAD>
<BODY>
<H1>Using The OR Operator</H1>
<pre>
<DIV STYLE="LAYOUT:FIXED;WIDTH:488pt;HEIGHT:260pt;">
    <OBJECT ID="Label1"
     CLASSID="CLSID:978C9E23-D4B0-11CE-BF2D-00AA003F40D0"
     STYLE="TOP:17pt;LEFT:116pt;WIDTH:239pt;
     HEIGHT:41pt;ZINDEX:0;">
        <PARAM NAME="Caption"
          VALUE="People Who Might Have Paper Clips">
        <PARAM NAME="Size" VALUE="8440;1455">
        <PARAM NAME="FontName" VALUE="Times New Roman">
        <PARAM NAME="FontHeight" VALUE="320">
        <PARAM NAME="FontCharSet" VALUE="0">
        <PARAM NAME="FontPitchAndFamily" VALUE="2">
        <PARAM NAME="FontWeight" VALUE="0">
    </OBJECT>
    <OBJECT ID="CB_Joe"
     CLASSID="CLSID:8BD21D40-EC42-11CE-9E0D-00AA006002F3"
     STYLE="TOP:74pt;LEFT:116pt;WIDTH:124pt;
     HEIGHT:17pt;TABINDEX:1;ZINDEX:1;">
        <PARAM NAME="BackColor" VALUE="-2147483633">
        <PARAM NAME="ForeColor" VALUE="-2147483630">
        <PARAM NAME="DisplayStyle" VALUE="4">
        <PARAM NAME="Size" VALUE="4365;582">
        <PARAM NAME="Value" VALUE="False">
        <PARAM NAME="Caption" VALUE="Joe">
        <PARAM NAME="FontCharSet" VALUE="0">
        <PARAM NAME="FontPitchAndFamily" VALUE="2">
        <PARAM NAME="FontWeight" VALUE="0">
    </OBJECT>
    <OBJECT ID="CB_Jane"
     CLASSID="CLSID:8BD21D40-EC42-11CE-9E0D-00AA006002F3"
     STYLE="TOP:107pt;LEFT:116pt;WIDTH:132pt;
     HEIGHT:17pt;TABINDEX:2;ZINDEX:2;">
        <PARAM NAME="BackColor" VALUE="-2147483633">
        <PARAM NAME="ForeColor" VALUE="-2147483630">
        <PARAM NAME="DisplayStyle" VALUE="4">
        <PARAM NAME="Size" VALUE="4656;582">
        <PARAM NAME="Value" VALUE="False">
        <PARAM NAME="Caption" VALUE="Jane">
        <PARAM NAME="FontCharSet" VALUE="0">
        <PARAM NAME="FontPitchAndFamily" VALUE="2">
        <PARAM NAME="FontWeight" VALUE="0">
    </OBJECT>
    <OBJECT ID="CB_Sally"
```

```
        CLASSID="CLSID:8BD21D40-EC42-11CE-9E0D-00AA006002F3"
        STYLE="TOP:140pt;LEFT:116pt;WIDTH:140pt;
        HEIGHT:21pt;TABINDEX:3;ZINDEX:3;">
            <PARAM NAME="BackColor" VALUE="-2147483633">
            <PARAM NAME="ForeColor" VALUE="-2147483630">
            <PARAM NAME="DisplayStyle" VALUE="4">
            <PARAM NAME="Size" VALUE="4947;741">
            <PARAM NAME="Value" VALUE="False">
            <PARAM NAME="Caption" VALUE="Sally">
            <PARAM NAME="FontCharSet" VALUE="0">
            <PARAM NAME="FontPitchAndFamily" VALUE="2">
            <PARAM NAME="FontWeight" VALUE="0">
    </OBJECT>
    <OBJECT ID="Cmd_Borr"
     CLASSID="CLSID:D7053240-CE69-11CD-A777-00DD01143C57"
     STYLE="TOP:182pt;LEFT:140pt;WIDTH:173pt;
     HEIGHT:41pt;TABINDEX:4;ZINDEX:4;">
            <PARAM NAME="Caption"
              VALUE="Can I borrow a paper clip?">
            <PARAM NAME="Size" VALUE="6112;1455">
            <PARAM NAME="FontCharSet" VALUE="0">
            <PARAM NAME="FontPitchAndFamily" VALUE="2">
            <PARAM NAME="ParagraphAlign" VALUE="3">
            <PARAM NAME="FontWeight" VALUE="0">
    </OBJECT>
</DIV>
</pre>

<script language="VBS">
<!--

sub Cmd_Borr_Click

    if CB_Joe or CB_Jane or CB_Sally then
        MsgBox "Yes, someone is sure to have one.",,"OR Demonstration"
    else
        MsgBox "No, nobody has any paper clips. Sorry.",,"OR Demonstration"
    end if
end sub

-->
</script>
</BODY>
</HTML>
```

The code in Listing 4.4 poses the musical question, "Can I borrow some paper clips?" It sets up a Web page with three check boxes, each corresponding to a person in your office who might have some paper clips. If any one of those people has some paper clips, then you can borrow some. The only case in which you can't borrow any paper clips is if no one else in your office has any, either.

This is the situation embodied in the central code line of the **Click** event sub for the command button, as follows.

```
if CB_Joe or CB_Jane or CB_Sally then
```

The expression *CB_Joe or CB_Jane or CB_Sally* is true if at least one of its terms is true: that is, if the user checked at least one of the check boxes. Of course, there's nothing special about three terms: you could have only two, or you could have fifteen. The results of clicking the command button are shown in Figures 4.9 and 4.10.

Logical Conjunction

Logical conjunction is the flip side of logical disjunction. A disjunctive expression is false only if all of its terms are false, while a *conjunctive* expression is *true* only if both of its terms are *true*. That means if even one term in a conjunctive expression is false, then the whole thing is false. The truth table for conjunction is shown in Table 4.6.

As with disjunction, the inclusion of null values makes things a little messy, but the big rule stays the same: The only way for a conjunctive expression to be true, is for all of its terms to be true. Otherwise, if all of its terms have truth values, then a conjunctive expression is false. If all of its terms aren't true, and some of its terms are null, then the expression as a whole takes a null value.

Listing 4.5 shows an example of VBScript code that puts the conjunction operator to work. In this case, the user is trying to assemble a meeting that must include Joe, Jane, and Sally. Figure 4.11 shows the Web page created by the code.

Figure 4.9   The disjunctive expression is true.

Figure 4.10   The disjunctive expression is false.

Table 4.6   The truth table for conjunction.

p	q	p and q
true	true	true
true	false	false
false	true	false
false	false	false

Listing 4.5   Using the conjunction operator in VBScript.

```
<HTML>
<HEAD>
<TITLE>Some Simple Operator Demonstrations</TITLE>
</HEAD>
<BODY>
<H1>Using The AND Operator</H1>
<pre>
<DIV STYLE="LAYOUT:FIXED;WIDTH:488pt;HEIGHT:260pt;">
    <OBJECT ID="Label1"
     CLASSID="CLSID:978C9E23-D4B0-11CE-BF2D-00AA003F40D0"
     STYLE="TOP:17pt;LEFT:116pt;WIDTH:239pt;HEIGHT:41pt;ZINDEX:0;">
        <PARAM NAME="Caption"
          VALUE="People Who Must Be At The Meeting">
        <PARAM NAME="Size" VALUE="8440;1455">
        <PARAM NAME="FontName" VALUE="Times New Roman">
        <PARAM NAME="FontHeight" VALUE="320">
        <PARAM NAME="FontCharSet" VALUE="0">
        <PARAM NAME="FontPitchAndFamily" VALUE="2">
        <PARAM NAME="FontWeight" VALUE="0">
    </OBJECT>
    <OBJECT ID="CB_Joe"
     CLASSID="CLSID:8BD21D40-EC42-11CE-9E0D-00AA006002F3"
     STYLE="TOP:74pt;LEFT:116pt;WIDTH:124pt;
     HEIGHT:17pt;TABINDEX:1;ZINDEX:1;">
        <PARAM NAME="BackColor" VALUE="-2147483633">
        <PARAM NAME="ForeColor" VALUE="-2147483630">
        <PARAM NAME="DisplayStyle" VALUE="4">
        <PARAM NAME="Size" VALUE="4365;582">
        <PARAM NAME="Value" VALUE="False">
        <PARAM NAME="Caption" VALUE="Joe">
        <PARAM NAME="FontCharSet" VALUE="0">
        <PARAM NAME="FontPitchAndFamily" VALUE="2">
        <PARAM NAME="FontWeight" VALUE="0">
    </OBJECT>
    <OBJECT ID="CB_Jane"
     CLASSID="CLSID:8BD21D40-EC42-11CE-9E0D-00AA006002F3"
     STYLE="TOP:107pt;LEFT:116pt;WIDTH:132pt;
```

```
         HEIGHT:17pt;TABINDEX:2;ZINDEX:2;">
            <PARAM NAME="BackColor" VALUE="-2147483633">
            <PARAM NAME="ForeColor" VALUE="-2147483630">
            <PARAM NAME="DisplayStyle" VALUE="4">
            <PARAM NAME="Size" VALUE="4656;582">
            <PARAM NAME="Value" VALUE="False">
            <PARAM NAME="Caption" VALUE="Jane">
            <PARAM NAME="FontCharSet" VALUE="0">
            <PARAM NAME="FontPitchAndFamily" VALUE="2">
            <PARAM NAME="FontWeight" VALUE="0">
        </OBJECT>
        <OBJECT ID="CB_Sally"
         CLASSID="CLSID:8BD21D40-EC42-11CE-9E0D-00AA006002F3"
         STYLE="TOP:140pt;LEFT:116pt;WIDTH:140pt;
         HEIGHT:21pt;TABINDEX:3;ZINDEX:3;">
            <PARAM NAME="BackColor" VALUE="-2147483633">
            <PARAM NAME="ForeColor" VALUE="-2147483630">
            <PARAM NAME="DisplayStyle" VALUE="4">
            <PARAM NAME="Size" VALUE="4947;741">
            <PARAM NAME="Value" VALUE="False">
            <PARAM NAME="Caption" VALUE="Sally">
            <PARAM NAME="FontCharSet" VALUE="0">
            <PARAM NAME="FontPitchAndFamily" VALUE="2">
            <PARAM NAME="FontWeight" VALUE="0">
        </OBJECT>
        <OBJECT ID="Cmd_Borr"
         CLASSID="CLSID:D7053240-CE69-11CD-A777-00DD01143C57"
         STYLE="TOP:182pt;LEFT:140pt;WIDTH:173pt;
         HEIGHT:41pt;TABINDEX:4;ZINDEX:4;">
            <PARAM NAME="Caption"
              VALUE="Can everyone attend a meeting at 9am?">
            <PARAM NAME="Size" VALUE="6112;1455">
            <PARAM NAME="FontCharSet" VALUE="0">
            <PARAM NAME="FontPitchAndFamily" VALUE="2">
            <PARAM NAME="ParagraphAlign" VALUE="3">
            <PARAM NAME="FontWeight" VALUE="0">
        </OBJECT>
</DIV>
</pre>

<script language="VBS">
<!--

sub Cmd_Borr_Click

    if CB_Joe and CB_Jane and CB_Sally then
      MsgBox "Yes, everyone is available for the meeting." _
             ,,"AND Demonstration"
    else
      MsgBox "No, some people can't make the meeting. Pick another time." _
             ,,"AND Demonstration"
```

```
    end if
end sub

-->
</script>
</BODY>
</HTML>
```

If you've already perused the previous example (disjunction), then the concept here should be familiar. The central line of code appears in the event sub for the command button, as shown in the following code line.

```
if CB_Joe and CB_Jane and CB_Sally then
```

If any of the check boxes is *not* checked, then the whole expression takes a value of false, meaning that at least one person can't attend the meeting, and it must be rescheduled. The results of the program are shown in Figures 4.12 and 4.13.

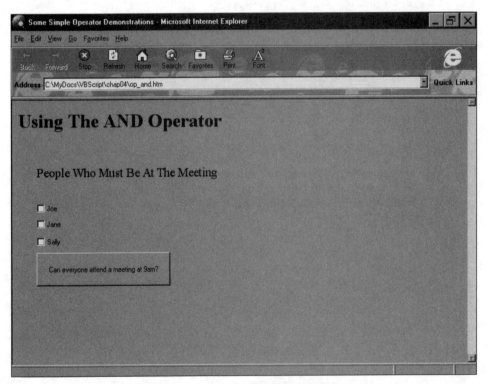

Figure 4.11   The Web page created by Listing 4.5.

Figure 4.12 All the boxes are checked, so the expression is true.

Figure 4.13 Not all of the boxes are checked, so the expression is false.

XOr, Equivalence, And Implication

Logical exclusion (exclusive "or"), logical equivalence, and logical implication are operators you'll use less often, but they do have their applications. An exclusive-or expression is true if only *one* of its terms is true: In all other cases, it's false. An equivalence expression is true only if its terms have the *same* truth value: In all other cases, it's false. And a logical implication expression is false only if its first term is true and its second term is false: In all other cases, it's true. The truth tables for these operators are shown in Tables 4.7, 4.8, and 4.9.

Table 4.7 The truth table for logical exclusion (exclusive or).

p	q	p xor q
true	true	false
true	false	true
false	true	true
false	false	false

Table 4.8 The truth table for equivalence.

p	q	p eqv q
true	true	true
true	false	false
false	true	false
false	false	true

Table 4.9 The truth table for implication.

p	q	p imp q
true	true	true
true	false	false
false	true	true
false	false	true

Comparison (Relational) Operators

Comparison operators, often called "relational" operators, compare the values of two or more expressions. These operators are all so familiar to anyone who made it past sixth grade that we won't rehearse them here in any great detail. Their meaning and use are the same in VBScript as everywhere else. An expression with a comparison operator takes a value of true, false, or null. The operators are summarized in Table 4.10.

Equal (=) doesn't always mean "equal".
It might have occurred to you that VBScript uses the same character ("=") for both the equality operator and the assignment operator. But if you're inclined to worry about the situation, don't. VBScript automatically looks at the context and determines if a particular instance of "=" should be interpreted as the equality operator or the assignment operator.

Table 4.10 Comparison (relational) operators in VBScript.

Operator	Meaning	Example
=	Equality	a = b, true if a and b are equal
<>	Inequality	a <> b, true if a and b are not equal
<	Less than	a < b, true if a is less than b

Continued

Table 4.10 Comparison (relational) operators in VBScript (Continued).

Operator	Meaning	Example
>	Greater than	a > b, true if a is greater than b
<=	Less than or equal to	a <= b, true if a is less than or equal to b
>	Greater than or equal to	a >= b, true if a is greater than or equal to b
Is	Object equivalence	a Is b, true if a and b refer to the same object

The only comparison operator that's at all unfamiliar is the object equivalence operator. It's used to determine whether two expressions refer to the same object. We'll discuss object equivalence in detail later in the book.

V
MAKING YOUR PROGRAM MAKE DECISIONS

Are you just a teensy
bit indecisive? At least
you can get away with
it: Your VBScript pro-
gram can't. Here's how
your program decides
how to respond to
things that happen
while it's running.

In Chapters 3 and 4, we looked at the various kinds of data, variables, and expressions you can use in VBScript. But we didn't really talk a lot about *what* you use them for. In this chapter, we'll look at how all these program elements work with special kinds of VBScript statements, called *control structures*.

These control structures allow your program to respond in different ways to different events. In fact, you've seen one control structure—the **if...then** statement—several times already. If the value of a variable is one thing, the **if** statement makes your program take action X; if the value is something else, your program takes action Y. Almost all uses of control structures are variations on that theme.

Types Of Control Structures

Control structures fall into two general categories: *branching statements* and *looping statements*. Branching statements make the program take one path or another based on the value of a variable or expression—just like the **if** statements you've already seen. Looping statements, on the other hand, make the program repeat a sequence of actions until a certain condition is reached.

In VBScript, branching statements are variations on **if...then**, as follows:

☆ **if.** This simply tells your program that if a certain condition is true (such as *Name* = *"Scott"* or a number being over 10), then it should carry out a certain statement or sequence of statements.

☆ **if...else.** Just like a plain **if** statement, this tells your program that if a certain condition is true, it should carry out a certain statement or sequence of statements. But it adds another instruction: If the condition is *not* true, then the program should do some other statement or sequence of statements. That's the **else** clause.

☆ **if...elseif.** With a simple **if** statement, your program decides its next move based on a single condition: the **if** clause. With an **if...else** statement, there are two conditions: the **if** clause and the **else** clause. With an **if...elseif** statement, there are multiple conditions: if A is true, then do B, **else if** C is true, then do D, **else if** E is true, then do F, and so on. Frankly, **if...elseif** statements are confusing and error-prone: they can usually be replaced by a sequence of simpler **if...else** statements, which is a good idea when possible.

☆ **select case.** This is a very sleek and economical replacement for a series of **if...else** statements when you have to deal with multiple alternatives. It's a special kind of branching statement that we'll cover at the end of the chapter.

Those are the branching statements. What about the looping statements? There are several of them, as follows:

☆ **for...next.** This allows you to set up a loop that will execute a specified number of times. Each time the loop executes, any statements in it are carried out. This type of loop is most useful when you know in advance how many times the loop should execute.

☆ **do...loop.** This repeats a statement or sequence of statements until a certain condition becomes true or false, depending on how you set up the loop.

☆ **while...wend.** Like a **do** loop, this repeats a statement or sequence of statements as long as a certain condition is true. It's not used too much, because anything you can do with **while...wend**, you can do with a **do** loop. It's included mainly because old-time Basic programmers still like it.

Using if Statements

You've seen **if** statements often enough by now that the concept should be familiar. There are just a few wrinkles you need to know. In particular, there are variations on the **if** statement. The important ones are the single-line **if** statement, the multiple-line **if** statement, and the **if...else** statement.

Single-Line if Statements

Single-line **if** statements, as their name implies, require only a single line of code. More significant is that when their **if** clause is true, they only carry out a single statement in their **then** clause. Here are a couple of examples:

```
if a = 10 then MsgBox "The value is 10."
if (temp > 212 and substance = "water") then CoffeeIsReady = true
```

The key factor is that there's only a single statement in the **then** clause. The syntax of a single-line **if** statement is **if** *X* **then** *Y.*

Multi-Line if Statements

Multiple-line **if** statements contain more than one statement in their **then** clause. As a result, they need an **end if** at the end to tell VBScript that the **then** clause is over and that the next line of code is not subject to the **if** clause.

That's a little abstract, so let's look at a specific code example. Suppose that we wanted to write some VBScript-like code to tell us things to do on Sunday afternoon. Consider how it might look with **if...then...endif**.

```
if Temperature > 100 then
    Say "The temperature is over 100."
    AdjustThermostat
end if
VacuumRug
GoShopping
WalkTheDog
```

It's fairly easy to see what's going on. If the temperature is over 100, announce the fact, then adjust the thermostat. After that, in completely unrelated business, vacuum the rug, go shopping, and walk the dog.

But suppose that we forgot to include the **end if** part of the **if** statement. The pseudocode would then look like this:

```
if Temperature > 100 then
    Say "The temperature is over 100."
    AdjustThermostat
VacuumRug
GoShopping
WalkTheDog
```

As a person, you can make a guess that vacuuming the rug, going shopping, and walking the dog have nothing to do with the temperature being over 100. But VBScript (and PCs generally) aren't that smart. All VBScript knows is that it saw an **if** statement and is busily carrying out the statements following the **then**. If the temperature were not over 100, then none of the non-temperature-related items would get done—because VBScript would think they were part of the **then** clause. That's why **end if** is needed in multi-line **if** statements. The syntax of a multi-line **if** statement is

```
if X then
    Y
    Z
    (etc.)
end if
```

if...else Statements

The final type of **if** statement is the **if...then...else** statement. This is usually a multi-line **if** statement, though it doesn't have to be: You can combine **if**, **then**, and **else** in a single-line **if** statement. The big difference is that after the **then** clause, there's an **else** clause that tells VBScript what to do if the **if** condition isn't true. The syntax of an **if...then...else** statement is:

```
if A then B else C
```

For a multi-line **if...then...else** statement you make the obvious changes, as shown in the following:

```
if A then
    B
    C
else
    D
    E
end if
```

A Wizardly if Example

You've seen enough simple examples of **if** statements that you'd probably be bored by another simple one. So let's look at a somewhat wizardly example. This will not only show you a few neat tricks, but will prove how much VBScript power you *already* have at your disposal. With **if** statements and a few other simple things you've learned, we're going to create a "Trivial Pursuit"-style game for a Web page. We'll call it "Trivia, Forsooth," because we don't want to get sued by the makers of Trivial Pursuit. The Web page from which a user can play Trivia, Forsooth is shown in Figure 5.1.

Playing the game is easy. The user first clicks on the "Set Up A New Game" button. That loads the questions and answers. Then, to get a question, the user clicks on the "Get A Question" button. A question appears in the text area at the left. At the right, the captions of the three option buttons change to the possible answers to the question. The user clicks in the option button he/she thinks gives the correct answer, then clicks on the "Give Your Answer" button. If the answer is correct, a congratulatory message box appears. If it's incorrect, a "wrong answer" message box appears, as shown in Figure 5.2.

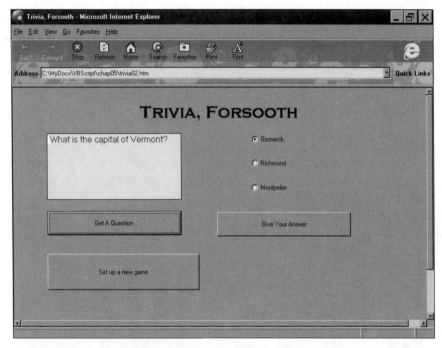

Figure 5.1 The Trivia, Forsooth game page.

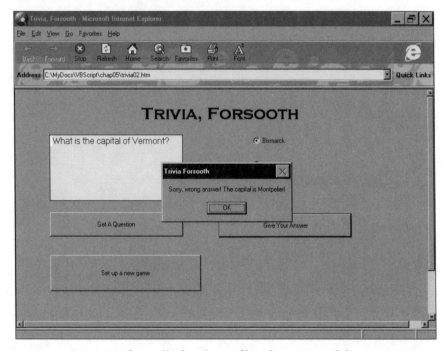

Figure 5.2 A message box tells the player if he/she answered the question correctly.

Okay, so it's not Doom. It's still a pretty snazzy game created with some fairly simple VBScript programming techniques. I created the page layout itself with Microsoft's ActiveX Control Pad, which is explained in a later chapter. The code that sets up the Web page is shown in Listing 5.1: It uses the HTML layout control to position the various ActiveX controls on the page. The layout code itself, including the VBScript code that actually runs the game, is shown in Listing 5.2.

Don't worry too much about the ActiveX and layout issues right now: We'll cover those fully in the chapter on the ActiveX Control Pad.

Listing 5.1　Code to create the Web page for the game.

```
<HTML>
<HEAD>
<TITLE>Trivia, Forsooth</TITLE>
</HEAD>
<BODY>

<OBJECT CLASSID="CLSID:812AE312-8B8E-11CF-93C8-00AA00C08FDF"
ID="trivia2" STYLE="LEFT:0;TOP:0">
<PARAM NAME="ALXPATH" REF VALUE="trivia2.alx">
 </OBJECT>

</BODY>
</HTML>
```

Listing 5.2　The VBScript code and ActiveX control layout.

```
<SCRIPT LANGUAGE="VBScript">
<!--
dim Questions(5)
dim Choices(5,3)
dim QuestionNum
dim GameSetUp

Sub Cmd_Setup_Click()
   GameSetUp = True

   QuestionNum = 0

   Questions(0) = "What is the capital of Vermont?"
   Questions(1) = "What is the best movie ever made?"
   Questions(2) = "What is the best scripting language?"
   Questions(3) = "Who played ""Blossom Russo"" on TV?"
   Questions(4) = "Who was the Lone Ranger's sidekick?"
```

```
      Choices(0,0) = "Bismarck"
      Choices(0,1) = "Richmond"
      Choices(0,2) = "Montpelier"

      Choices(1,0) = "Casablanca"
      Choices(1,1) = "The NeverEnding Story"
      Choices(1,2) = "Waterworld"

      Choices(2,0) = "VBScript"
      Choices(2,1) = "JavaScript"
      Choices(2,2) = "Eszterhas"

      Choices(3,0) = "Kellie Martin"
      Choices(3,1) = "Jodie Foster"
      Choices(3,2) = "Mayim Bialik"

      Choices(4,0) = "Kato"
      Choices(4,1) = "Tonto"
      Choices(4,2) = "Snoop Doggy Dogg"

      QuestionNum = -1
end sub

Sub Cmd_Question_Click()
   if not GameSetUp then
      msgbox "You must click the Setup button first."
      exit sub
   else
      QuestionNum = (QuestionNum + 1) mod 5
      Lbl_Question.caption = Questions(QuestionNum)
      OB_Answer1.value = true
      OB_Answer1.caption = Choices(QuestionNum, 0)
      OB_Answer2.caption = Choices(QuestionNum, 1)
      OB_Answer3.caption = Choices(QuestionNum, 2)
   end if
end sub

Sub Cmd_Answer_Click()
   if QuestionNum = 0 then
      if OB_Answer3.value = true then
         msgbox "That's right! It's Montpelier!",, _
               "Trivia Forsooth"
      else
         msgbox "Sorry, wrong answer! The capital is Montpelier!",, _
             "Trivia Forsooth"
      end if
   end if
```

```
    if QuestionNum = 1 then
        if OB_Answer2.value = true then
            msgbox "That's right! It's ""The NeverEnding Story!""",,
                "Trivia Forsooth"
        else
            msgbox "Sorry, wrong answer! It's ""The NeverEnding Story!""",,
                "Trivia Forsooth"
        end if
    end if

    if QuestionNum = 2 then
        if OB_Answer1.value = true then
            msgbox "That's right! It's VBScript!",,"Trivia Forsooth"
        else
            msgbox "Sorry, wrong answer! It's VBScript!",,
                "Trivia Forsooth"
        end if
    end if

    if QuestionNum = 3 then
        if OB_Answer3.value = true then
            msgbox "That's right! It's Mayim Bialik!",,"Trivia Forsooth"
        else
            msgbox "Sorry, wrong answer! It's Mayim Bialik!",,
                "Trivia Forsooth"
        end if
    end if

    if QuestionNum = 4 then
        if OB_Answer2.value = true then
            msgbox "That's right! It was Tonto!",,"Trivia Forsooth"
        else
            msgbox "Sorry, wrong answer! It was Tonto!",,
                "Trivia Forsooth"
        end if
    end if

end sub

-->
</SCRIPT>

<DIV STYLE="LAYOUT:FIXED;WIDTH:597pt;HEIGHT:370pt;">
    <OBJECT ID="Label1"
     CLASSID="CLSID:978C9E23-D4B0-11CE-BF2D-00AA003F40D0"
     STYLE="TOP:8pt;LEFT:173pt;WIDTH:231pt;HEIGHT:33pt;ZINDEX:0;">
        <PARAM NAME="Caption" VALUE="Trivia, Forsooth">
        <PARAM NAME="Size" VALUE="8149;1164">
        <PARAM NAME="FontName" VALUE="Copperplate Gothic Bold">
        <PARAM NAME="FontEffects" VALUE="1073741825">
```

```
    <PARAM NAME="FontHeight" VALUE="480">
    <PARAM NAME="FontCharSet" VALUE="0">
    <PARAM NAME="FontPitchAndFamily" VALUE="2">
    <PARAM NAME="FontWeight" VALUE="700">
</OBJECT>

<OBJECT ID="Lbl_Question"
 CLASSID="CLSID:978C9E23-D4B0-11CE-BF2D-00AA003F40D0"
 STYLE="TOP:50pt;LEFT:41pt;WIDTH:190pt;HEIGHT:91pt;ZINDEX:1;">
    <PARAM NAME="BackColor" VALUE="16777215">
    <PARAM NAME="Size" VALUE="6703;3210">
    <PARAM NAME="BorderStyle" VALUE="1">
    <PARAM NAME="FontHeight" VALUE="240">
    <PARAM NAME="FontCharSet" VALUE="0">
    <PARAM NAME="FontPitchAndFamily" VALUE="2">
    <PARAM NAME="FontWeight" VALUE="0">
</OBJECT>

<OBJECT ID="Cmd_Question"
 CLASSID="CLSID:D7053240-CE69-11CD-A777-00DD01143C57"
 STYLE="TOP:157pt;LEFT:41pt;WIDTH:190pt;
      HEIGHT:33pt;TABINDEX:2;ZINDEX:2;">
    <PARAM NAME="Caption" VALUE="Get A Question">
    <PARAM NAME="Size" VALUE="6703;1164">
    <PARAM NAME="FontCharSet" VALUE="0">
    <PARAM NAME="FontPitchAndFamily" VALUE="2">
    <PARAM NAME="ParagraphAlign" VALUE="3">
    <PARAM NAME="FontWeight" VALUE="0">
</OBJECT>

<OBJECT ID="OB_Answer1"
 CLASSID="CLSID:8BD21D50-EC42-11CE-9E0D-00AA006002F3"
 STYLE="TOP:50pt;LEFT:330pt;WIDTH:139pt;HEIGHT:17pt;
    TABINDEX:3;ZINDEX:3;">
    <PARAM NAME="BackColor" VALUE="-2147483633">
    <PARAM NAME="ForeColor" VALUE="-2147483630">
    <PARAM NAME="DisplayStyle" VALUE="5">
    <PARAM NAME="Size" VALUE="4904;600">
    <PARAM NAME="Value" VALUE="True">
    <PARAM NAME="Caption" VALUE="Answer #1">
    <PARAM NAME="FontCharSet" VALUE="0">
    <PARAM NAME="FontPitchAndFamily" VALUE="2">
    <PARAM NAME="FontWeight" VALUE="0">
</OBJECT>

<OBJECT ID="OB_Answer2"
 CLASSID="CLSID:8BD21D50-EC42-11CE-9E0D-00AA006002F3"
 STYLE="TOP:83pt;LEFT:329pt;WIDTH:132pt;HEIGHT:16pt;
      TABINDEX:4;ZINDEX:4;">
    <PARAM NAME="BackColor" VALUE="-2147483633">
```

```
    <PARAM NAME="ForeColor" VALUE="-2147483630">
    <PARAM NAME="DisplayStyle" VALUE="5">
    <PARAM NAME="Size" VALUE="4657;564">
    <PARAM NAME="Value" VALUE="False">
    <PARAM NAME="Caption" VALUE="Answer #2">
    <PARAM NAME="FontCharSet" VALUE="0">
    <PARAM NAME="FontPitchAndFamily" VALUE="2">
    <PARAM NAME="FontWeight" VALUE="0">
</OBJECT>

<OBJECT ID="OB_Answer3"
 CLASSID="CLSID:8BD21D50-EC42-11CE-9E0D-00AA006002F3"
 STYLE="TOP:116pt;LEFT:329;WIDTH:132pt;HEIGHT:17pt;
     TABINDEX:5;ZINDEX:5;">
    <PARAM NAME="BackColor" VALUE="-2147483633">
    <PARAM NAME="ForeColor" VALUE="-2147483630">
    <PARAM NAME="DisplayStyle" VALUE="5">
    <PARAM NAME="Size" VALUE="4657;600">
    <PARAM NAME="Value" VALUE="False">
    <PARAM NAME="Caption" VALUE="Answer #3">
    <PARAM NAME="FontCharSet" VALUE="0">
    <PARAM NAME="FontPitchAndFamily" VALUE="2">
    <PARAM NAME="FontWeight" VALUE="0">
</OBJECT>

<OBJECT ID="Cmd_Answer"
 CLASSID="CLSID:D7053240-CE69-11CD-A777-00DD01143C57"
 STYLE="TOP:158pt;LEFT:281pt;WIDTH:190pt;HEIGHT:33pt;
     TABINDEX:6;ZINDEX:6;">
    <PARAM NAME="Caption" VALUE="Give Your Answer">
    <PARAM NAME="Size" VALUE="6703;1164">
    <PARAM NAME="FontCharSet" VALUE="0">
    <PARAM NAME="FontPitchAndFamily" VALUE="2">
    <PARAM NAME="ParagraphAlign" VALUE="3">
    <PARAM NAME="FontWeight" VALUE="0">
</OBJECT>

<OBJECT ID="Cmd_Setup"
 CLASSID="CLSID:D7053240-CE69-11CD-A777-00DD01143C57"
 STYLE="TOP:215pt;LEFT:41pt;WIDTH:215pt;HEIGHT:50pt;
     TABINDEX:7;ZINDEX:7;">
    <PARAM NAME="Caption" VALUE="Set up a new game">
    <PARAM NAME="Size" VALUE="7585;1764">
    <PARAM NAME="FontCharSet" VALUE="0">
    <PARAM NAME="FontPitchAndFamily" VALUE="2">
    <PARAM NAME="ParagraphAlign" VALUE="3">
    <PARAM NAME="FontWeight" VALUE="0">
</OBJECT>

</DIV>
```

Setup Tasks In The "Trivia, Forsooth" Code

This program example uses **if...then...else** statements, as well as many of the concepts you learned in chapters 3 and 4. The first thing that the code does is to declare some global variables. Normally, variables should be hidden inside subs or functions, but these variables need to be used by several different subs: That's why they have to be global. The variables are declared as follows:

```
dim Questions(5)
dim Choices(5,3)
dim QuestionNum
dim GameSetUp
```

The variables **Questions** and **Choices** are all arrays—that is, variables which have slots to hold multiple variables. Arrays are covered in Chapter 3. The variables do the following jobs:

☆ **Questions** holds the text of questions to be displayed on the Web page in the question box.

☆ **Choices** holds the possible answers to the questions. The only thing that's a little odd is that the **Choices** array is followed by *two* numbers in parentheses: This means that it's a two-dimensional array. The first number indicates the question number. For each question, we want to display three possible answers as captions for the three option buttons on the Web page. Therefore, for each value in the question-number slot of the array, there are three corresponding values in the answer slots of the array.

☆ **QuestionNum** keeps track of the current question number.

☆ **GameSetUp** is a true-false variable that keeps track of whether or not the user has clicked on the Setup button.

Once the variables are declared, the next step required to play the game is for the user to click on the Cmd_Setup button. The Click event for the button loads the questions and answers into the **Questions** and **Choices** arrays, as well as setting values for **GameSetUp** and **QuestionNum**. From the code, you can see that you access array slots by using the name of the array and the number of the slot: Other than that, you can treat them just as you would any other variable.

At the end of the **Cmd_Setup_Click** sub, the code sets the **QuestionNum** variable to −1. That's so that when the user clicks on the "Get A Question" button, the value can always be increased by 1 and display the correct question.

Getting A Question

The next step for the user is to click on the "Get A Question" button. The code for this button's **Click** event is shown in the following code snippet:

```
Sub Cmd_Question_Click()
    if not GameSetUp then
        msgbox "You must click the Setup button first."
        exit sub
    else
        QuestionNum = (QuestionNum + 1) mod 5
        Lbl_Question.caption = Questions(QuestionNum)
        OB_Answer1.value = true
        OB_Answer1.caption = Choices(QuestionNum, 0)
        OB_Answer2.caption = Choices(QuestionNum, 1)
        OB_Answer3.caption = Choices(QuestionNum, 2)
    end if
end sub
```

The first thing that the sub does is check to see if the game has been set up properly—in particular, if the user has already clicked on the Cmd_Setup button. If the user hasn't done so, then the sub displays a message telling the user about the problem. It then uses the statement **exit sub** to, well, exit from the sub. That way, if the game hasn't been set up, VBScript won't waste its time carrying out the rest of the code lines in the sub. Notice that the code in the **Cmd_Question_Click** sub is a classic example of a multi-line **if...then...else** statement, complete with an **end if** at the end.

The **else** clause is where the action begins. First, the code adds 1 to the **QuestionNum** variable. We've allowed room in the **Questions** array for five questions. That leaves us with the problem of what to do when the user clicks on the "Get A Question" button but has already reached the last question. In this case, we've decided to send the user back to the first question. Remember in Chapter 4 when we looked at the **mod** operator? Any number **mod** will give you a repeating sequence of values, as follows:

```
0
1
2
3
4
0
1
2
3
4
(and so on)
```

As it happens, 0, 1, 2, 3, 4 are the numbers of the slots in the **Questions** array. After the last question has been played, the **mod** operator makes the game cycle back to the first question.

The next line of code displays the current question in the label control at the left side of the Web page:

```
Lbl_Question.caption = Questions(QuestionNum)
```

Notice that we assigned text from the current **Questions** array slot to the **caption** property of the label control.

At the right side of the Web page, of course, we have three option buttons (radio buttons) where the player can select an answer to the question. The next lines of code set up these buttons, as shown in the following.

```
OB_Answer1.value = true
OB_Answer1.caption = Choices(QuestionNum, 0)
OB_Answer2.caption = Choices(QuestionNum, 1)
OB_Answer3.caption = Choices(QuestionNum, 2)
```

The **value** property of an option button indicates whether or not it appears checked—that is, whether or not there's a black dot in the center of the button. When a question is first loaded, we always want the first option button to be selected. Therefore, we assign **true** to its **value** property.

Next, we load possible answers into the **caption** properties of the option buttons. For each question, there are three possible answers. Thus, for each value in the **QuestionNum** slot of the array, we cycle through all the slots containing answers—0, 1, 2. Each slot contains text (assigned when the user clicked on the Cmd_SetUp button) with a possible answer to the current question. Each possible answer is now displayed next to an option button.

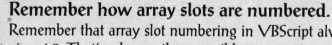

Remember how array slots are numbered.
Remember that array slot numbering in VBScript always begins at 0. That's why our three possible answers to each Trivia, Forsooth question are in slots numbered 0, 1, and 2.

After that, an **end if** statement ends the **if** statement. That's all there is in the sub for getting a question.

Giving An Answer

When the user clicks on the "Give Your Answer" button, the event code for that button is carried out. It's a long sub, but it's really quite simple because it repeats the same code pattern for each different question. The code for the first question is shown in the following code snippet:

```
if QuestionNum = 0 then
    if OB_Answer3.value = true then
        msgbox "That's right! It's Montpelier!",, _
            "Trivia Forsooth"
    else
        msgbox "Sorry, wrong answer! The capital is Montpelier!",, _
            "Trivia Forsooth"
    end if
end if
```

Essentially, this is just another **if...then...else** statement. The **if** clause checks the value of the option button that holds the correct answer for the current question number. If the player has checked that option button, then its value will be true. The sub displays a message box congratulating the player on giving the right answer.

If the correct option button is not checked, then the **else** clause kicks in. VBScript displays a message box telling the player that his/her answer was incorrect, and giving the correct answer.

There's only one other thing about this code pattern that's kind of interesting. Notice that we've embedded one **if..then..else** statement inside a multi-line **if** statement. First, the "big" **if** statement checks the current question number. If the question number doesn't match—in the code snippet, if it's not 0 and we're not on the first question—then VBScript skips everything else in that particular **if** statement and goes on to the next big **if** statement. The next big **if** statement asks if *QuestionNum = 1,* meaning, are we on the second question in the game, and so on.

Embedding one **if** statement inside another is something you'll do very often. All you need to remember is that an **if** statement is a statement. When you're embedding it inside another **if** statement, you follow the same rules as you would if you were embedding any other statement, such as a **MsgBox** statement.

And that's it for Trivia, Forsooth! I hope that this example has not only given you a better understanding of how **if** statements work, but also shown you the immense VBScript power that you already have in your hands.

Looping Statements

A different kind of control structure is the *looping statement*. This causes a statement or sequence of statements to repeat. The most common kinds of looping statement are the **for** loop and the **do** loop.

for Loops

A **for** loop usually counts from one number to another number, and on each count, carries out the statements inside the loop. That's why it's ideal when you know in advance how many times the loop should repeat. Here's a typical example of a **for** loop.

```
for i = 0 to 9
    AnArray(i) = ""
next
```

This **for** loop initializes an array by inserting a blank value in each array slot. The syntax of the **for** loop is as follows.

```
for x=1 to y
    A
    B
    C
next
```

Here, *x* is a loop counter variable that you have to declare separately from the loop itself. On each pass through the loop, the loop statements (A, B, and C) are carried out. Then, **next** sends VBScript back to the top of the loop, the value of the loop counter variable is increased by 1, and the loop statements execute again. This process continues until the loop counter variable's value *exceeds* the value of *y*. At that point, the program drops out of the loop and goes on with whatever statement (if any) comes after **next**.

There's also an optional **step** part of the loop statement. With **step**, you can control how much the loop counter variable increases on each pass through the loop. The following code snippet gives an example:

```
for x = 0 to 25 step 5
   MsgBox "The current loop number is " & x & "."
next
```

Without the **step** option, this loop would display the following sequence of messages:

```
The current loop number is 0.
The current loop number is 1.
The current loop number is 2.
The current loop number is 3.
The current loop number is 4.
The current loop number is 5.
(and so on)
```

However, with the **step** option set to 5, the following messages would be displayed:

```
The current loop number is 0.
The current loop number is 5.
The current loop number is 10.
The current loop number is 15.
The current loop number is 20.
The current loop number is 25.
```

A Simple for Loop Example

That's all abstract, so let's look at a specific example. Listing 5.3 gives the HTML code for a page that demonstrates a simple **for** loop, while Listing 5.4 gives the ActiveX layout and the VBScript code. The resulting Web page is shown in Figure 5.3.

Listing 5.3   HTML code for the Web page in Figure 5.3.

```
<HTML>
<HEAD>
<TITLE>For Loop Demonstration</TITLE>
</HEAD>
<BODY>

<OBJECT CLASSID="CLSID:812AE312-8B8E-11CF-93C8-00AA00C08FDF"
ID="forloop1" STYLE="LEFT:0;TOP:0">
<PARAM NAME="ALXPATH" REF VALUE="file:C:\MyDocs\VBScript\chap05\forloop1.alx">
 </OBJECT>

</BODY>
</HTML>
```

Listing 5.4 VBScript code and ActiveX layout for the Web page.

```
<SCRIPT LANGUAGE="VBScript">
<!--
Sub Cmd_DoLoops_Click()
dim LoopCounter, NumLoops
if TB_NumberOfLoops.text = "" then
   msgbox "You must enter the number of loops first.",, _
      "For Loop Demonstration"
else
   NumLoops = TB_NumberOfLoops.text
   for LoopCounter = 1 to NumLoops
      Lbl_LoopDisplay.caption = LoopCounter
   next
end if

end sub
-->
</SCRIPT>
<DIV STYLE="LAYOUT:FIXED;WIDTH:597pt;HEIGHT:370pt;">
    <OBJECT ID="Lbl_LoopDisplay"
     CLASSID="CLSID:978C9E23-D4B0-11CE-BF2D-00AA003F40D0"
     STYLE="TOP:41pt;LEFT:281pt;WIDTH:74pt;HEIGHT:58pt;ZINDEX:0;">
        <PARAM NAME="BackColor" VALUE="16777215">
        <PARAM NAME="Size" VALUE="2611;2046">
        <PARAM NAME="BorderStyle" VALUE="1">
        <PARAM NAME="FontName" VALUE="Times New Roman">
        <PARAM NAME="FontHeight" VALUE="480">
        <PARAM NAME="FontCharSet" VALUE="0">
        <PARAM NAME="FontPitchAndFamily" VALUE="2">
        <PARAM NAME="FontWeight" VALUE="0">
    </OBJECT>
    <OBJECT ID="TB_NumberOfLoops"
     CLASSID="CLSID:8BD21D10-EC42-11CE-9E0D-00AA006002F3"
     STYLE="TOP:41pt;LEFT:17pt;WIDTH:74pt;HEIGHT:58pt;
        TABINDEX:1;ZINDEX:1;">
        <PARAM NAME="VariousPropertyBits" VALUE="746604571">
        <PARAM NAME="Size" VALUE="2611;2046">
        <PARAM NAME="FontName" VALUE="Times New Roman">
        <PARAM NAME="FontHeight" VALUE="480">
        <PARAM NAME="FontCharSet" VALUE="0">
        <PARAM NAME="FontPitchAndFamily" VALUE="2">
        <PARAM NAME="FontWeight" VALUE="0">
    </OBJECT>
    <OBJECT ID="Label2"
     CLASSID="CLSID:978C9E23-D4B0-11CE-BF2D-00AA003F40D0"
        STYLE="TOP:17pt;LEFT:17pt;WIDTH:248pt;
            HEIGHT:17pt;ZINDEX:2;">
        <PARAM NAME="Caption"
            VALUE="Enter the number of loops you want:">
        <PARAM NAME="Size" VALUE="8749;600">
```

```
            <PARAM NAME="FontHeight" VALUE="280">
            <PARAM NAME="FontCharSet" VALUE="0">
            <PARAM NAME="FontPitchAndFamily" VALUE="2">
            <PARAM NAME="FontWeight" VALUE="0">
        </OBJECT>
        <OBJECT ID="Label3"
         CLASSID="CLSID:978C9E23-D4B0-11CE-BF2D-00AA003F40D0"
         STYLE="TOP:17pt;LEFT:281pt;WIDTH:239pt;HEIGHT:17pt;ZINDEX:3;">
            <PARAM NAME="Caption" VALUE="Here's where the loops count off">
            <PARAM NAME="Size" VALUE="8431;600">
            <PARAM NAME="FontHeight" VALUE="280">
            <PARAM NAME="FontCharSet" VALUE="0">
            <PARAM NAME="FontPitchAndFamily" VALUE="2">
            <PARAM NAME="FontWeight" VALUE="0">
        </OBJECT>
        <OBJECT ID="Cmd_DoLoops"
         CLASSID="CLSID:D7053240-CE69-11CD-A777-00DD01143C57"
         STYLE="TOP:157pt;LEFT:281pt;WIDTH:198pt;
             HEIGHT:41pt;TABINDEX:4;ZINDEX:4;">
            <PARAM NAME="Caption" VALUE="Count off the loops">
            <PARAM NAME="Size" VALUE="6985;1446">
            <PARAM NAME="FontCharSet" VALUE="0">
            <PARAM NAME="FontPitchAndFamily" VALUE="2">
            <PARAM NAME="ParagraphAlign" VALUE="3">
            <PARAM NAME="FontWeight" VALUE="0">
        </OBJECT>
</DIV>
```

This program uses a fairly simple—if somewhat atypical—**for** loop. The user enters a number in the text box on the left side of the Web page. Then, when he/she clicks the command button, the **for** loop executes. On each pass through the loop, it displays the current loop number in the label on the right side of the Web page.

Now, if you run this program, all you're likely to see displayed is the last number in the sequence—*i.e.,* the same number the user entered in the text box. That's because the loop runs so blindingly fast that the other numbers whiz by too quickly for you to see them. It's not a big worry, because **for** loops are used most often to initialize arrays and for other tasks that don't need to be slowed down for human eyes.

do Loops

The other major kind of loop in VBScript (apart from **while...wend**, which we won't cover here) is the **do** loop. This type of loop is normally used when you do *not* know in advance how many times the loops should execute: All you know is that it should execute either (a) as long as a certain condition is true, in which

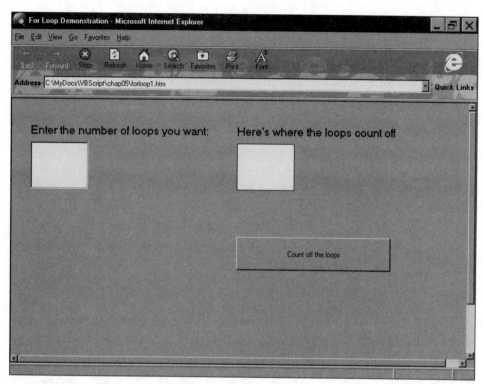

Figure 5.3 Demonstrating a very fast **for** loop.

case, you'd add a **while** clause; or (b) until a certain condition *becomes* true, in which case, you'd add an **until** clause.

Whether you use **while** or **until**, there are two basic varieties of the **do** loop. When you're setting up a **do** loop, you need to ask if the loop should always execute at least once, no matter what. For example, suppose that you set up a loop to execute *while x < 10.* Suppose that the program gets to the **do** loop and *x* already equals 15? Do you still need the loop statements to be carried out at least once?

Your answer to that question will determine which kind of **do** statement you use. If you don't want the loop statements to execute at all if the loop condition is false when the program gets to the loop, you put **while** or **until** at the top of the loop, as shown in the following code snippet:

```
do while x < 10
    A
    B
    C
loop
```

When the program reaches this loop, it first checks to see if *x* is less than 10. If it is, then the program carries out statements A, B, C, and $x = x + 1$. The **loop** keyword then sends the program back to the first line of the loop, and the *x* check is repeated. This process continues as long as *x* is less than 10. The value of *x* might be set by a user clicking a button: Make absolutely sure that you always include a way for your loop to terminate. Otherwise, your program will go into an endless loop, and you'll miss dinner.

If you want the loop to execute at least once, whether or not the loop condition is true when the program gets to the loop, you put **while** or **until** at the bottom of the loop. This is shown in the following code snippet:

```
do
    A
    B
    C
loop while x < 10
```

In this case, when the program gets to the loop, it does not first check to see if the loop condition is true. That means it will always execute the statements in the loop at least once. After executing the loop statements, the program gets to the **loop while** clause and checks to see if the loop condition is true. If it is, then it goes back to the top of the loop and repeats the process. Otherwise, it goes on to the next statement following the loop.

Using select case Statements

VBScript's **if** statements are fine, but you saw how involved and repetitive they could get with only five alternatives—the five questions in Trivia, Forsooth. If you wanted to increase the number of questions to 15 or 20, your VBScript code would get terribly cluttered with all those **if...else** statements.

Fortunately, there's an alternative: **select case**. This type of branching statement, often called simply a "case" statement for short, gives you a neat and economical way to handle multiple alternatives. The basic syntax of a **select case** statement is as follows:

```
select case ControlVariable
    case X
        ' Some VBScript statements
    case Y
        ' Some VBScript statements
```

```
    case Z
        ' Some VBScript statements
    case else
        ' Some VBScript statements
end select
```

The **select case** statement tests the value of the control variable—here, rather unimaginatively called **ControlVariable**. Each case has a list of one or more constants, which can be numbers, strings, or any valid VBScript data type. When the value of the control variable matches a particular case, VBScript does all the statements for that case. If the control variable doesn't match a value in any of the cases, then VBScript does the statements that go with **case else**. Finally, the program drops out of the **select case** statement and moves on to the next statement after **end select**.

Each case, by the way, can include more than one value. You can have a list of values, or a range, or even an inequality, as shown in the following code lines:

```
case 10, 20, 25, 31
case 10 to 20
case 21 to 30, 75 to 80
case is < 15       ' When specifying a range, use the word IS.
```

Obviously, you wouldn't see all of those cases in a single **select case** statement, inasmuch as there's quite a bit of overlap. But they show what you can do in setting up cases for a **select case** statement.

A Simple select case Example

Let's look at a simple example of a **select case** statement in action. Listing 5.5 shows the VBScript code and ActiveX layout for a Web page that gets the user's first name, then makes a comment about it. Listing 5.6 shows the HTML code that uses the layout. Figure 5.4 shows the Web page set up by the code.

Listing 5.5 A simple **select case** example.

```
<SCRIPT LANGUAGE="VBScript">
<!--
Sub Cmd_Ask_Click()
    dim UserName

    UserName = TB_UserName.text

    select case UserName
```

```
      case "Scott"
        msgbox "Are you the author of this book?",,"Select Case Statements"
      case "Ludwig"
        msgbox "Are you of Germanic ancestry?",,"Select Case Statements"
      case "Fabio"
        msgbox "Are you a total and utter geek?",,"Select Case Statements"
      case else
        msgbox "That's a very nice name!",,"Select Case Statements"
      end select

end sub
-->

</SCRIPT>

<DIV STYLE="LAYOUT:FIXED;WIDTH:597pt;HEIGHT:370pt;">
    <OBJECT ID="Label1"
     CLASSID="CLSID:978C9E23-D4B0-11CE-BF2D-00AA003F40D0"
     STYLE="TOP:99pt;LEFT:116pt;WIDTH:140pt;HEIGHT:25pt;ZINDEX:0;">
        <PARAM NAME="Caption" VALUE="Enter your first name:">
        <PARAM NAME="Size" VALUE="4948;873">
        <PARAM NAME="FontName" VALUE="Times New Roman">
        <PARAM NAME="FontHeight" VALUE="320">
        <PARAM NAME="FontCharSet" VALUE="0">
        <PARAM NAME="FontPitchAndFamily" VALUE="2">
        <PARAM NAME="FontWeight" VALUE="0">
    </OBJECT>
    <OBJECT ID="TB_UserName"
     CLASSID="CLSID:8BD21D10-EC42-11CE-9E0D-00AA006002F3"
     STYLE="TOP:99pt;LEFT:272pt;WIDTH:140pt;
            HEIGHT:25pt;TABINDEX:1;ZINDEX:1;">
        <PARAM NAME="VariousPropertyBits" VALUE="746604571">
        <PARAM NAME="Size" VALUE="4948;873">
        <PARAM NAME="FontHeight" VALUE="360">
        <PARAM NAME="FontCharSet" VALUE="0">
        <PARAM NAME="FontPitchAndFamily" VALUE="2">
        <PARAM NAME="FontWeight" VALUE="0">
    </OBJECT>
    <OBJECT ID="Cmd_Ask"
     CLASSID="CLSID:D7053240-CE69-11CD-A777-00DD01143C57"
     STYLE="TOP:157pt;LEFT:182pt;WIDTH:182pt;
            HEIGHT:33pt;TABINDEX:2;ZINDEX:2;">
        <PARAM NAME="Caption" VALUE="Ask VBScript about your name">
        <PARAM NAME="Size" VALUE="6403;1164">
        <PARAM NAME="FontCharSet" VALUE="0">
        <PARAM NAME="FontPitchAndFamily" VALUE="2">
        <PARAM NAME="ParagraphAlign" VALUE="3">
        <PARAM NAME="FontWeight" VALUE="0">
    </OBJECT>
    <OBJECT ID="Label2"
```

```
CLASSID="CLSID:978C9E23-D4B0-11CE-BF2D-00AA003F40D0"
STYLE="TOP:33pt;LEFT:83pt;WIDTH:380pt;HEIGHT:41pt;ZINDEX:3;">
    <PARAM NAME="Caption"
      VALUE="A Demonstration of Select Case Statements">
    <PARAM NAME="Size" VALUE="13388;1455">
    <PARAM NAME="FontName" VALUE="Times New Roman">
    <PARAM NAME="FontEffects" VALUE="1073741825">
    <PARAM NAME="FontHeight" VALUE="400">
    <PARAM NAME="FontCharSet" VALUE="0">
    <PARAM NAME="FontPitchAndFamily" VALUE="2">
    <PARAM NAME="FontWeight" VALUE="700">
  </OBJECT>
</DIV>
```

Listing 5.6 HTML code for the layout in Listing 5.5.

```
<HTML>
<HEAD>
<TITLE>Select Case Statements</TITLE>
</HEAD>
<BODY>

<OBJECT CLASSID="CLSID:812AE312-8B8E-11CF-93C8-00AA00C08FDF"
ID="select1" STYLE="LEFT:0;TOP:0">
<PARAM NAME="ALXPATH" REF VALUE=
    "file:C:\MyDocs\VBScript\chap06\select1.alx">
 </OBJECT>

</BODY>
</HTML>
```

Let's take a look at how **select case** works in this program. The command button's click event sub begins with two code lines, as follows:

```
dim UserName
UserName = TB_UserName.text
```

The first line declares a local variable to hold the name that the user enters in the text box. The second line assigns the text box's **text** property to the variable. We'll then use the variable to control the action of the **select case** statement, as follows:

```
select case UserName
   case "Scott"
     msgbox "Are you the author of this book?",, _
        "Select Case Statements"
```

This pattern is repeated for each case, until we get to the optional **case else** clause. That clause is simply a way to catch any cases that we haven't anticipated.

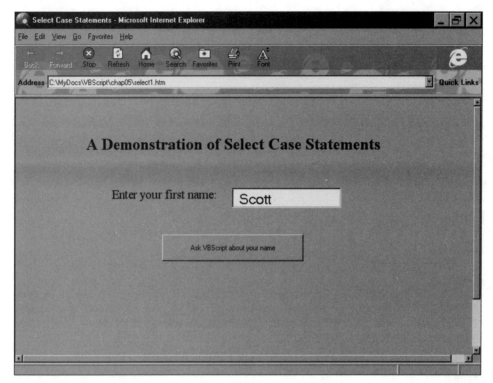

Figure 5.4   The Web page set up by Listings 5.5 and 5.6.

At the end of all the cases, we use an **end select** statement to tell VBScript that no more cases are coming.

When the user enters his or her name and clicks on the command button, a message box is displayed like the one shown in Figure 5.5.

What, no break?

If you're coming to VBScript from C or C++, you might wonder why the statements for each case don't end with something like **break**, and why the whole **select case** statement seems devoid of the punctuation (colons, semicolons, etc.) that you use to parse **case** statements in C and C++.

The answer is that because of the way VBScript processes **select case** statements, a **break** statement is unnecessary. Moreover,

Figure 5.5   The program displays a message box.

> unlike most other languages such as C, C++, and Pascal, VBScript is a line-oriented language. As a result, no extra punctuation is necessary to distinguish one line from another, whether in a **select case** statement or elsewhere.

A More Wizardly select case Example

Let's apply this **select case** technique to "Trivia, Forsooth" to see how it might smooth out our code if we increased the number of questions to 15. Listing 5.7 shows how our VBScript code would change for a game with 15 questions if we used a **select case** statement instead of a series of **if...else** statements. (The HTML code that appears in Listing 5.1 doesn't change, so we won't reproduce it here.) The game works exactly the same as before, but you can imagine how long and cluttered the code would be with three times as many **if...else** statements as appeared earlier in Listing 5.2!

Listing 5.7   Using **select case** in the Trivia, Forsooth code.

```
<SCRIPT LANGUAGE="VBScript">
<!--
dim Questions(15)
dim Choices(15,3)
dim QuestionNum
dim GameSetUp

Sub Cmd_Setup_Click()

    GameSetUp = True
    MsgBox "The game is ready to play! Click " & _
       ""Get a Question"" to begin.",,"Trivia Forsooth"

    Questions(0) = "What is the capital of Vermont?"
    Questions(1) = "What is the best movie ever made?"
    Questions(2) = "What is the best scripting language?"
    Questions(3) = "Who played ""Blossom Russo"" on TV?"
    Questions(4) = "Who was the Lone Ranger's sidekick?"
```

```
Questions(5) = "How many biblical commandments are " & _
    "recognized by Orthodox Judaism?"
Questions(6) = "What is Pee-Wee Herman's real name?"
Questions(7) = "Which Constitutional amendment reserves " & _
    "powers to the states or the people?"
Questions(8) = "How many pounds are in a kilogram?"
Questions(9) = "In what year did Jodie Foster act in the " & _
    " TV series ""Paper Moon""?"

Questions(10) = "In what year did the Germans bomb Pearl Harbor?"
Questions(11) = "Selenium is .. ?"
Questions(12) = "What is the sixth planet in the solar system?"
Questions(13) = "In Norse mythology, where did the gods live?"
Questions(14) = "Who invented the Pascal programming language?"


Choices(0,0) = "Bismarck"
Choices(0,1) = "Richmond"
Choices(0,2) = "Montpelier"

Choices(1,0) = "Casablanca"
Choices(1,1) = "The NeverEnding Story"
Choices(1,2) = "Waterworld"

Choices(2,0) = "VBScript"
Choices(2,1) = "JavaScript"
Choices(2,2) = "Eszterhas"

Choices(3,0) = "Kellie Martin"
Choices(3,1) = "Jodie Foster"
Choices(3,2) = "Mayim Bialik"

Choices(4,0) = "Kato"
Choices(4,1) = "Tonto"
Choices(4,2) = "Snoop Doggy Dogg"

Choices(5,0) = "10"
Choices(5,1) = "613"
Choices(5,2) = "5,280"

Choices(6,0) = "Marion Mercer"
Choices(6,1) = "Paul Rubenfeld"
Choices(6,2) = "Archibald Leach"

Choices(7,0) = "The 5th"
Choices(7,1) = "The 2nd"
Choices(7,2) = "The 10th"

Choices(8,0) = "2.2"
Choices(8,1) = "1.77"
Choices(8,2) = "5"
```

```
      Choices(9,0) = "1980"
      Choices(9,1) = "1961"
      Choices(9,2) = "1974"

      Choices(10,0) = "1945"
      Choices(10,1) = "1941"
      Choices(10,2) = "1918"

      Choices(11,0) = "A planet"
      Choices(11,1) = "A chemical element"
      Choices(11,2) = "The capital of Moldavia"

      Choices(12,0) = "Saturn"
      Choices(12,1) = "Neptune"
      Choices(12,2) = "Mars"

      Choices(13,0) = "Mt. Olympus"
      Choices(13,1) = "Valhallah"
      Choices(13,2) = "Asgard"

      Choices(14,0) = "Antony Hoare"
      Choices(14,1) = "Niklaus Wirth"
      Choices(14,2) = "Mary Worth"

      QuestionNum = -1
   end sub

Sub Cmd_Question_Click()
   if not GameSetUp then
      msgbox "You must click the Setup button first.",, _
         "Trivia Forsooth"
      exit sub
   else
      QuestionNum = (QuestionNum + 1) mod 15
      Lbl_Question.caption = Questions(QuestionNum)
      OB_Answer1.value = true
      OB_Answer1.caption = Choices(QuestionNum, 0)
      OB_Answer2.caption = Choices(QuestionNum, 1)
      OB_Answer3.caption = Choices(QuestionNum, 2)
   end if
end sub

Sub Cmd_Answer_Click()

   Select Case QuestionNum
   case 2, 8, 12
      if OB_Answer1.value = true then
         MsgBox "That's right! The answer is " & _
            Choices(QuestionNum, 0) & "!",,"Trivia, Forsooth"
      else
         MsgBox "Sorry, wrong! The answer is " & _
            Choices(QuestionNum, 0) & "!",,"Trivia, Forsooth"
```

```
      end if
   case 1, 4, 5, 6, 11, 14
      if OB_Answer2.value = true then
         MsgBox "That's right! The answer is " & _
            Choices(QuestionNum, 1) & "!",,"Trivia, Forsooth"
      else
         MsgBox "Sorry, wrong! The answer is " & _
            Choices(QuestionNum, 1) & "!",,"Trivia, Forsooth"
      end if
   case 0, 3, 7, 9, 13
      if OB_Answer3.value = true then
         MsgBox "That's right! The answer is " & _
            Choices(QuestionNum, 2) & "!",,"Trivia, Forsooth"
      else
         MsgBox "Sorry, wrong! The answer is " & _
            Choices(QuestionNum, 2) & "!",,"Trivia, Forsooth"
      end if
   case 10
      MsgBox "SUCKER! It was the Japanese who bombed " & _
         "Pearl Harbor, not the Germans!",,"Trivia, Forsooth"
   case else
      MsgBox "Warning! Program error! Run for your lives!",, _
         "Trivia, Forsooth"
   end select

   Cmd_Question_Click

end sub

-->

</SCRIPT>
<DIV STYLE="LAYOUT:FIXED;WIDTH:597pt;HEIGHT:370pt;">
   <OBJECT ID="Label1"
    CLASSID="CLSID:978C9E23-D4B0-11CE-BF2D-00AA003F40D0"
    STYLE="TOP:8pt;LEFT:173pt;WIDTH:231pt;HEIGHT:33pt;ZINDEX:0;">
      <PARAM NAME="Caption" VALUE="Trivia, Forsooth">
      <PARAM NAME="Size" VALUE="8149;1164">
      <PARAM NAME="FontName" VALUE="Copperplate Gothic Bold">
      <PARAM NAME="FontEffects" VALUE="1073741825">
      <PARAM NAME="FontHeight" VALUE="480">
      <PARAM NAME="FontCharSet" VALUE="0">
      <PARAM NAME="FontPitchAndFamily" VALUE="2">
      <PARAM NAME="FontWeight" VALUE="700">
   </OBJECT>
   <OBJECT ID="Lbl_Question"
    CLASSID="CLSID:978C9E23-D4B0-11CE-BF2D-00AA003F40D0"
    STYLE="TOP:50pt;LEFT:41pt;WIDTH:190pt;HEIGHT:91pt;ZINDEX:1;">
      <PARAM NAME="BackColor" VALUE="16777215">
      <PARAM NAME="Size" VALUE="6703;3210">
      <PARAM NAME="BorderStyle" VALUE="1">
```

```
    <PARAM NAME="FontHeight" VALUE="240">
    <PARAM NAME="FontCharSet" VALUE="0">
    <PARAM NAME="FontPitchAndFamily" VALUE="2">
    <PARAM NAME="FontWeight" VALUE="0">
</OBJECT>
<OBJECT ID="Cmd_Question"
 CLASSID="CLSID:D7053240-CE69-11CD-A777-00DD01143C57"
 STYLE="TOP:157pt;LEFT:41pt;WIDTH:190pt;
     HEIGHT:33pt;TABINDEX:2;ZINDEX:2;">
    <PARAM NAME="Caption" VALUE="Get A Question">
    <PARAM NAME="Size" VALUE="6703;1164">
    <PARAM NAME="FontCharSet" VALUE="0">
    <PARAM NAME="FontPitchAndFamily" VALUE="2">
    <PARAM NAME="ParagraphAlign" VALUE="3">
    <PARAM NAME="FontWeight" VALUE="0">
</OBJECT>
<OBJECT ID="OB_Answer1"
 CLASSID="CLSID:8BD21D50-EC42-11CE-9E0D-00AA006002F3"
 STYLE="TOP:50pt;LEFT:330pt;WIDTH:139pt;
     HEIGHT:17pt;TABINDEX:3;ZINDEX:3;">
    <PARAM NAME="BackColor" VALUE="-2147483633">
    <PARAM NAME="ForeColor" VALUE="-2147483630">
    <PARAM NAME="DisplayStyle" VALUE="5">
    <PARAM NAME="Size" VALUE="4904;600">
    <PARAM NAME="Value" VALUE="True">
    <PARAM NAME="Caption" VALUE="Answer #1">
    <PARAM NAME="FontCharSet" VALUE="0">
    <PARAM NAME="FontPitchAndFamily" VALUE="2">
    <PARAM NAME="FontWeight" VALUE="0">
</OBJECT>
<OBJECT ID="OB_Answer2"
 CLASSID="CLSID:8BD21D50-EC42-11CE-9E0D-00AA006002F3"
 STYLE="TOP:83pt;LEFT:329pt;WIDTH:132pt;
     HEIGHT:16pt;TABINDEX:4;ZINDEX:4;">
    <PARAM NAME="BackColor" VALUE="-2147483633">
    <PARAM NAME="ForeColor" VALUE="-2147483630">
    <PARAM NAME="DisplayStyle" VALUE="5">
    <PARAM NAME="Size" VALUE="4657;564">
    <PARAM NAME="Value" VALUE="False">
    <PARAM NAME="Caption" VALUE="Answer #2">
    <PARAM NAME="FontCharSet" VALUE="0">
    <PARAM NAME="FontPitchAndFamily" VALUE="2">
    <PARAM NAME="FontWeight" VALUE="0">
</OBJECT>
<OBJECT ID="OB_Answer3"
 CLASSID="CLSID:8BD21D50-EC42-11CE-9E0D-00AA006002F3"
 STYLE="TOP:116pt;LEFT:329pt;WIDTH:132pt;
     HEIGHT:17pt;TABINDEX:5;ZINDEX:5;">
    <PARAM NAME="BackColor" VALUE="-2147483633">
    <PARAM NAME="ForeColor" VALUE="-2147483630">
    <PARAM NAME="DisplayStyle" VALUE="5">
```

```
            <PARAM NAME="Size" VALUE="4657;600">
            <PARAM NAME="Value" VALUE="False">
            <PARAM NAME="Caption" VALUE="Answer #3">
            <PARAM NAME="FontCharSet" VALUE="0">
            <PARAM NAME="FontPitchAndFamily" VALUE="2">
            <PARAM NAME="FontWeight" VALUE="0">
        </OBJECT>
        <OBJECT ID="Cmd_Answer"
         CLASSID="CLSID:D7053240-CE69-11CD-A777-00DD01143C57"
         STYLE="TOP:158pt;LEFT:281pt;WIDTH:190pt;
             HEIGHT:33pt;TABINDEX:6;ZINDEX:6;">
            <PARAM NAME="Caption" VALUE="Give Your Answer">
            <PARAM NAME="Size" VALUE="6703;1164">
            <PARAM NAME="FontCharSet" VALUE="0">
            <PARAM NAME="FontPitchAndFamily" VALUE="2">
            <PARAM NAME="ParagraphAlign" VALUE="3">
            <PARAM NAME="FontWeight" VALUE="0">
        </OBJECT>
        <OBJECT ID="Cmd_Setup"
         CLASSID="CLSID:D7053240-CE69-11CD-A777-00DD01143C57"
         STYLE="TOP:215pt;LEFT:41pt;WIDTH:215pt;
             HEIGHT:50pt;TABINDEX:7;ZINDEX:7;">
            <PARAM NAME="Caption" VALUE="Set up a new game">
            <PARAM NAME="Size" VALUE="7585;1764">
            <PARAM NAME="FontCharSet" VALUE="0">
            <PARAM NAME="FontPitchAndFamily" VALUE="2">
            <PARAM NAME="ParagraphAlign" VALUE="3">
            <PARAM NAME="FontWeight" VALUE="0">
        </OBJECT>
    </DIV>
```

Other than the **select case** statement, the code works the same as before, so let's focus on the **select case** statement. As in our simpler **select case** example, it begins by specifying the control variable:

```
Select Case QuestionNum
```

Each case corresponds to one of the possible answers to a question—answer 1, answer 2, or answer 3. For example, if you scan through the answers, you'll see that the user gives a correct answer to questions 2, 8, and 12 by clicking on the first option button—that is, by picking the first possible answer. Therefore, the first case in the **select case** statement is as follows:

```
case 2, 8, 12
    if OB_Answer1.value = true then
        MsgBox "That's right! The answer is " & _
            Choices(QuestionNum, 0) & "!",,"Trivia, Forsooth"
    else
```

```
    MsgBox "Sorry, wrong! The answer is " & _
        Choices(QuestionNum, 0) & "!",,"Trivia, Forsooth"
end if
```

The statements in this case, of course, will only be executed if the value of **QuestionNum** is 2, 8, or 12. VBScript then checks to see if the user selected the first option button. If so, then the user gave the correct answer and gets a congratulatory message box. Otherwise—as in the **else** clause—the user gave an incorrect answer and gets a message box about the error.

Notice that we've made one other enhancement in the code. In the original version, the message boxes were hard-coded with the specific answer to an individual question, as in the following:

```
msgbox "That's right! It's VBScript!",,"Trivia Forsooth"
```

When we're grouping together several questions in each case, that kind of hard coding isn't possible. Fortunately, it isn't necessary, either. All we needed to do was remember that the correct answer for each question is stored in a particular slot of the **Choices** array. Then, for each case, we simply pull the answer out of that slot and plug it into the message boxes we show to the user, as follows:

```
MsgBox "That's right! The answer is " & _
        Choices(QuestionNum, 0) & "!",,"Trivia, Forsooth"
```

That's it for control structures! In the next chapter, we'll take our first look at the ActiveX Control Pad and how you can use it to create snazzy Web page layouts like the one used in the "Trivia, Forsooth" game.

VI

USING SUBS AND FUNCTIONS

By now, you've seen
lots of subs and func-
tions. This chapter
gives you the complete
details on how, when,
and why to create
them.

We've been using subs and functions all through the previous five chapters. But we've never really paused to examine what they are or how they work. Both subs and functions are named blocks of code. However, they differ in an important way. In a nutshell:

☆ Subs (procedures) *perform program tasks.*

☆ Functions *return values.*

VBScript comes with a large number of predefined subs and functions. You can also create your own for program-specific tasks.

Subs Vs. Functions: "Vive La Difference"

Subs do things like responding to events and directing the program to go in one direction or another. Every time the user clicks a command button, that button's **Click** sub fires, executing the statements it contains and performing a specific program action.

Functions, on the other hand, simply take values, massage them, and return new values based on the ones they received. For example, you might need to know the square root of a number. You could hand the number to VBScript's **sqr()** function, and the function would immediately hand back the square root.

A good way to visualize the contrast between subs and functions is to think of subs as complete sentences and think of functions as individual words. Consider **MsgBox**, which comes in both a sub version (the **MsgBox** statement) and a function version. A **MsgBox** statement (or sub) stands by itself on a code line, as follows.

```
MsgBox "This is the message box caption",,"This is the message box title."
```

A use of the **MsgBox** function, on the other hand, is part of a program statement, just as an English word is part of a statement. This is illustrated in the following code line:

```
UserChoice = MsgBox("This is the message box caption.",3, _
    "This is the message box title.")
```

There are a couple of other differences, but the main point should be clear. A sub is like a complete sentence, whereas a function is like a word.

The MsgBox Sub Vs. The MsgBox Function

Let's look at an example that illustrates this contrast. In previous chapters, we've used the **MsgBox** statement several times to display message boxes on the user's screen. But these message boxes really don't do anything but display a message. Often, that's plenty.

But suppose you want to display a message box that gets a value from the user. By using the **MsgBox** function instead of the message box statement, you can display a message box that has multiple buttons and immediately hands back a value indicating which button the user clicked. Listing 6.1 shows the VBScript code and ActiveX layout for a program that uses both the **MsgBox** statement and the **MsgBox** function; Listing 6.2 shows the HTML code that sets up the containing Web page. Figure 6.1 shows the Web page created by Listings 6.1 and 6.2.

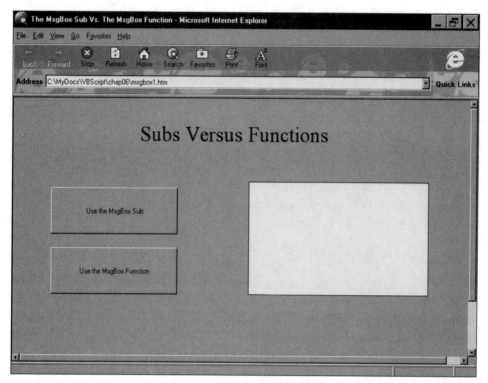

Figure 6.1 A Web page that uses both the **MsgBox** statement and the **MsgBox** function.

Listing 6.1 VBScript code and ActiveX layout for a **MsgBox** demonstration.

```
<SCRIPT LANGUAGE="VBScript">
<!--
Sub Cmd_Function_Click()
dim UserChoice

UserChoice = MsgBox("This is displayed by the MsgBox function. " & _
   "It gets a value from the user. Do you want to display your " & _
   "answer in the label control at the right?",3,"Subs vs. Functions")

   select case UserChoice
      case 6
         Lbl_Answer.caption = "Yes!"
      case 7
         lbl_Answer.caption = "No!"
      case 2
         lbl_Answer.caption = ""
   end select

end sub

Sub Cmd_Sub_Click()
MsgBox "This is displayed by the MsgBox sub. It simply " & _
   "displays information: It doesn't get a value back from " & _
   "the user.",,"Subs vs. Functions"
end sub
-->
</SCRIPT>

<DIV STYLE="LAYOUT:FIXED;WIDTH:597pt;HEIGHT:370pt;">
    <OBJECT ID="Label1"
     CLASSID="CLSID:978C9E23-D4B0-11CE-BF2D-00AA003F40D0"
     STYLE="TOP:17pt;LEFT:157pt;WIDTH:256pt;HEIGHT:33pt;ZINDEX:0;">
        <PARAM NAME="Caption" VALUE="Subs Versus Functions">
        <PARAM NAME="Size" VALUE="9031;1164">
        <PARAM NAME="FontName" VALUE="Times New Roman">
        <PARAM NAME="FontHeight" VALUE="520">
        <PARAM NAME="FontCharSet" VALUE="0">
        <PARAM NAME="FontPitchAndFamily" VALUE="2">
        <PARAM NAME="FontWeight" VALUE="0">
    </OBJECT>
    <OBJECT ID="Cmd_Sub"
     CLASSID="CLSID:D7053240-CE69-11CD-A777-00DD01143C57"
     STYLE="TOP:99pt;LEFT:41pt;WIDTH:165pt;HEIGHT:58pt;
         TABINDEX:1;ZINDEX:1;">
        <PARAM NAME="Caption" VALUE="Use the MsgBox Sub">
        <PARAM NAME="Size" VALUE="5821;2046">
        <PARAM NAME="FontCharSet" VALUE="0">
        <PARAM NAME="FontPitchAndFamily" VALUE="2">
```

```
        <PARAM NAME="ParagraphAlign" VALUE="3">
        <PARAM NAME="FontWeight" VALUE="0">
    </OBJECT>
    <OBJECT ID="Cmd_Function"
     CLASSID="CLSID:D7053240-CE69-11CD-A777-00DD01143C57"
     STYLE="TOP:173pt;LEFT:41pt;WIDTH:165pt;HEIGHT:58pt;
            TABINDEX:2;ZINDEX:2;">
        <PARAM NAME="Caption" VALUE="Use the MsgBox Function">
        <PARAM NAME="Size" VALUE="5821;2046">
        <PARAM NAME="FontCharSet" VALUE="0">
        <PARAM NAME="FontPitchAndFamily" VALUE="2">
        <PARAM NAME="ParagraphAlign" VALUE="3">
        <PARAM NAME="FontWeight" VALUE="0">
    </OBJECT>
    <OBJECT ID="Lbl_Answer"
     CLASSID="CLSID:978C9E23-D4B0-11CE-BF2D-00AA003F40D0"
            STYLE="TOP:91pt;LEFT:297pt;WIDTH:231pt;
            HEIGHT:140pt;ZINDEX:3;">
        <PARAM NAME="BackColor" VALUE="16777215">
        <PARAM NAME="Size" VALUE="8149;4939">
        <PARAM NAME="BorderStyle" VALUE="1">
        <PARAM NAME="FontName" VALUE="Times New Roman">
        <PARAM NAME="FontHeight" VALUE="720">
        <PARAM NAME="FontCharSet" VALUE="0">
        <PARAM NAME="FontPitchAndFamily" VALUE="2">
        <PARAM NAME="FontWeight" VALUE="0">
    </OBJECT>
</DIV>
```

Listing 6.2 HTML code for the Web page that uses Listing 6.1.

```
<HTML>
<HEAD>
<TITLE>The MsgBox Sub Vs. The MsgBox Function</TITLE>
</HEAD>
<BODY>

<OBJECT CLASSID="CLSID:812AE312-8B8E-11CF-93C8-00AA00C08FDF"
ID="msgbox1" STYLE="LEFT:0;TOP:0">
<PARAM NAME="ALXPATH" REF
    VALUE="file:C:\MyDocs\VBScript\chap06\msgbox1.alx">
 </OBJECT>

</BODY>
</HTML>
```

The most immediate difference is visual. When the user clicks on the button labeled "Use the **MsgBox** Sub," a simple message box appears, as shown in Figure 6.2. It has only an OK button. Clicking on the OK button simply closes the message box.

Figure 6.2   The message box displayed by the **MsgBox** sub.

But when the user clicks on the button labeled "Use the MsgBox Function," a different result appears. This time, the message box has three buttons: Yes, No, and Cancel, as shown in Figure 6.3. Clicking on the Yes button causes the user's choice to be displayed in the label control at the right, as shown in Figure 6.4.

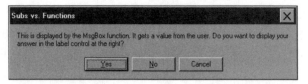

Figure 6.3   The message box displayed by the **MsgBox** function.

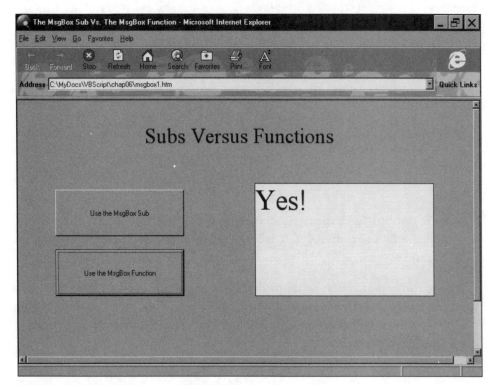

Figure 6.4   The label control displays the user's choice.

Differences In The Code

Let's see how the code differs when we compare the sub versus function versions of **MsgBox**. In Listing 6.1, the **Click** event sub for the first command button goes like this.

```
Sub Cmd_Sub_Click()
MsgBox "This is displayed by the MsgBox sub. It simply " & _
    "displays information: it doesn't get a value back from " & _
    "the user.",,"Subs vs. Functions"
end sub
```

This is the same pattern we've seen over and over in previous chapters. First, there's the word **MsgBox**, then the message text, then two commas indicating that a parameter has been omitted, and finally the title of the message box itself. Nothing really new there. But look at the **Click** event sub for the second command button, which uses the **MsgBox** function instead of the sub version.

```
Sub Cmd_Function_Click()
dim UserChoice

UserChoice = MsgBox("This is displayed by the MsgBox function. " & _
    "It gets a value from the user. Do you want to display your " & _
    "answer in the label control at the right?",3,"Subs vs. Functions")

    select case UserChoice
        case 6
            Lbl_Answer.caption = "Yes!"
        case 7
            lbl_Answer.caption = "No!"
        case 2
            lbl_Answer.caption = ""
    end select

end sub
```

This code not only gets the user's choice, but it stores that choice in a variable and then displays the choice in a label control on the Web page. Let's take it from the top.

The first thing that the sub has to do is declare a variable to catch the value returned by the **MsgBox** function—something you don't need to do with the sub version, because it doesn't return a value. **UserChoice** is the variable that will catch the value.

Next, we actually use the **MsgBox** function. Unlike the sub version, however, it doesn't stand on its own in the program statement. Instead, the whole **MsgBox** expression is the right side of an assignment statement. There are two other important differences in the use of the **MsgBox** function itself:

☆ With the **MsgBox** function, you must put parentheses around the parameter list. You don't have to do that with the **MsgBox** sub.

☆ With the **MsgBox** function, you should include a parameter for the buttons to be displayed in the message box. That's the parameter after the message text. We usually omit it from calls to the **MsgBox** sub, indicating the omission with ",,". You don't have to include this parameter, but inasmuch as the whole point of using the **MsgBox** function is to get a response from the user, it makes little sense to leave it out.

Finally, we set up a **select case** statement to process the value returned by the message box. If the user clicks on the Yes button, the message box returns a value of 6; if the user clicks on the No button, it returns a value of 7; and if the user clicks on the Cancel button, it returns a value of 2. Depending on which value is returned, the **select case** statement takes an appropriate action.

VALUES TO DISPLAY BUTTONS OR ICONS IN A MESSAGE BOX

If you're using the **MsgBox** function, you need to know which values will display which buttons. The values are shown in Table 6.1, along with the buttons displayed by each. Some of the values also display icons such as exclamation marks in the message box.

But wait! There's more to the story. You aren't limited to the specific entries in the table: You can add them together to display multiple table entries. For example, suppose that you wanted to display a message box with Yes, No, and Cancel buttons, along with a Critical Message icon. The value to display Yes, No, and Cancel buttons is 3; the value to display a Critical Message icon is 16. Therefore, as the second parameter in the **MsgBox** function call, you'd put 3 + 16, or 19.

In addition to the values that display various things in a message box, there are other values that control how the message box operates. For example, suppose that the user simply presses Enter instead of clicking on a button. Which button

Table 6.1   Values to display buttons in message boxes.

Value	Buttons Displayed In Message Box
0	OK
1	OK, Cancel
2	Abort, Retry, Ignore
3	Yes, No, Cancel
4	Yes, No
5	Retry, Cancel
16	Critical Message icon
32	Warning Query icon
48	Warning Message icon
64	Information Message icon

should that select? The value to set a "default" button, along with several other values, is shown in Table 6.2.

By adding the desired values from Table 6.1 to the desired values (if any) from Table 6.2, you can make your message box work in quite a few different ways.

Table 6.2   Values to control the operation of message boxes.

Value	Result
0	First button is the default.
256	Second button is the default.
512	Third button is the default.
768	Fourth button is the default.
0	The message box is "application modal:" The user must respond to the message box before he/she can do anything else in the current program.
4096	The message box is "system modal:" The user must respond to the message box before he/she can do anything in this program or any other.

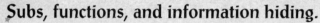

Subs, functions, and information hiding.
Here's a trick question: How does the **MsgBox** function work?
You don't know? Fine. You don't need to know. And that
spotlights a very important feature of properly-designed subs
and functions. Other parts of the program should be able to
use a sub or function without needing to know anything about
its internal workings. All that should be necessary to use a sub
or function is its name and parameter list.

Creating Your Own Subs

Most of the subs we've seen so far have been event handlers for specific controls—in particular, for the click events of various command buttons. That's a
very important kind of sub, but not the only kind. You can create your own subs
that aren't associated with any particular ActiveX controls. These subs can perform tasks that are needed by several controls or other parts of your program.
When you create and use your own sub, there are two parts in the process:

☆ First, you *declare* the sub, in much the same way as you'd declare a variable.

☆ Second, you *call* the sub, just as you'd call any of VBScript's built-in subs
(statements).

To declare a sub, you use the following syntax:

```
Sub ThisIsTheSubName(ParameterName1, ParameterName2, ...)
   ' The code that performs the sub's tasks.
End sub
```

To call the sub, you use its name as a statement in VBScript, adding the desired
values as parameters, as follows:

```
ThisIsTheSubName("Joe", 15)
```

Inside the sub, the values **Joe** and **15** will be known by their parameter names—
ParameterName1 and **ParameterName2**. Listing 6.3 shows the VBScript code
and ActiveX layout for a program demonstrating such a sub. Listing 6.4 shows
the HTML code that sets up the Web page. Figure 6.5 shows the Web page
created by the listings.

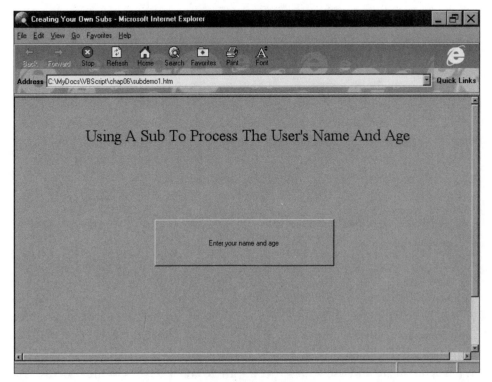

Figure 6.5   The Web page created by Listings 6.3 and 6.4.

Listing 6.3   VBScript code with a sub to get name and age.

```
<SCRIPT LANGUAGE="VBScript">
<!--
dim UserName, UserAge

Sub ProcessNameAndAge(Name, Age)

    If Name = "Larry" then msgbox "Are you Larry Laffer?",, _
       "Sub Demonstration"

    if age < 16 then
       msgbox "Sorry, " & Name & ", you must be at least 16.",, _
          "Sub Demonstration"
    end if

    if age > 15 and age < 31 then
       msgbox "Have fun, " & Name & "!",,"Sub Demonstration"
    end if

    if age > 30 then
       msgbox Name & ", it's good to see older people using PCs.",, _
```

```
            "Sub Demonstration"
        end if

end sub

Sub CommandButton1_Click()

    UserName = InputBox("Enter your name","Sub Demonstration","")
    UserAge = InputBox("Enter your age","Sub Demonstration","")
    ProcessNameAndAge UserName, UserAge

end sub
-->
</SCRIPT>
<DIV STYLE="LAYOUT:FIXED;WIDTH:597pt;HEIGHT:370pt;">
    <OBJECT ID="CommandButton1"
     CLASSID="CLSID:D7053240-CE69-11CD-A777-00DD01143C57"\
     STYLE="TOP:140pt;LEFT:173pt;WIDTH:231pt;HEIGHT:58pt;
     TABINDEX:0;ZINDEX:0;">
        <PARAM NAME="Caption" VALUE="Enter your name and age">
        <PARAM NAME="Size" VALUE="8149;2037">
        <PARAM NAME="FontCharSet" VALUE="0">
        <PARAM NAME="FontPitchAndFamily" VALUE="2">
        <PARAM NAME="ParagraphAlign" VALUE="3">
        <PARAM NAME="FontWeight" VALUE="0">
    </OBJECT>
    <OBJECT ID="Label1"
     CLASSID="CLSID:978C9E23-D4B0-11CE-BF2D-00AA003F40D0"
     STYLE="TOP:25pt;LEFT:83pt;WIDTH:421pt;HEIGHT:33pt;ZINDEX:1;">
        <PARAM NAME="Caption"
          VALUE="Using A Sub To Process The User's Name And Age">
        <PARAM NAME="Size" VALUE="14843;1164">
        <PARAM NAME="FontName" VALUE="Times New Roman">
        <PARAM NAME="FontHeight" VALUE="400">
        <PARAM NAME="FontCharSet" VALUE="0">
        <PARAM NAME="FontPitchAndFamily" VALUE="2">
        <PARAM NAME="FontWeight" VALUE="0">
    </OBJECT>
</DIV>
```

Listing 6.4   HTML code that sets up the Web page.

```
<HTML>
<HEAD>
<TITLE>Creating Your Own Subs</TITLE>
</HEAD>
<BODY>

<OBJECT CLASSID="CLSID:812AE312-8B8E-11CF-93C8-00AA00C08FDF"
ID="subdemo1" STYLE="LEFT:0;TOP:0">
<PARAM NAME="ALXPATH" REF
```

```
    VALUE="file:C:\MyDocs\VBScript\chap06\subdemo1.alx">
</OBJECT>

</BODY>
</HTML>
```

When the user clicks on the command button, he/she is first confronted with an input box asking for his/her name, as shown in Figure 6.6. Then, another input box asks for age, as shown in Figure 6.7. Finally, a message box responds to the information, as shown in Figure 6.8.

All subs can be called, even event subs.

In our examples so far, the **Click** event subs for command buttons have been activated only when the user clicks on the command buttons. But any sub can be called from another sub, so you can artificially "click" a command button simply by using the name of its **Click** event sub. For example, if a command button were named Cmd_Jump, you could make your code click the button by using the statement Cmd_Jump_Click. Then, all the event code inside the sub would execute, just as if the user had actually clicked the button.

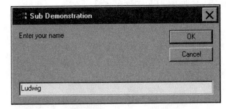

Figure 6.6 Asking for the user's name.

Figure 6.7 Asking for the user's age.

Figure 6.8 Responding to the user's name and age.

Inside The Sub Code

The sub in this case is a very simple one. As parameters, it takes the user's name and age. Then, it looks at the name and age values and gives a response. The code inside the sub is unremarkable, so we won't tarry over it here. But this example makes two very important points that need to be emphasized.

The first point is that a sub is declared, then used. Let's put the header line of the sub declaration next to the line where the sub is called. That should spotlight how they differ:

```
Sub ProcessNameAndAge(Name, Age)
ProcessNameAndAge UserName, UserAge
```

The header line from the **sub** declaration begins, as you'd expect, with the word **sub**. It then gives the name of the sub, and a parameter list. The names of the parameters are how the values passed to the sub will be known *inside* the sub. The parameters are in parentheses.

The line that calls the sub is somewhat different. It doesn't begin with the word **sub** and its parameters aren't in parentheses. Moreover, the parameters aren't the same as the parameter names in the sub declaration: Instead, they're the names of variables which are passed to the sub for processing.

Watch for needless parentheses!

If you're coming to VBScript from C, C++, or Pascal, you'll have an ingrained habit of putting parameters in parentheses when you call a sub or function. This isn't wrong in VBScript, but if you include the parentheses when you call the sub or function, you must begin the statement with the word **call**. If you include the parentheses but don't include the word **call**, it can cause hard-to-diagnose errors in your program.

> The easiest solution is simply to remember not to include parentheses when you call a sub or function.

Inside the sub, the variables passed to the sub are known by their parameter names, as if traveling under an alias in a foreign land:

```
If Name = "Larry" then msgbox "Are you Larry Laffer?",,"Sub Demonstration"

   if age < 16 then
      msgbox "Sorry, " & Name & ", you must be at least 16.",, _
         "Sub Demonstration"
   end if
```

And, Of Course, The InputBox Function

There's one other new wrinkle in Listing 6.3, and we've deferred it until last because it has no particular connection with creating your own subs. That's the **InputBox** function used to get the user's name and age. We've usually obtained that kind of information by putting text boxes on the Web page, and I felt it was time for a change.

The **InputBox** function works a lot like the **MsgBox** function, except that it has fewer options. Just like the **MsgBox** function, it gets a value from the user and gives it back to your VBScript program. VBScript will look at the value and automatically decide if it's text, a number, or some other subtype of the basic VBScript **variant** data type. The syntax of the **InputBox** function is as follows:

```
ValueCatcher = InputBox(Prompt, Title, Default Text, Xpos, Ypos)
```

There are two other parameters, but you'll very seldom use them, so they're omitted here. The parameters are mostly self-explanatory. The default text is the text displayed in the input box's blank, where the user enters his/her information.

Creating Your Own Functions

Home-made functions are quite similar to home-made subs, except that they're lower in fat and cholesterol. There's an even more important difference, though: At some point in every function—usually the last line—there's a statement that assigns a value to the function *itself.* That's because the function is a "word" in a larger program statement, and when you assign a value to the function itself, you tell VBScript which value to use for that word. To declare a function, you use the following syntax. It's almost exactly like the syntax for declaring a sub, except that you use the word **function:**

```
Function FunctionName(ParameterName1, ParameterName2, ..)
   ' Code that does the processing inside the function
end function
```

Like most abstract explanations, that still sounds a little murky. Let's look at a specific example of a home-made function. Listing 6.5 gives the VBScript code and ActiveX layout for a program that uses a function to multiply two numbers. Listing 6.6 gives the HTML code that sets up the Web page. And Figure 6.9 shows the Web page created by the listings.

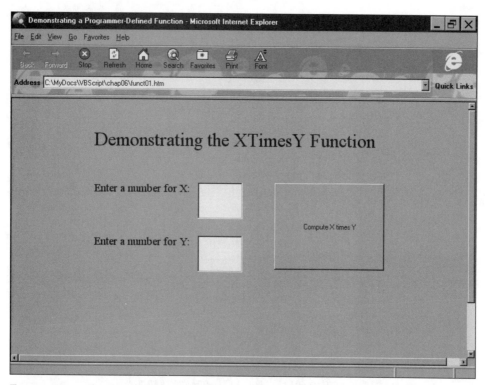

Figure 6.9 The Web page created by Listings 6.5 and 6.6.

Listing 6.5   VBScript code and ActiveX layout to use a home-made function.

```
<SCRIPT LANGUAGE="VBScript">
<!--

Function XTimesY(NumX, NumY)

   XTimesY = NumX * NumY

end function

Sub Cmd_ComputeXTimesY_Click()
   dim TheAnswer

   TheAnswer = XTimesY(TB_X, TB_Y)
   MsgBox "X times Y is " & TheAnswer & ".",,"Function Demonstration"
end sub

-->
</SCRIPT>
<DIV STYLE="LAYOUT:FIXED;WIDTH:597pt;HEIGHT:370pt;">
    <OBJECT ID="Label1"
     CLASSID="CLSID:978C9E23-D4B0-11CE-BF2D-00AA003F40D0"
     STYLE="TOP:25pt;LEFT:99pt;WIDTH:363pt;HEIGHT:33pt;ZINDEX:0;">
        <PARAM NAME="Caption"
          VALUE="Demonstrating the XTimesY Function">
        <PARAM NAME="Size" VALUE="12806;1164">
        <PARAM NAME="FontName" VALUE="Times New Roman">
        <PARAM NAME="FontHeight" VALUE="480">
        <PARAM NAME="FontCharSet" VALUE="0">
        <PARAM NAME="FontPitchAndFamily" VALUE="2">
        <PARAM NAME="FontWeight" VALUE="0">
    </OBJECT>
    <OBJECT ID="Label2"
     CLASSID="CLSID:978C9E23-D4B0-11CE-BF2D-00AA003F40D0"
     STYLE="TOP:91pt;LEFT:99pt;WIDTH:124pt;HEIGHT:17pt;ZINDEX:1;">
        <PARAM NAME="Caption" VALUE="Enter a number for X:">
        <PARAM NAME="Size" VALUE="4365;583">
        <PARAM NAME="FontName" VALUE="Times New Roman">
        <PARAM NAME="FontHeight" VALUE="280">
        <PARAM NAME="FontCharSet" VALUE="0">
        <PARAM NAME="FontPitchAndFamily" VALUE="2">
        <PARAM NAME="FontWeight" VALUE="0">
    </OBJECT>
    <OBJECT ID="Label3"
     CLASSID="CLSID:978C9E23-D4B0-11CE-BF2D-00AA003F40D0"
     STYLE="TOP:157pt;LEFT:99pt;WIDTH:124pt;HEIGHT:17pt;ZINDEX:2;">
        <PARAM NAME="Caption" VALUE="Enter a number for Y:">
        <PARAM NAME="Size" VALUE="4365;582">
        <PARAM NAME="FontName" VALUE="Times New Roman">
        <PARAM NAME="FontHeight" VALUE="280">
```

```
        <PARAM NAME="FontCharSet" VALUE="0">
        <PARAM NAME="FontPitchAndFamily" VALUE="2">
        <PARAM NAME="FontWeight" VALUE="0">
    </OBJECT>
    <OBJECT ID="TB_X"
     CLASSID="CLSID:8BD21D10-EC42-11CE-9E0D-00AA006002F3"
     STYLE="TOP:91pt;LEFT:231pt;WIDTH:58pt;HEIGHT:45pt;
         TABINDEX:3;ZINDEX:3;">
        <PARAM NAME="VariousPropertyBits" VALUE="746604571">
        <PARAM NAME="Size" VALUE="2037;1588">
        <PARAM NAME="FontHeight" VALUE="480">
        <PARAM NAME="FontCharSet" VALUE="0">
        <PARAM NAME="FontPitchAndFamily" VALUE="2">
        <PARAM NAME="FontWeight" VALUE="0">
    </OBJECT>
    <OBJECT ID="TB_y"
     CLASSID="CLSID:8BD21D10-EC42-11CE-9E0D-00AA006002F3"
     STYLE="TOP:157pt;LEFT:231pt;WIDTH:58pt;HEIGHT:45pt;
         TABINDEX:4;ZINDEX:4;">
        <PARAM NAME="VariousPropertyBits" VALUE="746604571">
        <PARAM NAME="Size" VALUE="2037;1588">
        <PARAM NAME="FontHeight" VALUE="480">
        <PARAM NAME="FontCharSet" VALUE="0">
        <PARAM NAME="FontPitchAndFamily" VALUE="2">
        <PARAM NAME="FontWeight" VALUE="0">
    </OBJECT>
    <OBJECT ID="Cmd_ComputeXTimesY"
     CLASSID="CLSID:D7053240-CE69-11CD-A777-00DD01143C57"
     STYLE="TOP:91pt;LEFT:330pt;WIDTH:140pt;HEIGHT:107pt;
         TABINDEX:5;ZINDEX:5;">
        <PARAM NAME="Caption" VALUE="Compute X times Y">
        <PARAM NAME="Size" VALUE="4947;3784">
        <PARAM NAME="FontCharSet" VALUE="0">
        <PARAM NAME="FontPitchAndFamily" VALUE="2">
        <PARAM NAME="ParagraphAlign" VALUE="3">
        <PARAM NAME="FontWeight" VALUE="0">
    </OBJECT>
</DIV>
```

Listing 6.6 HTML code that sets up the Web page.

```
<HTML>
<HEAD>
<TITLE>Demonstrating a Programmer-Defined Function</TITLE>
</HEAD>
<BODY>

<OBJECT CLASSID="CLSID:812AE312-8B8E-11CF-93C8-00AA00C08FDF"
ID="funct01" STYLE="LEFT:0;TOP:0">
<PARAM NAME="ALXPATH" REF
    VALUE="file:C:\MyDocs\VBScript\chap06\funct01.alx">
 </OBJECT>
```

```
</BODY>
</HTML>
```

When the user enters a number in each of the text boxes on the Web page, then clicks the command button, the VBScript program displays a message box. The message box is shown in Figure 6.10.

Inside The Function Demo Code

This is a very simple example, which makes it a good one for showing the key features of declaring and using a function. Let's start out by looking at the function declaration itself:

```
Function XTimesY(NumX, NumY)

    XTimesY = NumX * NumY

end function
```

As expected, the first line of the declaration starts with the word **function**, gives the name of the function, and then gives the parameter list. Inside the function, there's only one statement: It assigns the product of X and Y as the value of the function itself. Then an **end function** ends the declaration. That's it.

Now, let's see how this fits into the actual call to the function. This occurs in the **Click** event sub for the command button, as follows:

```
Sub Cmd_ComputeXTimesY_Click()
    dim TheAnswer

    TheAnswer = XTimesY(TB_X, TB_Y)
    MsgBox "X times Y is " & TheAnswer & ".",,"Function Demonstration"
end sub
```

First, of course, we declare a local variable to catch the value returned by the function. Then, we embed the function call as a "word" in the statement assigning its value to the **TheAnswer** variable. The assignment statement makes it plain why

Figure 6.10 The product of X and Y.

the last line *inside* the function sets the value of the function itself: What gets assigned to **TheAnswer** is the value of the function itself.

As Rabbi Akiva remarked after summarizing *The Bible* with the statement "Do unto others as you'd want them to do unto you," the rest is commentary. Those are the really important points to remember about creating your own functions. (And about doing unto others.)

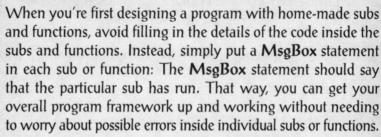

Designing a program with home-made subs and functions.

When you're first designing a program with home-made subs and functions, avoid filling in the details of the code inside the subs and functions. Instead, simply put a **MsgBox** statement in each sub or function: The **MsgBox** statement should say that the particular sub has run. That way, you can get your overall program framework up and working without needing to worry about possible errors inside individual subs or functions.

Once you have the framework established, code the subs and functions one at a time, testing the program after you finish each one to make sure that no errors have been introduced. That can dramatically reduce the time you have to spend "bug hunting" later on.

Using VBScript's Built-In Subs And Functions

This book is meant to show you wizardly tricks, not to be an exhaustive reference about the VBScript language. However, we can give you a flavor of the amazing things you can do with some of the subs and functions that come ready-to-use with VBScript.

Let's create what, in the 1980s, would have been called an "artificial intelligence" (AI) program with VBScript. Now, the idea of artificial intelligence is a moving target: It seems to mean whatever is currently at the leading edge of computer science. But parsing and natural language has always been an important field of AI research. And that's pretty much what we're going to do here. Once again, we'll create an amazingly simple program that demonstrates some amazingly powerful techniques. These are the same kinds of techniques, on a much smaller scale, as are used in some of the most sophisticated programs for natural language processing (NLP).

To keep it simple, let's get a two-word text string from the user. We'll then parse the string into its constituent words. As you can imagine, this technique applied on a larger scale is the first step toward making a computer program understand English. Listing 6.7 shows the VBScript code and ActiveX layout for the program, while Listing 6.8 shows the HTML code that sets up the Web page. And Figure 6.11 shows the Web page created by the code.

Listing 6.7 VBScript code and ActiveX layout to parse a text string.

```
<SCRIPT LANGUAGE="VBScript">
<!--
Sub Cmd_Separate_Click()

    dim SpacePos, FirstName, LastName
    SpacePos = InStr(TB_Names.text, " ")

    FirstName = Mid(TB_Names.text, 1, SpacePos - 1)
    LastName = Mid(TB_Names.text, SpacePos + 1)

    MsgBox "Your first name is " & FirstName & chr(13) & _
        "and your last name is " & LastName & ".",,"Parsing a Text String"

end sub
-->
</SCRIPT>
<DIV STYLE="LAYOUT:FIXED;WIDTH:597pt;HEIGHT:370pt;">
    <OBJECT ID="Label1"
      CLASSID="CLSID:978C9E23-D4B0-11CE-BF2D-00AA003F40D0"
      STYLE="TOP:17pt;LEFT:83pt;WIDTH:388pt;HEIGHT:25pt;ZINDEX:0;">
        <PARAM NAME="Caption"
          VALUE="Using Functions To Parse A Text String">
        <PARAM NAME="Size" VALUE="13688;882">
        <PARAM NAME="FontName" VALUE="Times New Roman">
        <PARAM NAME="FontHeight" VALUE="480">
        <PARAM NAME="FontCharSet" VALUE="0">
        <PARAM NAME="FontPitchAndFamily" VALUE="2">
        <PARAM NAME="FontWeight" VALUE="0">
    </OBJECT>
    <OBJECT ID="TB_Names"
```

```
    CLASSID="CLSID:8BD21D10-EC42-11CE-9E0D-00AA006002F3"
    STYLE="TOP:74pt;LEFT:132pt;WIDTH:281pt;HEIGHT:41pt;
        TABINDEX:1;ZINDEX:1;">
      <PARAM NAME="VariousPropertyBits" VALUE="746604571">
      <PARAM NAME="Size" VALUE="9913;1446">
      <PARAM NAME="FontHeight" VALUE="480">
      <PARAM NAME="FontCharSet" VALUE="0">
      <PARAM NAME="FontPitchAndFamily" VALUE="2">
      <PARAM NAME="FontWeight" VALUE="0">
  </OBJECT>
  <OBJECT ID="Label2"
    CLASSID="CLSID:978C9E23-D4B0-11CE-BF2D-00AA003F40D0"
    STYLE="TOP:124pt;LEFT:140pt;WIDTH:264pt;HEIGHT:25pt;ZINDEX:2;">
      <PARAM NAME="Caption"
        VALUE="Type your first and last name, separated by a space.">
      <PARAM NAME="Size" VALUE="9313;882">
      <PARAM NAME="FontName" VALUE="Times New Roman">
      <PARAM NAME="FontEffects" VALUE="1073741825">
      <PARAM NAME="FontHeight" VALUE="240">
      <PARAM NAME="FontCharSet" VALUE="0">
      <PARAM NAME="FontPitchAndFamily" VALUE="2">
      <PARAM NAME="FontWeight" VALUE="700">
  </OBJECT>
  <OBJECT ID="Cmd_Separate"
    CLASSID="CLSID:D7053240-CE69-11CD-A777-00DD01143C57"
    STYLE="TOP:173pt;LEFT:149pt;WIDTH:248pt;HEIGHT:58pt;
        TABINDEX:3;ZINDEX:3;">
      <PARAM NAME="Caption" VALUE="Separate the names">
      <PARAM NAME="Size" VALUE="8749;2046">
      <PARAM NAME="FontCharSet" VALUE="0">
      <PARAM NAME="FontPitchAndFamily" VALUE="2">
      <PARAM NAME="ParagraphAlign" VALUE="3">
      <PARAM NAME="FontWeight" VALUE="0">
  </OBJECT>
</DIV>
```

Listing 6.8   HTML code that sets up the Web page.

```
<HTML>
<HEAD>
<TITLE>Using Functions To Parse A Text String</TITLE>
</HEAD>
<BODY>

<OBJECT CLASSID="CLSID:812AE312-8B8E-11CF-93C8-00AA00C08FDF"
ID="parse01" STYLE="LEFT:0;TOP:0">
<PARAM NAME="ALXPATH" REF
    VALUE="file:C:\MyDocs\VBScript\chap06\parse01.alx">
 </OBJECT>

</BODY>
</HTML>
```

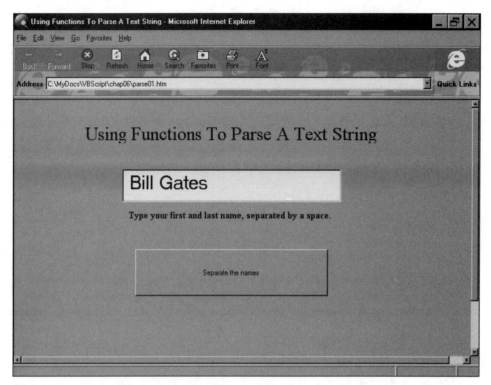

Figure 6.11   A Web page that parses a text string.

Inserting a line break in message box text.

In Listing 6.7's sub for the command button, you might have noticed something new in the middle of the message box text: **chr**(13). That calls VBScript's **chr** function to insert a line break in the message box text. The ASCII number for a carriage return-line feed is 13, and the **chr** function returns the character associated with the number it gets as a parameter. So when you insert **chr**(13) in the middle of a text string, it starts a new line at that point.

When the user types his/her name in the text box, then clicks on the command button, the program parses the name, separating the first and last names. Then, it displays the result, as shown in Figure 6.12.

Figure 6.12   The message box shows the first and last names of the user.

Inside The String-Parsing Code

The code that parses the text string is in the **Click** event sub for the command button. It uses two built-in VBScript functions—**InStr** and **Mid**:

- ☆ **InStr** searches a text string for a particular sub-string. In this case, it's simply the space that separates the user's first and last names.

- ☆ **Mid** pulls sub-strings out of a larger string. To use it, you give it the starting position of each substring, along with the number of characters you want it to get.

Let's see how these functions are used in Listing 6.7. First, the sub declares some local variables:

```
dim SpacePos, FirstName, LastName
```

The **FirstName** and **LastName** variables are self-explanatory. The **SpacePos** variable will hold the position of the space character in the text string entered by the user. Now, we make a call to the **InStr** function:

```
SpacePos = InStr(TB_Names.text, " ")
```

This tells VBScript to look in the **text** property of **TB_Names**—that's the text box on the Web page—and find the position of the space character. If the user entered the name "Bill Gates," then the space character would be at position 5, because the first four positions in the string are occupied by the word "Bill."

Once we have the position of the space character, we can use it to break the string. We call the **Mid** function twice—first to get the first name, then to get the last name, as follows:

```
FirstName = Mid(TB_Names.text, 1, SpacePos - 1)
LastName = Mid(TB_Names.text, SpacePos + 1)
```

In both cases, we tell **Mid** to look at the text string that's in the **text** property of **TB_Names**. To get the first name, we tell **Mid** to start at position 1, then pull out *SpacePos – 1* characters from the big text string. To get the last name, we tell **Mid** to start at position *SpacePos + 1*. We don't need to specify how many characters it should get, because we want it to go all the way to the end of the text string.

Once the first and last names are loaded into separate variables, we use a message box to display them on the user's screen.

As simple as this example is, you can see how the same techniques can be extended to parse any number of words from text input. It's a powerful—indeed, wizardly—technique that you'll probably use from time to time in your VBScript career.

That's it for subs and functions! In Chapter 7, we'll take a closer look at how ActiveX controls fit into your Web pages and VBScript programs.

VII

USING ACTIVEX CONTROLS WITH VBSCRIPT

We've used ActiveX controls in most of our VBScript sample programs so far. But what are ActiveX controls, anyway? In this chapter, you'll learn the concepts and techniques for using any ActiveX control, whether or not you're already familiar with ActiveX.

N

ext to the VBScript language itself, ActiveX controls are probably the most important tool for developing programs with VBScript. And though we've used ActiveX controls very often in the previous chapters, we've never really talked about what they are. If you want to get the most out of using ActiveX controls, you need that knowledge.

Objects, Properties, and Events

ActiveX controls are program *objects*. They are pre-packaged capsules of program functionality that you can simply plug into a Web page or a Visual Basic form and use. You don't have to worry about how they were created—unless you want to create them yourself. And you don't have to worry about how they work "inside:" All you need to know is how your VBScript programs can work *with* them.

Just like real-world objects, ActiveX controls have properties and events to which they can respond. Think about that for a moment. A grizzly bear has certain properties: seven feet tall, 400 pounds, big sharp teeth, and a hearty appetite. It also has events to which it can respond. If a hapless VBScript programmer annoys a grizzly bear at dinner time, the bear will eat the programmer. (We can at least hope that he'll get an upset stomach for his trouble.) There are also certain events to which a grizzly bear can't respond. If a sound truck started blasting the latest heavy metal songs into the forest, the bear would be unable to sing along or dance to the music. It would only, as would most of us, run away in abject terror.

ActiveX controls are a lot like grizzly bears. Sure, they lack the teeth, the fur, and the smell, but each ActiveX control has certain properties, as well as a list of events to which it can respond. When you click on a command button and it executes the statements in its *Click* event sub, it's responding to an event. On the other hand, if you started speaking French at the computer screen, the command button would be oblivious and wouldn't respond at all.

Therefore, when you encounter a new ActiveX control, there are a few important questions to ask about it:

☆ What's it good for? That is, how are you most likely to use it—and *are* you likely to use it?

☆ What events will it respond to? Of those events, which are going to be the most often used?

☆ What properties does it have? Of those properties, which are going to be the most often used?

☆ What is its default property—the property that is used if you simply give the control name and don't specify a property?

A gallery of some of the most important ActiveX controls is shown in Figure 7.1.

Important Properties Of ActiveX Controls

There are certain properties of ActiveX controls that you'll use again and again. Knowing these properties in advance can save you programming time later on. In order of importance—not an exact ranking, but good enough for government work—the properties are as follows.

☆ **ID.** This is a value you should *always* set before you write any code in VBScript. The reason is that your VBScript code will refer to each ActiveX control by its **ID** property. If later on, you change that property—*i.e.,* change the name of the control—then you'll have to rewrite all your code.

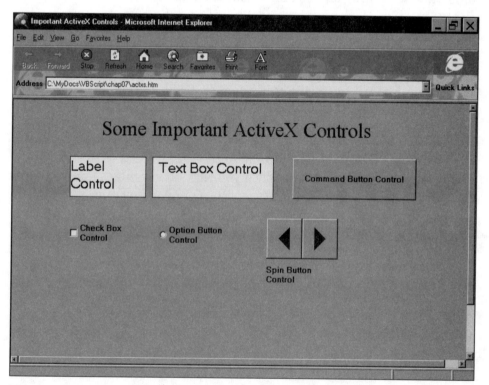

Figure 7.1   Important ActiveX controls.

The **ID** property should reflect two things: the type of control, and the purpose of the control. For example, a command button to multiply two numbers might be named *Cmd_Multiply*, while a text box intended to get a user's name might be called *TB_UserName*. Having a consistent and sensible way to name your controls makes the names easier to remember when you're writing code.

☆ **Value.** This indicates whether check boxes and option buttons are selected. If the value is **true** (-1), then the control is selected. If it's **false** (0), the control is not selected.

☆ **Caption.** This is the text displayed in a label control or command button. For a text box control, the corresponding property is the **text** property: text box controls do not have a caption property. As you've seen in many of the program examples, changing the **caption** or **text** property of a control is one way to display information in response to events.

☆ **Tabindex.** If an HTML layout has several controls, this property controls the order in which a user can "tab" from one to another. The first **tabindex** value is 0, and each control in the tab order has a **tabindex** value 1 higher than the control before it.

☆ **Font.** This controls the type face, size, and style of the text displayed in a control. In the ActiveX Control Pad, you can double-click on this property in the Properties window to see a dialog box in which you can select the type face, size, and style you want.

☆ **Enabled.** This determines whether a control is active or not. If a control's **enabled** property is set to false, it won't respond to events. You've already seen one use of the **enabled** property: In Listing 2.3, we turned a Timer control on and off by manipulating its **enabled** property.

Important ActiveX Controls

With that general introduction, let's look at some of the ActiveX controls you'll use most often, along with their most important properties.

The Label and Text Box Controls

In previous chapters, you've seen many examples of label and text box controls. And you might have wondered—if all we're using them for is to display text on a Web page—why we bother using two kinds of control instead of just one.

There's a very simple answer. Although both label and text box controls can display text on a Web page, *only* the text box control allows the user to type text directly into the control. Thus, if you want to allow the user to enter text into the control, use a text box control. If you want to display text but not allow the user to change it—at least, not directly, by typing it into the control—then use a label control.

Table 7.1 shows the most important properties of label controls, while Table 7.2 shows the most important properties of text box controls.

The Command Button Control

The command button control is also quite familiar by now. Its most often-used event is its **Click** event, and it's used almost exclusively to get input from the user. The most important properties of command button controls are listed in Table 7.3.

The Option Button Control

The option button control is helpful when you want the user to choose one— and only one—from a group of mutually-exclusive alternatives. For example, you might want a text message to be red, or green, or purple, but not all of those colors. In such a case, a group of option buttons is appropriate.

Table 7.1   Important properties of label controls.

Property	Explanation
BackColor	Color of label background.
BorderStyle	Determines if label has a visible border.
Caption	Text displayed in label.
ForeColor	Color of label text.
Font	Type face, size, and style of label text.
ID	Name by which VBScript code refers to label.
Left, Top	Determine the position of the label in the HTML layout. You will usually position the label by dragging it in the ActiveX Control Pad.
Height, Width	Determine the size of the label. You will usually size the label by dragging its borders in the ActiveX Control Pad.
WordWrap	Determines if label can display multiple lines of text.

Table 7.2 Important properties of text box controls.

Property	Explanation
BackColor	Color of text box background.
BorderStyle	Determines if text box has a visible border.
ForeColor	Color of text box text.
Font	Type face, size, and style of text box text.
ID	Name by which VBScript code refers to text box.
Left, Top	Determine the position of the text box in the HTML layout. You will usually position the text box by dragging it in the ActiveX Control Pad.
Height, Width	Determine the size of the text box. You will usually size the text box by dragging its borders in the ActiveX Control Pad.
Text	Text displayed in text box.
WordWrap	Determines if text box can display multiple lines of text.

Table 7.3 Important properties of command button controls.

Property	Explanation
Caption	Text displayed on the command button.
Enabled	Determines if command button will respond to events.
Font	Type face, size, and style of text displayed on the command button.
ID	Name by which VBScript code refers to the command button.
Left, Top	Determine the position of the command button in the HTML layout. You will usually position the command button by dragging it in the ActiveX Control Pad.
Height, Width	Determine the size of the command button. You will usually size the command button by dragging its borders in the ActiveX Control Pad.
WordWrap	Determines if command button can display multiple lines of text.

You've already seen a fairly realistic example of option buttons in the "Trivia, Forsooth" game that was developed in Chapter 5. The most important properties of option buttons are shown in Table 7.4.

The Check Box Control

Check boxes are similar to option buttons, but with an important difference. In a group of check boxes, more than one check box can be selected at the same time. This makes check boxes good for allowing the user to select non-exclusive alternatives, such as ordering one or more books from a bookstore. The important properties of check boxes are shown in Table 7.5.

The Spin Button Control

The spin button control is useful when you want the user to be able to increase or decrease a value by clicking on a button. The spin button control is actually two buttons with arrows pointing in opposite directions. Click one button, and the number in the spin control's **value** property increases by a specific amount. Click the other button, and the spin control's **value** property decreases by the same amount. The important properties of the spin button control are shown in Table 7.6.

Table 7.4 Important properties of option buttons.

Property	Explanation
BackColor	Color of option button background.
Caption	Text displayed next to option button.
ForeColor	Color of option button text.
Font	Type face, size, and style of option button text.
ID	Name by which VBScript code refers to option button.
Left, Top	Determine the position of the option button in the HTML layout. You will usually position the option button by dragging it in the ActiveX Control Pad.
Height, Width	Determine the size of the option button. You will usually size the option button by dragging its borders in the ActiveX Control Pad.
Value	Determines whether or not the option button is selected. In any group of option buttons, only one can have its value property set to true. The others are automatically false.
WordWrap	Determines if option button can display multiple lines of text.

Table 7.5   Important properties of check box controls.

Property	Explanation
BackColor	Color of check box background.
Caption	Text displayed next to check box.
ForeColor	Color of check box text.
Font	Type face, size, and style of check box text.
ID	Name by which VBScript code refers to check box.
Left, Top	Determine the position of the check box in the HTML layout. You will usually position the check box by dragging it in the ActiveX Control Pad.
Height, Width	Determine the size of the check box. You will usually size the check box by dragging its borders in the ActiveX Control Pad.
Value	Determines whether or not the check box is selected. In any group of check boxes, any number can be selected. A checkmark appears in any check box that is selected.
WordWrap	Determines if check box can display multiple lines of text.

Table 7.6   Important properties of the spin button control.

Property	Explanation
Enabled	Determines whether or not the control will respond to events.
ID	Name by which VBScript code refers to the spin control.
Left, Top	Determine the position of the spin control in the HTML layout. You will usually position the spin control by dragging it in the ActiveX Control Pad.
Height, Width	Determine the size of the spin control. You will usually size the spin button by dragging its borders in the ActiveX Control Pad.
Min, Max	Determine the top and bottom values that the spin control can have.
SmallChange	Determines how much the value of the spin control changes (up or down) when one of the buttons is clicked.
Value	The current number associated with the spin control. This is increased by clicking one of the buttons and decreased by clicking the other.

You're Not Limited To ActiveX Controls

With the release of VBScript and Microsoft's Internet Explorer 3.0, there are going to be some fairly basic ActiveX controls available. It might be a while, however, before there are as many ActiveX controls as there are now standard OCX controls.

But there's good news: You can often use existing OCX controls with VBScript and Internet Explorer. Figure 7.2 shows an example of a Web page that uses VBScript with OCX controls: a command button and a spin control.

These controls were designed by Crescent Software for use with Visual Basic 4. As a result, they're highly—but not totally—compatible with VBScript and Internet Explorer. You can often use some of their properties but not others. But if you have some OCX controls on hand that do what you need, give it a try—they'll often work just fine.

In Chapter 8, we'll take an in-depth look at using the ActiveX Control Pad to create HTML layouts with ActiveX controls.

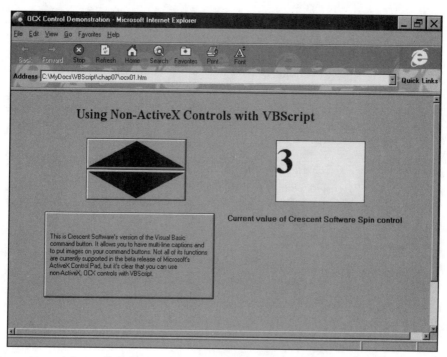

Figure 7.2   Using OCX controls with VBScript and Internet Explorer.

VIII

Using The ActiveX Control Pad

The ActiveX Control
Pad is the first of
many tools for visual
design of Web pages
with ActiveX controls
and Visual Basic
scripting. Once you
learn to use it, you'll
be creating wizardly
Web pages in no time!

So far, our focus has been mainly on VBScript itself. We've examined scripts that work with some hot-looking Web pages, but have deferred the question of how to create those Web pages. Until now. The answer is shown in Figure 8.1.

In this chapter, you'll learn how to create Web page layouts with Microsoft's new ActiveX Control Pad. Even at this early stage of its evolution, the ActiveX Control Pad is a remarkably powerful and easy-to-understand tool for laying out Web pages with ActiveX controls. In addition, many of its features are expected to be in the next releases of Visual Basic and Microsoft's FrontPage Web page editor, so when you learn about the ActiveX Control Pad, you're getting a jump on them, too.

You can download the ActiveX Control Pad from Microsoft's Web site: **http://www.microsoft.com/intdev/**. It's free.

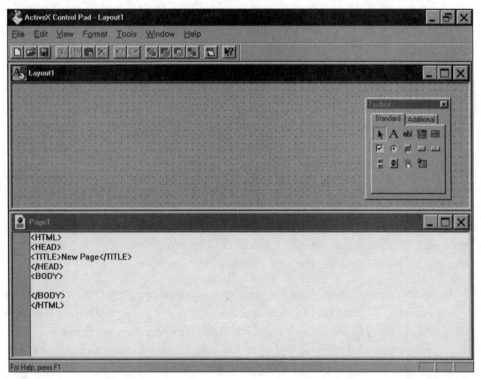

Figure 8.1 The ActiveX Control Pad.

Parts Of The ActiveX Control Pad

Although the most important thing you can do with the ActiveX Control Pad is to create HTML layouts for your Web pages, there's a lot more you can do. Let's take inventory of all the different features offered by the ActiveX Control Pad. It includes:

☆ A text editor for creating and editing HTML documents. This is essentially the same as Windows Notepad with a built-in template for HTML documents.

☆ An ActiveX insertion tool. This lets you insert the correct **<object>** tags for ActiveX controls into HTML documents. This tool is appropriate when you want to set the ActiveX control properties "manually" with code instead of using the ActiveX Control Pad's Properties window.

☆ A Visual Basic-like visual editor that lets you lay out HTML pages by selecting ActiveX controls from a toolbox, then drawing them on the screen. This is the powerhouse of the ActiveX Control Pad: It makes Web page creation incredibly easy.

☆ A toolbox ("palette") of ActiveX controls that are ready to use in your Web page layouts. As you acquire new ActiveX controls, you can add them to the toolbox.

☆ A script wizard that makes it easy to add VBScript code to ActiveX controls and to your HTML document.

Creating An HTML Layout

Let's start by creating a simple HTML layout in the ActiveX Control Pad. Before we get down to the specific steps, it's worthwhile to remember what happens when we create a layout and incorporate it into a Web page:

1. Using the ActiveX Control Pad, some other tool, or even a plain text editor, we create an HTML layout and save it in a file with the extension ALX. The HTML layout consists largely of **<object>** tags that specify the properties and positions of particular ActiveX controls in the layout.

2. Using the ActiveX Control Pad, some other tool, or even a plain text editor, we insert an **<object>** tag for the HTML Layout control—an ActiveX control—in the **<body>** area of the HTML document.

When the user loads the HTML document into his/her Web browser, it's the HTML Layout control—not the Web browser itself—that formats the layout in the Web page. This is a departure from HTML's historic approach, which was to let the Web browser do the work of interpreting the HTML document. The drawback of the old approach was that every Web browser had to support every new HTML coding trick anyone could devise.

With the new approach, however, a Web browser only needs to know how to work with ActiveX controls. If it does, then the ActiveX controls *themselves* can provide the special features—such as layouts—for the Web page.

Your version of ActiveX Control Pad might differ.
As this book was being written, the ActiveX Control Pad was still in beta testing. Therefore, some of the features discussed here—or their appearance on the screen—might have changed by the time you read this. In particular, it's likely that Microsoft will make the HTML Layout window appear automatically when you first load the ActiveX Control Pad.

The bottom line, however, is that you shouldn't panic if there are slight differences between what you see here and what you see on your screen. Everything in the ActiveX Control Pad should work as expected.

Drawing A Control

Let's create a simple Web page layout to see how it's done. When you first start the ActiveX Control Pad, you see a blank HTML document, as shown in Figure 8.2.

To create a Web page layout, open the File menu and select New HTML Layout. An HTML layout window will appear on your screen. When you maximize the window, it should look something like Figure 8.3.

How to find the control you want.
If you're not sure which Toolbox control is the one you want, just position the mouse pointer over a control and leave it there. In a moment, a "tip box" will appear, telling you the name of that control.

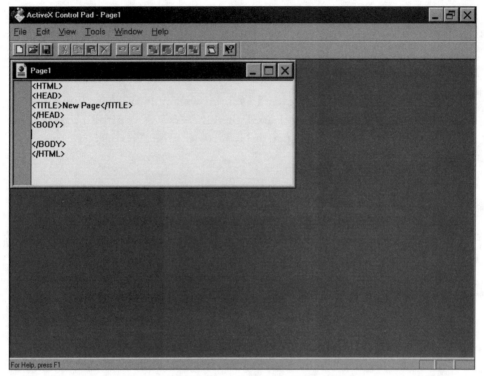

Figure 8.2   The ActiveX Control Pad's initial window.

The first step in drawing a control is to select the control in the Toolbox, shown in Figure 8.4. To keep things simple, let's draw a command button and a label. Follow these steps:

1. In the Toolbox, click on the label control. That's the one with a big "A."

    Your mouse pointer will change to an A with a small cross. The cross marks the point in the layout area where the label will be inserted when you click the mouse.

2. In the top left quadrant of the layout area, click the left mouse button and hold it down.

    This anchors the top left corner of the label control.

3. Still holding down the mouse button, drag the mouse pointer down and to the right on your screen until the label outline is big enough to hold a sentence of text.

    This sets the size of the control in the layout.

Figure 8.3   The HTML Layout window.

4.   Release the mouse button.

   The control is now located and sized on the HTML layout.

If it doesn't look too impressive so far, don't worry. It will *be* impressive very shortly. Now, let's add another control. This time, we'll draw a command button underneath the label control. In the Toolbox, select the command button control: It's the one that looks like a plain gray button. Then, follow the same procedure as in steps 2 to 4 to position the command button. When you're finished, your screen should look something like Figure 8.5.

Figure 8.4   The ActiveX Control Pad Toolbox.

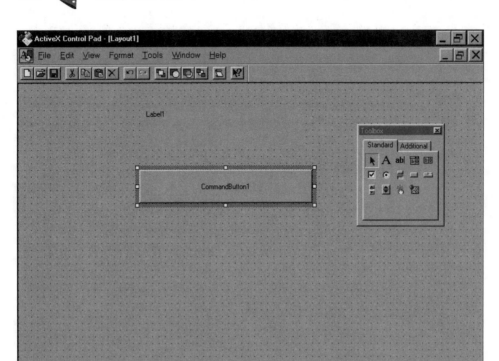

Figure 8.5   An HTML layout with label control and command button.

Changing the mouse pointer back to an arrow.
If you select a control in the Toolbox and then draw the control on the layout, the mouse pointer automatically changes back to an arrow. However, if you decide not to draw the control, you can change the mouse pointer back to an arrow by clicking on the Arrow button in the Toolbox.

CHANGING THE SIZE OR POSITION OF A CONTROL
If you're not totally satisfied with the size of a control or its location on the HTML layout, they're easy to change. To change the size of a control, follow these steps:

1. Click on the control to select it.

    A gray border will appear around the control. In the border are little white squares, as shown in Figure 8.6.

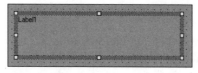

Figure 8.6   You can drag the white squares to resize the control.

2. Position the mouse pointer over one of the squares.

    The mouse pointer will change to a double arrow. The arrows indicate the directions in which you can drag the control's border, thereby resizing the control.

3. Click the left mouse button to "grab" the square you want.

4. Holding down the mouse button, drag the square (and thus, the control's border) in the direction you want to resize the control.

    For example, to make a control wider, you would drag its right border farther to the right; to make it narrower, you would drag its right border to the left.

5. When the control is the size you want, release the mouse button.

    The control appears on the layout with its new size.

Changing the position of a control is even easier. Simply select the control and, with the mouse pointer in the middle of the control, hold down the left mouse button and drag the control to the desired position. Then, release the mouse button. Presto! The control has been moved to its new location in the layout.

With label and text box controls, there's just one thing to be aware of.

When you select a label or text box control, sometimes the ActiveX Control Pad will think that you want to change the control's **caption** or **text** property. If that happens, you'll see a little text cursor inside the control and you won't be able to drag the control, resize it, or open its Properties window.

The solution is simply to click somewhere else in the layout area—that de-selects the control—and then click on the control a second time. This should select the control in the normal way so that you can drag it or perform other operations on it.

Using The Properties Window

Yes, the HTML layout we've created so far looks pretty drab. Let's see if we can spruce it up a bit by using the Properties window to set properties of the controls we've drawn. There are three ways to view the Properties window for a control:

☆ Double-click on the control. The Properties window will appear. This is the easiest method, but it occasionally fails to work because the ActiveX Control Pad thinks you want to change the control's caption or do something else with it.

☆ Right-click on the control. The shortcut menu for that control will appear, as shown in Figure 8.7. In the menu, select Properties. The Properties window will appear.

☆ Click on the control to select it. Then, open the View menu and select Properties. The Properties window will appear.

The Properties window always looks about the same, but it contains different properties depending on the type of control you've selected. Let's change the properties of the label control first. Follow these steps:

1. Double-click on the label control in the layout.

    The label control's Properties window will appear, as shown in Figure 8.8.

2. Double-click in the line for the **caption** property.

    The current caption will appear, highlighted, in the blank at the top of the Properties window, as shown in Figure 8.9. At this point, anything you type will replace the current caption.

Figure 8.7   The shortcut menu for an ActiveX control.

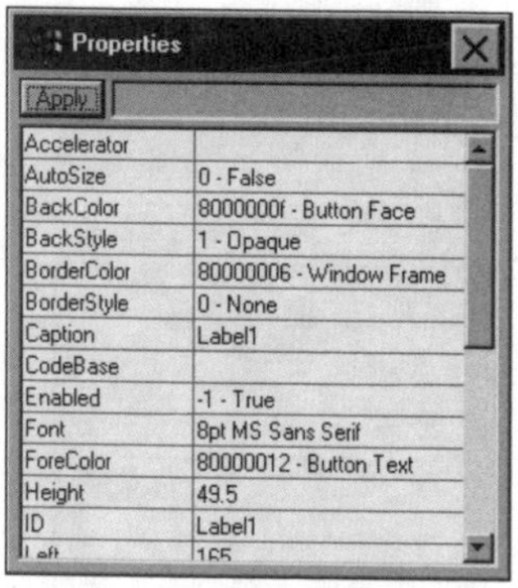

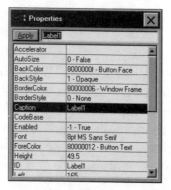

Figure 8.8 The Properties window for the label control.

3. Tap the Delete key to delete the current caption.

   We want the label control to be blank when the Web page loads.

4. Press the Enter key.

   The caption text disappears from the **caption** property line, indicating that the **caption** property is now blank.

5. Double-click in the line for the **borderstyle** property.

   The **borderstyle** changes from *0 - None* to *1- Single*. A single line will now show the edges of the label control in the layout.

6. Single-click in the line for the **backcolor** property.

   The current label background color appears in the blank at the top of the Properties window. But there's something more important to notice. At the right end of the blank, a button with three dots has appeared.

7. Click on the new three-dotted button.

   The Color Palette will appear, as shown in Figure 8.10.

Figure 8.9 Replacing the text in the **caption** property.

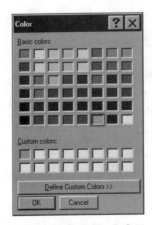

Figure 8.10   The ActiveX Control Pad Color Palette.

8. In the Color Palette, click in the white-color square. Then click on OK.

    The label's **backcolor** property changes to white, setting it off from the gray background of the Web page layout. You will probably be able to see it peeking out from behind the Properties window.

9. Close the Properties window by clicking on the Close-Window button.

    Your screen should look something like Figure 8.11.

Now, let's use the Properties window to change the **caption** property of the command button. Using the same method as in steps 1 and 2, select the command button control, open its Properties window, and select the **caption** property. This time, change the caption to *Display some text in the label control.*

It's a good time to save your work. Open the File menu and select Save. Give the layout a name that indicates its role in your set of Web pages, then put it in the appropriate directory. ActiveX Control Pad will automatically save it with an ALX file extension.

Learning about the Properties window.
You've seen a little bit of how to use the Properties window, but the best way to learn about it—and also about the properties of various controls—is simply to experiment. The more you use the Properties window, the more adept you'll become at using ActiveX controls in HTML layouts.

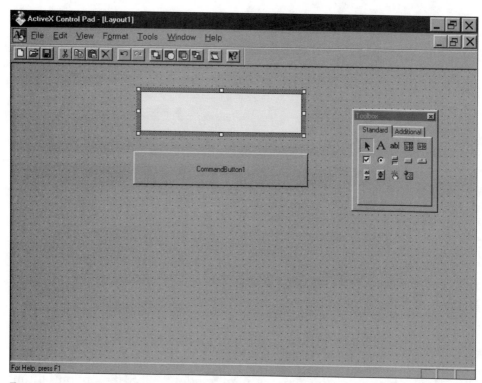

Figure 8.11   The label control's properties have changed.

Adding Code With The Script Wizard

So far, our Web page layout looks nice, but it doesn't do much. Let's add some event code to the command button. When a user clicks on the command button, we want it to display some text in the label control. Follow these steps:

1. Click on the command button to select it.

2. Open the Tools menu and select Script Wizard.

   The Script Wizard window will appear, as shown in Figure 8.12. Notice that on the left, the window lists items to which you can add code: the command button, the label control, and the HTML layout itself. On the right, it shows a list of actions that those items can perform.

3. In the list at the left, double-click on the entry for the command button.

   Under the command button entry, a list opens, showing the events to which code can be added.

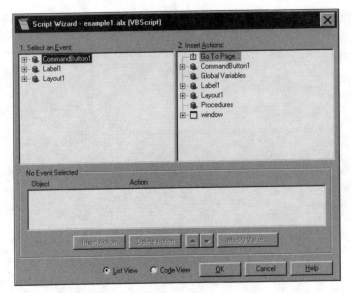

Figure 8.12 The Script Wizard window.

4. In the event list for the command button, click on the entry for the **Click** event.

5. At the bottom of the Script Wizard window, select the option button labeled **Code View**.

   A code window for the command button's **click** sub will appear, as shown in Figure 8.13.

6. In the code window, under the *Sub CommandButton1_Click()/*, enter the following code: *label1.caption = "This text is displayed by a sub created in the Script Wizard."*

7. Click on OK.

   The Script Wizard adds the code to the command button.

8. Save your Web page layout.

9. Close the layout window.

   This closes the layout file so you can insert it into an HTML document.

There's one more step in creating a Web page that includes an HTML layout: inserting the layout into the "master" Web document via the HTML Layout control. That's what you'll learn how to do in the next section.

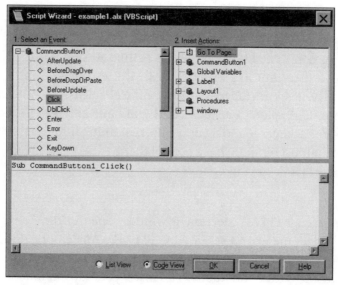

Figure 8.13 The code window for the command button's **click** sub.

Learning more about properties and events.
Curious about the properties of different ActiveX controls, and the events to which they can respond? A great way to learn about both is to browse through the Properties window and Script Wizard with different kinds of controls. By double-clicking on a particular control, you can open its Properties window to view and experiment with its various properties. By opening the Script Wizard for a page with several controls, you can see which events each control supports, and write simple test subs to see how each control behaves.

Inserting A Layout In An HTML Document

Once you've created a layout, you need to insert it into the **<body>** section of an HTML document. To do this, you use the HTML Layout control, which is an ActiveX control. The ActiveX Control Pad makes it easy.

You already have the HTML Layout control.
You don't need to worry about getting a copy of the HTML Layout control. It's included with the ActiveX Control Pad, and will be included with the official release of Microsoft's Internet Explorer version 3.0. If you have either of those software packages—and if you've been working through this book, you almost certainly have both of them—then you already have the HTML Layout control.

If you don't have an HTML document window open in the ActiveX Control Pad, open the File menu and select New HTML. An "empty" HTML document window will appear: All it contains is a simple HTML template, including tags for document **\<title\>** and **\<body\>**. To insert your layout, follow these steps:

1. Position the text cursor on the line between the **\<body\>** and **\</body\>** HTML tags.

2. Open the Edit menu and select I<u>n</u>sert HTML Layout, as shown in Figure 8.14.

   A File Open dialog box will appear.

3. In the dialog box, select the layout file you want to insert. Then click on OK.

   The ActiveX Control Pad inserts an object tag for the HTML Layout control at the cursor location in your HTML document window. If you look at the object tag, you'll see that it gives the directory path and file name of your HTML layout.

4. Add title text between the **\<title\>** and **\</title\>** tags.

Figure 8.14 Inserting an HTML layout.

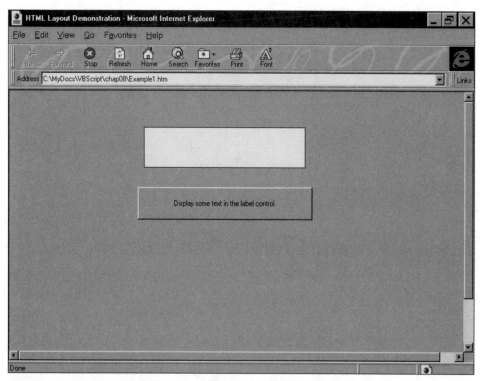

Figure 8.15 The Web page created by our HTML layout.

In this case, title the Web page *HTML Layout Demonstration* or something equally soporific.

5. Save the HTML document file and close the ActiveX Control Pad.

Your final step is to view the result of your hard work. Start up Internet Explorer and load the HTML document file. Your screen should look something like Figure 8.15.

When you click on the command button, it fires the sub you created in the Script Wizard. The result is shown in Figure 8.16.

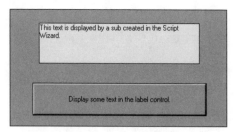

Figure 8.16 The command button's Click event sub displays text in the label control.

ActiveX Control Pad Tips And Techniques

There are three other tricks you can use to make the ActiveX Control Pad even more effective:

☆ You can add new ActiveX (or OCX) controls to the Toolbox.

☆ You can delete controls from the Toolbox.

☆ By switching to List View, you can make the Script Wizard write event code for you.

Adding Controls To The Toolbox

As you get new ActiveX controls, you'll want to add them to the ActiveX Control Pad Toolbox. It's quite easy to do so. In the ActiveX Control Pad, simply display an HTML layout window. Then, follow these steps:

1. Click on the Toolbox, but in a spot that's outside any of the pages with controls on them.

    A shortcut menu will appear, as shown in Figure 8.17.

2. In the menu, select New Page.

    A new, blank control page will appear in the Toolbox.

3. Right-click on the new page.

    A shortcut menu will appear.

4. Select Additional Controls.

    The Additional Controls dialog box will appear, as shown in Figure 8.18. It lists the ActiveX controls available on your PC.

5. In the dialog box, select the checkbox next to the control you want to add to the Toolbox.

6. Click on OK.

    The new control appears in the blank Toolbox page.

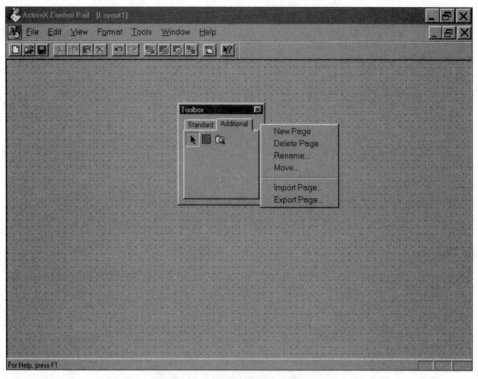

Figure 8.17   Preparing to add a new page to the Toolbox.

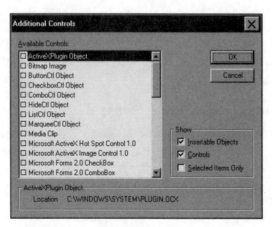

Figure 8.18   The Additional Controls dialog box.

Deleting Controls From The Toolbox

Deleting controls from the Toolbox is even easier than adding them. To delete a control, follow these steps:

1. Right-click the control you want to delete from the Toolbox.

    A shortcut menu will appear. Two of the menu choices are to delete or to customize the control on which you clicked.

2. In the menu, select the Delete menu choice.

    The control is deleted from the Toolbox.

Automatic Coding With The Script Wizard's List View

Earlier, you saw how easy it is to create event subs in the Script Wizard's Code View. But if you need to create an event sub that performs a very common VBScript task, there's an even easier way: use the Script Wizard's List View.

Consider the example we created earlier in this chapter: a Web page with a command button that displays some text in a label control. Wizardly VBScript programmers that we are, we had no trouble writing the appropriate line of code for the command button's **click** event:

```
Label1.caption = "This text is displayed by a sub created in the Script Wizard."
```

But amazing as it might seem, the Script Wizard—through its List View—can even do *that* for us. To create the same sub code using the List View, we would have followed these steps:

1. Open the Tools menu and select Script Wizard.

    The Script Wizard window appears. List View is actually the default.

2. In the list at the left, double-click on the control for which you want to create or edit an event sub.

    In this case, that's *CommandButton1*. A list of available events appears under the control name.

3. Click on the event for which you want to create a sub.

    In this case, that's the **click** event.

4. In the list on the right, double-click on the control or object that the event sub should affect.

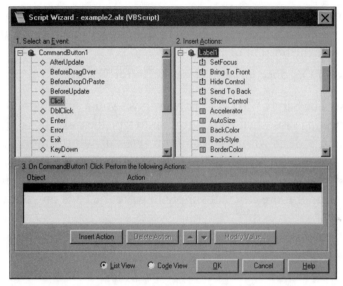

Figure 8.19 Preparing to create an event sub for the command button.

In this case, that's the *Label1* control. A list of available properties appears under the control name, as shown in Figure 8.19.

5. In the property list, double-click on the property you want the event sub to affect.

In this case, we double-click on the label control's **caption** property. A dialog box appears, asking for the new value of the property, as shown in Figure 8.20.

6. In the dialog box, enter the new value you want in the control's property.

In this case, we'd enter "This text is displayed by a sub created in the Script Wizard." as the new caption of the label control.

7. Click on OK.

Figure 8.20 The Script Wizard asks for the new property value.

The caption property change is added—in plain English—to the box showing the result of the sub selected in the left-hand list. This is shown at the bottom of Figure 8.21.

8. Click on OK once more to close the Script Wizard.

And that's it! The Script Wizard's List view gives you a simple point-and-shoot method of creating subs when you don't want to type the code. The only limitation is that because it deals with very common types of sub operations, the Script Wizard won't create highly specialized sub code for you. In those situations—and in most situations, as you become a highly proficient VBScript programmer—you'll find it more efficient simply to write the code on your own.

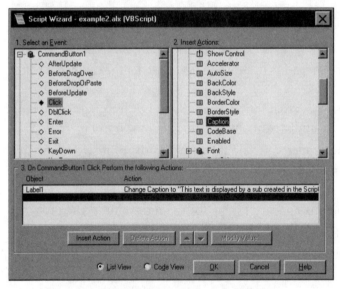

Figure 8.21 The Script Wizard has created the sub for you.

IX

THE SCRIPTING OBJECT MODEL

It's not just for Visual
Basic Script, but the
Internet Explorer
scripting object model
lets your code commu-
nicate with different
parts of the Web page.
That gives you the
foundation for some
pretty neat tricks.

If you're like most people—even most programmers, who are, of course, a different breed—your first question is, "What the heck is a scripting object model, anyway?" Your second question is, "Do I really need to know about this?"

In order, the answers to your questions are: Something Really Important, Yes, and 42. Oh, wait, you didn't ask about the ultimate question: Forget that third answer.

The scripting object model isn't part of VBScript: It's part of Microsoft's Internet Explorer Web browser. As a result, the scripting object model works equally well with VBScript or JavaScript, the other major scripting language for Web pages.

Objects, Properties, And Events

Internet Explorer treats each Web page as an object. But what is an object? An object is simply a thing that has properties and can react to certain external events. The ActiveX controls we've been using—and even the ordinary-seeming HTML controls—are objects. So are apples, bridges, PCs, and, at a higher level, human beings. Take your PC, for example. It has the following properties, among many others:

☆ Color

☆ Texture

☆ Weight

☆ Shape

A PC can also respond to some external events, such as the following:

☆ Typing on the keyboard

☆ Electronic impulses from the modem

☆ Movements of the mouse over the mouse pad

On the other hand, there are also properties that your PC does *not* have and events to which it cannot respond. For example, your PC doesn't have blood pressure because it doesn't have any blood. Moreover, if you talk out loud to your PC, it will usually not react at all—at least, not in 1996.

Objects in the Internet Explorer scripting object model are almost exactly like that. They have certain properties and not others; they react to certain events and not others.

The Object Hierarchy

But what objects are we talking about here? Well, inasmuch as Internet Explorer is a Web browser, you might guess—correctly—that the relevant objects are Web pages and their contents. In essence, anything that can appear in a Web page is included in the scripting object model. In addition, the model includes a few other objects that are part of Internet Explorer itself. The objects are as follows:

☆ **Window.** This is the top level object that holds everything else. You can think of it as the Web page itself.

☆ **Frame.** The main window can hold multiple, independent frames. The whole set of a window's frames is kept in an array and stored in the window's **frames** property. Each frame can be referred to by its array index, starting with **frames[0]**.

☆ **History.** This object is used to get the history list from Internet Explorer in case you need to back up to a Web page that the user visited earlier.

☆ **Navigator.** This object holds information about the browser program itself, i.e., about Internet Explorer.

☆ **Location.** This object holds the URL (Web address, or Uniform Resource Locator) of the current Web page.

☆ **Script.** This object holds any script code that's embedded in the current window.

☆ **Document.** This is the object you'll use most often. It's the "writing area" of the current window. If you want your Web page to change its background color or display new text in response to a user's actions, you can use the document object to accomplish those tasks—among many others.

☆ **Link.** This object is an array of links contained in the current document. It's part of the document object.

☆ **Anchor.** This object is an array of anchor tags (**<a>**) contained in the current document. It's part of the document object.

☆ **Form.** This object is a form (if any) contained in the current document. If you give the form a name in the **<form>** tag, you can refer to this object by name. It's part of the document object.

☆ **Element.** This object is a control contained in the current form or document. It can be either a standard HTML control (created with the **<input>** tag) or an ActiveX control. Depending on where the control is located—

in a form, or just in the document outside of any form—it can be part of either the form or the document object.

The object hierarchy is shown in Figure 9.1.

Attaching Scripts To Objects

Given that introduction, let's take a look at how you can use VBScript (or JavaScript, if you are so inclined) with the various objects which can appear in a window. There are three ways to attach script code to objects:

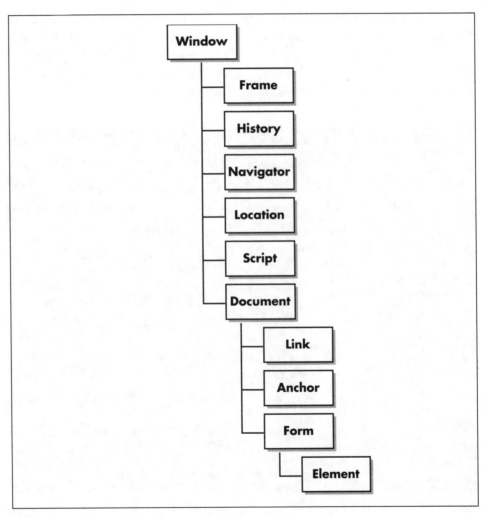

Figure 9.1 The scripting object hierarchy.

☆ Use the **script** element. This means using the HTML **<script>** tag exactly as we've been doing so far. The script code appears in its own separate section of the HTML document. Various event subs are linked to controls by their names, such as *CmdDoIt.Click()*.

☆ Name a particular sub in the HTML tag for a form control. This means, for example, including an **OnClick** clause in the HTML tag for an input button.

☆ Embedding a script in a hyperlink. This allows you to execute script code when the user clicks on a link to another Web page.

Only the first two methods were supported for VBScript in the beta release of Internet Explorer, so we'll demonstrate them here and explain the third in general terms. Listing 9.1 shows the first two methods of attaching script code to objects. Figure 9.2 shows the Web page created by the code in Listing 9.1, while Figure 9.3 shows the result of clicking on one of the buttons.

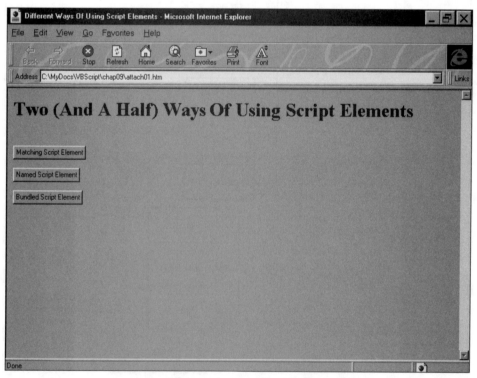

Figure 9.2   The Web page created by the code in Listing 9.1.

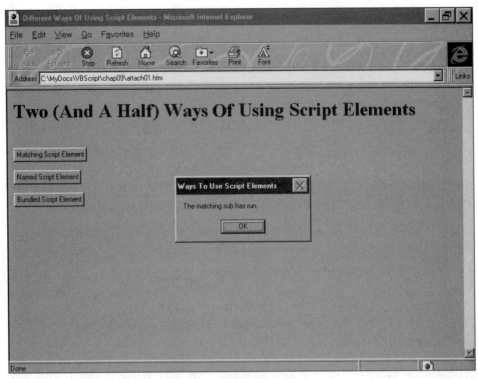

Figure 9.3 The result of clicking a button in the Web page.

Listing 9.1 Using different methods to attach script code to objects.

```
<HTML>
<HEAD>
<TITLE>Different Ways Of Using Script Elements</TITLE>
</HEAD>
<H1>Two (And A Half) Ways Of Using Script Elements</H1>
<BODY>
<script language="vbs">
<!--
Sub MScript_OnClick
    msgbox "The matching sub has run.",,"Ways To Use Script Elements"
end sub

sub NSub
    msgbox "The named sub has run.",,"Ways To Use Script Elements"
end sub
-->
</script>
<pre>
<form name="SForm">
<input type="button" name="MScript" value="Matching Script Element"><br>
```

```
<input type="button" name="NScript" value="Named Script Element"
    onClick="NSub"><br>
<input type="button" name="BScript" value="Bundled Script Element"><br>
    <script for="BScript" event="onClick" language="VBScript">
    msgbox "The bundled sub has run.",,"Ways To Use Script Elements."
    </script>
</form>
</pre>

</BODY>
</HTML>
```

The first method is to match the name of the VBScript sub to the control and event. That's the approach used by the following part of Listing 9.1:

```
<input type="button" name="MScript" value="Matching Script Element"><br>
Sub MScript_OnClick
    msgbox "The matching sub has run.",,"Ways To Use Script Elements"
end sub
```

It's pretty easy to see what's happening. To match the sub to the control, you simply name the sub so that it combines the control name (MScript) with the event name (OnClick).

The second method comes in two varieties. The first, familiar variety is shown in the following code snippet:

```
<input type="button" name="NScript" value="Named Script Element"
    onClick="NSub">
sub NSub
    msgbox "The named sub has run.",,"Ways To Use Script Elements"
end sub
```

In this case, the names don't match, but it doesn't matter. Inside the **<input>** tag, you've specified the name of the sub that should run when the user clicks on the button.

A variation on this method is to bundle the sub code right inside the HTML form, nestled snugly under the control tag that activates it. This is shown in the following code snippet:

```
<input type="button" name="BScript" value="Bundled Script Element"><br>
    <script for="BScript" event="onClick" language="VBScript">
    msgbox "The bundled sub has run.",,"Ways To Use Script Elements."
    </script>
```

The third method is to embed script code in a hypertext link. This method was not yet supported in the beta version of Internet Explorer for VBScript. However, when the final version of Internet Explorer is released, it should work as shown in the following code line:

```
<a href="vbscript: script code here"> hyperlink caption </a>
```

First, you have the standard HTML tags for anchor and hypertext reference. Then, in quote marks, you have the name of the scripting engine (VBScript or JavaScript), a colon, and the script code. A closing angle bracket terminates the **<a href=** tag. Then, you put in the text for the link caption, and finally, **</a>** to terminate the anchor.

Referring To Objects

In your script code, you'll often need to refer to objects—getting values from them, assigning values to their properties, calling their built-in methods, and so on. The general way you refer to object properties and methods is as follows:

```
ObjectName.property
```

or

```
ObjectName.method
```

The main exception to this rule is when you need to refer to the window object of the current Web page. Because the window object is the top-level object that contains all the other objects, you can leave out the word **window** when you use it. For instance, with either of these code lines, you can get the name of the current window and assign it to the **NameString** variable:

```
NameString = window.name
NameString = name
```

If you want to refer to other objects, however, you need to include the object in your code line. To call the document object's **writeln** method, for example, you'd use this code line:

```
document.writeln("Howdy, world.")
```

To assign a value to **Btn1** in a form that's contained in your document (contained in the main window object), you'd write

```
Document.FormName.Btn1.value = "New text in the button"
```

where **FormName** is the form name you assigned with the **<form>** tag. This is, of course, a way you'll use the object model very often: to refer to controls on your Web page.

The Objects Themselves

With that introduction, let's look at some of the things you can do with the objects themselves. This isn't meant to be an exhaustive reference to all the objects and their properties—merely to show you how it's done, so you can experiment on your own. We'll look at a few of the more interesting and useful properties and methods.

The Window Object

The window object is the top-level object that holds your Web page. It has two events, **onLoad** and **onUnload**, that you can use to do setup and shutdown work. Listing 9.2 shows an example of using these events, while Listing 9.3 shows code for an essentially blank Web page that just gives us a way to leave the first Web page. Figure 9.4 shows the result when the user loads the Web page created by Listing 9.2; the result of unloading is similar.

Listing 9.2 Using the window object's **onLoad** and **onUnload** events.

```
<HTML>
<HEAD>
<TITLE> Window OnLoad Event Demonstration</TITLE>
</HEAD>

<H1>The Window OnLoad Event</H1>

<BODY language="vbs" onLoad="DisplayMsg" onUnload="ByeBye">

<p>The Window object's OnLoad event can be used
to perform setup tasks when the user first loads your HTML
document into his/her Web browser. In this case, it displays
a simple message box.</p> <br><br>

<a href="Page2.htm">Go to a different page.</a>

<script language="vbs">

sub DisplayMsg
    msgbox "The window has loaded.",,"OnLoad Event Demonstration"
end sub
```

```
sub ByeBye
    msgbox "The window is unloading.",,"OnUnload Event Demonstration"
end sub

</script>

</BODY>
</HTML>
```

Listing 9.3   A blank Web page to which we can jump.

```
<HTML>
<HEAD>
<TITLE> Page Two</TITLE>
</HEAD>
<H1>Page Two</H1>
<BODY>
<p>This page doesn't really do anything. It simply gives you a
way to leave the other page so you can see the sub run for the
window object's Unload event.</p><br><br>
<a href="onload1.htm">Go back to the original page.</a>
</BODY>
</HTML>
```

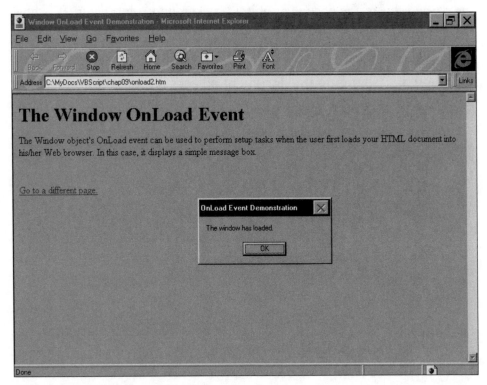

Figure 9.4   Using the window object's **onLoad** event.

The relevant HTML code line in Listing 9.2 is the **<body>** tag, as follows:

```
<BODY language="vbs" onLoad="DisplayMsg" onUnLoad="ByeBye">
```

To use the **onLoad** and **onUnload** events, you add information to the HTML document's **<body>** tag: the scripting engine (VBScript), the sub to execute when the **onLoad** event fires, and the sub to execute when the **onUnload** event fires. Of course, you don't have to use both events: You can use only one if that's appropriate.

In Listing 9.2, the event subs simply display message boxes. But in real-world Web pages, you can make them declare variables, set initial values, or change the text in a Web page based on the value of an already-existing variable.

The Document Object

You change document properties pretty much as you'd expect: by using the **document** object name and property in an assignment statement. Listing 9.4 shows an example of how you can change the color of your Web page by assigning a new value to the document object's background color. Figure 9.5 shows the Web page created by the code in Listing 9.5, while Figure 9.6 shows the *new* Web page displayed by the **document.writeln** calls.

Listing 9.4　Changing the document object's background color.

```
<HTML>
<HEAD>
<TITLE> type_Document_Title_here </TITLE>
</HEAD>
<BODY>
<script language="VBScript">
    sub Pressed
        document.bgColor = "Blue"
    end sub
</script>
<form>
<input type="button" value="Change Web page color" onclick="Pressed">
</form>
</BODY>
</HTML>
```

As you'd expect, in the **Pressed** sub, you just specify the object (**document**), the property (**bgColor**), and assign the new value. Baby simple.

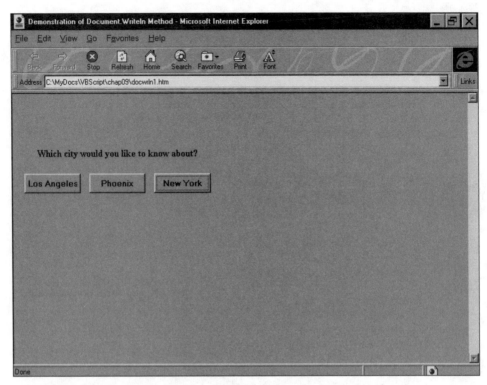

Figure 9.5 Web page created by the code in Listing 9.5.

USING DOCUMENT METHODS

Using the document object's **write** or **writeln** methods is even more interesting. You can use these methods to write new text into your Web page's underlying HTML document. In response to user actions, you can display new text or even new controls on your Web page. Listing 9.5 shows an example of using ActiveX controls and the document object's **writeln** method to answer a user's question about city statistics for Phoenix, Arizona.

Listing 9.5 Using the document object's **writeln** method.

```
<HTML>
<HEAD>
<TITLE> Demonstration of Document.Writeln Method</TITLE>
</HEAD>
<BODY>
<pre>
<br><br><br>
<TABLE WIDTH=200 HEIGHT=100 CELLPADDING=5 CELLSPACING=5>
<CAPTION ALIGN=top><b>Which city would you like to know about?</b></CAPTION>
```

```
<TR><TD>
<SCRIPT LANGUAGE="VBScript">
<!--
Sub CmdLA_Click()
document.open
document.writeln("<pre>")
document.writeln("<br><br><br><br>City of Los Angeles")
document.writeln("-----------------------------")
document.writeln("Population: 3.5 million")
document.writeln ("Area: 465 square miles")
document.writeln ("Per capita income: $19,906")
document.writeln ("Unemployment rate: 7.3 percent.")
document.writeln("</pre>")
document.close
end sub
-->
</SCRIPT>
     <OBJECT ID="CmdLA" WIDTH=96 HEIGHT=32
      CLASSID="CLSID:D7053240-CE69-11CD-A777-00DD01143C57">
        <PARAM NAME="Caption" VALUE="Los Angeles">
        <PARAM NAME="Size" VALUE="2540;846">
        <PARAM NAME="FontEffects" VALUE="1073741825">
        <PARAM NAME="FontHeight" VALUE="200">
        <PARAM NAME="FontCharSet" VALUE="0">
        <PARAM NAME="FontPitchAndFamily" VALUE="2">
        <PARAM NAME="ParagraphAlign" VALUE="3">
        <PARAM NAME="FontWeight" VALUE="700">
    </OBJECT>
</TD><TD>
<SCRIPT LANGUAGE="VBScript">
<!--
Sub CmdPhoenix_Click()
document.open
document.writeln("<pre>")
document.writeln("<br><br><br><br>City of Phoenix")
document.writeln("-----------------------------")
document.writeln("Population: 983,400")
document.writeln ("Area: 324 square miles")
document.writeln ("Per capita income: $17,705")
document.writeln ("Unemployment rate: 4.6 percent.")
document.writeln("</pre>")
document.close
end sub
-->
</SCRIPT>
    <OBJECT ID="CmdPhoenix" WIDTH=96 HEIGHT=32
     CLASSID="CLSID:D7053240-CE69-11CD-A777-00DD01143C57">
        <PARAM NAME="Caption" VALUE="Phoenix">
        <PARAM NAME="Size" VALUE="2540;846">
        <PARAM NAME="FontEffects" VALUE="1073741825">
        <PARAM NAME="FontHeight" VALUE="200">
```

```
            <PARAM NAME="FontCharSet" VALUE="0">
            <PARAM NAME="FontPitchAndFamily" VALUE="2">
            <PARAM NAME="ParagraphAlign" VALUE="3">
            <PARAM NAME="FontWeight" VALUE="700">
    </OBJECT>
</TD><TD>
<SCRIPT LANGUAGE="VBScript">
<!--
Sub CmdNYC_Click()
document.open
document.writeln("<pre>")
document.writeln("<br><br><br><br>City of New York")
document.writeln("----------------------------")
document.writeln("Population: 7,325,000")
document.writeln ("Area: 301 square miles")
document.writeln ("Per capita income: $22,064")
document.writeln ("Unemployment rate: 7.4 percent.")
document.writeln("</pre>")
document.close
end sub
-->
</SCRIPT>
    <OBJECT ID="CmdNYC" WIDTH=96 HEIGHT=32
     CLASSID="CLSID:D7053240-CE69-11CD-A777-00DD01143C57">
        <PARAM NAME="Caption" VALUE="New York">
        <PARAM NAME="Size" VALUE="2540;846">
        <PARAM NAME="FontEffects" VALUE="1073741825">
        <PARAM NAME="FontHeight" VALUE="200">
        <PARAM NAME="FontCharSet" VALUE="0">
        <PARAM NAME="FontPitchAndFamily" VALUE="2">
        <PARAM NAME="ParagraphAlign" VALUE="3">
        <PARAM NAME="FontWeight" VALUE="700">
    </OBJECT>
</TD></TR>
</TABLE>
</pre>
</BODY>
</HTML>
```

We're getting a little fancy with our HTML code, here—using a table instead of an ActiveX layout to position our ActiveX command buttons. The main point of the listing, however, is contained in the **click** event subs for the command buttons, as follows:

```
Sub CmdPhoenix_Click()
document.open
document.writeln("<pre>")
document.writeln("<br><br><br><br>City of Phoenix")
document.writeln("----------------------------")
document.writeln("Population: 983,400")
```

```
document.writeln ("Area: 324 square miles")
document.writeln ("Per capita income: $17,705")
document.writeln ("Unemployment rate: 4.6 percent.")
document.writeln("</pre>")
document.close
end sub
```

To write to a document object, you must first open it, much as—in a "regular" PC program—you would open a file before writing to it. Once you've opened the document object for writing, you insert a **<pre>** (preformatted text) tag. Without it, VBScript won't distinguish between the document object's **writeln** method, which inserts a line break at the end of each line, and the document object's **write** method, which doesn't.

After that, you make repeated calls to **document.writeln** to insert your text into the HTML document. Note that the text goes right into the HTML code, and must be formatted with the appropriate HTML tags. If that seems like a pain, consider the result: You can insert not only text, but **<input>** or **<object>** tags to display new controls on the rewritten Web page.

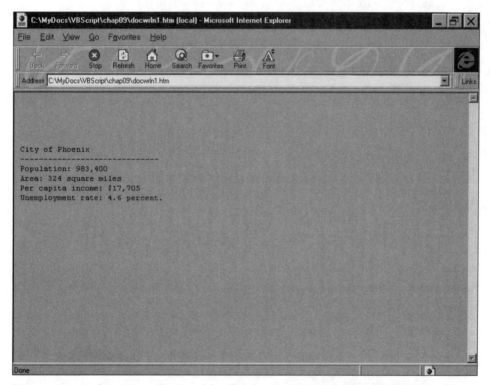

Figure 9.6 Information displayed by the **document.writeln** method.

When you're finished, you call **document.close** to close the document object and update the Web page. If you forget this step, your new Web page won't display—the old one will just sit there.

The Form Object

The next most important object in the scripting object model is the form object. If you want to submit data from your Web page to a server—for example, to allow users to order products—you'll need to use the form object and standard HTML form controls.

At this time, Internet Explorer and its scripting model do not allow you to submit values directly from ActiveX controls to a server via the HTML **submit** method. However, by a trick that combines standard form **<input>** controls with ActiveX controls, you can have the power and convenience of ActiveX controls and layouts while still using the **submit** method. All you need to do is refer to form elements. Creating such order forms—and using VBScript for client-side data validation—is the subject of Chapter 10.

X

Client-Side Data Validation

Now, you'll use all the skills you've learned to combine HTML, Visual Basic Script, and ActiveX in one of the Web's most common needs: validating data from order forms. You can do it on the user's PC, with VBScript, or you can do it on your Web server, with CGI programs. The choice is yours.

Ohne of the most common uses of the Web is to let customers order products from your Web page. But that entails a rather thorny problem: how to make sure that each customer enters all the data required to process his or her order. Moreover, you often need to make sure that the data is not only *present,* but that it fits some general guidelines: for example, that the customer's last name isn't all digits, or that a customer's credit-card number is in the correct format.

Creating a Web-page order form with data validation is an ideal exercise, because you'll use every concept and skill you've learned so far—as well as a few brand new ones:

☆ Creating an ActiveX layout

☆ Using the Internet Explorer scripting object model to access controls on the Web page

☆ Writing subs and functions to process the data on the order form

☆ Checking the data to make sure it's complete

☆ Sending data from a Web page to a Web server

Client-Side Vs. Server-Side Data Validation

If a user of your Web page is going to send you some data—whether it's to order a product or for some other purpose—you can choose one of three strategies (shown in Figure 10.1) for checking the data:

☆ Don't check the data at all.

☆ Check the data after it gets to your Web server (server-side data validation).

☆ Check the data on the user's own machine, before it's submitted to your Web server (client-side data validation).

For serious Web applications, it's simply not an option to skip checking the data. That leaves only two choices: Either you check the data on your Web server, or you check it on the user's machine—the client.

Historically, most Web ordering systems have used server-side data validation because that's what was available with current technology. To validate data when it gets to your Web server, you write a CGI (Common Gateway Interface) program

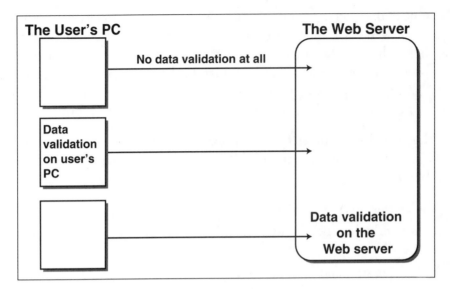

Figure 10.1 Strategies for Web data validation.

that actually runs on your Web server. Normally, this type of program will check the data, then process it to fulfill the customer's order. In Chapter 15, you'll learn how to use Visual Basic 4 to create this type of program and run it on your Web server.

VBScript, however, makes it easy to validate data on the client machine, before it ever gets to your Web server. If you're going to process a lot of orders, this can be a much more efficient way to check the data.

Client-Side Validation With VBScript And HTML

The simplest way to do client-side data validation is to use VBScript with standard HTML forms and controls. That's not nearly as easy or powerful as using an ActiveX layout and ActiveX controls, but it's much simpler, so it's a good place to start.

The concept is simple: Before you submit the data to the Web server, you run it through a few VBScript routines to check it. Then, you submit it. This approach is shown in Listing 10.1. As before, we had to break a few lines to fit the

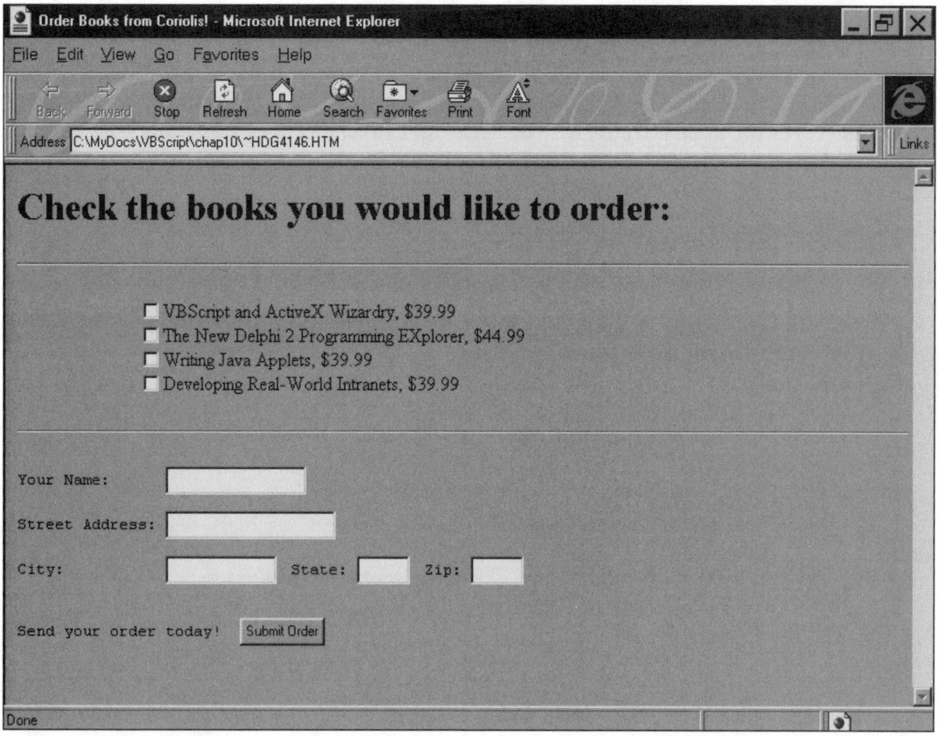

Figure 10.2 A Web page order form.

code into the page margins of this book. As a result, the material between the **<pre>** and **</pre>** (preformatted text) tags won't display properly on your screen unless you reformat it. The Web page created by the HTML code in Listing 10.1 is shown in Figure 10.2.

Listing 10.1 HTML code to create a Web page order form.

```
<HTML>
<HEAD>
<TITLE>Order Books from Coriolis!</TITLE>
<!--
    This version of the Web page order form shows the beginnings of how to
    incorporate error-checking into a simple HTML document without using an
    ActiveX layout or controls.
-->
</HEAD>
<BODY>
<h1>Check the books you would like to order:</h1>
<FORM name="OrderForm" method=post ACTION="http://localhost/cgi-win/
    cgitest32.exe/Form">
<hr>
```

```
<ul><ul><ul><ul><ul>
<INPUT NAME="CB_VBScriptWiz" TYPE="CHECKBOX" VALUE="1"
   ALIGN=left>VBScript and ActiveX Wizardry, $39.99<br>
<INPUT NAME="CB_DelphiExp" TYPE="CHECKBOX" VALUE="1"
   ALIGN=left>The New Delphi 2 Programming EXplorer, $44.99<br>
<INPUT NAME="CB_JavaApp" TYPE="CHECKBOX" VALUE="1"
   ALIGN=left>Writing Java Applets, $39.99<br>
<INPUT NAME="CB_Intranet" TYPE="CHECKBOX" VALUE="1"
   ALIGN=left>Developing Real-World Intranets, $39.99<br>
</ul></ul></ul></ul></ul>
<hr>
<pre>
Your Name:       <INPUT NAME="TB_Customer" TYPE="" SIZE="20"
   ALIGN=right><br>
Street Address: <INPUT NAME="TB_Street" TYPE="" SIZE="25" ALIGN=right><br>
City:            <INPUT NAME="TB_City" TYPE="TEXT" SIZE="15"
   ALIGN=right> State: <INPUT NAME="TB_State" TYPE="TEXT"
   SIZE="5" ALIGN=right> Zip: <INPUT NAME="TB_Zip"
   TYPE="TEXT" SIZE="5" ALIGN=right>
<br>
Send your order today!  <INPUT NAME="Btn_Order" TYPE="Button"
   value="Submit Order" ALIGN=right >
</pre>
</FORM>

<script language="VBS">
<!--

function DataOkay
   MsgBox "The data has been checked, and it's okay.",, _
      "Client-Side Data Validation"
end function

sub Btn_Order_onClick
   OrderForm.Submit
end sub

-->
</script>
</BODY>
</HTML>
```

Stepping Through The Example Code

Before we construct a fully-functional example, let's take a look at the broad outlines of what's going on in Listing 10.1. Later, when we do the same thing with an ActiveX layout, you'll need a firm understanding of these basic moves.

The first step is to create an HTML form by using the **<form>** tag. The specific code that sets up the HTML form is as follows:

```
<FORM name="OrderForm" method=post ACTION="http://localhost/cgi-win/
    cgitest32.exe/Form">
```

This line does several jobs. First, of course, it tells the Web browser that this is the beginning of a form. Then, it does the following:

✯ *name="OrderForm"* tells the Web browser that the form is named *OrderForm.* You'll use that name to refer to the form and its controls later on.

✯ *method=post* tells the Web browser that this form will be used to send data to the Web server.

✯ Finally, *ACTION="http://localhost/cgi-win/cgitest32.exe/Form"* tells the Web browser what action it should perform when the user submits the data to the Web server. This action will normally be a CGI program that runs on the server. Here, instead of a regular CGI program, we're using *cgitest,* a simple program bundled with O'Reilly & Associates' Website server software. The *cgitest* program just verifies that your Web page is sending data to the server and shows you what data the server received. It's explained in detail in Chapter 15.

The next code lines just do a little formatting for us:

```
<hr>
<ul><ul><ul><ul><ul>
```

The <HR> tag draws a horizontal line on the Web page, while the repeated <UL> (un-numbered list) tags indent the material that follows them on the page. You can see the effect of both of these code lines in Figure 10.2, which appeared earlier.

The next lines set up a series of HTML check box controls, each of which corresponds to a book that a Web page user might order from the Coriolis Group:

```
<INPUT NAME="CB_VBScriptWiz" TYPE="CHECKBOX" VALUE="1"
    ALIGN=left>VBScript and ActiveX Wizardry, $39.99<br>
…and so on
```

The code is fairly self-explanatory, but there's one point worth noting if you haven't used HTML check boxes very much: The **value** property is set to 1. This does *not* mean what you might expect: that the check box has a value of 1 as soon as it appears on the Web page. Instead, it means that if and when the user checks the check box, it *will* have a value of 1—in other words, 1 is the value of its "checked" state. By testing to see if a check box control has a value of 1, you can determine whether or not it has been checked.

The next code removes the indents created by the <UL> tags, draws another horizontal line, and tells the browser to display the next material as it's formatted in the HTML document:

```
</ul></ul></ul></ul></ul>
<hr>
<pre>
```

Following the <PRE> tag, we use essentially the same techniques to create a series of labeled text boxes in which the user can enter his/her name and address for order shipment:

```
<INPUT NAME="CB_VBScriptWiz" TYPE="CHECKBOX" VALUE="1"
   ALIGN=left>VBScript and ActiveX Wizardry, $39.99<br>
…and so on.
```

As before, these are native HTML controls, not ActiveX controls. Next, we create a submit button. When the user clicks on this button, the data will be sent from the Web page to the server, where the order will be processed by a CGI program:

```
Send your order today!  <INPUT NAME="Btn_Order" TYPE="Button"
   value="Submit Order" ALIGN=right >
</pre>
</FORM>
```

Ordinarily, the **type** of this control would be **submit**, so that clicking it would automatically submit the data to the server. However, we're bundling the call to the **form.submit** method into the **OnClick** sub for the button control. Therefore, the button control is coded simply as a plain vanilla **button**. The reason for bundling the call to **form.submit** into the sub is that it enables us to validate the data before submitting it.

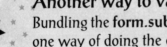

Another way to validate before submitting.

Bundling the **form.submit** call into a button's **click** sub is only one way of doing the data validation. Another is to build the data validation into a sub for the form's **onsubmit** event. This event was not supported in the beta test 2 version of Internet Explorer, but should be supported in the final release.

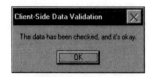

Figure 10.3 The VBScript data-checking framework is running.

Finally, we create the framework for our data-validation script, as follows:

```
<script language="VBS">
<!--
function DataOkay
   MsgBox "The data has been checked, and it's okay.",, _
      "Client-Side Data Validation"
end function

sub Btn_Order_onClick
   OrderForm.Submit
end sub
-->
</script>
```

In the next version of our code, we'll build the actual data validation into the **DataOkay** function and will call that function in the **Btn_Order_onClick** sub. At present, there really isn't any data checking. However, if the user clicks on the submit button, a message box will appear, as shown in Figure 10.3. That, at least, shows us that the VBScript code framework is up and running.

Creating A Data-Checking Function

Our next step is to fill in the blanks that we left in Listing 10.1—mainly by writing the actual VBScript code that does the data checking. Listing 10.2 shows the modified HTML document with the data-checking code.

Listing 10.2 Data-checking code for the Web page.

```
<HTML>
<HEAD>
<TITLE>Order Books from Coriolis!</TITLE>
<!--
   This version of the Web page order form builds in some simple error-
   checking. The DataOkay function is activated when the user clicks on the
   button to submit the order to the Web server.
-->
</HEAD>
<BODY>
<h1>Check the books you would like to order:</h1>
```

```
<FORM name="OrderForm" method=post ACTION="http://localhost/cgi-win/
   cgitest32.exe/Form">
<hr>
<ul><ul><ul><ul><ul>
<INPUT NAME="CB_VBScriptWiz" TYPE="CHECKBOX" VALUE="1"
   ALIGN=left>VBScript and ActiveX Wizardry, $39.99<br>
<INPUT NAME="CB_DelphiExp" TYPE="CHECKBOX" VALUE="1"
   ALIGN=left>The New Delphi 2 Programming EXplorer, $44.99<br>
<INPUT NAME="CB_JavaApp" TYPE="CHECKBOX" VALUE="1"
   ALIGN=left>Writing Java Applets, $39.99<br>
<INPUT NAME="CB_Intranet" TYPE="CHECKBOX" VALUE="1"
   ALIGN=left>Developing Real-World Intranets, $39.99<br>
</ul></ul></ul></ul></ul>
<hr>
<pre>
Your Name:        <INPUT NAME="TB_Customer" TYPE="" SIZE="20"
   ALIGN=right><br>
Street Address: <INPUT NAME="TB_Street" TYPE="" SIZE="25" ALIGN=right><br>
City:             <INPUT NAME="TB_City" TYPE="TEXT" SIZE="15"
   ALIGN=right> State: <INPUT NAME="TB_State" TYPE="TEXT"
   SIZE="5" ALIGN=right> Zip: <INPUT NAME="TB_Zip"
   TYPE="TEXT" SIZE="5" ALIGN=right>
<br>
Send your order today!  <INPUT NAME="Btn_Order" TYPE="Button"
    value="Submit Order" ALIGN=right >
</pre>
</FORM>

<script language="VBS">
<!--

function DataOkay
   if (OrderForm.CB_VBScriptWiz.checked) or _
      (OrderForm.CB_DelphiExp.checked)  or _
      (OrderForm.CB_JavaApp.checked) or _
      (OrderForm.CB_Intranet.checked) then
      DataOkay = true
      MsgBox "The data has been checked, and it's okay.",, _
        "Client-Side Data Validation"
   else
      DataOkay = false
      MsgBox "The data isn't adequate to process the order.",, _
        "Client-Side Data Validation"
   end if
end function

sub Btn_Order_onClick
   If DataOkay then
      OrderForm.Submit
   else
      MsgBox "You haven't provided adequate data to process your" & _
         "order.",,"Client-Side Data Validation"
```

```
    end if
end sub

-->
</script>
</BODY>
</HTML>
```

Let's take a look at how the VBScript code works. The **onClick** event code for the submit button consists of a simple **if...then...else** statement:

```
If DataOkay then
     OrderForm.Submit
   else
     MsgBox _
        "You haven't provided adequate data to process your order."_
        ,, "Client-Side Data Validation"
end if
```

The **if** statement checks to see if the data is okay—that is, if the **DataOkay()** function returns a value of **true**. If so, the **then** clause calls **OrderForm.submit** to send the data to the Web server. If not, then the **else** clause displays a message box informing the user that there's a problem.

The **DataOkay()** function, too, is pretty straightforward. It consists of another **if...then...else** statement:

```
if (OrderForm.CB_VBScriptWiz.checked) or _
     (OrderForm.CB_DelphiExp.checked)  or _
     (OrderForm.CB_JavaApp.checked) or _
     (OrderForm.CB_Intranet.checked) then
     DataOkay = true
     MsgBox "The data has been checked, and it's okay.",,_
        "Client-Side Data Validation"
else
     DataOkay = false
     MsgBox "The data isn't adequate to process the order.",,_
        "Client-Side Data Validation"
end if
```

Notice that, in accordance with Internet Explorer's scripting object model, we refer to the check boxes by prefacing each check box name with the name of the form in which it appears, for example:

```
OrderForm.CB_VBScriptWiz.checked
```

The **if** part of the statement checks to see if at least one of the check boxes has been checked. If none has been checked, then the user didn't select any books to

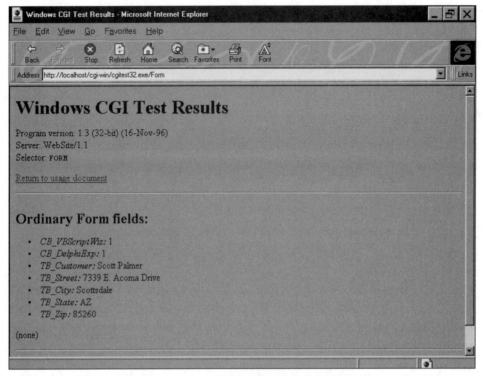

Figure 10.4   The order data was received by the Web server.

order, and there's no point in sending the rest of the data (if any) to the server. If at least one book is being ordered, the order goes through, and the data is sent to the server. Figure 10.4 shows the report we get back from the Website *cgitest* program if we order *VBScript and ActiveX Wizardry* and *The New Delphi 2 Programming EXplorer.*

To keep things simple in this example, we only verified that at least one check box was checked. However, you can use the same techniques to build other data checks into the **DataOkay**() function.

Client-Side Data Validation With An ActiveX Layout

As noted earlier, the HTML-only implementation of client-side data validation has two very important virtues: First, it's simple; second, it works. But when you compare it to the attractive Web page layouts we can create with the ActiveX Control Pad, and the power we can get from ActiveX controls, it seems a bit lame.

Doing client-side data validation with ActiveX layouts and controls is much more complicated than plain HTML data validation, but the results are spectacular—even wizardly. And once you've mastered the necessary concepts and techniques, you'll be able to create better-looking order forms much faster than you could by hand-coding everything in HTML.

Let's take a "first pass" at creating an order entry form with the ActiveX Control Pad. It will do some basic data checking, but won't yet submit the data to the Web server. The HTML container code is shown in Listing 10.3, while the ActiveX layout code is shown in Listing 10.4. The Web page created by Listings 10.3 and 10.4 is shown in Figure 10.5.

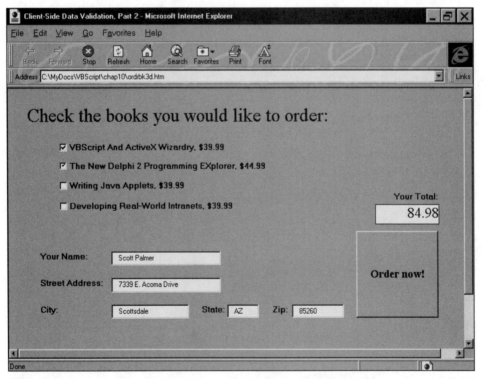

Figure 10.5 A Web order entry form that uses an ActiveX layout.

Listing 10.3 HTML code for the order entry form.

```
<HTML>
<HEAD>
<TITLE>Client-Side Data Validation, Part 1</TITLE>
</HEAD>
<BODY>

<OBJECT CLASSID="CLSID:812AE312-8B8E-11CF-93C8-00AA00C08FDF"
ID="ordrbk2_alx" STYLE="LEFT:0;TOP:0">
<PARAM NAME="ALXPATH" REF VALUE="ordrbk2.alx">
 </OBJECT>
</BODY>
</HTML>
```

Listing 10.4 ActiveX layout for the order entry form.

```
<SCRIPT LANGUAGE="VBScript">
<!--
Sub CmdOrder_Click()
dim OrderComplete

if (CBApp or CBDelphi or CBIntra or CBVBS) then
   OrderComplete = true
else
   msgbox "You must select a book to order."
   OrderComplete = false
end if

if (TBName.text = "") or _
   (TBStreet.text = "") or _
   (TBCity.text = "") or _
   (TBState.text = "") or _
   (TBZip.text = "") then
   msgbox "You didn't fill in all the address information."
   OrderComplete = false
else
   OrderComplete = true
end if

If OrderComplete then
   MsgBox "Order accepted!"
else
   MsgBox "You didn't include all the necessary information."
end if

end sub
-->
</SCRIPT>
<SCRIPT LANGUAGE="VBScript">
<!--
Sub CBApp_Change()
if CBApp then
```

```
      LblTotal.caption = LblTotal.caption + 39.99
else
      LblTotal.caption = LblTotal.caption - 39.99
end if
end sub
-->
</SCRIPT>
<SCRIPT LANGUAGE="VBScript">
<!--
Sub CBVBS_Change()
if CBVBS then
      LblTotal.caption = LblTotal.caption + 39.99
else
      LblTotal.caption = LblTotal.caption - 39.99
end if
end sub
-->
</SCRIPT>
<SCRIPT LANGUAGE="VBScript">
<!--
Sub CBIntra_Change()
if CBIntra then
      LblTotal.caption = LblTotal.caption + 39.99
else
      LblTotal.caption = LblTotal.caption - 39.99
end if
end sub
-->
</SCRIPT>
<SCRIPT LANGUAGE="VBScript">
<!--
Sub CBDelphi_Change()
if CBDelphi then
      LblTotal.caption = LblTotal.caption + 44.99
else
      LblTotal.caption = LblTotal.caption - 44.99
end if
end sub
-->
</SCRIPT>
<DIV ID="Layout1" STYLE="LAYOUT:FIXED;WIDTH:597pt;HEIGHT:370pt;">
    <OBJECT ID="Label1"
      CLASSID="CLSID:978C9E23-D4B0-11CE-BF2D-00AA003F40D0"
      STYLE="TOP:8pt;LEFT:17pt;WIDTH:396pt;HEIGHT:32pt;ZINDEX:0;">
        <PARAM NAME="Caption"
          VALUE="Check the books you would like to order:">
        <PARAM NAME="Size" VALUE="13970;1129">
        <PARAM NAME="FontName" VALUE="Times New Roman">
        <PARAM NAME="FontHeight" VALUE="480">
        <PARAM NAME="FontCharSet" VALUE="0">
        <PARAM NAME="FontPitchAndFamily" VALUE="2">
        <PARAM NAME="FontWeight" VALUE="0">
    </OBJECT>
```

```
<OBJECT ID="CBVBS"
 CLASSID="CLSID:8BD21D40-EC42-11CE-9E0D-00AA006002F3"
 STYLE="TOP:50pt;LEFT:58pt;WIDTH:281pt;HEIGHT:22pt;
    TABINDEX:1;ZINDEX:1;">
   <PARAM NAME="BackColor" VALUE="2147483663">
   <PARAM NAME="ForeColor" VALUE="2147483666">
   <PARAM NAME="DisplayStyle" VALUE="4">
   <PARAM NAME="Size" VALUE="9913;776">
   <PARAM NAME="Value" VALUE="False">
   <PARAM NAME="Caption"
    VALUE="VBScript And ActiveX Wizardry, $39.99">
   <PARAM NAME="FontEffects" VALUE="1073741825">
   <PARAM NAME="FontHeight" VALUE="200">
   <PARAM NAME="FontCharSet" VALUE="0">
   <PARAM NAME="FontPitchAndFamily" VALUE="2">
   <PARAM NAME="FontWeight" VALUE="700">
</OBJECT>

<OBJECT ID="CBDelphi"
 CLASSID="CLSID:8BD21D40-EC42-11CE-9E0D-00AA006002F3"
    STYLE="TOP:74pt;LEFT:58pt;WIDTH:281pt;HEIGHT:20pt;
    TABINDEX:2;ZINDEX:2;">
   <PARAM NAME="BackColor" VALUE="2147483663">
   <PARAM NAME="ForeColor" VALUE="2147483666">
   <PARAM NAME="DisplayStyle" VALUE="4">
   <PARAM NAME="Size" VALUE="9913;706">
   <PARAM NAME="Value" VALUE="False">
   <PARAM NAME="Caption"
    VALUE="The New Delphi 2 Programming EXplorer, $44.99">
   <PARAM NAME="FontEffects" VALUE="1073741825">
   <PARAM NAME="FontHeight" VALUE="200">
   <PARAM NAME="FontCharSet" VALUE="0">
   <PARAM NAME="FontPitchAndFamily" VALUE="2">
   <PARAM NAME="FontWeight" VALUE="700">
</OBJECT>

<OBJECT ID="CBApp"
 CLASSID="CLSID:8BD21D40-EC42-11CE-9E0D-00AA006002F3"
    STYLE="TOP:99pt;LEFT:58pt;WIDTH:281pt;HEIGHT:19pt;
    TABINDEX:3;ZINDEX:3;">
   <PARAM NAME="BackColor" VALUE="2147483663">
   <PARAM NAME="ForeColor" VALUE="2147483666">
   <PARAM NAME="DisplayStyle" VALUE="4">
   <PARAM NAME="Size" VALUE="9913;670">
   <PARAM NAME="Value" VALUE="False">
   <PARAM NAME="Caption"
    VALUE="Writing Java Applets, $39.99">
   <PARAM NAME="FontEffects" VALUE="1073741825">
   <PARAM NAME="FontHeight" VALUE="200">
   <PARAM NAME="FontCharSet" VALUE="0">
   <PARAM NAME="FontPitchAndFamily" VALUE="2">
   <PARAM NAME="FontWeight" VALUE="700">
```

```
</OBJECT>

<OBJECT ID="CBIntra"
 CLASSID="CLSID:8BD21D40-EC42-11CE-9E0D-00AA006002F3"
     STYLE="TOP:124pt;LEFT:58pt;WIDTH:281pt;HEIGHT:20pt;
     TABINDEX:4;ZINDEX:4;">
   <PARAM NAME="BackColor" VALUE="2147483663">
   <PARAM NAME="ForeColor" VALUE="2147483666">
   <PARAM NAME="DisplayStyle" VALUE="4">
   <PARAM NAME="Size" VALUE="9913;706">
   <PARAM NAME="Value" VALUE="False">
   <PARAM NAME="Caption"
     VALUE="Developing Real-World Intranets, $39.99">
   <PARAM NAME="FontEffects" VALUE="1073741825">
   <PARAM NAME="FontHeight" VALUE="200">
   <PARAM NAME="FontCharSet" VALUE="0">
   <PARAM NAME="FontPitchAndFamily" VALUE="2">
   <PARAM NAME="FontWeight" VALUE="700">
</OBJECT>

<OBJECT ID="Label2"
 CLASSID="CLSID:978C9E23-D4B0-11CE-BF2D-00AA003F40D0"
     STYLE="TOP:190pt;LEFT:33pt;WIDTH:66pt;
     HEIGHT:17pt;ZINDEX:5;">
   <PARAM NAME="Caption" VALUE="Your Name:">
   <PARAM NAME="Size" VALUE="2328;600">
   <PARAM NAME="FontEffects" VALUE="1073741825">
   <PARAM NAME="FontHeight" VALUE="200">
   <PARAM NAME="FontCharSet" VALUE="0">
   <PARAM NAME="FontPitchAndFamily" VALUE="2">
   <PARAM NAME="FontWeight" VALUE="700">
</OBJECT>

<OBJECT ID="Label3"
 CLASSID="CLSID:978C9E23-D4B0-11CE-BF2D-00AA003F40D0"
     STYLE="TOP:223pt;LEFT:33pt;WIDTH:83pt;
     HEIGHT:17pt;ZINDEX:6;">
   <PARAM NAME="Caption" VALUE="Street Address:">
   <PARAM NAME="Size" VALUE="2928;600">
   <PARAM NAME="FontEffects" VALUE="1073741825">
   <PARAM NAME="FontHeight" VALUE="200">
   <PARAM NAME="FontCharSet" VALUE="0">
   <PARAM NAME="FontPitchAndFamily" VALUE="2">
   <PARAM NAME="FontWeight" VALUE="700">
</OBJECT>

<OBJECT ID="Label4"
 CLASSID="CLSID:978C9E23-D4B0-11CE-BF2D-00AA003F40D0"
     STYLE="TOP:256pt;LEFT:33pt;WIDTH:33pt;
     HEIGHT:17pt;ZINDEX:7;">
   <PARAM NAME="Caption" VALUE="City:">
   <PARAM NAME="Size" VALUE="1164;600">
```

```
        <PARAM NAME="FontEffects" VALUE="1073741825">
        <PARAM NAME="FontHeight" VALUE="200">
        <PARAM NAME="FontCharSet" VALUE="0">
        <PARAM NAME="FontPitchAndFamily" VALUE="2">
        <PARAM NAME="FontWeight" VALUE="700">
    </OBJECT>

    <OBJECT ID="TBName"
     CLASSID="CLSID:8BD21D10-EC42-11CE-9E0D-00AA006002F3"
        STYLE="TOP:190pt;LEFT:124pt;WIDTH:140pt;
        HEIGHT:17pt;TABINDEX:8;ZINDEX:8;">
        <PARAM NAME="VariousPropertyBits" VALUE="746604571">
        <PARAM NAME="Size" VALUE="4939;600">
        <PARAM NAME="FontCharSet" VALUE="0">
        <PARAM NAME="FontPitchAndFamily" VALUE="2">
        <PARAM NAME="FontWeight" VALUE="0">
    </OBJECT>

    <OBJECT ID="TBStreet"
     CLASSID="CLSID:8BD21D10-EC42-11CE-9E0D-00AA006002F3"
        STYLE="TOP:223pt;LEFT:124pt;WIDTH:140pt;HEIGHT:18pt;
        TABINDEX:9;ZINDEX:9;">
        <PARAM NAME="VariousPropertyBits" VALUE="746604571">
        <PARAM NAME="Size" VALUE="4939;635">
        <PARAM NAME="FontCharSet" VALUE="0">
        <PARAM NAME="FontPitchAndFamily" VALUE="2">
        <PARAM NAME="FontWeight" VALUE="0">
    </OBJECT>

    <OBJECT ID="TBCity"
     CLASSID="CLSID:8BD21D10-EC42-11CE-9E0D-00AA006002F3"
        STYLE="TOP:256pt;LEFT:124pt;WIDTH:99pt;HEIGHT:17pt;
        TABINDEX:10;ZINDEX:10;">
        <PARAM NAME="VariousPropertyBits" VALUE="746604571">
        <PARAM NAME="Size" VALUE="3493;600">
        <PARAM NAME="FontCharSet" VALUE="0">
        <PARAM NAME="FontPitchAndFamily" VALUE="2">
        <PARAM NAME="FontWeight" VALUE="0">
    </OBJECT>

    <OBJECT ID="Label5"
     CLASSID="CLSID:978C9E23-D4B0-11CE-BF2D-00AA003F40D0"
        STYLE="TOP:256pt;LEFT:239pt;WIDTH:33pt;
        HEIGHT:17pt;ZINDEX:11;">
        <PARAM NAME="Caption" VALUE="State:">
        <PARAM NAME="Size" VALUE="1164;600">
        <PARAM NAME="FontEffects" VALUE="1073741825">
        <PARAM NAME="FontHeight" VALUE="200">
        <PARAM NAME="FontCharSet" VALUE="0">
        <PARAM NAME="FontPitchAndFamily" VALUE="2">
        <PARAM NAME="FontWeight" VALUE="700">
    </OBJECT>
```

```
<OBJECT ID="TBState"
 CLASSID="CLSID:8BD21D10-EC42-11CE-9E0D-00AA006002F3"
     STYLE="TOP:256pt;LEFT:272pt;WIDTH:41pt;HEIGHT:16pt;
     TABINDEX:12;ZINDEX:12;">
   <PARAM NAME="VariousPropertyBits" VALUE="746604571">
   <PARAM NAME="Size" VALUE="1446;564">
   <PARAM NAME="FontCharSet" VALUE="0">
   <PARAM NAME="FontPitchAndFamily" VALUE="2">
   <PARAM NAME="FontWeight" VALUE="0">
</OBJECT>

<OBJECT ID="Label6"
 CLASSID="CLSID:978C9E23-D4B0-11CE-BF2D-00AA003F40D0"
     STYLE="TOP:256pt;LEFT:330pt;WIDTH:25pt;
     HEIGHT:17pt;ZINDEX:13;">
   <PARAM NAME="Caption" VALUE="Zip:">
   <PARAM NAME="Size" VALUE="882;600">
   <PARAM NAME="FontEffects" VALUE="1073741825">
   <PARAM NAME="FontHeight" VALUE="200">
   <PARAM NAME="FontCharSet" VALUE="0">
   <PARAM NAME="FontPitchAndFamily" VALUE="2">
   <PARAM NAME="FontWeight" VALUE="700">
</OBJECT>

<OBJECT ID="TBZip"
 CLASSID="CLSID:8BD21D10-EC42-11CE-9E0D-00AA006002F3"
     STYLE="TOP:256pt;LEFT:355pt;WIDTH:66pt;HEIGHT:16pt;
     TABINDEX:14;ZINDEX:14;">
   <PARAM NAME="VariousPropertyBits" VALUE="746604571">
   <PARAM NAME="Size" VALUE="2328;564">
   <PARAM NAME="FontCharSet" VALUE="0">
   <PARAM NAME="FontPitchAndFamily" VALUE="2">
   <PARAM NAME="FontWeight" VALUE="0">
</OBJECT>

<OBJECT ID="CmdOrder"
 CLASSID="CLSID:D7053240-CE69-11CD-A777-00DD01143C57"
     STYLE="TOP:165pt;LEFT:437pt;WIDTH:107pt;HEIGHT:107pt;
     TABINDEX:15;ZINDEX:15;">
   <PARAM NAME="Caption" VALUE="Order now!">
   <PARAM NAME="Size" VALUE="3775;3775">
   <PARAM NAME="FontName" VALUE="Times New Roman">
   <PARAM NAME="FontEffects" VALUE="1073741825">
   <PARAM NAME="FontHeight" VALUE="280">
   <PARAM NAME="FontCharSet" VALUE="0">
   <PARAM NAME="FontPitchAndFamily" VALUE="2">
   <PARAM NAME="ParagraphAlign" VALUE="3">
   <PARAM NAME="FontWeight" VALUE="700">
</OBJECT>

<OBJECT ID="Label7"
 CLASSID="CLSID:978C9E23-D4B0-11CE-BF2D-00AA003F40D0"
```

```
        STYLE="TOP:116pt;LEFT:470pt;WIDTH:74pt;
        HEIGHT:17pt;ZINDEX:16;">
    <PARAM NAME="Caption" VALUE="Your Total:">
    <PARAM NAME="Size" VALUE="2611;600">
    <PARAM NAME="FontEffects" VALUE="1073741825">
    <PARAM NAME="FontHeight" VALUE="240">
    <PARAM NAME="FontCharSet" VALUE="0">
    <PARAM NAME="FontPitchAndFamily" VALUE="2">
    <PARAM NAME="ParagraphAlign" VALUE="2">
    <PARAM NAME="FontWeight" VALUE="700">
</OBJECT>

<OBJECT ID="LblTotal"
 CLASSID="CLSID:978C9E23-D4B0-11CE-BF2D-00AA003F40D0"
        STYLE="TOP:132pt;LEFT:462pt;WIDTH:83pt;
        HEIGHT:25pt;ZINDEX:17;">
    <PARAM NAME="BackColor" VALUE="16777215">
    <PARAM NAME="Caption" VALUE="0.00">
    <PARAM NAME="Size" VALUE="2928;882">
    <PARAM NAME="BorderStyle" VALUE="1">
    <PARAM NAME="FontName" VALUE="Times New Roman">
    <PARAM NAME="FontHeight" VALUE="360">
    <PARAM NAME="FontCharSet" VALUE="0">
    <PARAM NAME="FontPitchAndFamily" VALUE="2">
    <PARAM NAME="ParagraphAlign" VALUE="2">
    <PARAM NAME="FontWeight" VALUE="0">
</OBJECT>
</DIV>
```

Stepping Through The Example Code

Let's see how the code works. As usual, the HTML document itself functions as a container for the ActiveX layout, to which it's connected by the **<object>** tag for the HTML Layout control. The layout creates a Web page that's quite similar to the one we created earlier: There are check boxes for the books, text boxes for the customer's name and address, and a command button to send the order. One new wrinkle is the addition of a dynamically-updated label control that shows the current total due for the customer's order. We'll look at that first. The relevant VBScript code is as follows:

```
Sub CBApp_Change()
if CBApp then
   LblTotal.caption = LblTotal.caption + 39.99
else
   LblTotal.caption = LblTotal.caption - 39.99
end if

end sub
```

```
Sub CBVBS_Change()
if CBVBS then
   LblTotal.caption = LblTotal.caption + 39.99
else
   LblTotal.caption = LblTotal.caption - 39.99
end if
end sub

Sub CBIntra_Change()
if CBIntra then
   LblTotal.caption = LblTotal.caption + 39.99
else
   LblTotal.caption = LblTotal.caption - 39.99
end if
end sub

Sub CBDelphi_Change()
if CBDelphi then
   LblTotal.caption = LblTotal.caption + 44.99
else
   LblTotal.caption = LblTotal.caption - 44.99
end if
end sub
```

The various "CB" controls, of course, are the check boxes, and the **change** event is fired whenever the value of the check box *changes*. Inside the **change** event code, each sub performs a check on the new value of the check box. If the check box is now checked—which means that before, it *wasn't* checked—then the sub adds the appropriate dollar amount to the label that displays the order total. If the check box is now unchecked—meaning that it *was* checked before—then the code subtracts the same amount from the total in the label control. That keeps the customer's current order total up to date.

Now, let's get back to our central problem: client-side data validation. The data-checking code is in the **click** event sub for the command button, as follows:

```
Sub CmdOrder_Click()
dim OrderComplete

if (CBApp or CBDelphi or CBIntra or CBVBS) then
   OrderComplete = true
else
   msgbox "You must select a book to order."
   OrderComplete = false
end if

if (TBName.text = "") or _
   (TBStreet.text = "") or _
```

```
      (TBCity.text = "") or _
      (TBState.text = "") or _
      (TBZip.text = "") then
      msgbox "You didn't fill in all the address information."
      OrderComplete = false
   else
      OrderComplete = true
   end if

   If OrderComplete then
      MsgBox "Order accepted!"
   else
      MsgBox "You didn't include all the necessary information."
   end if

   end sub
```

First, we declare a variable called **OrderComplete**: This will indicate whether or not the user has provided the data needed to process the order. The value of **OrderComplete** is set by two **if...then** statements. The first **if...then** statement looks to see if at least one check box has been checked, indicating that at least one book is being ordered. The second **if...then** statement makes sure that *all* of the name and address blanks have been filled in—none of them is empty. If all the data has been provided, then **OrderComplete** is set to **true** and the order is accepted.

As before, this is fairly simple data checking. Using the same techniques, you can easily build in more sophisticated data validation for your Web order forms.

Another thing to notice is that, at this point, we're still talking only about the client side of things. We haven't yet attempted to *send* the data to the server. That's what we'll do in the next section.

Sending Data From An ActiveX Layout To The Web Server

There are two ways you might try to send data from an HTML document with an ActiveX layout. One is obvious but doesn't work. The other one is wizardly—and *does* work. Let's examine the obvious solution first: After that, it will be easier to understand the non-obvious (but correct) solution. The obvious solution is embodied in the Web page created by Listings 10.5 and 10.6, which constitute our "first draft" version of a Web page that sends data to the server. The Web page itself looks the same, as you can see in Figure 10.6.

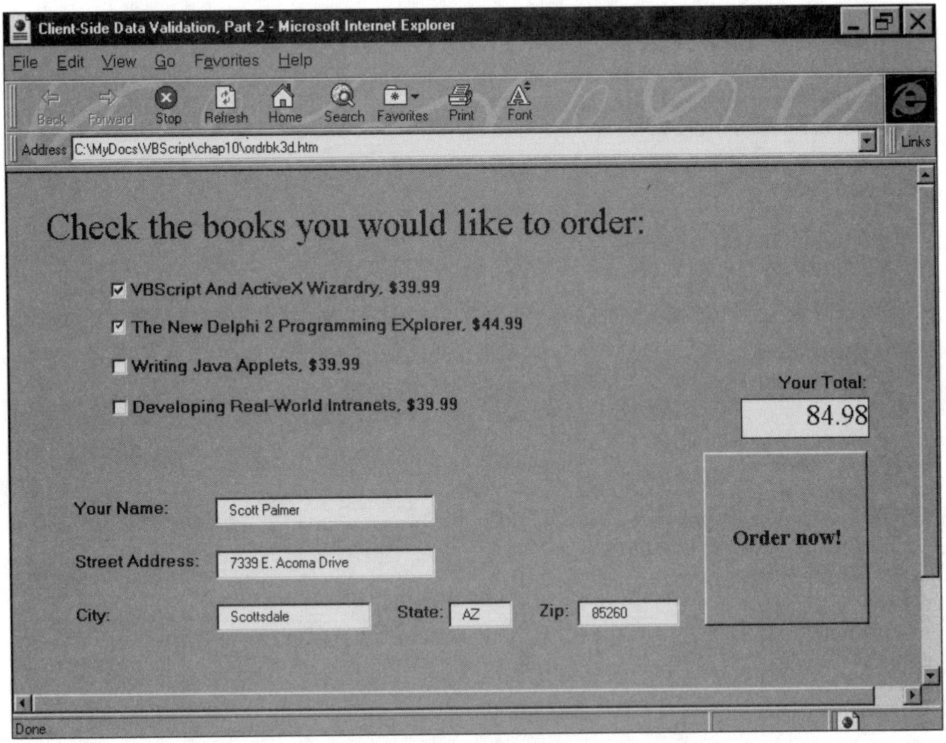

Figure 10.6   The Web page created by Listings 10.5 and 10.6.

Listing 10.5   HTML code for the "first draft" data submission.

```
<HTML>
<HEAD>
<TITLE>Client-Side Data Validation, Part 2</TITLE>
</HEAD>
<BODY>

<OBJECT CLASSID="CLSID:812AE312-8B8E-11CF-93C8-00AA00C08FDF"
ID="cantsubm_alx" STYLE="LEFT:0;TOP:0">
<PARAM NAME="ALXPATH" REF VALUE="cantsubm.alx">
 </OBJECT>

</BODY>
</HTML>
```

Listing 10.6   ActiveX layout for the "first draft" data submission.

```
<SCRIPT LANGUAGE="VBScript">
<!--
Sub CmdOrder_Click()
dim OrderComplete
dim TheForm
```

```
if LblTotal.caption > 0 then
    OrderComplete = true
else
    msgbox "You must select a book to order."
    OrderComplete = false
end if


if (TBName.text = "") or _
   (TBStreet.text = "") or _
   (TBCity.text = "") or _
   (TBState.text = "") or _
   (TBZip.text = "") then
    msgbox "You didn't fill in all the address information."
    OrderComplete = false
else
    OrderComplete = true
end if


If OrderComplete then
    MsgBox "Order accepted!"
    TheForm.submit
else
    MsgBox "You didn't include all the necessary information."
end if



end sub
-->
</SCRIPT>
<SCRIPT LANGUAGE="VBScript">
<!--
Sub CBApp_Change()
if CBApp then
    LblTotal.caption = LblTotal.caption + 39.99
else
    LblTotal.caption = LblTotal.caption - 39.99
end if



end sub
-->
</SCRIPT>
<SCRIPT LANGUAGE="VBScript">
<!--
Sub CBVBS_Change()
if CBVBS then
    LblTotal.caption = LblTotal.caption + 39.99
else
    LblTotal.caption = LblTotal.caption - 39.99
end if
end sub
```

```
-->
</SCRIPT>
<SCRIPT LANGUAGE="VBScript">
<!--
Sub CBIntra_Change()
if CBIntra then
    LblTotal.caption = LblTotal.caption + 39.99
else
    LblTotal.caption = LblTotal.caption - 39.99
end if
end sub
-->
</SCRIPT>
<SCRIPT LANGUAGE="VBScript">
<!--
Sub CBDelphi_Change()
if CBDelphi then
    LblTotal.caption = LblTotal.caption + 44.99
else
    LblTotal.caption = LblTotal.caption - 44.99
end if
end sub
-->
</SCRIPT>

<DIV ID="Layout1" STYLE="LAYOUT:FIXED;WIDTH:597pt;HEIGHT:370pt;">
    <OBJECT ID="Label1"
     CLASSID="CLSID:978C9E23-D4B0-11CE-BF2D-00AA003F40D0"
     STYLE="TOP:8pt;LEFT:17pt;WIDTH:396pt;HEIGHT:32pt;ZINDEX:0;">
        <PARAM NAME="Caption"
          VALUE="Check the books you would like to order:">
        <PARAM NAME="Size" VALUE="13970;1129">
        <PARAM NAME="FontName" VALUE="Times New Roman">
        <PARAM NAME="FontHeight" VALUE="480">
        <PARAM NAME="FontCharSet" VALUE="0">
        <PARAM NAME="FontPitchAndFamily" VALUE="2">
        <PARAM NAME="FontWeight" VALUE="0">
    </OBJECT>

    <OBJECT ID="CBVBS"
     CLASSID="CLSID:8BD21D40-EC42-11CE-9E0D-00AA006002F3"
     STYLE="TOP:50pt;LEFT:58pt;WIDTH:281pt;HEIGHT:22pt;
         TABINDEX:1;ZINDEX:1;">
        <PARAM NAME="BackColor" VALUE="2147483663">
        <PARAM NAME="ForeColor" VALUE="2147483666">
        <PARAM NAME="DisplayStyle" VALUE="4">
        <PARAM NAME="Size" VALUE="9913;776">
        <PARAM NAME="Value" VALUE="False">
        <PARAM NAME="Caption"
          VALUE="VBScript And ActiveX Wizardry, $39.99">
        <PARAM NAME="FontEffects" VALUE="1073741825">
```

```
        <PARAM NAME="FontHeight" VALUE="200">
        <PARAM NAME="FontCharSet" VALUE="0">
        <PARAM NAME="FontPitchAndFamily" VALUE="2">
        <PARAM NAME="FontWeight" VALUE="700">
</OBJECT>

<OBJECT ID="CBDelphi"
 CLASSID="CLSID:8BD21D40-EC42-11CE-9E0D-00AA006002F3"
        STYLE="TOP:74pt;LEFT:58pt;WIDTH:281pt;HEIGHT:20pt;
        TABINDEX:2;ZINDEX:2;">
        <PARAM NAME="BackColor" VALUE="2147483663">
        <PARAM NAME="ForeColor" VALUE="2147483666">
        <PARAM NAME="DisplayStyle" VALUE="4">
        <PARAM NAME="Size" VALUE="9913;706">
        <PARAM NAME="Value" VALUE="False">
        <PARAM NAME="Caption"
        VALUE="The New Delphi 2 Programming EXplorer, $44.99">
        <PARAM NAME="FontEffects" VALUE="1073741825">
        <PARAM NAME="FontHeight" VALUE="200">
        <PARAM NAME="FontCharSet" VALUE="0">
        <PARAM NAME="FontPitchAndFamily" VALUE="2">
        <PARAM NAME="FontWeight" VALUE="700">
</OBJECT>

<OBJECT ID="CBApp"
 CLASSID="CLSID:8BD21D40-EC42-11CE-9E0D-00AA006002F3"
        STYLE="TOP:99pt;LEFT:58pt;WIDTH:281pt;HEIGHT:19pt;
        TABINDEX:3;ZINDEX:3;">
        <PARAM NAME="BackColor" VALUE="2147483663">
        <PARAM NAME="ForeColor" VALUE="2147483666">
        <PARAM NAME="DisplayStyle" VALUE="4">
        <PARAM NAME="Size" VALUE="9913;670">
        <PARAM NAME="Value" VALUE="False">
        <PARAM NAME="Caption"
        VALUE="Writing Java Applets, $39.99">
        <PARAM NAME="FontEffects" VALUE="1073741825">
        <PARAM NAME="FontHeight" VALUE="200">
        <PARAM NAME="FontCharSet" VALUE="0">
        <PARAM NAME="FontPitchAndFamily" VALUE="2">
        <PARAM NAME="FontWeight" VALUE="700">
</OBJECT>

<OBJECT ID="CBIntra"
 CLASSID="CLSID:8BD21D40-EC42-11CE-9E0D-00AA006002F3"
        STYLE="TOP:124pt;LEFT:58pt;WIDTH:281pt;HEIGHT:20pt;
        TABINDEX:4;ZINDEX:4;">
        <PARAM NAME="BackColor" VALUE="2147483663">
        <PARAM NAME="ForeColor" VALUE="2147483666">
        <PARAM NAME="DisplayStyle" VALUE="4">
        <PARAM NAME="Size" VALUE="9913;706">
        <PARAM NAME="Value" VALUE="False">
```

```
   <PARAM NAME="Caption"
     VALUE="Developing Real-World Intranets, $39.99">
   <PARAM NAME="FontEffects" VALUE="1073741825">
   <PARAM NAME="FontHeight" VALUE="200">
   <PARAM NAME="FontCharSet" VALUE="0">
   <PARAM NAME="FontPitchAndFamily" VALUE="2">
   <PARAM NAME="FontWeight" VALUE="700">
</OBJECT>

<OBJECT ID="Label2"
 CLASSID="CLSID:978C9E23-D4B0-11CE-BF2D-00AA003F40D0"
     STYLE="TOP:190pt;LEFT:33pt;WIDTH:66pt;
     HEIGHT:17pt;ZINDEX:5;">
   <PARAM NAME="Caption" VALUE="Your Name:">
   <PARAM NAME="Size" VALUE="2328;600">
   <PARAM NAME="FontEffects" VALUE="1073741825">
   <PARAM NAME="FontHeight" VALUE="200">
   <PARAM NAME="FontCharSet" VALUE="0">
   <PARAM NAME="FontPitchAndFamily" VALUE="2">
   <PARAM NAME="FontWeight" VALUE="700">
</OBJECT>

<OBJECT ID="Label3"
 CLASSID="CLSID:978C9E23-D4B0-11CE-BF2D-00AA003F40D0"
     STYLE="TOP:223pt;LEFT:33pt;WIDTH:83pt;
     HEIGHT:17pt;ZINDEX:6;">
   <PARAM NAME="Caption" VALUE="Street Address:">
   <PARAM NAME="Size" VALUE="2928;600">
   <PARAM NAME="FontEffects" VALUE="1073741825">
   <PARAM NAME="FontHeight" VALUE="200">
   <PARAM NAME="FontCharSet" VALUE="0">
   <PARAM NAME="FontPitchAndFamily" VALUE="2">
   <PARAM NAME="FontWeight" VALUE="700">
</OBJECT>

<OBJECT ID="Label4"
 CLASSID="CLSID:978C9E23-D4B0-11CE-BF2D-00AA003F40D0"
     STYLE="TOP:256pt;LEFT:33pt;WIDTH:33pt;
     HEIGHT:17pt;ZINDEX:7;">
   <PARAM NAME="Caption" VALUE="City:">
   <PARAM NAME="Size" VALUE="1164;600">
   <PARAM NAME="FontEffects" VALUE="1073741825">
   <PARAM NAME="FontHeight" VALUE="200">
   <PARAM NAME="FontCharSet" VALUE="0">
   <PARAM NAME="FontPitchAndFamily" VALUE="2">
   <PARAM NAME="FontWeight" VALUE="700">
</OBJECT>

<OBJECT ID="TBName"
 CLASSID="CLSID:8BD21D10-EC42-11CE-9E0D-00AA006002F3"
     STYLE="TOP:190pt;LEFT:124pt;WIDTH:140pt;
     HEIGHT:17pt;TABINDEX:8;ZINDEX:8;">
```

```
    <PARAM NAME="VariousPropertyBits" VALUE="746604571">
    <PARAM NAME="Size" VALUE="4939;600">
    <PARAM NAME="FontCharSet" VALUE="0">
    <PARAM NAME="FontPitchAndFamily" VALUE="2">
    <PARAM NAME="FontWeight" VALUE="0">
</OBJECT>

<OBJECT ID="TBStreet"
 CLASSID="CLSID:8BD21D10-EC42-11CE-9E0D-00AA006002F3"
    STYLE="TOP:223pt;LEFT:124pt;WIDTH:140pt;HEIGHT:18pt;
    TABINDEX:9;ZINDEX:9;">
    <PARAM NAME="VariousPropertyBits" VALUE="746604571">
    <PARAM NAME="Size" VALUE="4939;635">
    <PARAM NAME="FontCharSet" VALUE="0">
    <PARAM NAME="FontPitchAndFamily" VALUE="2">
    <PARAM NAME="FontWeight" VALUE="0">
</OBJECT>

<OBJECT ID="TBCity"
 CLASSID="CLSID:8BD21D10-EC42-11CE-9E0D-00AA006002F3"
    STYLE="TOP:256pt;LEFT:124pt;WIDTH:99pt;HEIGHT:17pt;
    TABINDEX:10;ZINDEX:10;">
    <PARAM NAME="VariousPropertyBits" VALUE="746604571">
    <PARAM NAME="Size" VALUE="3493;600">
    <PARAM NAME="FontCharSet" VALUE="0">
    <PARAM NAME="FontPitchAndFamily" VALUE="2">
    <PARAM NAME="FontWeight" VALUE="0">
</OBJECT>

<OBJECT ID="Label5"
 CLASSID="CLSID:978C9E23-D4B0-11CE-BF2D-00AA003F40D0"
    STYLE="TOP:256pt;LEFT:239pt;WIDTH:33pt;
    HEIGHT:17pt;ZINDEX:11;">
    <PARAM NAME="Caption" VALUE="State:">
    <PARAM NAME="Size" VALUE="1164;600">
    <PARAM NAME="FontEffects" VALUE="1073741825">
    <PARAM NAME="FontHeight" VALUE="200">
    <PARAM NAME="FontCharSet" VALUE="0">
    <PARAM NAME="FontPitchAndFamily" VALUE="2">
    <PARAM NAME="FontWeight" VALUE="700">
</OBJECT>

<OBJECT ID="TBState"
 CLASSID="CLSID:8BD21D10-EC42-11CE-9E0D-00AA006002F3"
    STYLE="TOP:256pt;LEFT:272pt;WIDTH:41pt;HEIGHT:16pt;
    TABINDEX:12;ZINDEX:12;">
    <PARAM NAME="VariousPropertyBits" VALUE="746604571">
    <PARAM NAME="Size" VALUE="1446;564">
    <PARAM NAME="FontCharSet" VALUE="0">
    <PARAM NAME="FontPitchAndFamily" VALUE="2">
    <PARAM NAME="FontWeight" VALUE="0">
</OBJECT>
```

```
<OBJECT ID="Label6"
 CLASSID="CLSID:978C9E23-D4B0-11CE-BF2D-00AA003F40D0"
      STYLE="TOP:256pt;LEFT:330pt;WIDTH:25pt;
      HEIGHT:17pt;ZINDEX:13;">
    <PARAM NAME="Caption" VALUE="Zip:">
    <PARAM NAME="Size" VALUE="882;600">
    <PARAM NAME="FontEffects" VALUE="1073741825">
    <PARAM NAME="FontHeight" VALUE="200">
    <PARAM NAME="FontCharSet" VALUE="0">
    <PARAM NAME="FontPitchAndFamily" VALUE="2">
    <PARAM NAME="FontWeight" VALUE="700">
</OBJECT>

<OBJECT ID="TBZip"
 CLASSID="CLSID:8BD21D10-EC42-11CE-9E0D-00AA006002F3"
      STYLE="TOP:256pt;LEFT:355pt;WIDTH:66pt;HEIGHT:16pt;
      TABINDEX:14;ZINDEX:14;">
    <PARAM NAME="VariousPropertyBits" VALUE="746604571">
    <PARAM NAME="Size" VALUE="2328;564">
    <PARAM NAME="FontCharSet" VALUE="0">
    <PARAM NAME="FontPitchAndFamily" VALUE="2">
    <PARAM NAME="FontWeight" VALUE="0">
</OBJECT>

<OBJECT ID="CmdOrder"
 CLASSID="CLSID:D7053240-CE69-11CD-A777-00DD01143C57"
      STYLE="TOP:165pt;LEFT:437pt;WIDTH:107pt;HEIGHT:107pt;
      TABINDEX:15;ZINDEX:15;">
    <PARAM NAME="Caption" VALUE="Order now!">
    <PARAM NAME="Size" VALUE="3775;3775">
    <PARAM NAME="FontName" VALUE="Times New Roman">
    <PARAM NAME="FontEffects" VALUE="1073741825">
    <PARAM NAME="FontHeight" VALUE="280">
    <PARAM NAME="FontCharSet" VALUE="0">
    <PARAM NAME="FontPitchAndFamily" VALUE="2">
    <PARAM NAME="ParagraphAlign" VALUE="3">
    <PARAM NAME="FontWeight" VALUE="700">
</OBJECT>

<OBJECT ID="Label7"
 CLASSID="CLSID:978C9E23-D4B0-11CE-BF2D-00AA003F40D0"
      STYLE="TOP:116pt;LEFT:470pt;WIDTH:74pt;
      HEIGHT:17pt;ZINDEX:16;">
    <PARAM NAME="Caption" VALUE="Your Total:">
    <PARAM NAME="Size" VALUE="2611;600">
    <PARAM NAME="FontEffects" VALUE="1073741825">
    <PARAM NAME="FontHeight" VALUE="240">
    <PARAM NAME="FontCharSet" VALUE="0">
    <PARAM NAME="FontPitchAndFamily" VALUE="2">
    <PARAM NAME="ParagraphAlign" VALUE="2">
    <PARAM NAME="FontWeight" VALUE="700">
</OBJECT>
```

```
<OBJECT ID="LblTotal"
  CLASSID="CLSID:978C9E23-D4B0-11CE-BF2D-00AA003F40D0"
      STYLE="TOP:132pt;LEFT:462pt;WIDTH:83pt;
      HEIGHT:25pt;ZINDEX:17;">
    <PARAM NAME="BackColor" VALUE="16777215">
    <PARAM NAME="Caption" VALUE="0.00">
    <PARAM NAME="Size" VALUE="2928;882">
    <PARAM NAME="BorderStyle" VALUE="1">
    <PARAM NAME="FontName" VALUE="Times New Roman">
    <PARAM NAME="FontHeight" VALUE="360">
    <PARAM NAME="FontCharSet" VALUE="0">
    <PARAM NAME="FontPitchAndFamily" VALUE="2">
    <PARAM NAME="ParagraphAlign" VALUE="2">
    <PARAM NAME="FontWeight" VALUE="0">
  </OBJECT>
</DIV>
```

The obvious solution is simply to do what you did before in the Web page that used only HTML controls: Call **form.submit** and thereby send the data in the various controls to the server. That's the approach taken in the **click** event sub for the command button, as follows:

```
Sub CmdOrder_Click()
dim OrderComplete
dim TheForm

' …some code omitted here

If OrderComplete then
   MsgBox "Order accepted!"
   TheForm.submit
else
   MsgBox "You didn't include all the necessary information."
end if

end sub
```

The fact that the ActiveX-layout Web page looks similar to the HTML-only page suggests that this will work. But there's a problem in this approach: **form.submit** is a method supported by the Internet Explorer scripting object model for *HTML forms*. What you've got in your ActiveX layout is not an HTML form. The controls in your ActiveX layout are not HTML form controls. And in that situation, calling **form.submit** in your VBScript code won't do anything but generate an error message, as shown in Figure 10.7.

Another problem is that your ActiveX layout is a separate file, inserted into the display of your Web page by the HTML Layout control. The ActiveX layout itself, however, is not part of your HTML document.

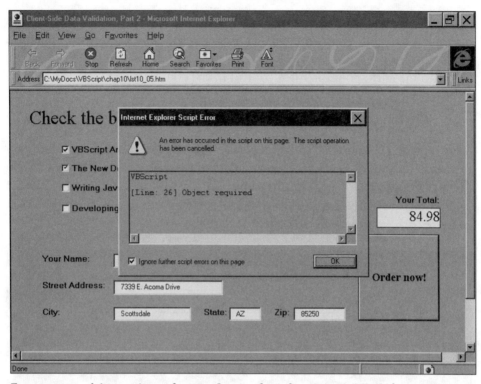

Figure 10.7   You can't use **form.submit** when there's no HTML form on your Web page.

The *most* crucial question that needs to be answered is this: How can you make your ActiveX layout communicate with your HTML document?

The Wizardly Secret: Use The Scripting Object Model

The secret is to use what you learned in Chapter 9 about the Internet Explorer scripting object model. From your ActiveX layout code, you assign values to elements in the HTML document by indicating which objects contain them. That suggests a three-step process for sending validated data to the Web server:

1. On the containing HTML document, create an HTML form with hidden form controls—controls that aren't visible when the user displays the Web page. There should be one hidden control for each data item that needs to be sent from the ActiveX layout to the server.

2. In the ActiveX layout, write code to validate the data entered by the user. Then, using the scripting object model as your guide, copy the data from each ActiveX data-entry control (in this case, check boxes and text boxes) to the corresponding form control in the containing HTML document.

3. Call **form.submit** to send the data from the HTML form controls to the Web server.

This approach is embodied in Listings 10.7 and 10.8, which create a fully-functional ActiveX order form that can send data to the Web server. When you fill in the blanks and click on the command button—sending the data to the Website *cgitest* program—you get a result that looks something like Figure 10.8. That indicates that your data arrived safely at the Web server.

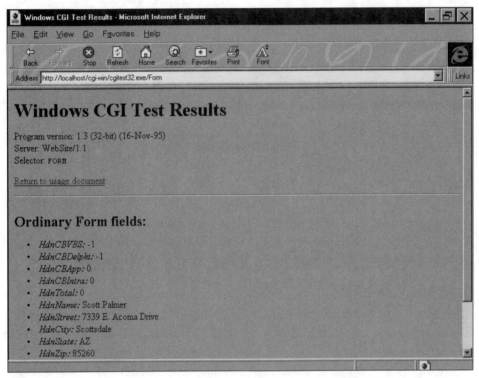

Figure 10.8　The cgitest program reports that your data was received by the Web server.

Communication goes both ways.

From your ActiveX layout code, you can refer to controls in your HTML document by identifying which controls contain them. Likewise, from within your HTML document, you can refer to controls in your ActiveX layout by prefacing the control names with the name of your ActiveX layout.

Listing 10.7 HTML code for sending data to the server.

```
<HTML>
<HEAD>
<TITLE>Client-Side Data Validation, Part 2</TITLE>
</HEAD>
<BODY>
<FORM name="HiddenForm" METHOD="POST"
    ACTION="http://localhost/cgi-win/cgitest32.exe/Form">

<INPUT NAME="HdnCBVBS" TYPE="HIDDEN" VALUE="0">
<INPUT NAME="HdnCBDelphi" TYPE="HIDDEN" VALUE="0">
<INPUT NAME="HdnCBApp" TYPE="HIDDEN" VALUE="0">
<INPUT NAME="HdnCBIntra" TYPE="HIDDEN" VALUE="0">
<INPUT NAME="HdnTotal" TYPE="HIDDEN" VALUE="0">

<INPUT NAME="HdnName" TYPE="HIDDEN" VALUE="">
<INPUT NAME="HdnStreet" TYPE="HIDDEN" VALUE="">
<INPUT NAME="HdnCity" TYPE="HIDDEN" VALUE="""">
<INPUT NAME="HdnState" TYPE="HIDDEN" VALUE="""">
<INPUT NAME="HdnZip" TYPE="HIDDEN" VALUE="""">

</FORM>

<OBJECT CLASSID="CLSID:812AE312-8B8E-11CF-93C8-00AA00C08FDF"
ID="ordrbk2b_alx" STYLE="LEFT:0;TOP:0">
<PARAM NAME="ALXPATH" REF VALUE="ordrbk2b.alx">
 </OBJECT>

</BODY>
</HTML>
```

Listing 10.8 ActiveX layout for sending data to the server.

```
<SCRIPT LANGUAGE="VBScript">
<!--
Sub CmdOrder_Click()
dim OrderComplete
dim TheForm
Set TheForm = window.Document.HiddenForm
```

```
if LblTotal.caption > 0 then
   OrderComplete = true
else
   msgbox "You must select a book to order."
   OrderComplete = false
end if

if (TBName.text = "") or _
   (TBStreet.text = "") or _
   (TBCity.text = "") or _
   (TBState.text = "") or _
   (TBZip.text = "") then
   msgbox "You didn't fill in all the address information."
   OrderComplete = false
else
   OrderComplete = true
end if

If OrderComplete then
   MsgBox "Order accepted!"
   window.Document.HiddenForm.HdnCBVBS.value = CBVBS.value
   window.Document.HiddenForm.HdnCBDelphi.value = CBDelphi.value
   window.Document.HiddenForm.HdnCBApp.value = CBApp.value
   window.Document.HiddenForm.HdnCBIntra.value = CBIntra.value
   window.Document.HiddenForm.HdnName.value = TBName.text
   window.Document.HiddenForm.HdnStreet.value = TBStreet.text
   window.Document.HiddenForm.HdnCity.value = TBCity.text
   window.Document.HiddenForm.HdnState.value = TBState.text
   window.Document.HiddenForm.HdnZip.value = TBZip.text
   TheForm.submit
else
   MsgBox "You didn't include all the necessary information."
end if

end sub
-->
</SCRIPT>
<SCRIPT LANGUAGE="VBScript">
<!--
Sub CBApp_Change()
if CBApp then
   LblTotal.caption = LblTotal.caption + 39.99
else
   LblTotal.caption = LblTotal.caption - 39.99
end if


end sub
-->
</SCRIPT>
<SCRIPT LANGUAGE="VBScript">
```

```
<!--
Sub CBVBS_Change()
if CBVBS then
   LblTotal.caption = LblTotal.caption + 39.99
else
   LblTotal.caption = LblTotal.caption - 39.99
end if
end sub
-->
</SCRIPT>
<SCRIPT LANGUAGE="VBScript">
<!--
Sub CBIntra_Change()
if CBIntra then
   LblTotal.caption = LblTotal.caption + 39.99
else
   LblTotal.caption = LblTotal.caption - 39.99
end if
end sub
-->
</SCRIPT>
<SCRIPT LANGUAGE="VBScript">
<!--
Sub CBDelphi_Change()
if CBDelphi then
   LblTotal.caption = LblTotal.caption + 44.99
else
   LblTotal.caption = LblTotal.caption - 44.99
end if
end sub
-->
</SCRIPT>

<DIV ID="Layout1" STYLE="LAYOUT:FIXED;WIDTH:597pt;HEIGHT:370pt;">
    <OBJECT ID="Label1"
     CLASSID="CLSID:978C9E23-D4B0-11CE-BF2D-00AA003F40D0"
     STYLE="TOP:8pt;LEFT:17pt;WIDTH:396pt;HEIGHT:32pt;ZINDEX:0;">
        <PARAM NAME="Caption"
         VALUE="Check the books you would like to order:">
        <PARAM NAME="Size" VALUE="13970;1129">
        <PARAM NAME="FontName" VALUE="Times New Roman">
        <PARAM NAME="FontHeight" VALUE="480">
        <PARAM NAME="FontCharSet" VALUE="0">
        <PARAM NAME="FontPitchAndFamily" VALUE="2">
        <PARAM NAME="FontWeight" VALUE="0">
    </OBJECT>

    <OBJECT ID="CBVBS"
     CLASSID="CLSID:8BD21D40-EC42-11CE-9E0D-00AA006002F3"
     STYLE="TOP:50pt;LEFT:58pt;WIDTH:281pt;HEIGHT:22pt;
         TABINDEX:1;ZINDEX:1;">
```

```
            <PARAM NAME="BackColor" VALUE="2147483663">
            <PARAM NAME="ForeColor" VALUE="2147483666">
            <PARAM NAME="DisplayStyle" VALUE="4">
            <PARAM NAME="Size" VALUE="9913;776">
            <PARAM NAME="Value" VALUE="False">
            <PARAM NAME="Caption"
             VALUE="VBScript And ActiveX Wizardry, $39.99">
            <PARAM NAME="FontEffects" VALUE="1073741825">
            <PARAM NAME="FontHeight" VALUE="200">
            <PARAM NAME="FontCharSet" VALUE="0">
            <PARAM NAME="FontPitchAndFamily" VALUE="2">
            <PARAM NAME="FontWeight" VALUE="700">
        </OBJECT>

        <OBJECT ID="CBDelphi"
         CLASSID="CLSID:8BD21D40-EC42-11CE-9E0D-00AA006002F3"
             STYLE="TOP:74pt;LEFT:58pt;WIDTH:281pt;HEIGHT:20pt;
             TABINDEX:2;ZINDEX:2;">
            <PARAM NAME="BackColor" VALUE="2147483663">
            <PARAM NAME="ForeColor" VALUE="2147483666">
            <PARAM NAME="DisplayStyle" VALUE="4">
            <PARAM NAME="Size" VALUE="9913;706">
            <PARAM NAME="Value" VALUE="False">
            <PARAM NAME="Caption"
             VALUE="The New Delphi 2 Programming EXplorer, $44.99">
            <PARAM NAME="FontEffects" VALUE="1073741825">
            <PARAM NAME="FontHeight" VALUE="200">
            <PARAM NAME="FontCharSet" VALUE="0">
            <PARAM NAME="FontPitchAndFamily" VALUE="2">
            <PARAM NAME="FontWeight" VALUE="700">
        </OBJECT>

        <OBJECT ID="CBApp"
         CLASSID="CLSID:8BD21D40-EC42-11CE-9E0D-00AA006002F3"
             STYLE="TOP:99pt;LEFT:58pt;WIDTH:281pt;HEIGHT:19pt;
             TABINDEX:3;ZINDEX:3;">
            <PARAM NAME="BackColor" VALUE="2147483663">
            <PARAM NAME="ForeColor" VALUE="2147483666">
            <PARAM NAME="DisplayStyle" VALUE="4">
            <PARAM NAME="Size" VALUE="9913;670">
            <PARAM NAME="Value" VALUE="False">
            <PARAM NAME="Caption"
             VALUE="Writing Java Applets, $39.99">
            <PARAM NAME="FontEffects" VALUE="1073741825">
            <PARAM NAME="FontHeight" VALUE="200">
            <PARAM NAME="FontCharSet" VALUE="0">
            <PARAM NAME="FontPitchAndFamily" VALUE="2">
            <PARAM NAME="FontWeight" VALUE="700">
        </OBJECT>

        <OBJECT ID="CBIntra"
```

```
    CLASSID="CLSID:8BD21D40-EC42-11CE-9E0D-00AA006002F3"
        STYLE="TOP:124pt;LEFT:58pt;WIDTH:281pt;HEIGHT:20pt;
        TABINDEX:4;ZINDEX:4;">
      <PARAM NAME="BackColor" VALUE="2147483663">
      <PARAM NAME="ForeColor" VALUE="2147483666">
      <PARAM NAME="DisplayStyle" VALUE="4">
      <PARAM NAME="Size" VALUE="9913;706">
      <PARAM NAME="Value" VALUE="False">
      <PARAM NAME="Caption"
       VALUE="Developing Real-World Intranets, $39.99">
      <PARAM NAME="FontEffects" VALUE="1073741825">
      <PARAM NAME="FontHeight" VALUE="200">
      <PARAM NAME="FontCharSet" VALUE="0">
      <PARAM NAME="FontPitchAndFamily" VALUE="2">
      <PARAM NAME="FontWeight" VALUE="700">
</OBJECT>

<OBJECT ID="Label2"
 CLASSID="CLSID:978C9E23-D4B0-11CE-BF2D-00AA003F40D0"
        STYLE="TOP:190pt;LEFT:33pt;WIDTH:66pt;
        HEIGHT:17pt;ZINDEX:5;">
      <PARAM NAME="Caption" VALUE="Your Name:">
      <PARAM NAME="Size" VALUE="2328;600">
      <PARAM NAME="FontEffects" VALUE="1073741825">
      <PARAM NAME="FontHeight" VALUE="200">
      <PARAM NAME="FontCharSet" VALUE="0">
      <PARAM NAME="FontPitchAndFamily" VALUE="2">
      <PARAM NAME="FontWeight" VALUE="700">
</OBJECT>

<OBJECT ID="Label3"
 CLASSID="CLSID:978C9E23-D4B0-11CE-BF2D-00AA003F40D0"
        STYLE="TOP:223pt;LEFT:33pt;WIDTH:83pt;
        HEIGHT:17pt;ZINDEX:6;">
      <PARAM NAME="Caption" VALUE="Street Address:">
      <PARAM NAME="Size" VALUE="2928;600">
      <PARAM NAME="FontEffects" VALUE="1073741825">
      <PARAM NAME="FontHeight" VALUE="200">
      <PARAM NAME="FontCharSet" VALUE="0">
      <PARAM NAME="FontPitchAndFamily" VALUE="2">
      <PARAM NAME="FontWeight" VALUE="700">
</OBJECT>

<OBJECT ID="Label4"
 CLASSID="CLSID:978C9E23-D4B0-11CE-BF2D-00AA003F40D0"
        STYLE="TOP:256pt;LEFT:33pt;WIDTH:33pt;
        HEIGHT:17pt;ZINDEX:7;">
      <PARAM NAME="Caption" VALUE="City:">
      <PARAM NAME="Size" VALUE="1164;600">
      <PARAM NAME="FontEffects" VALUE="1073741825">
      <PARAM NAME="FontHeight" VALUE="200">
```

```
      <PARAM NAME="FontCharSet" VALUE="0">
      <PARAM NAME="FontPitchAndFamily" VALUE="2">
      <PARAM NAME="FontWeight" VALUE="700">
  </OBJECT>

  <OBJECT ID="TBName"
   CLASSID="CLSID:8BD21D10-EC42-11CE-9E0D-00AA006002F3"
        STYLE="TOP:190pt;LEFT:124pt;WIDTH:140pt;
        HEIGHT:17pt;TABINDEX:8;ZINDEX:8;">
      <PARAM NAME="VariousPropertyBits" VALUE="746604571">
      <PARAM NAME="Size" VALUE="4939;600">
      <PARAM NAME="FontCharSet" VALUE="0">
      <PARAM NAME="FontPitchAndFamily" VALUE="2">
      <PARAM NAME="FontWeight" VALUE="0">
  </OBJECT>

  <OBJECT ID="TBStreet"
   CLASSID="CLSID:8BD21D10-EC42-11CE-9E0D-00AA006002F3"
        STYLE="TOP:223pt;LEFT:124pt;WIDTH:140pt;HEIGHT:18pt;
        TABINDEX:9;ZINDEX:9;">
      <PARAM NAME="VariousPropertyBits" VALUE="746604571">
      <PARAM NAME="Size" VALUE="4939;635">
      <PARAM NAME="FontCharSet" VALUE="0">
      <PARAM NAME="FontPitchAndFamily" VALUE="2">
      <PARAM NAME="FontWeight" VALUE="0">
  </OBJECT>

  <OBJECT ID="TBCity"
   CLASSID="CLSID:8BD21D10-EC42-11CE-9E0D-00AA006002F3"
        STYLE="TOP:256pt;LEFT:124pt;WIDTH:99pt;HEIGHT:17pt;
        TABINDEX:10;ZINDEX:10;">
      <PARAM NAME="VariousPropertyBits" VALUE="746604571">
      <PARAM NAME="Size" VALUE="3493;600">
      <PARAM NAME="FontCharSet" VALUE="0">
      <PARAM NAME="FontPitchAndFamily" VALUE="2">
      <PARAM NAME="FontWeight" VALUE="0">
  </OBJECT>

  <OBJECT ID="Label5"
   CLASSID="CLSID:978C9E23-D4B0-11CE-BF2D-00AA003F40D0"
        STYLE="TOP:256pt;LEFT:239pt;WIDTH:33pt;
        HEIGHT:17pt;ZINDEX:11;">
      <PARAM NAME="Caption" VALUE="State:">
      <PARAM NAME="Size" VALUE="1164;600">
      <PARAM NAME="FontEffects" VALUE="1073741825">
      <PARAM NAME="FontHeight" VALUE="200">
      <PARAM NAME="FontCharSet" VALUE="0">
      <PARAM NAME="FontPitchAndFamily" VALUE="2">
      <PARAM NAME="FontWeight" VALUE="700">
  </OBJECT>
```

```
<OBJECT ID="TBState"
 CLASSID="CLSID:8BD21D10-EC42-11CE-9E0D-00AA006002F3"
     STYLE="TOP:256pt;LEFT:272pt;WIDTH:41pt;HEIGHT:16pt;
     TABINDEX:12;ZINDEX:12;">
   <PARAM NAME="VariousPropertyBits" VALUE="746604571">
   <PARAM NAME="Size" VALUE="1446;564">
   <PARAM NAME="FontCharSet" VALUE="0">
   <PARAM NAME="FontPitchAndFamily" VALUE="2">
   <PARAM NAME="FontWeight" VALUE="0">
</OBJECT>

<OBJECT ID="Label6"
 CLASSID="CLSID:978C9E23-D4B0-11CE-BF2D-00AA003F40D0"
     STYLE="TOP:256pt;LEFT:330pt;WIDTH:25pt;
     HEIGHT:17pt;ZINDEX:13;">
   <PARAM NAME="Caption" VALUE="Zip:">
   <PARAM NAME="Size" VALUE="882;600">
   <PARAM NAME="FontEffects" VALUE="1073741825">
   <PARAM NAME="FontHeight" VALUE="200">
   <PARAM NAME="FontCharSet" VALUE="0">
   <PARAM NAME="FontPitchAndFamily" VALUE="2">
   <PARAM NAME="FontWeight" VALUE="700">
</OBJECT>

<OBJECT ID="TBZip"
 CLASSID="CLSID:8BD21D10-EC42-11CE-9E0D-00AA006002F3"
     STYLE="TOP:256pt;LEFT:355pt;WIDTH:66pt;HEIGHT:16pt;
     TABINDEX:14;ZINDEX:14;">
   <PARAM NAME="VariousPropertyBits" VALUE="746604571">
   <PARAM NAME="Size" VALUE="2328;564">
   <PARAM NAME="FontCharSet" VALUE="0">
   <PARAM NAME="FontPitchAndFamily" VALUE="2">
   <PARAM NAME="FontWeight" VALUE="0">
</OBJECT>

<OBJECT ID="CmdOrder"
 CLASSID="CLSID:D7053240-CE69-11CD-A777-00DD01143C57"
     STYLE="TOP:165pt;LEFT:437pt;WIDTH:107pt;HEIGHT:107pt;
     TABINDEX:15;ZINDEX:15;">
   <PARAM NAME="Caption" VALUE="Order now!">
   <PARAM NAME="Size" VALUE="3775;3775">
   <PARAM NAME="FontName" VALUE="Times New Roman">
   <PARAM NAME="FontEffects" VALUE="1073741825">
   <PARAM NAME="FontHeight" VALUE="280">
   <PARAM NAME="FontCharSet" VALUE="0">
   <PARAM NAME="FontPitchAndFamily" VALUE="2">
   <PARAM NAME="ParagraphAlign" VALUE="3">
   <PARAM NAME="FontWeight" VALUE="700">
</OBJECT>

<OBJECT ID="Label7"
 CLASSID="CLSID:978C9E23-D4B0-11CE-BF2D-00AA003F40D0"
```

```
        STYLE="TOP:116pt;LEFT:470pt;WIDTH:74pt;
        HEIGHT:17pt;ZINDEX:16;">
    <PARAM NAME="Caption" VALUE="Your Total:">
    <PARAM NAME="Size" VALUE="2611;600">
    <PARAM NAME="FontEffects" VALUE="1073741825">
    <PARAM NAME="FontHeight" VALUE="240">
    <PARAM NAME="FontCharSet" VALUE="0">
    <PARAM NAME="FontPitchAndFamily" VALUE="2">
    <PARAM NAME="ParagraphAlign" VALUE="2">
    <PARAM NAME="FontWeight" VALUE="700">
 </OBJECT>

<OBJECT ID="LblTotal"
 CLASSID="CLSID:978C9E23-D4B0-11CE-BF2D-00AA003F40D0"
        STYLE="TOP:132pt;LEFT:462pt;WIDTH:83pt;
        HEIGHT:25pt;ZINDEX:17;">
    <PARAM NAME="BackColor" VALUE="16777215">
    <PARAM NAME="Caption" VALUE="0.00">
    <PARAM NAME="Size" VALUE="2928;882">
    <PARAM NAME="BorderStyle" VALUE="1">
    <PARAM NAME="FontName" VALUE="Times New Roman">
    <PARAM NAME="FontHeight" VALUE="360">
    <PARAM NAME="FontCharSet" VALUE="0">
    <PARAM NAME="FontPitchAndFamily" VALUE="2">
    <PARAM NAME="ParagraphAlign" VALUE="2">
    <PARAM NAME="FontWeight" VALUE="0">
 </OBJECT>
</DIV>
```

Inside The Wizardly Example Code

Let's take the technique one step at a time. The first step is to create a standard HTML form in the containing HTML document (Listing 10.7). The relevant code is as follows:

```
<FORM name="HiddenForm" METHOD="POST"
    ACTION="http://localhost/cgi-win/cgitest32.exe/Form">

<INPUT NAME="HdnCBVBS" TYPE="HIDDEN" VALUE="0">
<INPUT NAME="HdnCBDelphi" TYPE="HIDDEN" VALUE="0">
<INPUT NAME="HdnCBApp" TYPE="HIDDEN" VALUE="0">
<INPUT NAME="HdnCBIntra" TYPE="HIDDEN" VALUE="0">
<INPUT NAME="HdnTotal" TYPE="HIDDEN" VALUE="0">

<INPUT NAME="HdnName" TYPE="HIDDEN" VALUE="">
<INPUT NAME="HdnStreet" TYPE="HIDDEN" VALUE="">
<INPUT NAME="HdnCity" TYPE="HIDDEN" VALUE="""">
<INPUT NAME="HdnState" TYPE="HIDDEN" VALUE="""">
<INPUT NAME="HdnZip" TYPE="HIDDEN" VALUE="""">

</FORM>
```

Once again, we've created a form whose **action** property sends data to the Website *cgitest* program. On the form, we've created one **<input>** control for each data item that needs to be transferred from the ActiveX layout to the Web server. Notice two things:

☆ The **type** of all the controls is **hidden**. That's so they won't be visible on the Web page.

☆ As a result, none of the HTML form control types match the control types in your ActiveX layout. The data from all your ActiveX controls, whether they are check boxes or text boxes, is sent to the **hidden**-type HTML form controls. This isn't a problem, because you're passing the data as text strings. For the Web server, you can write a CGI program (see Chapter 15) to interpret the data correctly.

Let's look at the VBScript code embedded in the ActiveX layout. The action takes place mainly in the **click** event sub for the command button. The data validation code itself is the same as before. The first new piece of code is as follows:

```
Sub CmdOrder_Click()
    dim OrderComplete
    dim TheForm
    Set TheForm = window.Document.HiddenForm
```

Here, at the beginning of the **click** sub, we declare the **OrderComplete** variable as well as **TheForm**, a variable by which our VBScript code will refer to the HTML form in the containing HTML document.

Having declared a variable for the form, we next set the variable's value so that it does, in fact, refer to the HTML form in the HTML document. We'll now be able to use the variable when we call the **form.submit** method.

The next step is to assign the values in the ActiveX controls to the corresponding form controls in the HTML document. That is accomplished by the following code:

```
If OrderComplete then
    MsgBox "Order accepted!"
    window.Document.HiddenForm.HdnCBVBS.value = CBVBS.value
    window.Document.HiddenForm.HdnCBDelphi.value = CBDelphi.value
    window.Document.HiddenForm.HdnCBApp.value = CBApp.value
    window.Document.HiddenForm.HdnCBIntra.value = CBIntra.value
    window.Document.HiddenForm.HdnName.value = TBName.text
    window.Document.HiddenForm.HdnStreet.value = TBStreet.text
    window.Document.HiddenForm.HdnCity.value = TBCity.text
    window.Document.HiddenForm.HdnState.value = TBState.text
    window.Document.HiddenForm.HdnZip.value = TBZip.text
```

Notice that each time we refer to a control on the form, we use the scripting object model to fully identify where the control is located. For example, the control for the first book's check box is named **HdnCBVBS** (for hidden check box, Visual Basic Script). It's on the hidden form, **HiddenForm**, which in turn is contained in the **Document** object, which in turn is contained in the **Window** object. Thus, the control is referred to like this:

```
window.Document.HiddenForm.HdnCBVBS.value = CBVBS.value
```

Once all the values have been copied from the ActiveX layout controls to the hidden HTML form controls, it's time for the final step: sending the data to the server. That's done with the following code line:

```
TheForm.submit
```

The result, as you saw earlier in Figure 10.8, is that the data is successfully transmitted to the Web server. Once it's on the Web server, you can subject it to further validation and processing as needed for your particular application.

You'll use this same general technique whenever you need to transfer data from an ActiveX layout to an HTML document, or from an HTML document to an ActiveX layout.

X1

AN ACTIVEX MISCELLANY

You've seen how to use a few ActiveX controls so far—mainly labels, text boxes, and command buttons. In this chapter, you'll learn about some of the others.

$\mathbf{B}$y the time you read this book, there will likely be more than a hundred ActiveX controls—one for every conceivable purpose. Even now, prior to the final release of Microsoft's Internet Explorer 3.0, there are dozens of ActiveX controls available.

Most of the new controls will address specialized needs. However, there are a few controls bundled with the ActiveX Control Pad that you'll use again and again in your Web projects. In this chapter, we'll take a look at those controls.

We've already seen many examples of the *most* often-used controls: labels, text boxes, command buttons, and check boxes. Now, get ready to meet the list box, combo box, option button, toggle button, and scrollbar controls. All of our examples in this chapter will be set up with the ActiveX Control Pad, though we won't deal with the specifics of using the ActiveX Control Pad. If you're hazy on that part of the discussion, refer back to Chapter 8.

The List Box Control

The list box control lets you present the user with a list of text items. Depending on how you set up the list box, the user can select one or more of those items by clicking on them in the list box. Figure 11.1 shows a Web page with an ActiveX list box control. Listing 11.1 is the containing HTML document, while Listing 11.2 is the ActiveX layout code.

Listing 11.1 HTML document to contain the ActiveX layout.

```
<HTML>
<HEAD>
<TITLE>List Box Demonstration</TITLE>
</HEAD>
<BODY>

<OBJECT CLASSID="CLSID:812AE312-8B8E-11CF-93C8-00AA00C08FDF"
ID="listbox1_alx" STYLE="LEFT:0;TOP:0">
<PARAM NAME="ALXPATH" REF
  VALUE="file:C:\MyBooks\VBS\ch11\listbox1.alx">
 </OBJECT>

</BODY>
</HTML>
```

Listing 11.2 ActiveX layout list box control and VBScript code.

```
<SCRIPT LANGUAGE="VBScript">
<!--
```

243

```
Sub Layout1_OnLoad()
    ListBox1.AddItem "Drew Barrymore"
    ListBox1.AddItem "Alicia Silverstone"
    ListBox1.AddItem "Alyssa Milano"
    ListBox1.AddItem "Alyson Hannigan"
    ListBox1.AddItem "Kellie Martin"
end sub

Sub CmdLunch_Click()
    msgbox "Have lunch with " & Listbox1.value & ".",, _
        "Listbox Demonstration"
end sub

Sub CmdAddFriend_Click()
    dim NewFriend
    NewFriend = inputbox( _
        "Enter the name of your new friend:", _
        "Listbox Demonstration")
    ListBox1.AddItem NewFriend
end sub
-->
</SCRIPT>

<DIV ID="Layout1" STYLE="LAYOUT:FIXED;WIDTH:597pt;HEIGHT:370pt;">
    <OBJECT ID="Label1"
     CLASSID="CLSID:978C9E23-D4B0-11CE-BF2D-00AA003F40D0"
     STYLE="TOP:33pt;LEFT:198pt;WIDTH:198pt;HEIGHT:
        33pt;ZINDEX:0;">
        <PARAM NAME="Caption" VALUE="My Best Friends">
        <PARAM NAME="Size" VALUE="6985;1164">
        <PARAM NAME="FontName" VALUE="Times New Roman">
        <PARAM NAME="FontHeight" VALUE="480">
        <PARAM NAME="FontCharSet" VALUE="0">
        <PARAM NAME="FontPitchAndFamily" VALUE="2">
        <PARAM NAME="FontWeight" VALUE="0">
    </OBJECT>

    <OBJECT ID="CmdLunch"
     CLASSID="CLSID:D7053240-CE69-11CD-A777-00DD01143C57"
     STYLE="TOP:198pt;LEFT:305pt;WIDTH:132pt;HEIGHT:83pt;
        TABINDEX:2;ZINDEX:1;">
        <PARAM NAME="Caption" VALUE="Let's do lunch.">
        <PARAM NAME="Size" VALUE="4657;2928">
        <PARAM NAME="FontEffects" VALUE="1073741825">
        <PARAM NAME="FontHeight" VALUE="240">
        <PARAM NAME="FontCharSet" VALUE="0">
        <PARAM NAME="FontPitchAndFamily" VALUE="2">
        <PARAM NAME="ParagraphAlign" VALUE="3">
        <PARAM NAME="FontWeight" VALUE="700">
    </OBJECT>
```

```
<OBJECT ID="CmdAddFriend"
  CLASSID="CLSID:D7053240-CE69-11CD-A777-00DD01143C57"
  STYLE="TOP:198pt;LEFT:157pt;WIDTH:132pt;HEIGHT:83pt;
      TABINDEX:3;ZINDEX:2;">
    <PARAM NAME="Caption" VALUE="Add a new friend">
    <PARAM NAME="Size" VALUE="4657;2928">
    <PARAM NAME="FontEffects" VALUE="1073741825">
    <PARAM NAME="FontHeight" VALUE="240">
    <PARAM NAME="FontCharSet" VALUE="0">
    <PARAM NAME="FontPitchAndFamily" VALUE="2">
    <PARAM NAME="ParagraphAlign" VALUE="3">
    <PARAM NAME="FontWeight" VALUE="700">
  </OBJECT>

<OBJECT ID="Listbox1"
  CLASSID="CLSID:8BD21D20-EC42-11CE-9E0D-00AA006002F3"
  STYLE="TOP:74pt;LEFT:198pt;WIDTH:198pt;HEIGHT:111pt;
      TABINDEX:0;ZINDEX:3;">
    <PARAM NAME="ScrollBars" VALUE="3">
    <PARAM NAME="DisplayStyle" VALUE="2">
    <PARAM NAME="Size" VALUE="6985;3914">
    <PARAM NAME="MatchEntry" VALUE="0">
    <PARAM NAME="FontEffects" VALUE="1073741825">
    <PARAM NAME="FontHeight" VALUE="280">
    <PARAM NAME="FontCharSet" VALUE="0">
    <PARAM NAME="FontPitchAndFamily" VALUE="2">
    <PARAM NAME="FontWeight" VALUE="700">
  </OBJECT>
</DIV>
```

Writing VBScript Code For The List Box Control

Of course, a list box control doesn't come with list items: You have to put them into the list. The most common way to do so is when your window or ActiveX layout loads. When the user loads your Web page into his or her browser, the **onLoad** event fires for both the containing Web page window and the ActiveX layout. Therefore, it's easy to put your initialization code in there. In this example, we loaded the list with the names of actresses who have fans in the Web-nerd community:

```
Sub Layout1_OnLoad()
    ListBox1.AddItem "Drew Barrymore"
    ListBox1.AddItem "Alicia Silverstone"
    ListBox1.AddItem "Alyssa Milano"
    ListBox1.AddItem "Alyson Hannigan"
    ListBox1.AddItem "Kellie Martin"
end sub
```

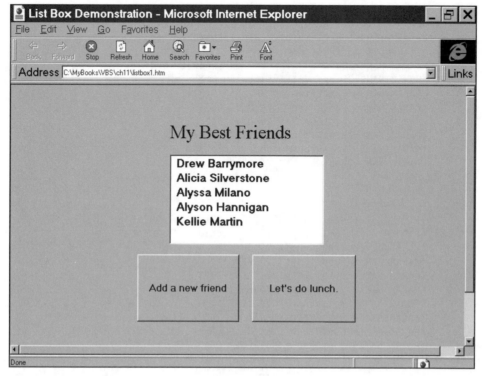

Figure 11.1 A Web page with a list box control.

It's the list box control's **AddItem** method that does the work. To add an item to the list, you just call the **AddItem** method and give it the text for the new item. When the user clicks on an item in the list, that item is assigned to the list box control's **value** property. It's then quite easy to use that value in your VBScript code, as in the **click** event sub for the "Let's do lunch" command button. As shown in Figure 11.2, this code displays a message box with the selected list item in the text:

```
Sub CmdLunch_Click()
    msgbox "Have lunch with " & Listbox1.value & ".",, _
        "Listbox Demonstration"
end sub
```

Of course, the **onLoad** event isn't the only time you can load new items into the list. As shown in Figure 11.3, the **click** event sub for the other command button uses the VBScript **InputBox()** function to prompt the user for a new name that will be added to the list:

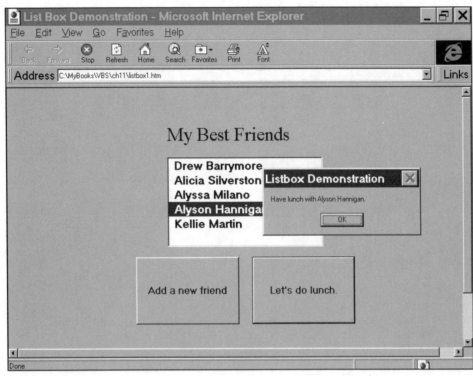

Figure 11.2   A message box with the selected list item in the text.

```
Sub CmdAddFriend_Click()
   dim NewFriend
   NewFriend = inputbox( _
      "Enter the name of your new friend:", _
      "Listbox Demonstration")
   ListBox1.AddItem NewFriend
end sub
```

Once the user has entered the new name in the input box, the sub calls the list box's **AddItem** method and adds the new item to the list. Simple.

List boxes are appropriate when you want the user to choose from a predefined set of choices, and do *not* want to allow a choice that isn't on the list. This contrasts with combo boxes, which are like list boxes but *do* allow the user to make a choice that isn't on the list.

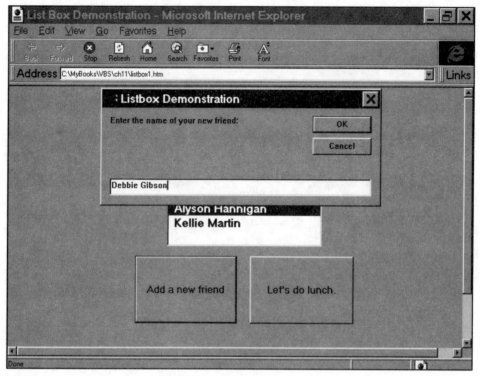

Figure 11.3 Adding a new item to the list box.

The Combo Box Control

The combo box control is like a cross between a text box and a list box—in fact, it *is* a cross between a text box and a list box. At the top of a combo box is a text box in which the user can type an entry. Underneath, a drop-down list appears with the regular list items. This allows a user either to select an item from the list, or type a new item in the text box.

Figure 11.4 shows the combo-box version of our Web page with names of people to call for lunch. Listing 11.3 shows the HTML container code for an ActiveX layout with a combo box, while Listing 11.4 shows the ActiveX layout and VBScript code.

Listing 11.3 HTML document to contain the layout with combo box.

```
<HTML>
<HEAD>
<TITLE>Combo Box Demonstration</TITLE>
</HEAD>
<BODY>
```

```
<OBJECT CLASSID="CLSID:812AE312-8B8E-11CF-93C8-00AA00C08FDF"
ID="combobx1_alx" STYLE="LEFT:0;TOP:0">
<PARAM NAME="ALXPATH" REF
  VALUE="file:C:\MyBooks\VBS\ch11\combobx1.alx">
 </OBJECT>


</BODY>
</HTML>
```

Listing 11.4　ActiveX layout with combo box and VBScript code.

```
<SCRIPT LANGUAGE="VBScript">
<!--
Sub Layout1_OnLoad()
ComboBox1.AddItem "Drew Barrymore"
ComboBox1.AddItem "Alicia Silverstone"
ComboBox1.AddItem "Alyssa Milano"
ComboBox1.AddItem "Alyson Hannigan"
ComboBox1.AddItem "Kellie Martin"
end sub

Sub CmdLunch_Click()
msgbox "Have lunch with " & ComboBox1.value & ".",, _
    "Listbox Demonstration"
end sub

Sub CmdAddFriend_Click()
dim NewFriend
NewFriend = inputbox( _
   "Enter the name of your new friend:","Listbox Demonstration")
ComboBox1.AddItem NewFriend
end sub
-->
</SCRIPT>

<DIV ID="Layout1" STYLE="LAYOUT:FIXED;WIDTH:597pt;HEIGHT:370pt;">
    <OBJECT ID="Label1"
     CLASSID="CLSID:978C9E23-D4B0-11CE-BF2D-00AA003F40D0"
         STYLE="TOP:33pt;LEFT:198pt;WIDTH:198pt;
         HEIGHT:33pt;ZINDEX:0;">
        <PARAM NAME="Caption" VALUE="My Best Friends">
        <PARAM NAME="Size" VALUE="6985;1164">
        <PARAM NAME="FontName" VALUE="Times New Roman">
        <PARAM NAME="FontHeight" VALUE="480">
        <PARAM NAME="FontCharSet" VALUE="0">
        <PARAM NAME="FontPitchAndFamily" VALUE="2">
        <PARAM NAME="FontWeight" VALUE="0">
    </OBJECT>

    <OBJECT ID="CmdLunch"
     CLASSID="CLSID:D7053240-CE69-11CD-A777-00DD01143C57"
         STYLE="TOP:198pt;LEFT:305pt;WIDTH:132pt;
```

```
         HEIGHT:83pt;TABINDEX:1;ZINDEX:1;">
      <PARAM NAME="Caption" VALUE="Let's do lunch.">
      <PARAM NAME="Size" VALUE="4657;2928">
      <PARAM NAME="FontEffects" VALUE="1073741825">
      <PARAM NAME="FontHeight" VALUE="240">
      <PARAM NAME="FontCharSet" VALUE="0">
      <PARAM NAME="FontPitchAndFamily" VALUE="2">
      <PARAM NAME="ParagraphAlign" VALUE="3">
      <PARAM NAME="FontWeight" VALUE="700">
   </OBJECT>

   <OBJECT ID="CmdAddFriend"
    CLASSID="CLSID:D7053240-CE69-11CD-A777-00DD01143C57"
       STYLE="TOP:198pt;LEFT:157pt;WIDTH:132pt;
       HEIGHT:83pt;TABINDEX:2;ZINDEX:2;">
      <PARAM NAME="Caption" VALUE="Add a new friend">
      <PARAM NAME="Size" VALUE="4657;2928">
      <PARAM NAME="FontEffects" VALUE="1073741825">
      <PARAM NAME="FontHeight" VALUE="240">
      <PARAM NAME="FontCharSet" VALUE="0">
      <PARAM NAME="FontPitchAndFamily" VALUE="2">
      <PARAM NAME="ParagraphAlign" VALUE="3">
      <PARAM NAME="FontWeight" VALUE="700">
   </OBJECT>

   <OBJECT ID="ComboBox1"
    CLASSID="CLSID:8BD21D30-EC42-11CE-9E0D-00AA006002F3"
       STYLE="TOP:74pt;LEFT:182pt;WIDTH:231pt;
       HEIGHT:21pt;TABINDEX:3;ZINDEX:3;">
      <PARAM NAME="VariousPropertyBits" VALUE="746604571">
      <PARAM NAME="DisplayStyle" VALUE="3">
      <PARAM NAME="Size" VALUE="8149;741">
      <PARAM NAME="MatchEntry" VALUE="1">
      <PARAM NAME="ShowDropButtonWhen" VALUE="2">
      <PARAM NAME="FontEffects" VALUE="1073741825">
      <PARAM NAME="FontHeight" VALUE="240">
      <PARAM NAME="FontCharSet" VALUE="0">
      <PARAM NAME="FontPitchAndFamily" VALUE="2">
      <PARAM NAME="FontWeight" VALUE="700">
   </OBJECT>
</DIV>
```

When a user clicks on the down-arrow button at the right end of the text box, a list appears underneath, as shown in Figure 11.5. If the user doesn't want to select any of the items on the list, he or she can type a new item in the text box and select it, as shown in Figure 11.6.

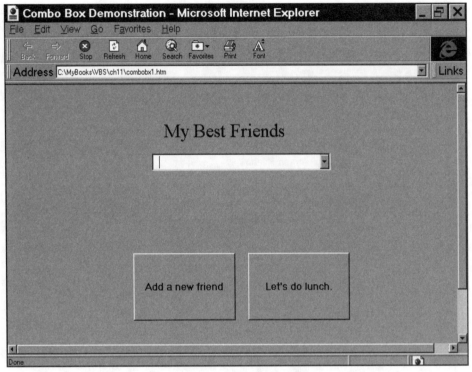

Figure 11.4   A combo box combines a text box with a drop-down list.

Writing VBScript Code For The Combo Box Control

As you can see from Listings 11.3 and 11.4, the VBScript code works exactly the same with a combo box as it does with a list box. The only real difference is in the way the controls work: The combo box lets the user enter a choice that isn't on the list, whereas the list box doesn't.

Typing a new choice in the combo box's text box does not, by the way, add the new item to the list. That still has to be done by calling the combo box's **AddItem** method.

The Option Button Control

Option buttons might look a lot different from list boxes, but they really aren't. Option buttons are another way to present the user with a list of choices and

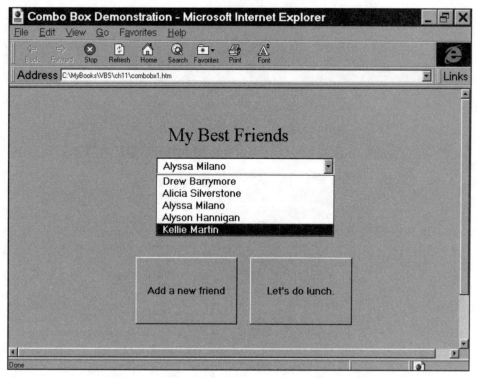

Figure 11.5   A list drops down underneath the text box.

require that he or she pick an item from the list. Figure 11.7 shows a simple Web page with three option buttons. Each option button corresponds to a CD that the user might want to play. Unlike check boxes, only *one* of a group of option buttons can be selected at a time.

Option buttons = radio buttons, but don't call them that.

Option buttons are also sometimes called "radio buttons"—in fact, historically, that's what they were originally called. However, there's also a native HTML form control called a radio button, so it's probably a good idea to avoid calling ActiveX option button controls "radio buttons." That way, you avoid any potential for confusion.

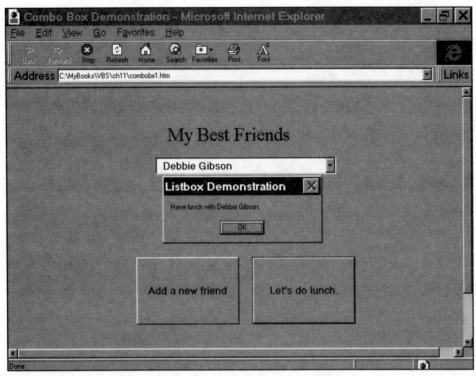

Figure 11.6   The user can type a new entry in the text box.

In spite of their functional similarity to list boxes, option buttons are coded quite differently in VBScript. Listing 11.5 shows the HTML container document for an ActiveX layout with option buttons, while Listing 11.6 shows the ActiveX layout and the VBScript code.

Listing 11.5   HTML document for a layout with option buttons.

```
<HTML>
<HEAD>
<TITLE>Option Button Demonstration</TITLE>
</HEAD>
<BODY>

<OBJECT CLASSID="CLSID:812AE312-8B8E-11CF-93C8-00AA00C08FDF"
ID="opt_btn1_alx" STYLE="LEFT:0;TOP:0">
<PARAM NAME="ALXPATH" REF VALUE="file:C:\MyBooks\VBS\ch11\opt_btn1.alx">
 </OBJECT>

</BODY>
</HTML>
```

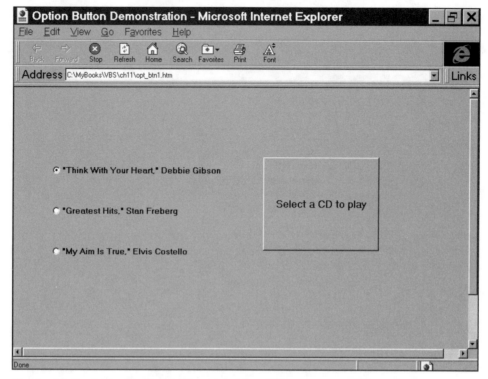

Figure 11.7 Using option buttons to pick a CD.

Listing 11.6 ActiveX layout with option buttons and VBScript code.

```
<SCRIPT LANGUAGE="VBScript">
<!--
Sub CommandButton1_Click()
   If OptionButton1 then
      msgbox "Play " & OptionButton1.caption & ".",, _
         "Option Button Demonstration"
   end if

   If OptionButton2 then
      msgbox "Play " & OptionButton2.caption & ".",, _
         "Option Button Demonstration"
   end if

   If OptionButton3 then
      msgbox "Play " & OptionButton3.caption & ".",, _
         "Option Button Demonstration"
   end if
end sub
-->
</SCRIPT>
<DIV ID="Layout3" STYLE="LAYOUT:FIXED;WIDTH:597pt;HEIGHT:370pt;">
```

```
<OBJECT ID="OptionButton1"
  CLASSID="CLSID:8BD21D50-EC42-11CE-9E0D-00AA006002F3"
  STYLE="TOP:74pt;LEFT:41pt;WIDTH:230pt;
  HEIGHT:34pt;TABINDEX:0;ZINDEX:0;">
    <PARAM NAME="BackColor" VALUE="2147483663">
    <PARAM NAME="ForeColor" VALUE="2147483666">
    <PARAM NAME="DisplayStyle" VALUE="5">
    <PARAM NAME="Size" VALUE="8114;1199">
    <PARAM NAME="Value" VALUE="True">
    <PARAM NAME="Caption"
      VALUE="&quot;Think With Your Heart,&quot; Debbie Gibson">
    <PARAM NAME="FontEffects" VALUE="1073741825">
    <PARAM NAME="FontHeight" VALUE="200">
    <PARAM NAME="FontCharSet" VALUE="0">
    <PARAM NAME="FontPitchAndFamily" VALUE="2">
    <PARAM NAME="FontWeight" VALUE="700">
</OBJECT>

<OBJECT ID="OptionButton2"
  CLASSID="CLSID:8BD21D50-EC42-11CE-9E0D-00AA006002F3"
  STYLE="TOP:124pt;LEFT:41pt;WIDTH:230pt;
  HEIGHT:35pt;TABINDEX:1;ZINDEX:1;">
    <PARAM NAME="BackColor" VALUE="2147483663">
    <PARAM NAME="ForeColor" VALUE="2147483666">
    <PARAM NAME="DisplayStyle" VALUE="5">
    <PARAM NAME="Size" VALUE="8114;1235">
    <PARAM NAME="Value" VALUE="False">
    <PARAM NAME="Caption"
      VALUE="&quot;Greatest Hits,&quot; Stan Freberg">
    <PARAM NAME="FontEffects" VALUE="1073741825">
    <PARAM NAME="FontHeight" VALUE="200">
    <PARAM NAME="FontCharSet" VALUE="0">
    <PARAM NAME="FontPitchAndFamily" VALUE="2">
    <PARAM NAME="FontWeight" VALUE="700">
</OBJECT>

<OBJECT ID="OptionButton3"
  CLASSID="CLSID:8BD21D50-EC42-11CE-9E0D-00AA006002F3"
  STYLE="TOP:173pt;LEFT:41pt;WIDTH:238pt;
  HEIGHT:37pt;TABINDEX:2;ZINDEX:2;">
    <PARAM NAME="BackColor" VALUE="2147483663">
    <PARAM NAME="ForeColor" VALUE="2147483666">
    <PARAM NAME="DisplayStyle" VALUE="5">
    <PARAM NAME="Size" VALUE="8396;1305">
    <PARAM NAME="Value" VALUE="False">
    <PARAM NAME="Caption"
      VALUE="&quot;My Aim Is True,&quot; Elvis Costello">
    <PARAM NAME="FontEffects" VALUE="1073741825">
    <PARAM NAME="FontHeight" VALUE="200">
    <PARAM NAME="FontCharSet" VALUE="0">
    <PARAM NAME="FontPitchAndFamily" VALUE="2">
    <PARAM NAME="FontWeight" VALUE="700">
</OBJECT>
```

```
<OBJECT ID="CommandButton1"
 CLASSID="CLSID:D7053240-CE69-11CD-A777-00DD01143C57"
 STYLE="TOP:74pt;LEFT:314pt;WIDTH:149pt;
 HEIGHT:116pt;TABINDEX:3;ZINDEX:3;">
    <PARAM NAME="Caption" VALUE="Select a CD to play">
    <PARAM NAME="Size" VALUE="5256;4092">
    <PARAM NAME="FontEffects" VALUE="1073741825">
    <PARAM NAME="FontHeight" VALUE="240">
    <PARAM NAME="FontCharSet" VALUE="0">
    <PARAM NAME="FontPitchAndFamily" VALUE="2">
    <PARAM NAME="ParagraphAlign" VALUE="3">
    <PARAM NAME="FontWeight" VALUE="700">
</OBJECT>
</DIV>
```

When you first set up option buttons in the ActiveX Control Pad, you need to go into the Properties window and set the **value** property of one of the buttons to **true**. This will automatically set the values of the other buttons to false. When the user loads your Web page, the button whose initial value you set to **true** will be selected. The user can then accept it, or select one of the other option buttons by clicking in it.

Writing VBScript Code For Option Button Controls

Apart from its **caption** property, which is self-explanatory, the most important property of an option button is its **value** property. The **value** property is also the default property of an option button. If you refer to an option button control but don't specify a property, VBScript assumes you are talking about the default property—its value.

If the button is selected, then its value is **true**; otherwise, its value is **false**. In VBScript, **false** equals 0 (zero), while **true** is any non-zero integer value—usually −1. That makes it easy to write code detecting which option button is selected, as in Listing 11.6:

```
If OptionButton1 then
    msgbox "Play " & OptionButton1.caption & ".",, _
        "Option Button Demonstration"
   end if
```

Notice that all the **if** clause says is "If OptionButton1…" That's because if the control is selected, its **value** property is **true**. And when you refer to the control without specifying a property, you get the value property. It would work fine if you instead wrote:

```
If OptionButton1.value = true then
    msgbox "Play " & OptionButton1.caption & ".",, _
        "Option Button Demonstration"
end if
```

but it wouldn't accomplish anything more, and would thus be a waste of time.

The Toggle Button Control

A toggle is essentially just an on-off switch, like a light switch. The ActiveX toggle button control works exactly as you'd expect: Each time it's clicked, it switches between "on" and "off."

Because a toggle button is like a light switch, our example gives you a chance to turn the lights on or off at The Coriolis Group. When you first arrive, the lights are on, as shown in Figure 11.8. When you leave our office, like any thoughtful guest, you click on the toggle button to turn off the lights, as shown in Figure 11.9.

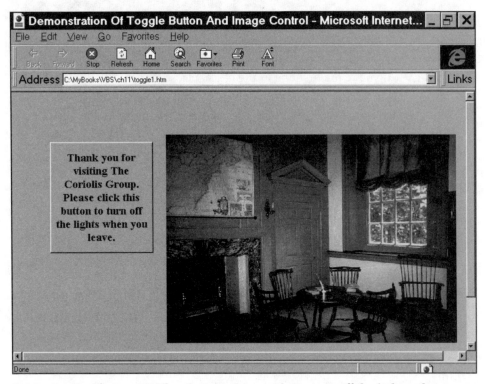

Figure 11.8 If you visit The Coriolis Group, please turn off the lights when you leave.

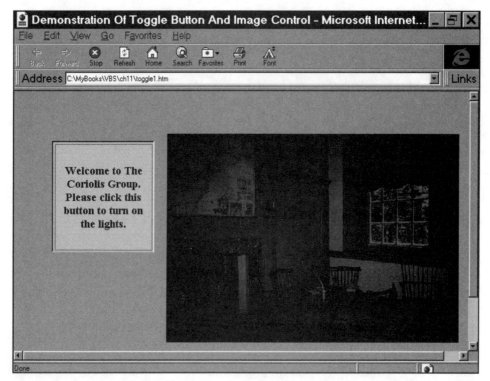

Figure 11.9 If you're the first one in the office, please turn on the lights.

This Web page uses a few tricks in addition to the toggle button itself. The HTML code for the containing Web page is shown in Listing 11.7, while the ActiveX layout and the VBScript code are shown in Listing 11.8.

Listing 11.7 HTML code for the containing Web page.

```
<HTML>
<HEAD>
<TITLE>Demonstration Of Toggle Button And Image Control</TITLE>
</HEAD>
<BODY>

<OBJECT CLASSID="CLSID:812AE312-8B8E-11CF-93C8-00AA00C08FDF"
ID="toggle1_alx" STYLE="LEFT:0;TOP:0">
<PARAM NAME="ALXPATH" REF VALUE="file:C:\MyBooks\VBS\ch11\toggle1.alx">
 </OBJECT>

</BODY>
</HTML>
```

Listing 11.8 ActiveX layout with toggle control, image control, and VBScript code.

```
<SCRIPT LANGUAGE="VBScript">
<!--
Sub ToggleButton1_Click()
If ToggleButton1 then
   Image1.picturepath = "c:\mybooks\vbs\ch11\office2.bmp"
   ToggleButton1.caption = "Welcome to The Coriolis Group." & _
      "Please click this button to turn on the lights."
else
   Image1.picturepath = "c:\mybooks\vbs\ch11\office1.bmp"
   ToggleButton1.caption = "Thank you for visiting The " & _
      "Coriolis Group. Please click this button to turn off " & _
      "the lights when you leave."
end if

end sub
-->
</SCRIPT>

<DIV ID="Layout4" STYLE="LAYOUT:FIXED;WIDTH:597pt;HEIGHT:370pt;">

    <OBJECT ID="ToggleButton1"
     CLASSID="CLSID:8BD21D60-EC42-11CE-9E0D-00AA006002F3"
     STYLE="TOP:50pt;LEFT:41pt;WIDTH:132pt;HEIGHT:138pt;
     TABINDEX:0;ZINDEX:0;">
        <PARAM NAME="BackColor" VALUE="2147483663">
        <PARAM NAME="ForeColor" VALUE="4194368">
        <PARAM NAME="DisplayStyle" VALUE="6">
        <PARAM NAME="Size" VALUE="4657;4868">
        <PARAM NAME="Value" VALUE="True">
        <PARAM NAME="Caption"
          VALUE="Thank you for visiting The Coriolis Group.
                Please click this button to turn off the lights when
                you leave.">
        <PARAM NAME="FontName" VALUE="Times New Roman">
        <PARAM NAME="FontEffects" VALUE="1073741825">
        <PARAM NAME="FontHeight" VALUE="280">
        <PARAM NAME="FontCharSet" VALUE="0">
        <PARAM NAME="FontPitchAndFamily" VALUE="2">
        <PARAM NAME="ParagraphAlign" VALUE="3">
        <PARAM NAME="FontWeight" VALUE="700">
    </OBJECT>

    <OBJECT ID="Image1"
     CLASSID="CLSID:D4A97620-8E8F-11CF-93CD-00AA00C08FDF"
     STYLE="TOP:41pt;LEFT:190pt;WIDTH:375pt;
     HEIGHT:260pt;ZINDEX:1;">
        <PARAM NAME="PicturePath"
          VALUE="c:\mybooks\vbs\ch11\office1.bmp">
```

```
        <PARAM NAME="BorderStyle" VALUE="0">
        <PARAM NAME="SizeMode" VALUE="3">
        <PARAM NAME="Size" VALUE="13229;9172">
        <PARAM NAME="PictureAlignment" VALUE="0">
        <PARAM NAME="VariousPropertyBits" VALUE="19">
    </OBJECT>
</DIV>
```

As you might have guessed from the figures, and confirmed by looking at the code, this example also uses an ActiveX Image control. We'll cover it only in passing here. Chapter 12 discusses in more detail how to handle images in your Web documents.

Writing VBScript Code For The Toggle Button Control

The code for the toggle button control is as simple as the control itself. Just like an option button, a toggle button's default property is its **value** property, and its value property is either on (**true**) or off (**false**). Thus, inside the button's **click** event, you set up a simple **if...then...else** statement, as follows:

```
Sub ToggleButton1_Click()
If ToggleButton1 then
    Image1.picturepath = "c:\mybooks\vbs\ch11\office2.bmp"
    ToggleButton1.caption = "Welcome to The Coriolis Group." & _
        "Please click this button to turn on the lights."
else
    Image1.picturepath = "c:\mybooks\vbs\ch11\office1.bmp"
    ToggleButton1.caption = "Thank you for visiting The " & _
        "Coriolis Group. Please click this button to turn off " & _
        "the lights when you leave."
end if
```

If the toggle button's value is already **true** when the user clicks on it, that means the lights are turned on at The Coriolis Group. Thus, **ToggleButton1** is **true** and the **then** part of the statement fires. This changes the image file name in the image control's **picturepath** property, causing a new image to display in the control.

If the toggle button's value is **false** when the button is clicked, then it means the lights are out. As a result, the **else** clause fires, using the same technique to swap a fully-lit photograph into the image control's **picturepath** property.

How the darkened photo was created.
To create the "dark" version of the office photo, I used JASC's
Paint Shop Pro 4. By adjusting the brightness and contrast of
the photo, I took a fully-lit scene and made it look darker.

The ScrollBar Control

You use scroll bars all the time—in your word processor, in utility programs—
any time there's some data that scrolls off the screen. What you might not have
realized is that scroll bars have other applications as well. They're a good way to
let users visually change values in a program. Figure 11.10 shows a Web page
with an ActiveX scrollbar control that displays its current value in a label control. The HTML code for the containing document is shown in Listing 11.9,
while the ActiveX layout and VBScript code is shown in Listing 11.10.

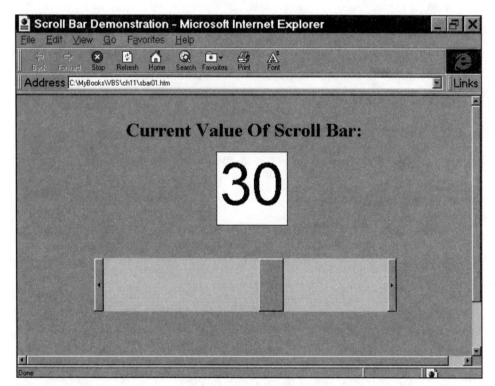

Figure 11.10 A Web page with a scrollbar control.

Listing 11.9   HTML code for the scroll bar layout.

```
<HTML>
<HEAD>
<TITLE>Scroll Bar Demonstration</TITLE>
</HEAD>
<BODY>

<OBJECT CLASSID="CLSID:812AE312-8B8E-11CF-93C8-00AA00C08FDF"
ID="sbar01_alx" STYLE="LEFT:0;TOP:0">
<PARAM NAME="ALXPATH" REF
  VALUE="file:C:\MyBooks\VBS\ch11\sbar01.alx">
 </OBJECT>


</BODY>
</HTML>
```

Listing 11.10   ActiveX layout with scrollbar control and VBScript code.

```
<SCRIPT LANGUAGE="VBScript">
<!--
Sub ScrollBar1_Change()
   Label1.caption = ScrollBar1.value
end sub
-->
</SCRIPT>

<DIV ID="Layout1" STYLE="LAYOUT:FIXED;WIDTH:597pt;HEIGHT:370pt;">

    <OBJECT ID="ScrollBar1"
      CLASSID="CLSID:DFD181E0-5E2F-11CE-A449-00AA004A803D"
      STYLE="TOP:190pt;LEFT:91pt;WIDTH:388pt;
      HEIGHT:66pt;TABINDEX:0;ZINDEX:0;">
        <PARAM NAME="Size" VALUE="13688;2328">
        <PARAM NAME="Max" VALUE="50">
        <PARAM NAME="LargeChange" VALUE="5">
    </OBJECT>

    <OBJECT ID="Label1"
     CLASSID="CLSID:978C9E23-D4B0-11CE-BF2D-00AA003F40D0"
     STYLE="TOP:58pt;LEFT:248pt;WIDTH:91pt;
     HEIGHT:91pt;ZINDEX:1;">
        <PARAM NAME="BackColor" VALUE="16777215">
        <PARAM NAME="Caption" VALUE="0">
        <PARAM NAME="Size" VALUE="3210;3210">
        <PARAM NAME="BorderStyle" VALUE="1">
        <PARAM NAME="FontName" VALUE="Arial">
        <PARAM NAME="FontHeight" VALUE="1440">
        <PARAM NAME="FontCharSet" VALUE="0">
        <PARAM NAME="FontPitchAndFamily" VALUE="2">
        <PARAM NAME="ParagraphAlign" VALUE="3">
```

```
        <PARAM NAME="FontWeight" VALUE="0">
    </OBJECT>

    <OBJECT ID="Label2"
     CLASSID="CLSID:978C9E23-D4B0-11CE-BF2D-00AA003F40D0"
     STYLE="TOP:17pt;LEFT:132pt;WIDTH:314pt;
     HEIGHT:33pt;ZINDEX:2;">
        <PARAM NAME="Caption"
          VALUE="Current Value Of Scroll Bar:">
        <PARAM NAME="Size" VALUE="11077;1164">
        <PARAM NAME="FontName" VALUE="Times New Roman">
        <PARAM NAME="FontEffects" VALUE="1073741825">
        <PARAM NAME="FontHeight" VALUE="480">
        <PARAM NAME="FontCharSet" VALUE="0">
        <PARAM NAME="FontPitchAndFamily" VALUE="2">
        <PARAM NAME="FontWeight" VALUE="700">
    </OBJECT>
</DIV>
```

When you set up the scrollbar control in the ActiveX Control Pad, you need to know about its four most important properties:

☆ **SmallChange.** This is the amount by which the scroll bar's **value** property changes when a user clicks on one of the arrow buttons at either end of the scroll bar. Clicking once on the right-hand arrow button increases the value by **SmallChange**, while clicking once on the left-hand arrow button *decreases* the value by **SmallChange**.

☆ **LargeChange.** This is the amount by which the scroll bar's **value** property changes when a user clicks on the area *within* the scroll bar. Clicking to the right of the value indicator increases the value by **LargeChange**, while clicking to the left of the value indicator *decreases* the value by the same amount.

☆ **Min.** This is the minimum value of the control's **value** property—by default, this is 0 (zero).

☆ **Max.** This is the maximum value of the control's **value** property. If you're testing the control and clicking doesn't seem to have much effect, you might have left the **Max** property at its default setting, which is 32,767.

Writing VBScript Code For The Scrollbar Control

The most important event that happens to the scrollbar control is its **change** event. Whenever the value of the scrollbar changes, its **change** event fires. By putting your VBScript code into the scrollbar control's **change** event, you can update any other controls with the scrollbar's new value. That's what was done in our example. The scrollbar control's **change** event assigned a new value to the label control's **caption** property:

```
Sub ScrollBar1_Change()
   Label1.caption = ScrollBar1.value
end sub
```

There are many applications of scroll bars, and you'll often find them useful in your Web pages.

XII

IMAGES, VIDEO, AND SOUND

There are plenty of ways to use images, video, and sound on your Web page— ActiveX is only one of them. In this chapter, you'll learn the most important tricks of the trade.

Command buttons, text boxes, and other standard controls make your Web page *work*. Images, animations, and video can help make it *fun*. There are several different controls and techniques you can use for different purposes. We'll start by taking another look at the ActiveX image control we used in Chapter 11's "toggle button" demonstration. Then, we'll look at some other ways you can incorporate images and video into your Web pages.

Using ActiveX Image Controls

If you recall from Chapter 11, the toggle-button demonstration used an ActiveX image control to show an office photograph from The Coriolis Group (at least, a fantasy version of our office). The Web page looked like Figure 12.1.

Like any other control, an image control has some properties that you'll use all the time, but others that you'll use less often. The most important properties are as follows:

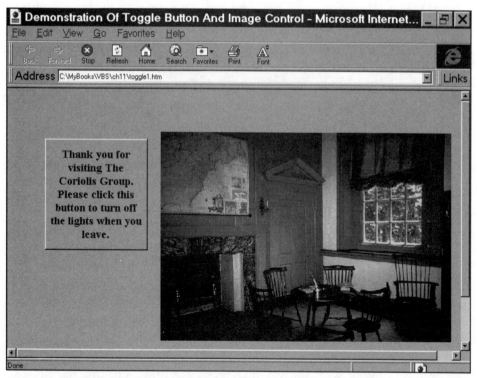

Figure 12.1   An image control displays a photo on the Web page.

☆ **Autosize**. This determines if the image control will resize itself to fit the picture that's loaded into it. If this property is set to **true**, then the image control will expand or shrink to fit the picture it contains. If the property is set to **false**, then the image control will remain the same size. If the image is bigger than the control, the right and bottom edges of the image might not be visible.

Normally, you'll set the **autosize** property to false. Once you've created a Web page layout, you probably won't want it disrupted by an image control whose size on the page is unpredictable. On the other hand, if you're loading a series of pictures into the control and want to be sure that the picture edges don't get "clipped" by the control borders, then set **autosize** to **true** and plan for size changes when you design your Web page.

☆ **Borderstyle**. This determines whether or not the image control will have a visible border on your Web page. The default value is usually 0, or "none." The Microsoft image control only lets you have a single-line border, but other image controls might give you more choices.

☆ **ID**. This, of course, is the name by which you refer to the image control in your VBScript code.

☆ **PicturePath**. This is the location and file name of the picture that the image control should display. With the Microsoft image control, you type this directly into the **picturepath** line of the Properties window. With other image controls, you can often browse through your disk directories and select a file instead of typing the path and file name.

The image control can display images from the following file types: GIF, JPG, BMP, WMF, and WVLET. If you have an image in a different kind of file, you need to convert it to a file type that the image control can use.

Try to minimize downloading time for images.

No matter what file type you use for your images, you should try to keep your image files as small as possible because they'll have to load across the Web into the user's PC. Bigger files mean longer download times. One way to shrink the file size is to select a compressed file type, such as JPG: a JPG file takes up far less disk space than a BMP file of the same image. Another way to shrink the file size is to reduce the number of colors in the image. Paint Shop Pro and other image processing programs allow you to do this quite easily.

Some images will display fine with only 16 colors, whereas others require 256 or even 65,000 colors to display properly. But the thing to remember is a Web version of "Ockham's Razor:" Don't multiply colors beyond necessity. (William of Ockham was a medieval philosopher who said that in explaining any phenomenon, we should not multiply entities beyond necessity—in other words, we should keep the explanation as simple as possible. Ditto for program code. Ditto for colors.)

The mechanics of writing VBScript code for the image control are similar to all other controls, as shown by this line from Listing 11.8:

```
Image1.picturepath = "c:\mybooks\vbs\ch11\office2.bmp"
```

Most of the time, when you write code for an image control, it will be to assign a new picture file to the control's **picturepath** property. Of course, you can make other changes in the control, but that's the most common. The default event for the image control is the **click** event: You can even use image controls as ersatz command buttons.

Other "image" controls are similar.

In this chapter, we're talking about the ActiveX image control from Microsoft. However, all image controls—whether they're called "image controls" or not, and whether they're from Microsoft or not—have the same basic properties in common. The reason is simple: They all do basically the same thing, which is to display images on a Web page or program window.

As a result, don't be too worried if you end up working with a different image control than the one we discuss here. All the basic concepts, properties, and techniques you learn in this chapter will probably apply to the new control, too.

Using Images In HTML

ActiveX and VBScript aside, HTML itself gives you quite a bit of flexibility in displaying images on your Web page. There are two HTML tags supported by Internet Explorer that are of particular interest:

☆ The **<body>** tag. This has a property called **background** that lets you use an image file as wallpaper for your Web page.

☆ The **<img>** tag. This has a property called **src** ("source") that lets you display an image on your Web page—in much the same way as you would with an ActiveX image control. The difference, of course, is that an image displayed with the **<img>** tag can't react to events and execute VBScript code like an ActiveX image control.

Listing 12.1 shows the HTML code for a Web page that uses the **<body background>** and **<img>** tags. Figure 12.2 shows the Web page it creates.

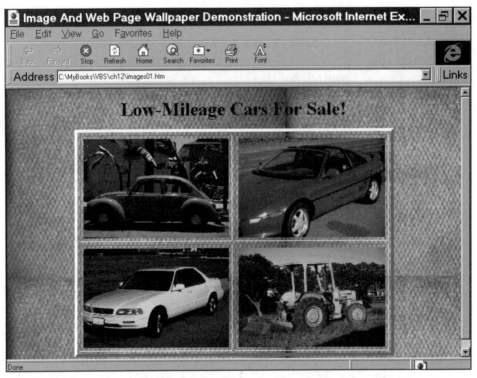

Figure 12.2 Selling cars on a Web page.

Listing 12.1 HTML code showing two ways to use images.

```
<HTML>
<HEAD>
<TITLE>Image And Web Page Wallpaper Demonstration</TITLE>
</HEAD>
<BODY background="orngbk1.gif">
<center>
<H1><STRONG>Low-Mileage Cars For Sale!</STRONG></H1>
<TABLE BORDER=5 WIDTH=250 HEIGHT=200 CELLPADDING=5 CELLSPACING=5>
<TR><TD><img src="car01.gif"></TD><TD><img src="car02.gif"></TD></TR>
<TR><TD><img src="car03.gif"></TD><TD><img src="car04.gif"></TD></TR>
</TABLE>
</center>

</BODY>
</HTML>
```

Compared to some of the code we've seen with ActiveX layouts, Listing 12.1 is remarkably simple. It does two things. First, it uses the **<body background=>** tag to load an image as Web-page wallpaper. The image is tiled so that it completely fills the Web page. The image itself is shown in Figure 12.3.

Your wallpaper shouldn't be too "busy."
Remember that people aren't visiting your Web page to look at the wallpaper. If your wallpaper has too many different colors or images, then it will be hard for people to read the text in the foreground of your Web page. Thus, scenes of astronauts or rock stars, interesting as they are, make very bad wallpaper. Solid colors, weave patterns, and other innocuous images make the best wallpaper.

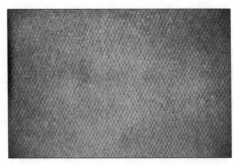

Figure 12.3 Background image for Web-page wallpaper.

Notice that the file name loaded into the **background** property needs to be in quotes. If the image file is in the same directory as the Web page, you can simply use the file name, as I did in Listing 12.1. If the image file is in a different location, you need to include the complete directory path with the file name.

Second, the HTML code sets up a table and uses the **<img src=>** tag to load a photo of a car into each cell of the table. As with the **<body>** tag's **background** property, you enclose the image file name in quotes and, if needed, give the full directory path of the file.

Playing Video With HTML

The HTML <IMG> tag is more powerful than you might expect. Not only does it allow you to display static images, but it also enables you to display video clips or virtual-reality simulations. The display isn't as flexible as what you get with ActiveX—as we'll see in the next part of the chapter—but it does work very well. Listing 12.2 shows the HTML code for a Web page that plays a video (AVI) clip, while Figure 12.4 shows the Web page that the HTML code creates. The video clip shown in the figure is from the movie *Eraser*, downloaded from the CompuServe ShowbizMedia Forum.

Listing 12.2   HTML code that plays a video clip.

```
<HTML>
<HEAD>
<TITLE>HTML Video Tag Demonstration</TITLE>
</HEAD>
<BODY>
<br><br><br>
<center>

<img dynsrc="eraser03.avi" start="mouseover">

<br><br>

<font size="5">
<p>This page demonstrates how you can embed video in your Web
pages even without using ActiveX controls. The HTML <img> tag has
a property called "dynsrc" that lets you specify a video clip or
VRML world to play. The "start" property lets you specify when
you want the video or virtual reality to start playing. In this
case, we set the start property so that the video would begin
when the user moved the mouse over the image control.</p>

</center>
```

```
</BODY>
</HTML>
```

The video doesn't play when the Web page first loads—only when the user passes the mouse pointer over the control. The relevant line of code is as follows:

```
<img dynsrc="eraser03.avi" start="mouseover">
```

In this **<img>** tag, we've used two new properties designed for handling video, virtual-reality simulations, and other "dynamic" images:

☆ **dynsrc.** This stands for "dynamic source," and is to video clips what **src** is to static images. To load a video clip, animation, or virtual-reality world, you just assign the file name (and directory path, if needed) to the **dynsrc** property of the **<img>** tag.

☆ **start.** This determines when the video clip (etc.) should begin to play. The default value is "fileopen," which causes the video to begin as soon as

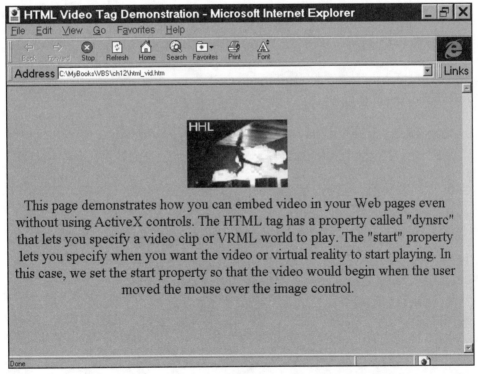

Figure 12.4 The HTML <IMG> tag can display video clips. The clip shown is from the movie Eraser, copyright 1996 by Warner Brothers.

the Web page and video file have finished loading. In Listing 12.2, we used the other possible value, "mouseover," which starts the video when the user passes the mouse pointer over the control on the Web page.

Playing Video With ActiveX

Just as with static images, ActiveX gives you a more flexible and powerful way to display video clips, animations, or virtual-reality worlds. Microsoft's ActiveMovie control (which you can download from http://www.microsoft.com) lets a user of your Web page:

- ☆ Start the video clip
- ☆ Stop the video clip
- ☆ Back up to a certain point in the video clip
- ☆ See the total length of the clip and the current time elapsed

It also lets you, the programmer, choose the size, position, and other features of the video display. Listing 12.3 shows the HTML code for a Web page that contains an ActiveX layout with the ActiveMovie control; Listing 12.4 shows the layout itself. Figure 12.5 shows the Web page with the video clip running. The video clip is from the movie *Eraser* and was downloaded from the CompuServe ShowbizMedia Forum.

Listing 12.3   HTML code for the Web page with the ActiveX layout.

```
<HTML>
<HEAD>
<TITLE>ActiveX Video Demonstration</TITLE>
</HEAD>
<BODY>

<OBJECT CLASSID="CLSID:812AE312-8B8E-11CF-93C8-00AA00C08FDF"
  ID="video01_alx" STYLE="LEFT:0;TOP:0">
<PARAM NAME="ALXPATH" REF
  VALUE="file:C:\MyBooks\VBS\ch12\video01.alx">
 </OBJECT>

</BODY>
</HTML>
```

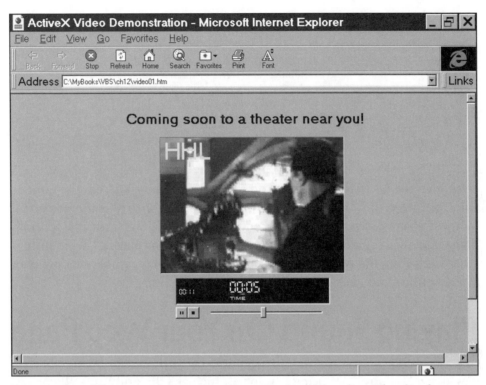

Figure 12.5 The ActiveMovie control can display video clips. The clip shown is from the movie Eraser, copyright 1996 by Warner Brothers.

Listing 12.4 ActiveX layout with the ActiveMovie control.

```
<DIV ID="Layout1" STYLE="LAYOUT:FIXED;WIDTH:597pt;HEIGHT:370pt;">

    <OBJECT ID="Label1"
     CLASSID="CLSID:978C9E23-D4B0-11CE-BF2D-00AA003F40D0"
     STYLE="TOP:8pt;LEFT:140pt;WIDTH:314pt;HEIGHT:25pt;ZINDEX:0;">
        <PARAM NAME="Caption"
          VALUE="Coming soon to a theater near you!">
        <PARAM NAME="Size" VALUE="11077;882">
        <PARAM NAME="FontEffects" VALUE="1073741825">
        <PARAM NAME="FontHeight" VALUE="360">
        <PARAM NAME="FontCharSet" VALUE="0">
        <PARAM NAME="FontPitchAndFamily" VALUE="2">
        <PARAM NAME="FontWeight" VALUE="700">
    </OBJECT>

    <OBJECT ID="ActiveMovie1"
     CLASSID="CLSID:05589FA1-C356-11CE-BF01-00AA0055595A"
     STYLE="TOP:41pt;LEFT:182pt;WIDTH:237pt;
     HEIGHT:229pt;TABINDEX:1;ZINDEX:1;">
```

```
        <PARAM NAME="_ExtentX" VALUE="8361">
        <PARAM NAME="_ExtentY" VALUE="8070">
        <PARAM NAME="MovieWindowSize" VALUE="1">
        <PARAM NAME="MovieWindowWidth" VALUE="312">
        <PARAM NAME="MovieWindowHeight" VALUE="224">
        <PARAM NAME="FileName"
          VALUE="c:\mybooks\vbs\ch12\eraser03.avi">
        <PARAM NAME="Volume" VALUE="-1185">
        <PARAM NAME="Balance" VALUE="0">
    </OBJECT>
</DIV>
```

Setting up the ActiveMovie control on an ActiveX layout proceeds the same as with the image control. The main thing you need to specify is the name and location of the video clip file: You enter this information into the control's **filename** property. Beyond that, you can make the movie playback window bigger by adjusting the **MovieWindowSize** property—making the window two, three, or four times the original size of the video clip image.

Playing Sound On Your Web Page

As far as sound and music go, ActiveX controls are still in their infancy. Several new ActiveX controls are being developed, such as DFL Software's "Light Lib Multimedia Sound" control. But the mainstay of your Web page sound and music, at least for the present, is likely to be—yes, you guessed it—HTML. The HTML <BGSOUND> tag lets you play background sound effects, spoken words, and music on your Web page.

Let's look at two simple examples. The first example will use <BGSOUND> to play a WAV file. The one I've chosen is a snippet of dialogue from the old *Dragnet* television series that I downloaded from the Web. You'll have to get your own WAV file to play, however, since I don't want to spend the next five years in court with the producers of *Dragnet*. The HTML code is shown in Listing 12.5.

Listing 12.5   Using <BGSOUND> to play a simple WAV file.

```
<HTML>
<HEAD>
<TITLE>Playing A Simple WAV Sound File</TITLE>
</HEAD>
<BODY>
<H1>Sgt. Friday speaks out on the dangers of marijuana</H1>
<bgsound src="harmless.wav">
</BODY>
</HTML>
```

There's really nothing to see, so we'll skip the usual figure showing the Web page. And since you can't *hear* the Web page talking from this book, you'll have to take it on faith that Sgt. Friday is really saying, "Marijuana is harmless."

As with the **<img>** tag, you use the **src** property to specify the name of the file you want to play—adding the directory path if the file isn't in the same directory as your Web page.

The **<bgsound>** tag can also be used to play MIDI music files, as shown in Listing 12.6.

Listing 12.6   Using **<bgsound>** to play a MIDI file.

```
<HTML>
<HEAD>
<TITLE>Playing A Simple MIDI File</TITLE>
</HEAD>
<BODY>
<p>This plays the CANYON.MID sound file that comes with Windows 95.
<bgsound src="canyon.mid">
</BODY>
</HTML>
```

One other property of the **<img>** tag that you will probably want to use is the **loop** property. This property lets you specify how many times the sound file should be played. For example,

```
<bgsound src="harmless.wav" loop=5>
```

will make the indefatigable Sgt. Friday say, "Marijuana is harmless," five times.

If you're playing a music file, you might want the music to play continuously as long as the user is viewing your Web page. To do that, you set the **loop** property either to **infinite** or to **–1**, as in the following:

```
<bgsound src="bach02.mid" loop="-1">
```

In either case, adding sound and music will add a *lot* of interest to your Web page.

XIII

A VBScript and ActiveX FAQ

Still have a question
about VBScript or
ActiveX? Here's
where you might find
the answer.

"F AQ" stands for "Frequently-Asked Questions." It's a list of questions and problems that come up over and over. In this chapter, you'll get answers to some of the questions that have been bugging VBScript users, but which haven't been answered in previous chapters. If you have additional questions you'd like answered in the next edition of this book, send them in!

Q: What's the difference between Visual Basic Script and Visual Basic?

A: Visual Basic Script is a subset of Visual Basic. It's designed to work inside a Web browser and work smoothly with HTML objects and controls. Because of this, it lacks the file I/O and some other advanced features offered by the Visual Basic language.

Q: My Web page loads too slowly. How can I speed it up?

A: Other than data transfer rates over the Web—which you can't do anything about—the most common reason for slow loading is that the Web page has too many images or the image files are too big. Try (a) cutting down on the number of images, (b) reducing the size of the images themselves, and (c) reducing the number of colors in the image files. Any or all of those moves should considerably improve your loading time.

Q: Can I combine VBScript and JavaScript on the same Web page?

A: Yes. Just make sure that you use <SCRIPT LANGUAGE=""> and </SCRIPT> tags to enclose each separate block of script code. The **language** property is very important. If you have multiple <SCRIPT>...</SCRIPT> blocks in your HTML document and do *not* specify the language for each block, then Internet Explorer assumes by default that the *first* script language you used in the document is the only one you're using. Each time you start a new <SCRIPT> block, you must specify which script language you're using.

Q: Can I do file I/O operations in VBScript?

A: No. For reasons of Web security, VBScript doesn't support any file I/O operations.

Q: How can I get the value of an HTML radio button and use it in VBScript code?

A: Just use the Internet Explorer scripting object model to guide how you refer to the radio button in VBScript. If the radio button is in an HTML form, preface the button name with the form name; if that doesn't work, try adding

document before the form name. This feature was a little rocky in the beta version of Internet Explorer 3.0, but should be working in the production version.

Q: How can I access HTML controls from within an ActiveX layout and vice versa?

A: As before, use the Internet Explorer scripting object model to guide how you refer to controls in the HTML document and the ActiveX layout. Remember that an ActiveX layout has a name, just like an ActiveX control has a name, or an HTML form can have a name. To refer to controls in an ActiveX layout from your HTML document, preface each control name with the name of the layout. To refer to controls in your HTML document from within the ActiveX layout, preface the control names with **window.document.** and any other object names that are needed to locate the controls.

This same procedure, by the way, enables you to call subs and functions between HTML documents and ActiveX layouts. Just preface the name of the sub or function with the name of the object in which it resides.

Q: How can I make my Web page play a greeting based on the time of day?

A: Use the VBScript **hour()** function to identify the current system time. Then use an **if...then...else** statement to control which greeting is played for the user. For example:

```
dim Greeting
dim h

h=hour(now)

if h < 12 then
    Greeting = "sound1.wav"
else
    Greeting = "sound2.wav"
end if
document.write "<bgsound src=" & Greeting & ">"
```

Q: How can I debug my VBScript code in Visual Basic 4?

A: It's not totally simple, but you can do it. Remember that much of VBScript code is engine code and has nothing particular to do with the Web. That code, you can debug in Visual Basic 4 almost without change. As for code that refers to HTML controls, you can include HTML controls in your Visual Basic 4 Toolbox by opening the Tools menu, selecting Custom Controls, and checking the box for *Microsoft Intrinsic HTML Controls.*

If you've created code in Visual Basic 4, take the word **private** out of sub and function headings, because that isn't used in VBScript. Remember that VBScript has only one data type, so you need to remove the type references to any variable declarations or sub/function parameters. Finally, remember that VBScript doesn't support **Initialize** or **Terminate** events. Instead, you can use the **onLoad** events of the Web page window or the ActiveX layout. If you stay alert for those differences between VBScript and Visual Basic 4, you should have few problems debugging—or even developing—VBScript code in Visual Basic 4.

Q: Can I play a WAV file when the user clicks on the Web page, but without using an ActiveX control?

A: Yes. Just embed the name of the WAV file in a hyperlink reference, as in the following code:

```
<a href="harmless.wav">Click this to hear something interesting.</a>
```

Q: How can I create a scrolling text marquee?

A: Use either the ActiveX Marquee control, included with the ActiveX Control Pad, or use the HTML **<marquee>** tag.

Q: How can I make an ActiveX layout initialize its controls and then make them perform actions?

A: Remember that, just like the **window** object in the Internet Explorer scripting object model, an ActiveX layout has an **onLoad** event. You can put code in that event to initialize any controls in the layout and, once they're initialized, to make them do things.

XIV

A Wizardly Web Game

Ready to stretch your VBScript abilities? In this chapter, you'll create a humorous Web game that uses almost all the wizardly tricks you've learned so far.

You've learned a lot in the previous 13 chapters. You've learned about the VBScript language, and how to use it with HTML and ActiveX controls. You've learned how to use the ActiveX Control Pad, and how it can help you create event code for the controls on a Web page. And you've learned some fairly neat tricks with VBScript and ActiveX controls.

Now, it's time to put all that knowledge together in a full-scale VBScript game for the Web. The game we'll develop is called "Sex C.P.A." Its ostensible purpose is to tell the player how much money he or she should spend on a date with a particular person. Its real purpose, of course, is somewhat different—to poke fun at male and female stereotypes and the bizarre rituals of dating in the 1990s.

Apart from its content, there's another reason why this game is a good way to learn about real-world VBScript: It shows how you can move a game from one programming platform to another. I originally developed Sex C.P.A. in 1984, using Microsoft Basic for the CP/M operating system—that's before you were born, kids. When IBM-style PCs overwhelmed the rest of the microcomputer world, I ported the game to GW-Basic, a version of Basic that came with Microsoft's operating system and was supposedly named after Greg Whitten (the "GW"), who was one of the company's software gurus at the time.

A few years later, I ported the game again, this time to Microsoft's QuickBasic, a compiled Basic language for MS-DOS PCs. When Windows superseded MS-DOS as the most popular operating system, I ported the game yet *again,* this time to Microsoft's Visual Basic.

And now, here we are in 1996, with the Web overshadowing everything else in the computer industry. We are porting Sex C.P.A. one last time—to VBScript— so that it will run on the Web. If anyone a few years from now wants to run Sex C.P.A. on his holographic nuclear-powered pocket technological whatsis, I leave it to you and other ingenious readers to perform the update.

General Game Concepts And Design

The basic structure of the game is pretty simple. The player is asked for the sex and name of the prospective date. After entering that information, the player answers a series of questions about that person: Different question lists are used for male and female dates.

Get tricky and expand your audience.
The first version of the game only allowed males to evaluate female dates. Some of my women friends complained about that inequity, so with their advice on what questions and answers to include, I added a module allowing women to evaluate male dates. But that still left one problem: how to avoid excluding gay men and lesbians from playing the game. Given that they make up only 10 percent of the potential audience for the game, adding two more quiz modules (one for gay men, one for lesbians) seemed like overkill.

The solution was surprisingly simple. The original version of the game asked for the sex of the player, assuming that male players would evaluate female dates and vice versa. The current, non-discriminatory version of the game asks for the sex of the date, thereby—at least in principle—allowing everyone to play the game.

Once all the questions are answered, the player is given the choice of either reviewing his/her answers or letting Sex C.P.A. calculate how much money should be spent on the date, at which point, the game is over. When the game is up and running, it will look like Figure 14.1. The "production" version of the game includes an R-rated game module, but we can't show that in a book meant to be read by the whole family.

Laying Out The Game In The ActiveX Control Pad

Our first job, of course, is to create the game window layout in the ActiveX Control Pad. To do that, we'll use the following ActiveX controls:

☆ One big label control to display game questions and explanatory text.

☆ One smaller text box control to display the player's answers. This is a text box instead of a label because, for at least one question (the name of the prospective date), the player must type the answer directly into the control window.

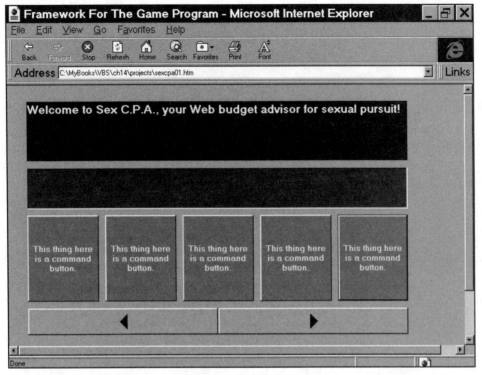

Figure 14.1 The Sex C.P.A. game, ready to play.

☆ Five command buttons, each of which will display a possible answer to the current game question.

☆ A SpinButton control that allows the player to move forward and backward in the question list.

☆ A timer control that presents a "slide show" to explain how the game works.

If you want to follow along as we assemble the game layout, start up the ActiveX Control Pad and join in. Otherwise, you can simply imbibe the ideas presented and use them to create your own games later on.

Setting Up The Game Controls

The question window, as noted previously, is a simple label control: All it does is display text. There's not much remarkable about it: black **backcolor**, yellow **forecolor**, adjust the font and type size so that it's to your liking and all the text can fit in the window. Name the control *LblTheQuestion*—that value should be in its **ID** property.

The answer window is a text box control and is equally unremarkable. You should assign the name **TBCurrentAnswer** to the control's **ID** property.

One thing that's kind of interesting about the text box is that when we arrive at the question asking for the name of the date, we'll call the control's **setfocus** method to position the text cursor inside the text box. When the user starts to type, the text will automatically go where it should.

Avoid the right and bottom edges of the layout. It's still a little unpredictable how much of your ActiveX layout will be displayed in the user's Web browser: Sometimes, the right and bottom edges will be clipped off just a little. For that reason, it's a good idea to allow plenty of distance between your ActiveX controls and those edges of the layout. A control that is too close to one of the edges might be obscured when the user displays your Web page.

The answer buttons are a bit more unusual. They're command buttons, but instead of using the same old drab gray and standard shape, we're making them blue and bigger. Because all the command buttons will have to display multiple lines of text (the possible answers to each question), set all their **wordwrap** properties to **true**. Set the **backcolor** property to blue and the **forecolor** property to yellow. If you have another color scheme that you prefer, use it instead. Give each command button an **ID** property that indicates the answer it displays, such as **CmdAnswer1**, **CmdAnswer2**, and so on.

The SpinButton control should be positioned as a long, horizontal rectangle underneath the command buttons, as shown in Figure 14.2. Its default properties will do just fine, inasmuch as there's only one SpinButton control on the layout.

Adding A Timer Control

The timer control is a little more involved, if only because in the beta 2 version of the ActiveX Control Pad, the timer control wasn't included in the toolbox.

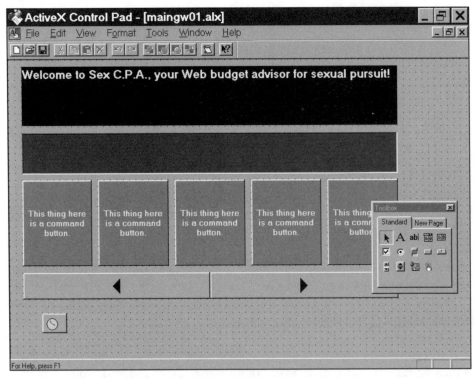

Figure 14.2 The ActiveX layout with all the controls in position.

However, the timer control—called "IETimer," if you want to get formal about it—is included with Microsoft's Internet Explorer Web browser. If you have Internet Explorer, you can easily add the timer control to the ActiveX Control Pad toolbox by following these steps:

1. In the ActiveX Control Pad, right-click on a page in the toolbox.
   A pop-up menu will appear.
2. In the menu, select Additional Controls.
   The Additional Controls dialog box will appear, as shown in Figure 14.3.
3. In the controls list, select the checkbox next to "Timer Object."
4. Click on OK.
   The timer control will appear in the ActiveX Control Pad toolbox.

Now that you've got the timer control, simply drop it on any empty area in the ActiveX layout. It won't be visible when the Web page is displayed. The only timer control property you really need to change is the **interval** property, whose

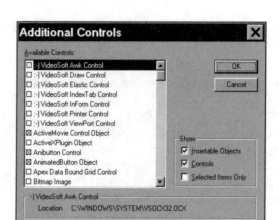

Figure 14.3   The Additional Controls dialog box.

default value is 0. The **interval** property determines how many milliseconds (thousandths of a second) elapse between each tick of the timer. If you set it to 1000, then the timer event will fire once a second; an **interval** value of 2500 means it will fire every two-and-a-half seconds, and so on.

For this game, the timer will display a slide show in the question window. Each slide will explain a different aspect of how the game is played. To give players enough time to read the text, I'd suggest an **interval** value of 4000. Much less than that, and players won't have enough time; much more than that, and the slide show will take too long.

Once you've created the layout, save it in its own directory under some descriptive name: I chose **maingw01.alx**, for "main game window, version 1." To load it into a Web browser, you should also create a containing HTML document, which should be old stuff for you by now.

Creating A Code Framework

Once you've created the ActiveX layout, it's time to write the VBScript code that actually runs the game. Listing 14.1 shows the basic framework of the game code so you can see the "big picture" without getting involved in the details just yet.

Listing 14.1   Basic VBScript code framework for Sex C.P.A.

```
<SCRIPT LANGUAGE="VBScript">
<!--
' This version of the program sets up the main framework for
```

```
' the controls and events on the ActiveX layout. Some "extra"
' code features are included that show how the program can be
' enhanced or expanded.

' arrays to hold game questions
dim MQ(10,8)
dim FQ(10,8)

' array to hold game answers
dim QuizAnswers(10)


dim MaxQ, MaxScore
dim FunScore, DatePercent, HowMuch
dim YesNo
dim LoopCounter
dim QuestionNum
dim GotAnswerNum
dim DateIsMale
dim timertick

dim HeShe, HisHer, HimHer, GuyGirl
dim NL ' variable for line break
dim Question, Ans1, Ans2, Ans3, Ans4, Ans5, AnsYN, AnsTyped
Question = 0
Ans1 = 1
Ans2 = 2
Ans3 = 3
Ans4 = 4
Ans5 = 5
AnsYN = 6
AnsTyped = 7

NL = chr(13)
FunScore = 0

' Initialize the QuizAnswers array slots.
for LoopCounter = 0 to 9
   QuizAnswers(LoopCounter) = ""
next

sub DoScoring
end sub

sub DisplayQuestion(QN)
end sub


sub NextQuestion(QN)
end sub
```

```
sub PrevQuestion(QN)
end sub

Sub Layout1_OnLoad()
end sub

Sub SpinButton1_SpinUp()
end sub

Sub SpinButton1_SpinDown()
end sub

Sub CmdAnswer5_Click()
end sub

Sub CmdAnswer4_Click()
end sub

Sub CmdAnswer3_Click()
end sub

Sub CmdAnswer2_Click()
end sub

Sub CmdAnswer1_Click()
end sub

Sub IeTimer1_Timer()
end sub

-->
</script>
```

Storing The Game Data

The VBScript code has the usual event subs associated with the controls in the ActiveX layout—including an event sub for the layout itself that will perform setup work when the game page loads. Once the game is being played, however, we need several places to keep data:

☆ Arrays to hold the question lists for the "male" and "female" versions of the game

☆ An array to hold the player's answers to the quiz questions

☆ A variable to hold the "score" for the prospective date

Let's see how these and other aspects of data storage are implemented in the VBScript code.

The first task is to create two arrays to store the questions for the male and female versions of the quiz. That's done by the following code lines:

```
dim MQ(10,8)
dim FQ(10,8)
```

These code lines set up two 10×8-slot arrays. Now, hardly anyone hates using multi-dimensional arrays more than I do. They're messy, they're error-prone, and they're an all-around pain in the rumpus room. But in this case, there's really no choice. For each question, we need to be able to store eight items of information:

☆ The question itself

☆ Each of the five possible answers to the question

☆ A control value indicating whether or not the question is a "yes/no" question

☆ A control value indicating whether or not the player must *type* the answer in the text box instead of clicking on a command button

In the QuickBasic and Visual Basic versions of the game, this was handled with a **type...end type** statement, as follows:

```
Type QARecord
    Question As String * 100
    Answer1 As String * 100
    Answer2 As String * 100
    Answer3 As String * 100
    Answer4 As String * 100
    Answer5 As String * 100
    YesNoAnswer As Integer
    TypedAnswer As Integer
End Type
```

Instead of using a multi-dimensional array, the Visual Basic code used an array of records. Each record held all the data for a particular question.

Sadly, VBScript doesn't include the **type...end type** statement, so you can't create user-defined types. The most sensible alternative is the one used here: an array of arrays. There are 10 rows in the array—one row for each question in the quiz. Each row has eight slots, enough to hold all the data for a particular question. And of course, VBScript only has the **variant** data type as an official type, so there are no type qualifiers added here.

Using an array in this manner lets us make our code more economical later on. Instead of having separate lines of code to load each question, we just use the same code to load all the questions. A control variable tells the code which question should be loaded at a specific time.

A simpler, one-dimensional array called **QuizAnswers** holds the player's answers to the questions in the quiz. The array slot that gets a particular answer is determined by the current value of the **QuestionNum** variable.

After setting up the arrays, we define and initialize a laundry-list of control variables, from **FunScore** to **TimerTick**. Some of these indicate ways that the code can be enhanced, such as using the **HeShe**, **HisHer**, **HimHer**, and **GuyGirl** variables to hold appropriate male or female pronouns for a particular session: That lets you use just one set of text strings for both male and female dates, as long as you substitute the appropriate variables for gender-specific pronouns.

Building The Complete Game Engine

Now that you've seen the "big picture," let's plunge into the details. Listing 14.2 shows the HTML containing document for the ActiveX game layout. Listing 14.3 shows the VBScript and ActiveX layout code for the full, working version of the game. As in earlier chapters, we've often had to use the Visual Basic line continuation character (_) to make the code lines fit into the page margins of this book. You don't have to use them unless you want to.

In the case of the **<object>** tags, there's one instance (the welcome message displayed in the label control) in which the line break printed in the book made the text indent oddly on the PC screen. If you include all the book's line breaks and that happens, simply remove the offending line break from your code.

Listing 14.2   HTML code to contain the ActiveX game layout.

```
<HTML>
<HEAD>
<TITLE>Sex C.P.A., Your Web Budget Advisor
   For Sexual Pursuit</TITLE>
</HEAD>
<BODY>
```

```
<OBJECT CLASSID="CLSID:812AE312-8B8E-11CF-93C8-00AA00C08FDF"
   ID="maingw14_alx" STYLE="LEFT:0;TOP:0">
<PARAM NAME="ALXPATH" REF VALUE="file:C:\game_sex\maingw14.alx">
 </OBJECT>

</BODY>
</HTML>
```

Listing 14.3   VBScript and ActiveX layout code for the game.

```
<SCRIPT LANGUAGE="VBScript">
<!--
' arrays to hold game questions
dim MQ(10,8)
dim FQ(10,8)

' array to hold game answers
dim QuizAnswers(10)

dim MaxQ, MaxScore
dim FunScore, DatePercent, HowMuch
dim YesNo
dim LoopCounter
dim QuestionNum
dim GotAnswerNum
dim DateIsMale
dim timertick

dim HeShe, HisHer, HimHer, GuyGirl
dim NL ' variable for line break

' Declare and initialize constants for array slots
dim Question, Ans1, Ans2, Ans3, Ans4, Ans5, AnsYN, AnsTyped
Question = 0
Ans1 = 1
Ans2 = 2
Ans3 = 3
Ans4 = 4
Ans5 = 5
AnsYN = 6
AnsTyped = 7

' Initialize constant for new line character
NL = chr(13)
FunScore = 0

' Initialize the QuizAnswers array slots.
for LoopCounter = 0 to 9
   QuizAnswers(LoopCounter) = ""
next
```

```
' Sub to calculate score based on answers
sub DoScoring

    dim AgeScore
    dim CurrentScore
    AgeScore = Left( QuizAnswers(1), 1)

    for LoopCounter = 2 to 9
        CurrentScore = Left( QuizAnswers(LoopCounter), 1)
        FunScore = FunScore + CurrentScore
    next

    if DateIsMale then
        select case AgeScore
        case "1"
            FunScore = FunScore + 2
        case "2"
            FunScore = FunScore + 4
        case "3"
            FunScore = FunScore + 5
        case "4"
            FunScore = FunScore + 4
        case "5"
            FunScore = FunScore + 3
        end select
    else
        select case AgeScore
        case "1"
            FunScore = FunScore + 4
        case "2"
            FunScore = FunScore + 5
        case "3"
            FunScore = FunScore + 4
        case "4"
            FunScore = FunScore + 3
        case "5"
            FunScore = FunScore + 2
        end select
    end if

    if Left( QuizAnswers(6), 1) = "1" then
        FunScore = FunScore + 4
    end if

    if Left( QuizAnswers(7), 1) = "1" then
        FunScore = FunScore + 4
    end if

    if Left( QuizAnswers(9), 1) = "1" then
        FunScore = FunScore + 4
    end if
```

```
        HowMuch = FunScore * 2

        MsgBox "Your date got " & FunScore & _
            " out of a possible 45 points.",,"Sex C.P.A."
        MsgBox "As your Sex C.P.A., I recommend that you spend $" _
            & HowMuch & " per date with " & QuizAnswers(0) & ".",, _
            "Sex C.P.A."
end sub


sub DisplayQuestion(QN)

    If DateIsMale then
        LblTheQuestion.caption = FQ(QN, Question)

        ' When we start using the array to hold answers
        ' to previously-answered questions, then the value
        ' in TBCurrentAnswer will be loaded from that array.
        TBCurrentAnswer = ""

        CmdAnswer1.caption = FQ(QN, Ans1)
        CmdAnswer2.caption = FQ(QN, Ans2)
        CmdAnswer3.caption = FQ(QN, Ans3)
        CmdAnswer4.caption = FQ(QN, Ans4)
        CmdAnswer5.caption = FQ(QN, Ans5)
    else
        LblTheQuestion.caption = MQ(QN, Question)

        ' When we start using the array to hold answers
        ' to previously-answered questions, then the value
        ' in TBCurrentAnswer will be loaded from that array.
        TBCurrentAnswer = ""

        CmdAnswer1.caption = MQ(QN, Ans1)
        CmdAnswer2.caption = MQ(QN, Ans2)
        CmdAnswer3.caption = MQ(QN, Ans3)
        CmdAnswer4.caption = MQ(QN, Ans4)
        CmdAnswer5.caption = MQ(QN, Ans5)
    end if

end sub


sub NextQuestion(QN)
    Select Case QN
    case -1
        If TBCurrentAnswer.text = "Male" then
            DateIsMale = true
        else
            DateIsMale = false
        end if
```

```
   TBCurrentAnswer.text = ""

   CmdAnswer1.caption = ""
   CmdAnswer2.caption = ""

   TBCurrentAnswer.setfocus
   if DateIsMale then
      LblTheQuestion = FQ(0,Question)

   else
      LblTheQuestion = MQ(0, Question)
   end if
case 0
   QuizAnswers(0) = TBCurrentAnswer.text
   DisplayQuestion 1
case 1
   DisplayQuestion 2
case 2
   DisplayQuestion 3
case 3
   DisplayQuestion 4
case 4
   DisplayQuestion 5
case 5
   DisplayQuestion 6
case 6
   DisplayQuestion 7
case 7
   DisplayQuestion 8
case 8
   DisplayQuestion 9
case 9
   YesNo = msgbox( _
      "That's the end of the quiz." & _
      "Would you like to see your date's score?", _
      4,"Sex C.P.A.")

    if YesNo = 6 then
      DoScoring
    end if

End Select

if QuestionNum < 9 then
   QuestionNum = QuestionNum + 1
end if

end sub


sub PrevQuestion(QN)
   Select Case QN
```

```
      case 0
         MsgBox "This is the first question. There aren't any before this."
      case 1
         DisplayQuestion 0
      case 2
         DisplayQuestion 1
      case 3
         DisplayQuestion 2
      case 4
         DisplayQuestion 3
      case 5
         DisplayQuestion 4
      case 6
         DisplayQuestion 5
      case 7
         DisplayQuestion 7
      case 8
         DisplayQuestion 7
      case 9
         DisplayQuestion 8
      case else
         DisplayQuestion 0
      End Select

      if QN > 0 then
         QuestionNum = QuestionNum -1
      end if

end sub


Sub Layout1_OnLoad()

   QuestionNum = -1
   MQ(0, Question) = "In the box, type the name of the girl, " & _
      "then click the Accept button."
   MQ(0, Ans1) = ""
   MQ(0, Ans2) = ""
   MQ(0, Ans3) = ""
   MQ(0, Ans4) = ""
   MQ(0, Ans5) = ""
   MQ(0, AnsYN) = "False"
   MQ(0, AnsTyped) = "True"

   MQ(1, Question) = "How old is she?"
   MQ(1, Ans1) = "1" & NL & "A real teeny-bopper! " & _
      "So young, she's illegal in 41 states."
   MQ(1, Ans2) = "2" & NL & "A little younger than me, " & _
      "but old enough to know what handcuffs are for."
   MQ(1, Ans3) = "3" & NL & "About the same age as me, " & _
      "but willing to date me, anyway."
```

```
MQ(1, Ans4) = "4" & NL & "A little older than me, " & _
    "but in shape and can hold her liquor (darn!)."
MQ(1, Ans5) = "5" & NL & "A lot older than me. " & _
    "But it's not an Oedipal thing. Honest!"
MQ(1, AnsYN) = "False"
MQ(1, AnsTyped) = "False"

MQ(2, Question) = "How would you rate her looks, " & _
    "from 1 (yucky) to 5 (totally hot)?"
MQ(2, Ans1) = "1" & NL & "Gag me with a fork! " & _
    "Someone get that geek out of here!"
MQ(2, Ans2) = "2" & NL & "Not bad, though in no danger " & _
    "of being mistaken for someone good-looking."
MQ(2, Ans3) = "3" & NL & "Okay-looking. " & _
    "I wouldn't be ashamed if people saw us together."
MQ(2, Ans4) = "4" & NL & "Very nice-looking. This could " & _
    "be the start of a beautiful three-day relationship."
MQ(2, Ans5) = "5" & NL & "WOW! This girl is " & _
    "absolutely awesome! I want her!"
MQ(2, AnsYN) = "False"
MQ(2, AnsTyped) = "False"

MQ(3, Question) = "How would you rate her personality, " & _
    "from 1 (raised by wolves) to 5 (fun city)?"
MQ(3, Ans1) = "1" & NL & "So obnoxious, she'd be " & _
    "unattractive even if she looked like Kellie Martin."
MQ(3, Ans2) = "2" & NL & "Seems to know which fork to " & _
    "use, but not much more than that."
MQ(3, Ans3) = "3" & NL & "About average. Prefers rap " & _
    "to Rachmaninoff, but okay."
MQ(3, Ans4) = "4" & NL & "Pretty nice. I might even " & _
    "pick up the check for dinner!"
MQ(3, Ans5) = "5" & NL & "So sweet that she's fun " & _
    "even WITHOUT sex!"
MQ(3, AnsYN) = "False"
MQ(3, AnsTyped) = "False"

MQ(4, Question) = "How would you rate her mind, from 1 " & _
    "(bimbo city) to 5 (Mayim Bialik)?"
MQ(4, Ans1) = "1" & NL & "DUH! Like, AS IF she " & _
    "could even find the mall without help!"
MQ(4, Ans2) = "2" & NL & "The finest fruit of public " & _
    "education. Has a condom in her purse, but can't " & _
    "read the label."
MQ(4, Ans3) = "3" & NL & "With six months' training, " & _
    "could qualify for a good McJob."
MQ(4, Ans4) = "4" & NL & "Reasonably bright. Knows " & _
    "more MTV than Milton, but okay."
MQ(4, Ans5) = "5" & NL & "Can discuss anything " & _
    "from classical music to quantum physics."
MQ(4, AnsYN) = "False"
MQ(4, AnsTyped) = "False"
```

```
MQ(5, Question) = "How compatible is she with you?"
MQ(5, Ans1) = "1" & NL & "Between spending time with " & _
    "her or a rabid wolverine, I'd pick her."
MQ(5, Ans2) = "2" & NL & "I could stand being around " & _
    "her for a while, as long as she didn't talk."
MQ(5, Ans3) = "3" & NL & "Unobjectionable. She says " & _
    """to-may-to"" to my ""to-mah-to"", but who cares?"
MQ(5, Ans4) = "4" & NL & "We fit together pretty well. " & _
    "Lots better than Bill and Hillary."
MQ(5, Ans5) = "5" & NL & "Any time I'm not with her " & _
    "is wasted time."
MQ(5, AnsYN) = "False"
MQ(5, AnsTyped) = "False"

MQ(6, Question) = "Does she kiss on the first date?"
MQ(6, Ans1) = "1" & NL & "Yes"
MQ(6, Ans2) = "2" & NL & "No"
MQ(6, Ans3) = ""
MQ(6, Ans4) = ""
MQ(6, Ans5) = ""
MQ(6, AnsYN) = "True"
MQ(6, AnsTyped) = "False"

MQ(7, Question) = "A French kiss?"
MQ(7, Ans1) = "1" & NL & "Yes, with dueling " & _
    "tongues all over the place."
MQ(7, Ans2) = "2" & NL & "No, it's more like " & _
    "kissing your sister."
MQ(7, Ans3) = ""
MQ(7, Ans4) = ""
MQ(7, Ans5) = ""
MQ(7, AnsYN) = "True"
MQ(7, AnsTyped) = "False"

MQ(8, Question) = "Is she rich? Rate her (and " & _
    "her family's) wealth."
MQ(8, Ans1) = "1" & NL & "She doesn't have a dime, " & _
    "but the welfare checks are a big help."
MQ(8, Ans2) = "2" & NL & "She works two jobs and makes " & _
    "almost enough to pay the rent."
MQ(8, Ans3) = "3" & NL & "She does okay. Works as a " & _
    "secretary and has her own (used) car."
MQ(8, Ans4) = "4" & NL & "She's got an MD from Stanford " & _
    "and a very comfortable Beverly Hills practice."
MQ(8, Ans5) = "5" & NL & "Bill Gates and Microsoft want " & _
    "to borrow money from her."
MQ(8, AnsYN) = "False"
MQ(8, AnsTyped) = "False"

MQ(9, Question) = "Realistically, will she EVER " & _
    """get horizontal"" with you?"
```

```
MQ(9, Ans1) = "1" & NL & "Yes, and it will be a deeply " & _
    "religious experience for both of us."
MQ(9, Ans2) = "2" & NL & "No, but what else is new? " & _
    "After my last time, the radio said that Nixon resigned."
MQ(9, Ans3) = ""
MQ(9, Ans4) = ""
MQ(9, Ans5) = ""
MQ(9, AnsYN) = "True"
MQ(9, AnsTyped) = "False"

FQ(0, Question) = "In the box, type the name of this " & _
    "guy, then click the Accept button."
FQ(0, Ans1) = ""
FQ(0, Ans2) = ""
FQ(0, Ans3) = ""
FQ(0, Ans4) = ""
FQ(0, Ans5) = ""
FQ(0, AnsYN) = "False"
FQ(0, AnsTyped) = "True"

FQ(1, Question) = "How old is he?"
FQ(1, Ans1) = "1" & NL & "A real teeny-bopper! " & _
    "So young, he's illegal in 41 states."
FQ(1, Ans2) = "2" & NL & "A little younger than me, but " & _
    "old enough to know what handcuffs are for."
FQ(1, Ans3) = "3" & NL & "About the same age as me, " & _
    "but willing to date me, anyway."
FQ(1, Ans4) = "4" & NL & "A little older than me, but " & _
    "in shape and can hold his liquor (darn!)."
FQ(1, Ans5) = "5" & NL & "A lot older than me. But it's " & _
    "not a father-figure thing. Honest!"
FQ(1, AnsYN) = "False"
FQ(1, AnsTyped) = "False"

FQ(2, Question) = "How would you rate his looks, from 1 " & _
    "(yucky) to 5 (totally hot)?"
FQ(2, Ans1) = "1" & NL & "Gag me with a fork! " & _
    "Someone get that geek out of here!"
FQ(2, Ans2) = "2" & NL & "Not bad, though in no danger " & _
    "of being mistaken for someone good-looking."
FQ(2, Ans3) = "3" & NL & "Okay-looking. I wouldn't " & _
    "be ashamed if people saw us together."
FQ(2, Ans4) = "4" & NL & "Very nice-looking. This could " & _
    "be the start of a beautiful three-day relationship."
FQ(2, Ans5) = "5" & NL & "WOW! This guy is absolutely " & _
    "awesome! I want him!"
FQ(2, AnsYN) = "False"
FQ(2, AnsTyped) = "False"

FQ(3, Question) = "How would you rate his personality, " & _
    "from 1 (raised by wolves) to 5 (fun city)?"
```

```
FQ(3, Ans1) = "1" & NL & "So obnoxious, he'd be " & _
    "unattractive even if he looked like David Duchovny."
FQ(3, Ans2) = "2" & NL & "Seems to know which fork to " & _
    "use, but not much more than that."
FQ(3, Ans3) = "3" & NL & "About average. Prefers rap to " & _
    "Rachmaninoff, but okay."
FQ(3, Ans4) = "4" & NL & "Pretty nice. I might even " & _
    "pick up the check for dinner!"
FQ(3, Ans5) = "5" & NL & "So sweet that he's fun even " & _
    "WITHOUT sex!"
FQ(3, AnsYN) = "False"
FQ(3, AnsTyped) = "False"

FQ(4, Question) = "How would you rate his mind, from 1 " & _
    "(steroid city) to 5 (Scott Palmer)?"
FQ(4, Ans1) = "1" & NL & "DUH! Like, AS IF he could " & _
    "even find the mall without help!"
FQ(4, Ans2) = "2" & NL & "The finest fruit of public " & _
    "education. Has a condom in his wallet, but can't " & _
    "read the label."
FQ(4, Ans3) = "3" & NL & "With six months' training, " & _
    "could qualify for a good McJob."
FQ(4, Ans4) = "4" & NL & "Reasonably bright. Knows more " & _
    "MTV than Milton, but okay."
FQ(4, Ans5) = "5" & NL & "Can discuss anything from " & _
    "classical music to quantum physics."
FQ(4, AnsYN) = "False"
FQ(4, AnsTyped) = "False"

FQ(5, Question) = "How compatible is he with you?"
FQ(5, Ans1) = "1" & NL & "Between spending time with " & _
    "him or a rabid wolverine, I'd pick him."
FQ(5, Ans2) = "2" & NL & "I could stand being around " & _
    "him for a while, as long as he didn't talk."
FQ(5, Ans3) = "3" & NL & "Okay. He says ""to-may-to"" " & _
    "to my ""to-mah-to"", but who cares?"
FQ(5, Ans4) = "4" & NL & "We fit together pretty well. " & _
    "Lots better than Bill and Hillary."
FQ(5, Ans5) = "5" & NL & "Any time I'm not with him " & _
    "is wasted time."
FQ(5, AnsYN) = "False"
FQ(5, AnsTyped) = "False"

FQ(6, Question) = "Does he ever suggest kinky stuff?"
FQ(6, Ans1) = "1" & NL & "Yes, but I'll get out my whips " & _
    "and give him a little surprise."
FQ(6, Ans2) = "2" & NL & "No, and I'd like to know " & _
    "why the heck not!"
FQ(6, Ans3) = ""
FQ(6, Ans4) = ""
FQ(6, Ans5) = ""
```

```
    FQ(6, AnsYN) = "True"
    FQ(6, AnsTyped) = "False"

    FQ(7, Question) = "Will he pay all the bills you ring up?"
    FQ(7, Ans1) = "1" & NL & "Yes. He'll complain, but as " & _
        "long as he pays, who cares?"
    FQ(7, Ans2) = "2" & NL & "No. And I think that's " & _
        "carrying sexual equality a little too far."
    FQ(7, Ans3) = ""
    FQ(7, Ans4) = ""
    FQ(7, Ans5) = ""
    FQ(7, AnsYN) = "True"
    FQ(7, AnsTyped) = "False"

    FQ(8, Question) = "Does he have good career and " & _
        "income prospects?"
    FQ(8, Ans1) = "1" & NL & "He blows his unemployment " & _
        "checks at the racetrack."
    FQ(8, Ans2) = "2" & NL & "He works two jobs and makes " & _
        "almost enough to pay the rent."
    FQ(8, Ans3) = "3" & NL & "He does okay. Works as a " & _
        "haircutter, so I'll get that free."
    FQ(8, Ans4) = "4" & NL & "He's got an MD from Stanford " & _
        "and a very comfortable Beverly Hills practice."
    FQ(8, Ans5) = "5" & NL & "Bill Gates and Microsoft want " & _
        "to borrow money from him."
    FQ(8, AnsYN) = "False"
    FQ(8, AnsTyped) = "False"

    FQ(9, Question) = "Realistically, will he EVER take you " & _
        "in his arms and ... you know ...?"
    FQ(9, Ans1) = "1" & NL & "Yes, and it will be a deeply " & _
        "religious experience for both of us."
    FQ(9, Ans2) = "2" & NL & "No, but what else is new? " & _
        "After my last time, the radio said that Nixon resigned."
    FQ(9, Ans3) = ""
    FQ(9, Ans4) = ""
    FQ(9, Ans5) = ""
    FQ(9, AnsYN) = "True"
    FQ(9, AnsTyped) = "False"

end sub
-->
</SCRIPT>

<SCRIPT LANGUAGE="VBScript">
<!--
Sub CmdAnswer2_Click()
   TBCurrentAnswer.text = CmdAnswer2.caption
end sub
-->
</SCRIPT>
```

```vbscript
<SCRIPT LANGUAGE="VBScript">
<!--
Sub CmdAnswer1_Click()
   TBCurrentAnswer.text = CmdAnswer1.caption
end sub
-->
</SCRIPT>

<SCRIPT LANGUAGE="VBScript">
<!--
Sub SpinButton1_SpinUp()
   PrevQuestion QuestionNum
   if QuestionNum >= 0 and QuestionNum <= 9 then
      TBCurrentAnswer.text = QuizAnswers(QuestionNum)
   end if
end sub

Sub SpinButton1_SpinDown()
   If QuestionNum = 0 _
   and TBCurrentAnswer.text <> QuizAnswers(0) then
      FunScore = 0
   end if

   if QuestionNum >= 0 and QuestionNum <= 9 then
      QuizAnswers(QuestionNum) = TBCurrentAnswer.text
   end if
   NextQuestion QuestionNum
end sub

-->
</SCRIPT>

<SCRIPT LANGUAGE="VBScript">
<!--
Sub CmdAnswer5_Click()
   TBCurrentAnswer.text = CmdAnswer5.caption
end sub
-->
</SCRIPT>

<SCRIPT LANGUAGE="VBScript">
<!--
Sub CmdAnswer4_Click()
   TBCurrentAnswer.text = CmdAnswer4.caption
end sub
-->
</SCRIPT>

<SCRIPT LANGUAGE="VBScript">
<!--
Sub CmdAnswer3_Click()
```

```
      TBCurrentAnswer.text = CmdAnswer3.caption
end sub
-->
</SCRIPT>

<SCRIPT LANGUAGE="VBScript">
<!--
Sub IeTimer1_Timer()
    timertick = timertick + 1
    select case timertick
        case 1
        LblTheQuestion.caption = "Sex C.P.A. will present " & _
            "you with a series of questions to help you " & _
            "evaluate a prospective date."

        case 2
        LblTheQuestion.caption = "Based on your answers to " & _
            "these questions, Sex C.P.A. will calculate how " & _
            "much you should spend per date."

        case 3
        LblTheQuestion.caption = "Click on a command button " & _
            "to select an answer. The Forward (>) button " & _
            "enters your answer and displays the next question."

        case 4
        LblTheQuestion.caption = "The Back (<) button allows " & _
            "you to review your answers."

        case 5
        LblTheQuestion.caption = "Remember that Sex C.P.A. " & _
            "is just a game. It is not meant as a serious " & _
            "statement about the merits or demerits of either sex."

        case 6
        LblTheQuestion.caption = "Ready to get started? " & _
          "Let's have some fun! Good luck ... "

        case 7
        LblTheQuestion.caption = "Is your date male or female?"
        CmdAnswer1.caption = "Male"
        CmdAnswer2.caption = "Female"
        CmdAnswer3.caption = ""
        CmdAnswer4.caption = ""
        CmdAnswer5.caption = ""

        QuestionNum = -1
        IeTimer1.enabled = false
    end select
end sub
-->
</SCRIPT>
```

```
<DIV ID="Layout1" STYLE="LAYOUT:FIXED;WIDTH:597pt;HEIGHT:370pt;">
    <OBJECT ID="LblTheQuestion"
     CLASSID="CLSID:978C9E23-D4B0-11CE-BF2D-00AA003F40D0"
     STYLE="TOP:8pt;LEFT:17pt;WIDTH:487pt;HEIGHT:74pt;ZINDEX:0;">
        <PARAM NAME="ForeColor" VALUE="8454143">
        <PARAM NAME="BackColor" VALUE="0">
        <PARAM NAME="Caption" VALUE=
          "Welcome to Sex C.P.A., your Web budget advisor
          for sexual pursuit!">
        <PARAM NAME="Size" VALUE="17180;2611">
        <PARAM NAME="BorderStyle" VALUE="1">
        <PARAM NAME="FontEffects" VALUE="1073741825">
        <PARAM NAME="FontHeight" VALUE="280">
        <PARAM NAME="FontCharSet" VALUE="0">
        <PARAM NAME="FontPitchAndFamily" VALUE="2">
        <PARAM NAME="FontWeight" VALUE="700">
    </OBJECT>

    <OBJECT ID="TBCurrentAnswer"
     CLASSID="CLSID:8BD21D10-EC42-11CE-9E0D-00AA006002F3"
     STYLE="TOP:91pt;LEFT:17pt;WIDTH:487pt;HEIGHT:51pt;
     TABINDEX:1;ZINDEX:1;">
        <PARAM NAME="VariousPropertyBits" VALUE="2894088219">
        <PARAM NAME="BackColor" VALUE="16711680">
        <PARAM NAME="ForeColor" VALUE="16777215">
        <PARAM NAME="Size" VALUE="17180;1799">
        <PARAM NAME="FontEffects" VALUE="1073741825">
        <PARAM NAME="FontHeight" VALUE="240">
        <PARAM NAME="FontCharSet" VALUE="0">
        <PARAM NAME="FontPitchAndFamily" VALUE="2">
        <PARAM NAME="FontWeight" VALUE="700">
    </OBJECT>

    <OBJECT ID="CmdAnswer1"
     CLASSID="CLSID:D7053240-CE69-11CD-A777-00DD01143C57"
     STYLE="TOP:149pt;LEFT:17pt;WIDTH:91pt;HEIGHT:107pt;
     TABINDEX:2;ZINDEX:2;">
        <PARAM NAME="ForeColor" VALUE="65535">
        <PARAM NAME="BackColor" VALUE="16744576">
        <PARAM NAME="VariousPropertyBits" VALUE="8388635">
        <PARAM NAME="Caption"
          VALUE="This thing here is a command button.">
        <PARAM NAME="Size" VALUE="3210;3775">
        <PARAM NAME="FontEffects" VALUE="1073741825">
        <PARAM NAME="FontHeight" VALUE="200">
        <PARAM NAME="FontCharSet" VALUE="0">
        <PARAM NAME="FontPitchAndFamily" VALUE="2">
        <PARAM NAME="ParagraphAlign" VALUE="3">
        <PARAM NAME="FontWeight" VALUE="700">
    </OBJECT>
```

```
<OBJECT ID="CmdAnswer2"
 CLASSID="CLSID:D7053240-CE69-11CD-A777-00DD01143C57"
 STYLE="TOP:149pt;LEFT:116pt;WIDTH:91pt;HEIGHT:107pt;
 TABINDEX:3;ZINDEX:3;">
    <PARAM NAME="ForeColor" VALUE="65535">
    <PARAM NAME="BackColor" VALUE="16744576">
    <PARAM NAME="VariousPropertyBits" VALUE="8388635">
    <PARAM NAME="Caption"
      VALUE="This thing here is a command button.">
    <PARAM NAME="Size" VALUE="3210;3775">
    <PARAM NAME="FontEffects" VALUE="1073741825">
    <PARAM NAME="FontHeight" VALUE="200">
    <PARAM NAME="FontCharSet" VALUE="0">
    <PARAM NAME="FontPitchAndFamily" VALUE="2">
    <PARAM NAME="ParagraphAlign" VALUE="3">
    <PARAM NAME="FontWeight" VALUE="700">
</OBJECT>

<OBJECT ID="CmdAnswer3"
 CLASSID="CLSID:D7053240-CE69-11CD-A777-00DD01143C57"
 STYLE="TOP:149pt;LEFT:215pt;WIDTH:91pt;HEIGHT:107pt;
 TABINDEX:4;ZINDEX:4;">
    <PARAM NAME="ForeColor" VALUE="65535">
    <PARAM NAME="BackColor" VALUE="16744576">
    <PARAM NAME="VariousPropertyBits" VALUE="8388635">
    <PARAM NAME="Caption"
      VALUE="This thing here is a command button.">
    <PARAM NAME="Size" VALUE="3210;3775">
    <PARAM NAME="FontEffects" VALUE="1073741825">
    <PARAM NAME="FontHeight" VALUE="200">
    <PARAM NAME="FontCharSet" VALUE="0">
    <PARAM NAME="FontPitchAndFamily" VALUE="2">
    <PARAM NAME="ParagraphAlign" VALUE="3">
    <PARAM NAME="FontWeight" VALUE="700">
</OBJECT>

<OBJECT ID="CmdAnswer4"
 CLASSID="CLSID:D7053240-CE69-11CD-A777-00DD01143C57"
 STYLE="TOP:149pt;LEFT:314pt;WIDTH:91pt;HEIGHT:107pt;
 TABINDEX:5;ZINDEX:5;">
    <PARAM NAME="ForeColor" VALUE="65535">
    <PARAM NAME="BackColor" VALUE="16744576">
    <PARAM NAME="VariousPropertyBits" VALUE="8388635">
    <PARAM NAME="Caption" VALUE="This thing here is a command button.">
    <PARAM NAME="Size" VALUE="3210;3775">
    <PARAM NAME="FontEffects" VALUE="1073741825">
    <PARAM NAME="FontHeight" VALUE="200">
    <PARAM NAME="FontCharSet" VALUE="0">
    <PARAM NAME="FontPitchAndFamily" VALUE="2">
    <PARAM NAME="ParagraphAlign" VALUE="3">
    <PARAM NAME="FontWeight" VALUE="700">
</OBJECT>
```

```
<OBJECT ID="CmdAnswer5"
 CLASSID="CLSID:D7053240-CE69-11CD-A777-00DD01143C57"
 STYLE="TOP:149pt;LEFT:413pt;WIDTH:91pt;HEIGHT:107pt;
 TABINDEX:6;ZINDEX:6;">
    <PARAM NAME="ForeColor" VALUE="65535">
    <PARAM NAME="BackColor" VALUE="16744576">
    <PARAM NAME="VariousPropertyBits" VALUE="8388635">
    <PARAM NAME="Caption"
      VALUE="This thing here is a command button.">
    <PARAM NAME="Size" VALUE="3210;3775">
    <PARAM NAME="FontEffects" VALUE="1073741825">
    <PARAM NAME="FontHeight" VALUE="200">
    <PARAM NAME="FontCharSet" VALUE="0">
    <PARAM NAME="FontPitchAndFamily" VALUE="2">
    <PARAM NAME="ParagraphAlign" VALUE="3">
    <PARAM NAME="FontWeight" VALUE="700">
</OBJECT>

<OBJECT ID="SpinButton1"
 CLASSID="CLSID:79176FB0-B7F2-11CE-97EF-00AA006D2776"
 STYLE="TOP:264pt;LEFT:17pt;WIDTH:487pt;HEIGHT:33pt;
 TABINDEX:7;ZINDEX:7;">
    <PARAM NAME="Size" VALUE="17180;1164">
</OBJECT>
<OBJECT ID="IeTimer1"
 CLASSID="CLSID:59CCB4A0-727D-11CF-AC36-00AA00A47DD2"
 STYLE="TOP:314pt;LEFT:41pt;WIDTH:33pt;HEIGHT:25pt;
 TABINDEX:8;ZINDEX:8;">
    <PARAM NAME="_ExtentX" VALUE="1164">
    <PARAM NAME="_ExtentY" VALUE="873">
    <PARAM NAME="Interval" VALUE="4000">
</OBJECT>
</DIV>
```

Doing Setup With The Layout.onLoad Event

The first task of the code—at least, when the game page loads into the player's Web browser—is to load the quiz data into the arrays. This is performed by event code for the ActiveX layout's **onLoad** event, which fires when the Web page containing the layout is loaded into the player's Web browser. The arrays are loaded pretty much as you'd expect:

```
MQ(0, Question) = "In the box, type the name of the girl, " & _
   "then click the Accept button."
MQ(0, Ans1) = ""
MQ(0, Ans2) = ""
MQ(0, Ans3) = ""
MQ(0, Ans4) = ""
MQ(0, Ans5) = ""
```

```
MQ(0, AnsYN) = "False"
MQ(0, AnsTyped) = "True"
```

Notice that each array slot is referred to by the question number and an easy-to-remember constant name declared earlier in the code:

```
' Declare and initialize constants for array slots
dim Question, Ans1, Ans2, Ans3, Ans4, Ans5, AnsYN, AnsTyped
Question = 0
Ans1 = 1
Ans2 = 2
Ans3 = 3
Ans4 = 4
Ans5 = 5
AnsYN = 6
AnsTyped = 7
```

Constants are just variables.

Remember that in VBScript, constants are just variables to which you assign a value that doesn't change—or at least, is not supposed to change—during the course of the program.

Aside from loading the quiz data, the **onLoad** code sets the initial value of the **QuestionNum** control variable to -1. Because the first quiz question is numbered 0, this lets us use the same code to move from the game's opening segment to the first quiz question as we use to move from one quiz question to the next.

Coding The Answer Buttons

In their **click** event, the answer buttons contain code that copies text from their caption property to the text box displaying the player's answer to a question, as shown in the following snippet:

```
Sub CmdAnswer1_Click()
   TBCurrentAnswer.text = CmdAnswer1.caption
end sub
```

Another way to do the same thing would be to copy the answer from the quiz data array to the text box, but that would be more complicated and wouldn't do the job any better.

Coding The SpinButton control

The code for the SpinButton control is a bit more interesting. There are two main events for which you need to write code: the **spindown** event, which moves the player forward in the quiz, and the **spinup** event, which moves backward.

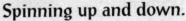

Spinning up and down.

You might have noticed that we coded the forward movement through the questions in the spin button's **spindown** event, and the backward movement in the **spinup** event. That's because when you position a spin button control horizontally, the right-pointing button is for **spindown** and the left-pointing button is for **spinup**—exactly the opposite of what you'd expect.

When the player clicks on the **spindown** part of the control, the activated event code is as follows:

```
Sub SpinButton1_SpinDown()
   If QuestionNum = 0 _
   and TBCurrentAnswer.text <> QuizAnswers(0) then
      FunScore = 0
   end if

   if QuestionNum >= 0 and QuestionNum <= 9 then
      QuizAnswers(QuestionNum) = TBCurrentAnswer.text
   end if
   NextQuestion QuestionNum
end sub
```

This code performs three main tasks:

☆ If the value of the **QuestionNum** variable indicates that the player is answering a quiz question, then it copies the answer from the text box into the appropriate slot of the **QuizAnswers** array.

☆ Calls a sub to display the next question in the quiz.

☆ If the player is at the first quiz question and enters a name different from that in the 0 slot of the **QuizAnswers** array, it sets the value of **FunScore** to 0. This allows the player to repeat the quiz with a different name.

Notice that when the **NextQuestion** sub is called, we pass it **QuestionNum** as a parameter so it will know which question comes next. The same method is used with the **PrevQuestion** sub, called in the code for the **spinup** event:

```
Sub SpinButton1_SpinUp()
   PrevQuestion QuestionNum
   if QuestionNum >= 0 and QuestionNum <= 9 then
      TBCurrentAnswer.text = QuizAnswers(QuestionNum)
   end if
end sub
```

Moving From One Question To Another

The heavy lifting of moving from question to question is done by the **NextQuestion** and **PrevQuestion** subs. They work in essentially the same way, as shown in the following code snippet:

```
sub NextQuestion(QN)
   Select Case QN
   case -1
      If TBCurrentAnswer.text = "Male" then
         DateIsMale = true
      else
         DateIsMale = false
      end if

      TBCurrentAnswer.text = ""

      CmdAnswer1.caption = ""
      CmdAnswer2.caption = ""

      TBCurrentAnswer.setfocus
      if DateIsMale then
         LblTheQuestion = FQ(0,Question)

      else
         LblTheQuestion = MQ(0, Question)
      end if
   case 0
      QuizAnswers(0) = TBCurrentAnswer.text
      DisplayQuestion 1
   case 1
      DisplayQuestion 2
   case 2
      DisplayQuestion 3
...and so on
```

Each sub, whether it's **NextQuestion** or **PrevQuestion**, is passed the current question number. It uses that question number in a **select case** statement to identify the question to which the program should go. The **NextQuestion** sub does carry a little extra baggage at the beginning, since it has to handle the case in which the player has just loaded the game and the question number is –1. The technique, however, remains very simple.

Displaying Quiz Questions And Answers

Both the **NextQuestion** and **PrevQuestion** subs call the **DisplayQuestion** sub to put the new question on the player's screen. **DisplayQuestion** gets a question number as a parameter, and uses that question number in a simple **if...then...else** statement, as follows:

```
If DateIsMale then
     LblTheQuestion.caption = FQ(QN, Question)
     TBCurrentAnswer = ""
     CmdAnswer1.caption = FQ(QN, Ans1)
     CmdAnswer2.caption = FQ(QN, Ans2)
     CmdAnswer3.caption = FQ(QN, Ans3)
     CmdAnswer4.caption = FQ(QN, Ans4)
     CmdAnswer5.caption = FQ(QN, Ans5)
   else
     LblTheQuestion.caption = MQ(QN, Question)
     TBCurrentAnswer = ""
     CmdAnswer1.caption = MQ(QN, Ans1)
     CmdAnswer2.caption = MQ(QN, Ans2)
     CmdAnswer3.caption = MQ(QN, Ans3)
     CmdAnswer4.caption = MQ(QN, Ans4)
     CmdAnswer5.caption = MQ(QN, Ans5)
   end if
```

The appropriate question and possible answers are loaded from the "male quiz" or "female quiz" data array, depending on the value of the **DateIsMale** variable—the sex of the prospective date. The text box is loaded with a blank value.

Coding With The Timer Control

The final piece of the puzzle is the code inside the timer control's **timer** event. This event fires every time the number of milliseconds in the timer's **interval** property has passed. The code works as follows:

```
timertick = timertick + 1
select case timertick
  case 1
  LblTheQuestion.caption = "Sex C.P.A. will present " & _
     "you with a series of questions to help you " & _
     "evaluate a prospective date."
```

```
case 2
LblTheQuestion.caption = "Based on your answers to " & _
    "these questions, Sex C.P.A. will calculate how " & _
    "much you should spend per date."

case 3
LblTheQuestion.caption = "Click on a command button " & _
    "to select an answer. The Forward (>) button " & _
    "enters your answer and displays the next question."

case 4
LblTheQuestion.caption = "The Back (<) button allows " & _
    "you to review your answers."

case 5
LblTheQuestion.caption = "Remember that Sex C.P.A. " & _
    "is just a game. It is not meant as a serious " & _
    "statement about the merits or demerits of either sex."

case 6
LblTheQuestion.caption = "Ready to get started? " & _
    "Let's have some fun! Good luck ... "

case 7
LblTheQuestion.caption = "Is your date male or female?"
CmdAnswer1.caption = "Male"
CmdAnswer2.caption = "Female"
CmdAnswer3.caption = ""
CmdAnswer4.caption = ""
CmdAnswer5.caption = ""

QuestionNum = -1
IeTimer1.enabled = false
```

The **TimerTick** variable starts out with a default value of 0. Each time that the **timer** event sub runs, it adds 1 to the value of **TimerTick**. A **select case** statement then uses this value to determine which text to display in the game's question window (in the label control).

After the **timer** event sub runs a few times and **TimerTick** reaches a value of 7, the timer displays the question that opens the quiz and sets the **QuestionNum** variable to its starting value of –1.

As its final act, when the **TimerTick** variable equals 7, the timer turns itself off, so that it doesn't play any further role in the action of the game. It's easy to forget to turn off the timer control, but it's important to do so. A running timer can make your program do odd things that drive you crazy, because you can't find the cause. It's better to be a little extra careful about turning off the timer.

Why The TimerTick Variable Has To Be Global.
You might wonder why the **TimerTick** variable is a global variable declared waaaay up at the top of the program, instead of being placed snugly inside the **timer** event code. The answer is simple: If the **TimerTick** variable were local to the **timer** event sub, it would come into existence each time the sub ran, and disappear each time the sub finished running. Thus, its value would never change. The simplest way to make **TimerTick** retain its value is to declare it outside the event code.

Playing Sex C.P.A.

Having gone through the code, let's take a quick run through the game itself so you can see the result. When the player first loads the Web page containing the game, the welcome message appears, as shown in Figure 14.4.

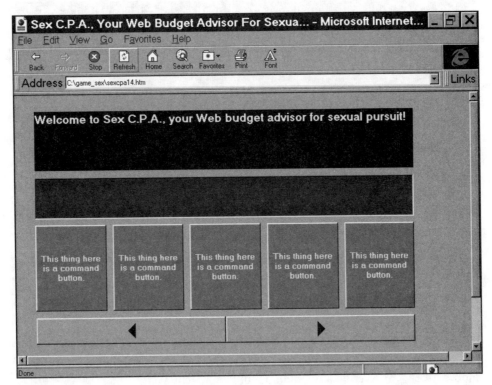

Figure 14.4 Sex C.P.A. greets the player.

The player works his or her way through the quiz questions by clicking on an answer button and then on the forward part of the **spinbutton** control. Each answer is displayed in the text box, as shown in Figure 14.5.

When the player has answered the last question in the quiz, clicking on the forward part of the **spinbutton** control displays a message box, as shown in Figure 14.6. The message box, coded with the **MsgBox()** function rather than the simple **MsgBox** statement, uses Yes/No buttons to ask if the player wants to see the score for the prospective date.

If the player answers "no," then the game just sits there, waiting. If the player clicks on the backward part of the **spinbutton** control, it will display the previous question. Repeatedly clicking on the backward **spinbutton** takes the player back to question 0, where he/she can type in a name of a prospective date and do the quiz all over again.

If the player answers "yes," then the game displays a message box with the date's score, as shown in Figure 14.7. When the player clicks on OK, the final message

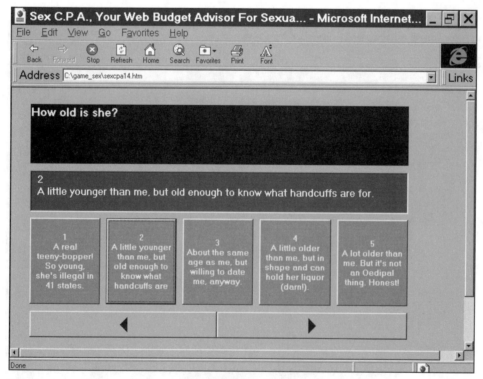

Figure 14.5　Answering a question about a prospective date.

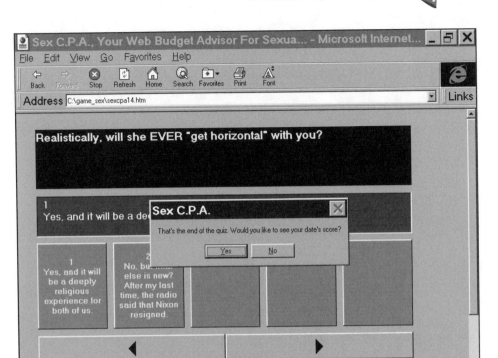

Figure 14.6   Does the player want to see the date's score?

box is displayed, telling the player how much money to spend on a date with the person in question. This message box is shown in Figure 14.8.

Figure 14.7   The prospective date's score.

Figure 14.8   How much to spend on the date.

XV

WRITING CGI PROGRAMS WITH VISUAL BASIC

If you know Visual Basic Script, you know a lot about the "regular" kind of Visual Basic. In this chapter, you'll learn how you can use Visual Basic to create server-side CGI programs that can process a user's form data.

VBScript is a powerful tool for writing scripts that activate your Web pages. But for many purposes—perhaps most—your Web pages must interact with programs on a Web server. And VBScript by itself won't enable you to do that.

If you've had some exposure to books and articles about writing programs that run on Web servers—such as Coriolis's excellent *Serving the Web* (Robert Jon Mudry, 1996)—you're probably a little intimidated by the idea. Web servers usually run on Unix machines and run programs (or scripts) written in oddball languages like Perl. And then there's all that talk about "CGI," as if you didn't have enough to learn, already.

Well, you're in luck. If you know VBScript, you're already familiar with a lot of Microsoft's "regular" Visual Basic programming language. And if you know Visual Basic, you can write CGI programs, as long as your Web server is running the right server software.

This isn't a book about CGI and Web servers, and we could easily fill up several chapters just giving you the fundamentals. To get you started as quickly as possible, we'll keep the technical details to a minimum and focus on the practical techniques you'll need. But you will need a little background information—otherwise, you'll have no idea what you're doing!

Web Servers And CGI: The Basics

In concept, the interaction between the Web browser on a user's PC and a CGI program on a Web server is a fairly simple process, shown in Figure 15.1. The process has several steps:

1. The Web browser has an HTML document loaded. This document contains a form to get input from the user and submit it to the Web server.

2. The user sends the form information to the Web server by clicking on a Submit button.

3. The Web server software sends the information to a CGI program that's on the Web server computer.

4. The CGI program processes the information. If needed, it looks up the answer in an external database.

5. The CGI program creates an appropriate response for the user's data or query. Then, it sends the response back to the Web server software.

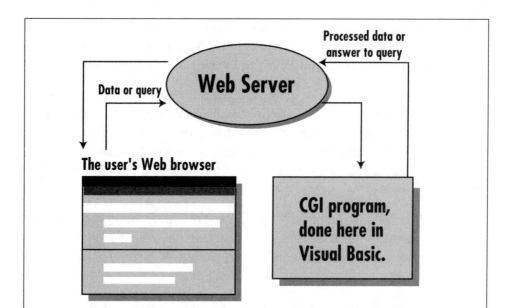

Figure 15.1   How a Web browser communicates with a CGI program.

6. The Web server software forwards the response to the Web browser on the user's PC, where it displays as an HTML document.

Now, this simplicity masks a few unanswered questions. First, the Web server might have access to a large number of CGI programs. How does it know which program to run? Second, what data does the Web browser have to provide to the server, and in what form? Third, what data does the CGI program have to give back to the server, and in what form?

All these questions are governed by HTTP, the Hypertext Transfer Protocol. It defines which information has to be provided, to whom, when, and in what form.

When you create a Web document and a CGI program that are meant to interact, you have to handle the arrangements for both ends of the conversation: from the user's Web browser to the CGI program on the server, and from your CGI program through the server back to the user's Web browser.

From the Web Browser To The Web Server.

This is the easier side of the conversation to set up. When you create an HTML form, you should—if it's going to be useful for interacting with a Web server—provide several pieces of information:

☆ The form method. Normally, this will be **post**.

☆ The protocol governing the communication between your software and the server. This will usually be HTTP, but it can also be FTP (File Transfer Protocol) or some other protocol.

☆ The URL (Web address) of the Web server.

☆ The URL of the CGI program, meaning, its location on the Web server computer.

If you think about this information, you can see that it answers some of our questions. **Post** tells the Web server what the browser means for it to do with the information from the user's HTML form. **HTTP** tells it what conventions the communication will follow, so that it knows what kind of message header information to expect. The Web server URL makes sure that the data is sent to the right Web server software on the right computer, and the CGI program's URL tells the Web server software where it should send the data it's received.

Thus, a bit later in the chapter, our first form to work with a CGI program will be started with the following tag in the user's HTML document:

```
<FORM method=post action="http://localhost/cgi-win/cgitest32.exe">
```

In the code line shown, the Web server's URL is *http://localhost*, while the location of the CGI program on the server computer is */cgi-win/cgitest32.exe*.

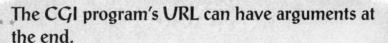

The CGI program's URL can have arguments at the end.

Depending on which Web server software you're using, you can often add arguments (parameters) at the end of the CGI program's URL. These will be parsed by the server and passed to the CGI program. Normally, these arguments are preceded by a question mark. Different types of servers handle this information in slightly different ways, so you need to check the server documentation, and write your CGI program to receive the parameters in the server's particular format.

In the form itself, of course, you'll probably have input fields that get data for the CGI program to process. If you've been creating HTML forms already, that part is familiar. And if you code the HTML document correctly, the user's Web browser will handle the details of sending a message to the Web server in the appropriate form, with required header information and so forth.

In essence, what happens is this. For each input field in your HTML document, the user enters a particular piece of information, such as his/her name or email address. When the user clicks on the Submit button, the Web browser sends this information to the Web server as a set of *name=value* pairs. If you have one input field called *CustomerName* and the user enters the name *Sylvester Stallone*, the *name=value* pair sent to the server would be *CustomerName="Sylvester Stallone"*.

The Web browser massages this data into a form that can be used by a CGI program. Then, it passes the data to the program. But everything is done behind the scenes: you don't have to worry too much about this part, as long as you set up your HTML form correctly in the first place.

From The CGI Program To The Web Server

It's on the other side of the conversation that you need slightly more knowledge of just how the server handles communication between the user's Web browser and the CGI program. The CGI program must give the server a message with an HTTP header indicating the type of data that the message contains. After that, the message might contain an HTML document like the ones we'll create with CGI programs in this chapter.

Setting Up To Test Your CGI Programs

If you want to write CGI programs in Visual Basic, the best Web server software to use is O'Reilly & Associates' WebSite. It runs under Windows 95 and Windows NT, has a Windows CGI interface for communicating with Windows CGI programs, and includes lots of CGI examples in Visual Basic. (It also includes a DOS CGI interface and a Standard CGI interface that lets you run programs in more traditional CGI languages such as Perl.)

To run CGI programs with WebSite, you first need a CGI program to run. The program should, of course, be designed to work with the WebSite WebServer. This chapter will show you how to develop such programs. You'll also need an HTML document that submits data to be processed by the CGI program. After that, you follow these steps:

1. Install the WebSite software on your PC.
2. Open a TCP/IP connection. The WebSite WebServer software needs this connection open even if you're not going to be communicating over the Internet.
3. Start up the WebSite WebServer software.
4. Start your Web browser and load the HTML document that collects data for the CGI program.
5. Submit the data to the WebSite WebServer software.
6. Get the response from the CGI program.

Let's see how this process would work with a simple example. The WebSite package comes with a ready-to-use CGI program called *cgitest32.exe*. After we see how the overall process works, we'll be ready to create our own CGI programs in Visual Basic.

Testing The Form-CGI Connection

Let's just create a basic HTML document that obtains the user's name and submits it to the Web server and thence to a CGI program. First, create the HTML document shown in Listing 15.1. The document's appearance in Internet Explorer is shown in Figure 15.2.

Listing 15.1 A simple HTML document to work with a CGI program.

```
<HTML>
<HEAD>
<TITLE> Form Test 1</TITLE>
</HEAD>
<BODY>
<h1>This is to test an input form with the Web server and CGI.</h1>
<br>
<hr>
<FORM METHOD="POST" ACTION="http://localhost/cgi-win/cgitest32.exe/Form">
Enter your name: <input type="text" name="UserName" size=25 value="">
<input type="submit" name="OK" value="Submit">
<input type="reset" name="Cancel" value="Oops">
```

```
</form>
<hr>
</BODY>
</HTML>
```

Most of the HTML code for the form will be familiar. Let's focus on the **<form>** tag itself. The form's method is **post**, and you should usually specify **post** as the method. The action part of the tag specifies the URL of the CGI program, as shown in the code line below.

```
http://localhost/cgi-win/cgitest32.exe/Form
```

Let's dissect this URL. It consists of the following:

http: tells the server what protocol is being used for the current message—*i.e.,* the data being sent from the form to the CGI program.

//localhost/ is the URL of the server itself. When WebSite's WebServer software is running, it defines this as the directory where the WebSite software is installed.

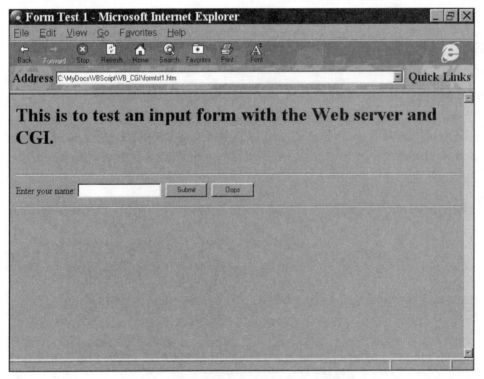

Figure 15.2   The HTML document loaded into Internet Explorer.

/cgi-win/ is the subdirectory under the WebSite directory where the Windows CGI software is installed.

cgitest32.exe is a ready-to-use CGI program that comes with WebSite. It was written in Visual Basic, and the Visual Basic project files are included as an example of CGI programming.

/Form is a parameter that gets passed to the *cgitest32.exe* program, telling it about the format in which it should return data to the user's Web browser. Note that this parameter is a little unusual, in that parameters at the end of a URL are normally preceded by a question mark.

Using the forward slash.

It might have struck you as odd that the URL uses a path name with forward slash characters ("/") when Windows 95 uses the backward slash ("\") to separate directories. However, the WebSite WebServer software "maps" standard Windows directory names onto the forward-slash expressions so that you can use the forward slash character, which is standard in URL notation.

If you load Listing 15.1's HTML document into a Web browser, then start up your TCP/IP connection and load the WebServer software, you can submit data from the HTML document to the *cgitest32.exe* program. The program, in turn, will send an HTML document back to your Web browser. It will look something like Figure 15.3.

In this case, the CGI program tells you that it received data from two form fields: *UserName,* which in the figure is matched with the value "Scott," and *OK,* which is the name of the Submit button—with a value, appropriately enough, of "Submit."

Assuming that you already know how to create forms, the *cgitest32.exe* program is a good way to verify that you have your WebServer software set up and running properly. Once you've done that, you can go on to create your own CGI programs. If something doesn't work right, you'll know that the problem is with your program, not with the way that the Web server software is set up.

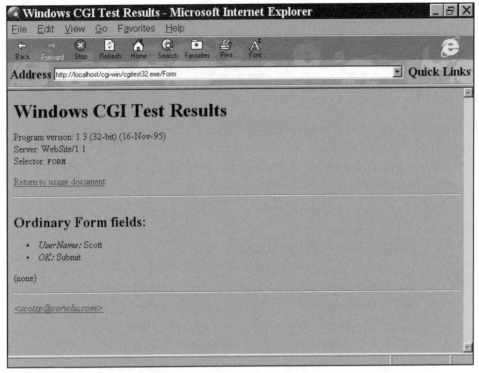

Figure 15.3   The cgitest32.exe program reports on what it received from your Web browser.

Writing A Simple CGI Program In Visual Basic

Now, let's create a simple—but practical—CGI program in Visual Basic. This program will process orders for Coriolis Group books. It will work with an HTML document that displays as an order form when loaded into a Web browser.

We're not going to tarry too long with the details of the HTML document, inasmuch as our main objective is to learn how to write a CGI program that will work with it. However, the HTML code is shown in Listing 15.2, while the Web page it creates is shown in Figure 15.4.

Listing 15.2   HTML code to create the order form in Figure 15.4.

```
<HTML>
<HEAD>
<TITLE>Order Books from Coriolis!</TITLE>
```

```
</HEAD>
<BODY>
<h1>Check the books you would like to order:</h1>
<FORM method=post action="http://localhost/cgi-win/orderbk1.exe">
<hr>
<ul><ul><ul><ul><ul>
<INPUT NAME="CB_VBScriptWiz" TYPE="CHECKBOX" VALUE="1"
        ALIGN=left>Visual Basic Script Wizardry, $39.99<br>
<INPUT NAME="CB_DelphiExp" TYPE="CHECKBOX" VALUE="1"
        ALIGN=left>The New Delphi 2 Programming EXplorer, $44.99<br>
<INPUT NAME="CB_JavaApp" TYPE="CHECKBOX" VALUE="1"
        ALIGN=left>Writing Java Applets, $39.99<br>
<INPUT NAME="CB_Intranet" TYPE="CHECKBOX" VALUE="1"
        ALIGN=left>Developing Real-World Intranets, $39.99<br>
</ul></ul> </ul></ul></ul>
<hr>
<pre>
Your Name:      <INPUT NAME="TB_Customer" TYPE="" SIZE="20"
        ALIGN=right><br>
Street Address: <INPUT NAME="TB_Street" TYPE="" SIZE="25"
        ALIGN=right><br>
City:           <INPUT NAME="TB_City" TYPE="TEXT" SIZE="15"
        ALIGN=right> State: <INPUT NAME="TB_State" TYPE="TEXT" SIZE="5"
        ALIGN=right> Zip: <INPUT NAME="TB_Zip" TYPE="TEXT" SIZE="5"
        ALIGN=right><br>

Send your order today!  <INPUT NAME="Btn_Order" TYPE="SUBMIT" ALIGN=right>
</pre>
</FORM>
</BODY>
</HTML>
```

As you can see, the HTML code in Listing 15.2 sets up a form with four checkboxes, each of which can be used (in theory) to order a book from The Coriolis Group. At the bottom of the form are text boxes for the customer's name and address.

The **action** part of the form tag specifies the usual URL path. Then, it specifies *orderbk1.exe,* the CGI program to process the form data—the CGI program we're now going to create.

Creating The CGI Program Itself

A CGI program needs routines to communicate with the server. In particular, it needs routines to:

☆ Get the names and values of various form fields passed to it by the server

☆ Determine if certain fields are present in the data stream or not

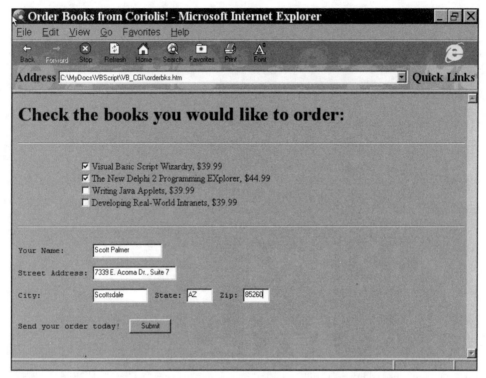

Figure 15.4   The Web page created by Listing 15.2 to order four Coriolis books.

☆ Send data back to the server in a format appropriate to the original request by the Web browser

That list, of course, is a bare minimum. Even so, if you had to write all those routines yourself, CGI programming would be a daunting task indeed.

WebSite, however, includes a ready-to-use Visual Basic code module called *cgi32.bas*. It defines all the procedures and functions you need to communicate with the WebSite WebServer software. That includes all three routines listed above, and quite a bit more. To use those routines, you need only add the *cgi32.bas* module to your Visual Basic program project.

With that little bit of introduction, let's go step by step through the creation of an order-processing CGI program with Visual Basic. Follow these steps:

1. Create a directory for your CGI programs.
2. Start up Visual Basic.

You can create CGI programs with Visual Basic 3, but you need a different version of WebSite.

3. Delete the form from the program project.

   Highlight the form in the Project window, then open the File menu and select Remove File.

4. Add the *cgi32.bas* code module to your program project.

   WebSite installs the *cgi32.bas* file in the directory \Website\cgi-src\: the "cgi-src" is for "CGI source code." To add the file to your project, open the File menu, select Add File, and then browse to the appropriate directory, where you can highlight and select the file.

5. Open the Tools menu and select Custom Controls.

   The Custom Controls dialog box will appear, as shown in Figure 15.5.

6. Uncheck all the custom controls. Then click on OK.

   This removes the custom controls from your program project.

7. Open the Insert menu and select Module.

   This creates a new Visual Basic code module and adds it to your program project. Save the module as *orderbk1.bas*.

8. Finally, save the whole project as *orderbk1.vbp*.

That gets you started. One thing you might do right now—it's optional, but you'll find it a deeply rewarding and spiritual experience—is peruse the code inside *cgi32.bas*. It defines all the routines your program will use to communicate with the Web server.

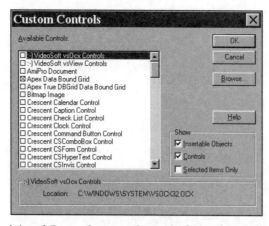

Figure 15.5 The Visual Basic Custom Controls dialog box.

Once you've set up the *Orderbk1* program project, you need to add three procedures to the *orderbk1.bas* code module:

☆ **CGI_Main()**. This is the main control procedure for the program. It's a lot like the **main()** function in a C program, in that it doesn't do much itself except call other routines that do the work of the program.

☆ **Inter_Main()**. Even though you're going to create an executable (.EXE) program, it will only do meaningful work when it's interacting with the Web server software. If someone tries to start the program from the Windows File Manager, this procedure will display a short message explaining the purpose of the program.

☆ **ProcessOrder()**. This is the routine that does the application-specific stuff. It gets the data from the server, processes it, and sends a response back to the server.

The complete code for the *orderbk1.bas* module is shown in Listing 15.3. Look over the listing to get a bird's-eye view: We'll discuss the details in a moment.

Listing 15.3 The orderbk1.bas code module.

```
Attribute VB_Name = "Orderbks"
'-----------------------------------------------------------------
' Orderbk1: example of writing a CGI program in Visual Basic.
' This simple program gets data from an HTML book-order form.
' It adds up the total amount owed by the customer, then sends an
' HTML document back to the user's Web browser. The HTML document
' shows the total amount owed, as well as the customer's name and
' address. It shows how a Visual Basic CGI program can get data from
' an HTML form and send data back to it.
'-----------------------------------------------------------------
Option Explicit


'-----------------------------------------------------------------
' This is the CGI_Main() sub. It's very much like the main() function in
' a C program: Its purpose is to call other subs that do the substantive
' work of the program.
'-----------------------------------------------------------------
Sub CGI_Main()
        ProcessOrder
        Beep
End Sub


'-----------------------------------------------------------------
' This gets the data from the various fields in the customer's order form.
' It then adds up the total amount due and sends a report to the customer
```

```
' in the form of an HTML document which appears in his/her Web browser.
'-----------------------------------------------------------------------
Sub ProcessOrder()

    Dim CustName, Street, City, State, Zip As String
    Dim Subtotal, Tax, Total As Single
    Dim VBScriptWiz, DelphiExp, JavaApp, Intranet As Boolean

    Subtotal = 0
    Tax = 0
    Total = 0

    VBScriptWiz = False
    DelphiExp = False
    JavaApp = False
    Intranet = False

    ' Get data from order form
    CustName = GetSmallField("TB_Customer")
    Street = GetSmallField("TB_Street")
    City = GetSmallField("TB_City")
    State = GetSmallField("TB_State")
    Zip = GetSmallField("TB_Zip")

    If FieldPresent("CB_VBScriptWiz") Then
        Subtotal = Subtotal + 39.99
        VBScriptWiz = True
    End If

    If FieldPresent("CB_DelphiExp") Then
        Subtotal = Subtotal + 44.99
        DelphiExp = True
    End If

    If FieldPresent("CB_JavaApp") Then
        Subtotal = Subtotal + 39.99
        JavaApp = True
    End If

    If FieldPresent("CB_Intranet") Then
        Subtotal = Subtotal + 39.99
        Intranet = True
    End If

    ' Compute the final amount.
    Tax = Subtotal * 1.5
    Total = Subtotal + Tax


    ' Report to the user on which books were ordered,
    ' where they will be sent, and how much he/she will
    ' be charged for them.
```

```
    Send ("Content-type: text/html")
    Send ("")
    Send ("<html><head><title>Thanks for your order!</title></head>")
    Send ("<body><h1>Books you will receive:</h1>")
    Send ("<ul><pre>")

    If VBScriptWiz Then
        Send ("<li>Visual Basic Script Wizardry         $39.99")
    End If

    If DelphiExp Then
        Send ("<li>The New Delphi 2 Programming EXplorer  $44.99")
    End If

    If JavaApp Then
        Send ("<li>Writing Java Applets                   $39.99")
    End If

    If Intranet Then
        Send ("<li>Developing Real-World Intranets        $39.99")
    End If
    Send ("                                  ----------")
    Send ("Subtotal:                         $" & Subtotal)
    Send ("<br>Tax:                           $" & Tax)
    Send ("                                  ----------")
    Send ("Total amount billed:              $" & Total)

    Send ("</ul><hr>")
    Send ("<h1>Books will be shipped to:</h1>")
    Send ("Name:    " & CustName)
    Send ("Address: " & Street)
    Send ("City:    " & City & "   State: " & State & _
        "   Zip: " & Zip)

    Send ("</pre></body></html>")

End Sub


'-------------------------------------------------------------------------
' Inter_Main: Because this is a CGI program, designed to work with the
' Web server, it makes no sense for someone to run it directly from the
' Windows File Manager. If someone attempts to run the program directly,
' this sub displays a message box explaining what kind of program it is.
'-------------------------------------------------------------------------
Sub Inter_Main()
    MsgBox "This is a CGI program for the Web Server.", 16, "Order Books"
End Sub
```

Inside The OrderBk1.bas Code Module

As noted earlier, there are only three procedures in the *orderbk1.bas* code module: **CGI_Main()**, **Inter_Main()**, and **ProcessOrder()**. Let's start with the first two, which are quite simple.

CGI_Main(), true to its mission as a control routine that simply calls other procedures, is only four lines long.

```
Sub CGI_Main()
        ProcessOrder
        Beep
End Sub
```

After calling the **ProcessOrder()** sub, it uses the Visual Basic **beep** statement to make the PC's speaker emit a tone. Then it terminates. In the next part of the chapter, this procedure will expand slightly to add server-side data validation.

Inter_Main() is similarly short and simple.

```
Sub Inter_Main()
    MsgBox "This is a CGI program for the Web Server.", 16, "Order Books"
End Sub
```

This uses the Visual Basic **msgbox** statement to display a message box in case anyone tries to run the program independently of a conversation with the Web server.

Now, let's get to the real heart of the program: the **ProcessOrder** sub. The first thing it does is declare some local variables: one for each of the fields in the order form, plus a couple of extras:

```
Dim CustName, Street, City, State, Zip As String
Dim Subtotal, Tax, Total As Single
Dim VBScriptWiz, DelphiExp, JavaApp, Intranet As Boolean
```

Once the variables are declared, the control variables are set to their initial values, as shown in the code snippet below. The variables for the money amounts in the order are set to zero. The boolean variables which show if particular books have been ordered are set to **false**.

```
Subtotal = 0
Tax = 0
Total = 0
```

```
VBScriptWiz = False
DelphiExp = False
JavaApp = False
Intranet = False
```

When the procedure gets the data from the form's text fields, it will put each data item into the variable that corresponds to its form field. To get the data from a text field, the program uses the **GetSmallField**() function defined in the *cgi32.bas* module, as shown in the code snippet below.

```
CustName = GetSmallField("TB_Customer")
Street = GetSmallField("TB_Street")
City = GetSmallField("TB_City")
State = GetSmallField("TB_State")
Zip = GetSmallField("TB_Zip")
```

The code is pretty easy to understand. If you look at the HTML document in Listing 15.2, you can see that *TB_Customer, TB_Street,* and so on are the names of the text box controls in the HTML form. Take one of the names, put it in quotes, pass it to the **GetSmallField**() function as a parameter, and the function returns whatever the form's user typed into that text box. Then, you just use a Visual Basic assignment statement to copy the value into the appropriate local variable.

Checkboxes, however, are handled differently. If the user checks a particular checkbox on the order form, then the checkbox's name-value pair will be passed by the server to the CGI program. However, if a particular checkbox is *not* checked, then it won't (like a text box control) have its name-value pair (with a null value) sent to the CGI program. If a particular checkbox is unchecked, then its name-value pair won't be sent to the CGI program at all. In that situation, trying to get its value by using **GetSmallField**() would cause a run-time error.

Fortunately, there's a simple and elegant solution. The value of a checkbox is really irrelevant in this context. If a checkbox is checked, then the WebServer software will send its name-value pair to the CGI program; If it's not checked, then its name-value pair will be absent from the data stream. As a result, you can use the **FieldPresent**() boolean function to see if a checkbox was checked, as shown in the code snippet below:

```
If FieldPresent("CB_VBScriptWiz") Then
        Subtotal = Subtotal + 39.99
        VBScriptWiz = True
    End If
```

This **if** statement uses **FieldPresent()** to determine if a book's checkbox was checked. If it was checked, then the next line adds the price of the book to the *subtotal* variable. Finally, the boolean variable for that book is set to **true**, indicating that the book has been ordered by the customer. At the end of this process, the *subtotal* variable will have the sum of the prices for the books the customer has ordered.

Sending A Report Back To The Customer's Web Browser

The final part of *ProcessOrder()* creates an HTML document with information about the customer's order. It then sends the document, with the required header information, back to the customer's Web browser. To do this, it uses the *Send()* procedure defined in *cgi32.bas. Send()* simply transmits a text string over the server to the user's Web browser.

The header information is absolutely required if the server is to get the message back to the customer's Web location. Two lines are mandatory: a content/type line, and a blank line to separate it from the body of the message. Other lines can be used for special cases, but we won't discuss them in this book. The two mandatory lines are shown in the code snippet below.

```
Send ("Content-type: text/html")
Send ("")
```

In this case, the content type line indicates that the CGI program is sending an HTML document back to the user. The blank line—well, it's a blank line. If you don't understand the concept, Zen meditation might help.

Next, the procedure sends the header information for an HTML document, along with some other initial formatting tags:

```
Send ("<html><head><title>Thanks for your order!</title></head>")
Send ("<body><h1>Books you will receive:</h1>")
Send ("<ul><pre>")
```

The **<ul>** tag, of course, marks the beginning of an unnumbered list in the HTML document. Then, the procedure uses successive **if** statements to test each boolean variable corresponding to a book that the customer might have ordered.

```
If VBScriptWiz Then
    Send ("<li>Visual Basic Script Wizardry        $39.99")
End If

If DelphiExp Then
    Send ("<li>The New Delphi 2 Programming EXplorer  $44.99")
End If
…and so on.
```

For each boolean variable with a value of **true**, the procedure sends a list item with the title and price of the corresponding book. After listing all the books ordered, the procedure sends the subtotal, tax, and total amount that will be billed to the customer. Note the use of the ampersand (&) to concatenate text strings and numeric values.

```
Send ("                        ----------")
Send ("Subtotal:                $" & Subtotal)
Send ("<br>Tax:                 $" & Tax)
Send ("                        ----------")
Send ("Total amount billed:     $" & Total)
```

Finally, the procedure sends back the name and address to which the books will be shipped, along with tags that mark the end of the HTML document.

```
Send ("</ul><hr>")
Send ("<h1>Books will be shipped to:</h1>")
Send ("Name:    " & CustName)
Send ("Address: " & Street)
Send ("City:    " & City & "   State: " & State & _
      "   Zip: " & Zip)

Send ("</pre></body></html>")
```

Use of the line continuation character "_".

In the listing, we've used the Visual Basic line continuation character "_" to keep the code lines from running too long for the book page margins. Obviously, in your own code, it's entirely optional. Use it only if you want to do so.

The HTML document sent back to the customer's Web browser is shown in Figure 15.6.

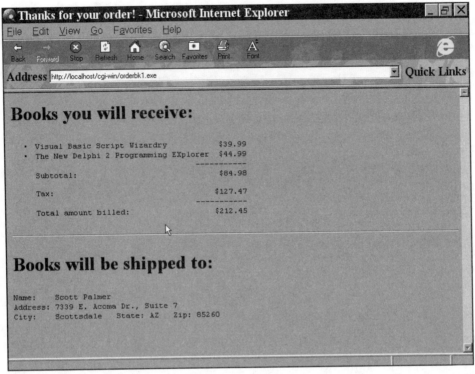

Figure 15.6   The HTML document sent back to the user by the CGI program.

Adding Server-Side Data Validation

Earlier in the book, you already saw how to use VBScript to handle client-side data validation—*i.e.*, to build a few simple error traps right into the Web page that appears in the user's Web browser. Sometimes, however, you'd like to do server-side data validation. You can accomplish that with a fairly easy modification of the *Orderbk1* program project and the HTML document with which the user places his/her order.

In essence, all you'll do is add two new routines to the CGI program:

☆ A boolean function called **OrderInfoPresent()**. This function will verify that in the order entry Web page, the user has filled in all the information required to process the order.

☆ A procedure called **RedisplayOrderForm()**. If any information is missing, this sub will send an HTML document back to the user's Web browser.

This document will redisplay the order form, along with a message explaining that some of the required information was missing from the original transmission.

The simplest part of the exercise is to modify the HTML document to work with the new CGI program, which we'll call *Orderbk2*. All you need to change is the name of the program in the **action** part of the form tag, as shown in Listing 15.4.

Listing 15.4 Changing the CGI program called by the HTML form.

```
<HTML>
<HEAD>
<TITLE>Order Books from Coriolis!</TITLE>
</HEAD>
<BODY>
<h1>Check the books you would like to order:</h1>
<FORM method=post action="http://localhost/cgi-win/orderbk2.exe">
<hr>
…and so on.
```

The next task is to change the *Orderbk1.bas* code module so that it contains and uses the new routines. The updated module, which you might want to save under the name of *orderbk2.bas,* is shown in Listing 15.5.

Listing 15.5 The Orderbk2.bas code module, with server-side data validation.

```
Attribute VB_Name = "Orderbks"
'-------------------------------------------------------------------
' Orderbks2: Demonstrates how to add server-side data validation
' to the CGI program in Orderbks1.
'-------------------------------------------------------------------
Option Explicit


'-------------------------------------------------------------------
' This is the CGI_Main() sub. It's very much like the main() function in
' a C program: Its purpose is to call other subs that do the substantive
' work of the program.
'-------------------------------------------------------------------
Sub CGI_Main()
    If OrderInfoPresent Then
        ProcessOrder
    Else
        RedisplayOrderForm
    End If
End Sub
```

```
'--------------------------------------------------------------------
' This gets the data from the various fields in the customer's order form.
' It then adds up the total amount due and sends a report to the customer
' in the form of an HTML document which appears in his/her Web browser.
'--------------------------------------------------------------------
Sub ProcessOrder()

    Dim CustName, Street, City, State, Zip As String
    Dim Subtotal, Tax, Total As Single
    Dim VBScriptWiz, DelphiExp, JavaApp, Intranet As Boolean

    Subtotal = 0
    Tax = 0
    Total = 0

    VBScriptWiz = False
    DelphiExp = False
    JavaApp = False
    Intranet = False

    ' Get data from order form
    CustName = GetSmallField("TB_Customer")
    Street = GetSmallField("TB_Street")
    City = GetSmallField("TB_City")
    State = GetSmallField("TB_State")
    Zip = GetSmallField("TB_Zip")

    If FieldPresent("CB_VBScriptWiz") Then
        Subtotal = Subtotal + 39.99
        VBScriptWiz = True
    End If

    If FieldPresent("CB_DelphiExp") Then
        Subtotal = Subtotal + 44.99
        DelphiExp = True
    End If

    If FieldPresent("CB_JavaApp") Then
        Subtotal = Subtotal + 39.99
        JavaApp = True
    End If

    If FieldPresent("CB_Intranet") Then
        Subtotal = Subtotal + 39.99
        Intranet = True
    End If

    ' Compute the final amount.
    Tax = Subtotal * 1.5
    Total = Subtotal + Tax
```

```
' Report to the user on which books were ordered,
' where they will be sent, and how much he/she will
' be charged for them.

Send ("Content-type: text/html")
Send ("")
Send ("<html><head><title>Thanks for your order!</title></head>")
Send ("<body><h1>Books you will receive:</h1>")
Send ("<ul><pre>")

If VBScriptWiz Then
    Send ("<li>Visual Basic Script Wizardry        $39.99")
End If

If DelphiExp Then
    Send ("<li>The New Delphi 2 Programming EXplorer  $44.99")
End If

If JavaApp Then
    Send ("<li>Writing Java Applets                $39.99")
End If

If Intranet Then
    Send ("<li>Developing Real-World Intranets      $39.99")
End If
Send ("                                    ----------")
Send ("Subtotal:                           $" & Subtotal)
Send ("<br>Tax:                            $" & Tax)
Send ("                                    ----------")
Send ("Total amount billed:                $" & Total)

Send ("</ul><hr>")
Send ("<h1>Books will be shipped to:</h1>")
Send ("Name:    " & CustName)
Send ("Address: " & Street)
Send ("City:    " & City & "   State: " & State & _
    "   Zip: " & Zip)

Send ("</pre></body></html>")

End Sub



'----------------------------------------------------------------------
' Inter_Main: Because this is a CGI program, designed to work with the
' Web server, it makes no sense for someone to run it directly from the
' Windows File Manager. If someone attempts to run the program directly,
' this sub displays a message box explaining what kind of program it is.
'----------------------------------------------------------------------
Sub Inter_Main()
    MsgBox "This is a CGI program for the Web Server.", 16, "Order Books"
End Sub
```

```
' -------------------------------------------------------------------
' RedisplayOrderForm: If the user doesn't provide all the required data,
' this procedure returns the order form with a "try again" message.
' -------------------------------------------------------------------
Public Sub RedisplayOrderForm()

    ' Send the header information.
    Send "Content-type: text/html"

    ' Here's the obligatory blank line
    ' to separate the header info from
    ' the body of the message.
    Send ""

    ' Redisplay the order form.
    Send ("<html><head><title>Order Books from Coriolis!")
    Send ("</title></head><body>")
    Send ("You didn't fill out the form completely. Try again.<br>")
    Send ("<h1>Check the books you would like to order:</h1>")
    Send ("<form method=post action=""http://localhost/cgi-win/ _
        orderbk2.exe"">")

    ' You can use the <ul> tag to indent text on a Web page.
    Send ("<hr><ul><ul><ul><ul>")

    ' Send the check boxes.
    ' HTML lines are broken up here to fit in
    ' the margins of this book. The user's Web
    ' browser doesn't care.
    Send ("<input name=""CB_VBScriptWiz"" type=""checkbox"" ")
    Send ("value=""1"" align=left> ")
    Send ("Visual Basic Script Wizardry, $39.99><br>")

    Send ("<input name=""CB_DelphiExp"" type=""checkbox"" ")
    Send ("value=""1"" align=left> ")
    Send ("The New Delphi 2 Programming EXplorer, $44.99<br>")

    Send ("<input name=""CB_JavaApp"" type=""checkbox"" ")
    Send ("value=""1"" align=left> ")
    Send ("Writing Java Applets, $39.99<br>")

    Send ("<input name=""CB_Intranet"" type=""checkbox"" ")
    Send ("value=""1"" align=left> ")
    Send ("Developing Real-World Intranets, $39.99<br>")

    ' Unindent and send a horizontal line. Use the
    ' <pre>formatted-text tag to make sure everything
    ' aligns as you want.
    Send ("</ul></ul></ul></ul></ul><hr><pre>")
```

```
' Send back the customer information fields.
Send ("Your Name:        <input name=""TB_Customer"" ")
Send ("type=""text"" size=""20"" align=right><br>")

Send ("Street Address: <input name=""TB_Street"" ")
Send ("type=""text"" size=""25"" align=right>")

' For the book's program listing ONLY, preformatted
' text needs to be turned off here. Otherwise, the
' hard carriage returns in the VB code will be included
' in the HTML document, and the City, State, and Zip
' fields will be displayed on separate lines. When you
' create a routine like this on your own, simply take out
' the next line ("Send("</pre>")") and send the City, State,
' and Zip fields in a single Send line. Then, turn off the
' preformatted-text tag at the end of the HTML form.
Send ("</pre>")
Send ("City:        <input name=""TB_City"" ")
Send ("type=""text"" size=""15"" align=right>")

Send ("State: <input name=""TB_State"" ")
Send ("type=""text"" size=""5"" align=right>")

Send ("Zip: <input name=""TB_Zip"" ")
Send ("type=""text"" size=""5"" align=right><br><br>")

Send ("Send your order today! <input name=""Btn_Order"" ")
Send ("type=""submit"" align=right>")
Send ("</form></body></html>")

End Sub

' ----------------------------------------------------------------
' OrderInfoPresent: This checks to see if the customer has sent all the
' information needed to process his/her order.
' ----------------------------------------------------------------
Public Function OrderInfoPresent()

    ' Set the function's value to false.
    ' The order will be processed ONLY IF
    ' all the required conditions are fulfilled,
    ' in which case, the function's value is set
    ' to true.
    OrderInfoPresent = False

    ' Notice that because we're using the "_" line
    ' continuation character, this is actually a
    ' single-line IF statement and doesn't require
    ' an ENDIF at the end.
```

```
' At least one of the book checkboxes must be checked.
' Therefore, we use OR here.
If (FieldPresent("CB_VBScriptWiz") _
    Or FieldPresent("CB_DelphiExp") _
    Or FieldPresent("CB_JavaApp") _
    Or FieldPresent("CB_Intranet")) _

' And ALL of the customer information has to be present.
' Therefore, we use AND here.
    And GetSmallField("TB_Customer") <> "" _
    And GetSmallField("TB_Street") <> "" _
    And GetSmallField("TB_City") <> "" _
    And GetSmallField("TB_State") <> "" _
    And GetSmallField("TB_Zip") <> "" Then OrderInfoPresent = True

End Function
```

Changing The CGI_Main() Procedure

Apart from the addition of the two new routines, which we'll get to in a moment, the first and most obvious change is in the **CGI_Main()** procedure, shown in the code snippet below.

```
Sub CGI_Main()
    If OrderInfoPresent Then
        ProcessOrder
    Else
        RedisplayOrderForm
    End If
End Sub
```

Previously, the **CGI_Main()** sub only called the **ProcessOrder()** routine. Now, it uses the **OrderInfoPresent()** function in an **if** statement to determine if the customer provided all the information needed to process the order. If so, then the program goes ahead with **ProcessOrder**, just as before. If not, then it calls the **RedisplayOrderForm** sub.

Checking The Order Data

The **OrderInfoPresent** function does only a basic data check: It makes sure that all the required data is present. In this case, that's all we really need. If a user were submitting more complex information, we might easily build in more extensive error trapping, such as making sure some of the values fell into a certain range.

Here, however, we're keeping it simple. The first thing that **OrderInfoPresent** does is to set itself to the value **false**. Only if all the required information is present will the function's value be set to **true**.

After that, there are two distinct steps in the data check. The first step verifies that at least one of the order form's book-order checkboxes has been checked. This is shown in the code snippet below.

```
If (FieldPresent("CB_VBScriptWiz") _
     Or FieldPresent("CB_DelphiExp") _
     Or FieldPresent("CB_JavaApp") _
     Or FieldPresent("CB_Intranet")) _
```

If no checkboxes are checked, then nothing has been ordered. Thus, only *one* of the checkboxes needs to be checked for this to be a valid order. We use parentheses to bundle together all four checkbox tests into a single expression. Inside the expression, we use **or** so that if the user checked at least one of the checkboxes, then the whole expression returns a value of **true**. As before, we use the line-continuation character to keep the Visual Basic code lines within the page margins of this book: For your own code, the line-continuation characters are totally optional.

The second step in the data check is to make sure that *all* of the customer information fields (name, street address, city, state, and zip code) have been filled in. To do that, we use the **and** operator so that the function will get a value of **true** only if all the blanks are filled in. This is shown in the code snippet below.

```
And GetSmallField("TB_Customer") <> "" _
     And GetSmallField("TB_Street") <> "" _
     And GetSmallField("TB_City") <> "" _
     And GetSmallField("TB_State") <> "" _
     And GetSmallField("TB_Zip") <> "" Then OrderInfoPresent = True
```

Redisplaying The Order Form

The procedure to redisplay the order form uses exactly the same approach as is used in the **ProcessOrder()** sub to send an order report back to the user. It starts out with the message header (content line, then a blank line). After that, it's just a matter of sending the appropriate text and HTML tags to redisplay the order form.

The only tricky part is using double and triple quote marks. Visual Basic strings are delimited by quote marks. Therefore, if you need to display a quote mark inside a Visual Basic string, you use two consecutive quote marks for each single quote mark you want to display. Yes, it's a simple idea, but it gets pretty messy in the code, as shown in the line below.

```
Send ("<form method=post action=""http://localhost/cgi-win/orderbk2.exe"">")
```

Where does that > go, again? Is it after all three quote marks at the end of the line, or between the second and third quote marks? You can answer those questions, but if you aren't careful, it's very easy to mess things up. Fortunately, a Web browser generally doesn't care how HTML code is formatted, so the messy-looking HTML document generated by the **RedisplayOrderForm**() sub works just fine. It's shown in Listing 15.6. The order form it displays in the Web browser is shown in Figure 15.7.

Listing 15.6   The HTML code sent by RedisplayOrderForm().

```
<html><head><title>Order Books from Coriolis!
</title></head><body>
You didn't fill out the form completely. Try again.<br>
<h1>Check the books you would like to order:</h1>
<form method=post action="http://localhost/cgi-win/orderbk2.exe">
<hr><ul><ul><ul><ul>
<input name="CB_VBScriptWiz" type="checkbox"
value="1" align=left>
Visual Basic Script Wizardry, $39.99<br>
<input name="CB_DelphiExp" type="checkbox"
value="1" align=left>
The New Delphi 2 Programming EXplorer, $44.99<br>
<input name="CB_JavaApp" type="checkbox"
value="1" align=left>
Writing Java Applets, $39.99<br>
<input name="CB_Intranet" type="checkbox"
value="1" align=left>
Developing Real-World Intranets, $39.99<br>
</ul></ul></ul></ul></ul><hr><pre>
Your Name:      <input name="TB_Customer"
type="text" size="20" align=right><br>
Street Address: <input name="TB_Street"
type="text" size="25" align=right>
</pre>
City:      <input name="TB_City"
type="text" size="15" align=right>
State: <input name="TB_State"
type="text" size="5" align=right>
```

```
Zip: <input name="TB_Zip"
type="text" size="5" align=right><br><br>
Send your order today! <input name="Btn_Order"
type="submit" align=right>
</form></body></html>
```

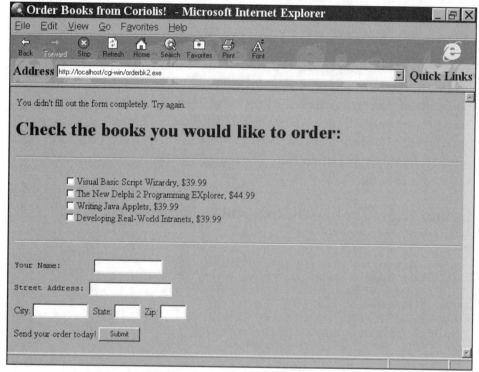

Figure 15.7 The redisplayed order form, sent from the CGI program to the user's Web browser.

APPENDICES

Appendix A
HTML 3 Reference Guide

To use Visual Basic Script effectively–especially with ActiveX layouts, you need to know HTML. HTML is essentially a basic ASCII *markup language* that can easily be composed and edited with any Windows or DOS editor.

As you probably know, HTML is the formatting language used by the World Wide Web. The acronym *HTML* stands for *Hypertext Markup Language*. The hypertext part means that an HTML document can contain references to other documents. This is why HTML makes a great platform for developing interactive multimedia applications. You can design HTML documents to link to other HTML documents or video, sound, and animation files. The other advantage of using HTML as a multimedia platform is that you can develop multimedia applications that can access and use the power of the Internet and the World Wide Web. This is a whole new field, one we like to call *virtual media*.

Originally, HTML was designed as a typesetting language for documents that were created using a computer. The "markup" part of its name comes from the days when book and magazine editors made special marks on the authors' manuscripts to instruct typesetters how to format the text. This process was called markup, and the term was adopted when people started inserting formatting instructions into their computer files.

This appendix provides a useful guide to most of the HTML features supported by leading Web browsers such as Internet Explorer.

HTML—The Language Of The Web

HTML is actually a subset of a language called *SGML*, which stands for *Standard Generalized Markup Language*. HTML commands are enclosed in angle brackets, <like this>. Most commands come in pairs that mark the beginning and end of a part of text. The end command is often identical to the start command, except that it includes a forward slash between the opening bracket and the command name. For example, the title of an HTML document called "Multimedia Adventures" would look like this:

```
<TITLE>Multimedia Adventures/TITLE>
```

Similarly, a word or phrase that you want to display in bold type would be indicated like this:

```
<B>Display this phrase in bold</B>
```

It's not too hard to mark up your text, but all the bracketed tags can make your source text hard to read and proofread. No one has created a true "Web processor," a WYSIWYG word processor that happens to read and write HTML files, but we're bound to see one soon. For now we have to use word processors, text editors, or simple HTML editors that display the tags, not their effects.

Using An HTML Editor

Many people do prefer using an HTML editor over a word processor like Microsoft Word or a simple text editor like Windows Notepad.

HTML Basics

All HTML files consist of a mixture of text to be displayed and HTML tags that describe how the text should be displayed. Normally, extra whitespace (spaces, tabs, and line breaks) is ignored, and text is displayed with a single space between each word. Text is always wrapped to fit within a browser's window in the reader's choice of fonts. Line breaks in the HTML source are treated as any other whitespace, that is, they're ignored—and a paragraph break must be marked with a <P> tag.

Tags are always set off from the surrounding text by angle brackets, the less-than and greater-than signs. Most tags come in *begin* and *end* pairs, for example, <I> ... </I>. The end tag includes a slash between the opening bracket and the tag name. There are a few tags that require only a start tag; we'll point out these tags as they come up.

HTML is case insensitive: <HTML> is the same as <html> or <hTmL>. However, many Web servers run on Unix systems, which *are* case sensitive. This will never affect HTML interpretation, but will affect your hyperlinks: My.gif is not the same file as my.gif or MY.GIF.

Some begin tags can take parameters, which come between the tag name and the closing bracket like this: **<DL COMPACT>**. Others, like description lists, have optional parameters. Still others, such as anchors and images, require certain parameters and can also take optional parameters.

The Structure Of An HTML Document

All HTML documents have a certain standard structure, but Netscape and most other Web browsers will treat any file that ends in .HTML (.HTM on PCs) as an HTML file, even if it contains no HTML tags. All HTML text and tags should be contained within this tag pair:

```
<HTML> ... </HTML>
```

<HEAD> ... </HEAD> Tag

All HTML documents are divided into a header that contains the title and other information about the document, and a body that contains the actual document text.

While you should not place display text outside the body section, this is currently optional since most Web browsers and HTML readers will format and display any text that's not in a tag. Also, while you can get away with not using the **<HEAD>** tag pair, we recommend you use it.

<BODY> ... </BODY> Tag

The tags that appear within the body of an HTML document do not separate the document into sections. Rather, they're either special parts of the text, like images or forms, or they're tags that say something about the text they enclose, like character attributes or paragraph styles.

Headings And Paragraphs

In some ways, HTML text is a series of paragraphs. Within a paragraph, the text will be wrapped to fit the reader's screen. In most cases, any line breaks that appear in the source file are totally ignored.

Paragraphs are separated either by an explicit paragraph break tag, <P>, or by paragraph style commands. The paragraph style determines both the font used for the paragraph and any special indenting. Paragraph styles include several levels of section headers, five types of lists, three different *block formats*, and the normal, or default, paragraph style. Any text outside of an explicit paragraph style command will be displayed in the normal style.

<ADDRESS> ... </ADDRESS> Tag

The last part of the document body should be an <ADDRESS> tag pair, which contains information about the author and, often, the document's copyright date and revision history. While the address block is not a required part of the document in the same way that the header or the body is, official style guides urge that all documents have one. In current practice, while most documents use the <HTML>, <HEAD>, and <BODY> tag pairs, almost all documents have address blocks—perhaps because the address block is visible.

The format for using the <ADDRESS> tag is as follows:

```
<ADDRESS>Address text goes here</ADDRESS>
```

Comments

Comments can be placed in your HTML documents using a special tag as shown:

```
<!-Comment text goes here->
```

Everything between the <> will be ignored by a browser when the document is displayed.

Header Elements

The elements used in the header of an HTML document include a title section and internal indexing information.

<TITLE> ... </TITLE> Tag

Every document should have a title. The manner in which a title is displayed varies from system to system and browser to browser. The title could be displayed as a window title, or it may appear in a pane within the window. The title should be short—64 characters or less—and should contain just text.

The title should appear in the header section, marked off with a <TITLE> tag pair; for example, <TITLE>Explore the Grand Canyon</TITLE>. Some Web browsers like Netscape are quite easy-going and will let you place the title anywhere in the document, even after the </HTML> tag, but future browsers might not be quite so accommodating. Including a title is important because many Web search engines will use the title to locate a document.

The format for using the <TITLE> tag is as follows:

```
<TITLE>Title text goes here</TITLE>
```

Other <HEAD> Elements

There are a few optional elements that may only appear in the document's header (<HEAD> tag pair). The header elements that browsers use are the <BASE> and <ISINDEX> tags. Both are empty or solitary tags that do not have a closing </...> tag and thus do not enclose any text.

The <BASE> tag contains the current document's URL, or Uniform Resource Locator; browsers can use it to find local URLs.

The <ISINDEX> tag tells browsers that this document is an index document, which means that the server can support keyword searches based on the document's URL. Searches are passed back to the Web server by concatenating a question mark and one or more keywords to the document URL and then requesting this extended URL. This is very similar to one of the ways that form data is returned. (See the section *Form Action and Method Attributes* for more information.)

HTML includes other header elements, such as <NEXTID> and <LINK>, which are included in HTML for the benefit of editing and cataloging software. They have no visible effect; browsers simply ignore them.

Normal Text

Most HTML documents are composed of plain, or normal, text. Any text not appearing between format tag pairs is displayed as normal text.

Normal text, like every other type of paragraph style except the preformatted style, is wrapped at display time to fit in the reader's window. A larger or smaller font or window size will result in a totally different number of words on each line, so don't try to change the wording of a sentence to make the line breaks come at appropriate places. It won't work.

 Tag

If line breaks are important, as in postal addresses or poetry, you can use the <BR> command to insert a line break. Subsequent text will appear one line down, on the left margin.

The general format for this tag is:

```
<BR CLEAR=[Left|Right]>
```

The section listed between the [] is optional. This is a feature introduced as an HTML enhancement and supported by newer versions of Netscape.

Let's look at an example of how <BR> is used. To keep

```
Coriolis Group Books
7339 East Acoma Drive, Suite 7
Scottsdale, Arizona 85260-6912
```

from coming out as

```
Coriolis Group Books 7339 East Acoma Drive, Suite 7 Scottsdale, Arizona
85260-6912
```

you would write:

```
Coriolis Group Books<BR>
7339 East Acoma Drive, Suite 7<BR>
Scottsdale, Arizona 85260-6912<BR>
```

The extended form of the <BR> tag allows you to control how text is wrapped. The **CLEAR** argument allows text to be broken so that it can flow to the right or to the left around an image. For example, this tag shows how text can be broken to flow to the left:

```
This text will be broken here.<BR CLEAR=Left>
```

This line will flow around to the right of an image that can be displayed with the **IMG** tag.

<NOBR> Tag

This tag stands for *No Break*. This is another HTML extension supported by Netscape. To keep text from breaking, you can include the **<NOBR>** tag at the beginning of the text you want to keep together.

<WBR> Tag

This tag stands for Word Break. If you use the **<NOBR>** tag to define a section of text without breaks, you can force a line break at any location by inserting the **<WBR>** tag followed by the **
** tag.

<P> Tag

The **
** command causes a line break within a paragraph, but more often we want to separate one paragraph from another. We can do this by enclosing each paragraph in a **<P>** tag pair, starting the paragraph with **<P>** and ending it with **</P>**. The actual appearance of the paragraphs will depend on your reader's Web browser: Paragraph breaks may be shown with an extra line or half line of spacing, a leading indent, or both.

The **</P>** tag is optional; most people include a single **<P>** at the beginning of each paragraph, at the end, or alone on a line between two paragraphs.

Physical And Logical Attributes

Character attribute tags let you emphasize words or phrases within a paragraph. HTML supports two different types of character attributes: physical and logical. Physical attributes include the familiar bold, italic, and underline, as well as a tty attribute for monospaced text.

Logical attributes are different. In keeping with the SGML philosophy of using tags to describe content and not the actual formatting, logical attributes let you describe what sort of emphasis you want to put on a word or phrase, but leave the actual formatting up to the browser. That is, where a word marked with a physical attribute like **<B>bold</B>** will always appear in bold type, an **<EM>emphasized</EM>** word may be italicized, underlined, bolded, or displayed in color.

Table A.1   List of physical attributes.

Attribute	Tag	Sample	Effect
Bold	`<B>`	Some `<B>`bold`</B>` text	Some **bold** text
Italic	`<I>`	Some `<I>`italicized`</I>` text	Some italicized text
Underline	`<U>`	Some `<U>`underlined`</U>` text	Some underlined text
TTY	`<TT>`	Some `<TT>`monospaced (tty)`</TT>` text	Some `monospaced (tty)` text

Web style guides suggest that you use logical attributes whenever you can, but there's a slight problem: Some current browsers only support some physical attributes, and few or no logical attributes. Since Web browsers simply ignore any HTML tag that they don't *understand*, when you use logical tags, you run the risk that your readers will not see any formatting at all!

The standard format for using any of the physical attributes tags is as follows:

```
<tag>text goes here</tag>
```

You can nest attributes, although the results will vary from browser to browser. For example, some browsers can display bold italic text, while others will only display the innermost attribute. (That is, **<B><I>bold italic</I></B>** may show up

Table A.2   List of logical attributes.

Attribute	Tag	Use or Interpretation	Typical Rendering
Citation	`<CITE>`	Titles of books and films	Italic
Code	`<CODE>`	Source code fragments	Monospaced
Definition	`<DFN>`	A word being defined	Italic
Emphasis	`<EM>`	Emphasize a word or phrase	Italic
PRE	`<PRE>`	Used for tables and text	Preformatted text
Keyboard	`<KBD>`	Something the user should type, word-for-word	Bold monospaced
Sample	`<SAMP>`	Computer status messages	Monospaced
Strong	`<STRONG>`	Strong emphasis	Bold
Variable	`<VAR>`	A description of something the user should type, like `<filename>`	Italic

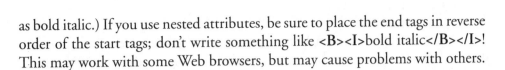

as bold italic.) If you use nested attributes, be sure to place the end tags in reverse order of the start tags; don't write something like <B><I>bold italic</B></I>! This may work with some Web browsers, but may cause problems with others.

Keep in mind that even if current browsers arbitrarily decide that <EM> text will be displayed as italic and <KBD> text will be displayed as Courier, future browsers will probably defer these attributes to a setting controlled by the user. So, don't conclude that citations, definitions, and variables all look alike and that you should ignore them and use italic.

<BLINK> ... </BLINK>

This is a new enhanced tag supported by Netscape. Text placed between this pair will blink on the screen. This feature is useful for attention-grabbing, but using it too much could get rather annoying. The format for this tag is:

```
<BLINK>This text will blink</BLINK>
```

<CENTER> ... </CENTER>

This HTML enhancement makes some Web page authors feel like they've died and gone to heaven. Any text (or images) placed between this pair is centered between the left and right margins of a page. The format for this tag is:

```
<CENTER>This text will be centered between the left and right margins</CENTER>
```

<FONT> ... </FONT>

This HTML enhancement allows you to control the sizes of the fonts displayed in your documents. The format for this tag is:

```
<FONT SIZE=font-size>text goes here</FONT>
```

where *font-size* must be a number from 1 to 7. A size of 1 produces the smallest font. The default font size is 3. Once the font size has been changed, it will remain in effect until the font size is changed by using another tag.

<BASEFONT>

To give you even greater control over font sizing, a new HTML tag has been added so that you can set the base font for all text displayed in a document. The format for this tag is:

```
<BASEFONT SIZE=font-size>
```

Again, *font-size* must be a number from 1 to 7. A size of 1 produces the smallest font. The default font size is 3. Once the base font size has been defined, you can display text in larger or smaller fonts using the + or - sign with the **<FONT>** tag. Here's an example of how this works:

```
<BASEFONT SIZE=4>
This text will be displayed as size 4 text.
<FONT SIZE=+2>
This text will be displayed as size 6.
</FONT>
This text will return to the base font size--size 4.
```

Headings

HTML provides six levels of section headers, **<H1>** through **<H6>**. While these are typically short phrases that fit on a line or two, the various headers are actually full-fledged paragraph types. They can even contain line and paragraph break commands.

You are not required to use a **<H1>** before you use a **<H2>**, or to make sure that a **<H4>** follows a **<H3>** or another **<H4>**.

The standard format for using one of the six heading tags is illustrated by this sample:

```
<H1>Text Goes Here</H1>
```

Lists

HTML supports five different list types. All five types can be thought of as a sort of paragraph type. The first four list types share a common syntax, and differ only in how they format their list elements. The fifth type, the *description* list, is unique in that each list element has two parts—a tag and a description of the tag.

All five list types display an element marker—whether it be a number, a bullet, or a few words—on the left margin. The marker is followed by the actual list elements, which appear indented. List elements do not have to fit on a single line or consist of a single paragraph—they may contain **<P>** and **
** tags.

Lists can be nested, but the appearance of a nested list depends on the browser. For example, some browsers use different bullets for inner lists than for outer lists, and some browsers do not indent nested lists. However, Netscape and Lynx, which are probably the most common graphical and text mode browsers, do indent nested lists; the tags of a nested list align with the elements of the outer list, and the elements of the nested list are further indented. For example,

```
• This is the first element of the main bulleted list.
  • This is the first element of a nested list.
  • This is the second element of the nested list.
• This is the second element of the main bulleted list.
```

The four list types that provide simple list elements use the list item tag, **<LI>**, to mark the start of each list element. The **<LI>** tag always appears at the start of a list element, not at the end.

Thus, all simple lists look something like this:

```
<ListType>

<LI>
There isn't really any ListType list, however the OL, UL, DIR, and
MENU lists all follow this format.

<LI>
Since whitespace is ignored, you can keep your source legible by
putting blank lines between your list elements. Sometimes, we like to put
the &lt;li&gt; tags on their own lines, too.

<LI>
(If we hadn't used the ampersand quotes in the previous list element,
the "&lt;li&gt;" would have been interpreted as the start of a new
list element.)

</ListType>
```

Numbered List

In HTML, numbered lists are referred to as *ordered lists*. The list type tag is **<OL>**. Numbered lists can be nested, but some browsers get confused by the close of a nested list, and start numbering the subsequent elements of the outer list from 1.

Bulleted List

If a numbered list is an ordered list, what else could an unnumbered, bulleted list be but an unordered list? The tag for an unordered (bulleted) list is **<UL>**.

While bulleted lists can be nested, you should keep in mind that the list nesting may not be visible; some browsers indent nested lists; some don't. Some use multiple bullet types; others don't.

Netscape List Extensions

Netscape has added a useful feature called **TYPE** that can be included with unordered and ordered lists. This feature allows you to specify the type of bullet or number that you use for the different levels of indentation in a list.

UNORDERED LIST WITH EXTENSIONS

When Netscape displays the different levels of indentation in an unordered list, it uses a solid disk (level 1) followed by a bullet (level 2) followed by a square (level 3). You can use the **TYPE** feature with the <UL> tag to override this sequence of bullets. Here's the format:

```
<UL TYPE=Disc|Circle|Square>
```

For example, here's a list defined to use circles as the bullet symbol:

```
<UL TYPE=Circle>
<LI>This is item 1
<LI>This is item 2
<LI>This is item 3
</UL>
```

ORDERED LIST WITH EXTENSIONS

When Netscape displays ordered (numbered) lists, it numbers each list item using a numeric sequence—1, 2, 3, and so on. You can change this setting by using the **TYPE** modifier with the <OL> tag. Here's how this feature is used with numbered lists:

```
<OL TYPE=A|a|I|i|1>
```

where **TYPE** can be assigned to any one of these values:

A   Mark list items with capital letters
a   Mark list items with lowercase letters
I   Mark list items with large roman numerals
i   Mark list items with small roman numerals
1   Mark list items with numbers (default)

Wait, there's more. You can also start numbering list items with a number other than 1. To do this, you use the **START** modifier as shown:

```
<OL START=starting-number>
```

where starting-number specifies the first number used. You can use the feature with the **TYPE** tag. For example, the tag

```
<OL TYPE=A START=4>
```

would start the numbered list with the roman numeral IV.

Using Modifiers With List Elements

In addition to supporting the **TYPE** modifier with the <UL> and <OL> tags, Netscape allows you to use this modifier with the <LI> tag to define list elements for ordered and unordered lists. Here's an example of how it can be used with an unordered list:

```
<H2>Useful Publishing Resources</H2>
<UL TYPE=Disc>
<LI>HTML Tips
<LI>Web Page Samples
<LI TYPE=Square>Images
<LI TYPE=Disc>Templates
</UL>
```

In this case, all the list items will have a disc symbol as the bullet, except the third item, *Images*, which will be displayed with a square bullet.

The **TYPE** modifier can be assigned the same values as those used to define lists with the <UL> and <OL> tags. Once it is used to define a style for a list item, all subsequent items in the list will be changed, unless another **TYPE** modifier is used.

If you are defining <LI> list elements for ordered lists <OL>, you can also use a new modifier named **VALUE** to change the numeric value of a list item. Here's an example:

```
<H2>Useful Publishing Resources</H2>
<OL>
<LI>HTML Tips
<LI>Web Page Samples
<LI VALUE=4>Images
<LI>Templates
</UL>
```

In this list, the third item would be assigned the number 4 and the fourth item would be assigned the number 5.

Directory And Menu Lists

The directory and menu lists are special types of unordered lists. The menu list, <MENU>, is meant to be visually more compact than a standard unordered list; menu list items should all fit on a single line. The directory list, <DIR>, is supposed to be even more compact; all list items should be less than 20 characters long, so that the list can be displayed in three (or more) columns.

We're not sure if we've ever actually seen these lists in use, and their implementation is still spotty; current versions of Netscape do not create multiple columns for a <DIR> list, and while they let you choose a directory list font and a menu list font, they do not actually use these fonts.

Description List

The description list, or <DL>, does not use the <LI> tag the way other lists do. Each description list element has two parts, a tag and its description. Each tag begins with a <DT> tag, and each description with a <DD> tag. These appear at the start of the list element, and are not paired with </DT> or </DD> tags.

The description list looks a lot like any other list, except that instead of a bullet or a number, the list tag consists of your text. Description lists are intended to be used for creating formats like a glossary entry, where a short tag is followed by an indented definition, but the format is fairly flexible. For example, a long tag will wrap, just like any other paragraph, although it should not contain line or paragraph breaks. (Netscape will indent any <DT> text after a line or paragraph, as if it were the <DD> text.) Further, you needn't actually supply any tag text; <DT><DD> will produce an indented paragraph.

Compact And Standard Lists

Normally, a description list puts the tags on one line, and starts the indented descriptions on the next:

```
Tag 1
Description 1.
Tag 2
Description 2.
```

For a tighter look, you can use a **<DL COMPACT>**. If the tags are very short, some browsers will start the descriptions on the same line as the tags:

```
Tag 1     Description 1
Tag 2     Description 2
```

However, most browsers do not support the compact attribute, and will simply ignore it. For example, with current versions of Windows Netscape, a **<DL COMPACT>** will always look like a **<DL>**, even if the tags are very short.

Inline Images

Using only text attributes, section headers, and lists, you can build attractive-looking documents. The next step is to add pictures.

<IMG ...> Tag

The <IMG> tag is a very useful HTML feature. It lets you insert inline images into your text. This tag is rather different from the tags we've seen so far. Not only is it an empty tag that always appears alone, it has a number of parameters between the opening **<IMG** and the closing **>**. Some of the parameters include the image file name and some optional modifiers. The basic format for this tag is:

```
<IMG SRC="URL" ALT="text"
     ALIGN=top|middle|bottom
     ISMAP>
```

Since HTML 3 has emerged and additional Netscape extensions have been added, this tag has expanded more than any other HTML feature. Here is the complete format for the latest and greatest version of the **<IMG>** tag:

```
<IMG SRC="URL" ALT="text"
     ALIGN=left|right|top|texttop|middle|absmiddle|
           baseline|bottom|absbottom
     WIDTH=pixels
     HEIGHT=pixels
     BORDER=pixels
     VSPACE=pixels
     HSPACE=pixels
     ISMAP>
```

The extended version allows you to specify the size of an image, better control image and text alignment, and specify the size of an image's border.

Every <IMG> tag must have a **SRC=** parameter. This specifies a URL, or Uniform Resource Locator, which points to a GIF or JPEG bitmap file. When the bitmap file is in the same directory as the HTML document, the file name is an adequate URL. For example, <IMG SRC=MySmilingFace.gif> would insert a picture of a smiling face.

Some people turn off inline images because they have a slow connection to the Web. This replaces all images, no matter what size, with a standard graphic. This isn't so bad if the picture is ancillary to your text, but if you've used small inline images as bullets in a list or as section dividers, the placeholder graphic will usually make your page look rather strange. For this reason, some people avoid using graphics as structural elements; others simply don't worry about people with slow connections; still others include a note at the top of the page saying that all the images on the page are small, and invite people with inline images off to turn them on and reload the page.

Keep in mind that some people use text-only browsers, like Lynx, to navigate the Web. If you include a short description of your image with the **ALT=** parameter, text-only browsers can show something in place of your graphic. For example, <IMG SRC=MySmilingFace.gif could be supplemented by the code: **ALT=**"A picture of the author">, so that no one feels left out.

Since the the value assigned to the **ALT** parameter has spaces in it, we have to put it within quotation marks. In general, you can put any parameter value in quotation marks, but you need to do so only if it includes spaces.

Table A.3 Summary of <IMG> parameters.

Parameter	Required?	Settings
SRC	Yes	URL
ALT	No	A text string
ALIGN	No	top, middle, bottom, left, right, texttop, absmiddle, baseline, absbottom
HEIGHT	No	Pixel setting
WIDTH	No	Pixel setting
BORDER	No	Pixel setting
VSPACE	No	Pixel setting
HSPACE	No	Pixel setting
ISMAP	No	None

Mixing Images And Text

You can mix text and images within a paragraph; an image does not constitute a paragraph break. However, some Web browsers, like earlier versions of Netscape, did not wrap paragraphs around images; they displayed a single line of text to the left or right of an image. Normally, any text in the same paragraph as an image would be lined up with the bottom of the image, and would wrap normally below the image. This works well if the text is essentially a caption for the image, or if the image is a decoration at the start of a paragraph. However, when the image is a part of a header, you may want the text to be centered vertically in the image, or to be lined up with the top of the image. In these cases, you can use the optional **ALIGN=** parameter to specify **ALIGN=top**, **ALIGN=middle**, or **ALIGN=bottom**.

Using Floating Images

With the extended version of the **<IMG>** tag, you can now create "floating" images that will align to the left or right margin of a Web page. Text that is displayed after the image will either wrap around the right-hand or left-hand side of the image. Here's an example of how an image can be displayed at the left margin with text that wraps to the right of the image:

```
<IMG SRC="limage.gif" ALIGN=left>
```

Text will be displayed to the right of the image.

Specifying Spacing For Floating Images

When you use floating images with wrap-around text, you can specify the spacing between the text and the image by using the **VSPACE** and **HSPACE** modifiers. **VSPACE** defines the amount of spacing in units of pixels between the top and bottom of the image and the text. **HSPACE** defines the spacing between the left or right edge of the image and the text that wraps.

Sizing Images

Another useful feature that has been added to the **<IMG>** tag is image sizing. The **WIDTH** and **HEIGHT** modifiers are used to specify the width and height for an image in pixels. Here's an example:

```
<IMG SRC="logo.gif" WIDTH=250 HEIGHT=310>
```

When a browser like Netscape displays an image, it needs to determine the size of the image before it can display a placeholder or bounding box for the image. If you include the image's size using **WIDTH** and **HEIGHT**, a Web page can be built much faster. If the values you specify for **WIDTH** and **HEIGHT** differ from the image's actual width and height, the image will be scaled to fit.

Using Multiple Images Per Line

Since an image is treated like a single (rather large) character, you can have more than one image on a single line. In fact, you can have as many images on a line as will fit in your reader's window! If you put too many images on a line, the browser will wrap the line and your images will appear on multiple lines. If you don't want images to appear on the same line, place a <BR> or <P> between them.

Defining An Image's Border

Typically, an image is displayed with a border around it. This is the border that is set to the color blue when the image is part of an anchor. Using the **BORDER** modifier, you can specify a border width for any image you display. Here's an example that displays an image with a five pixel border:

```
<IMG SRC="logo.gif" BORDER=5>
```

IsMap Parameter

The optional **ISMAP** parameter allows you to place hyperlinks to other documents in a bitmapped image. This technique is used to turn an image into a clickable map. (See the section *Using Many Anchors in an Image* for more detail.)

Horizontal Rules

The <HR> tag draws a horizontal rule, or line, across the screen. It's fairly common to put a rule before and after a form, to help set off the user entry areas from the normal text.

Many people use small inline images for decoration and separation, instead of rules. Although using images in this manner lets you customize your pages, it also takes longer for them to load—and it may make them look horrible when inline images are turned off.

The original **<HR>** tag simply displayed an engraved rule across a Web page. A newer version of the tag has been extended to add additional features including sizing, alignment, and shading. The format for the extended version of **<HR>** is:

```
<HR SIZE=pixels
    WIDTH=pixels|percent
    ALIGN=left|right|center
    NOSHADE>
```

The **SIZE** modifier sets the width (thickness) of the line in pixel units. The **WIDTH** modifier specifies the length of the line in actual pixel units or a percentage of the width of the page. The **ALIGN** modifier specifies the alignment for the line (the default is center) and the **NOSHADE** modifier allows you to display a solid line.

As an example of how some of these new features are used, the following tag displays a solid line, five pixels thick. The line is left justified and spans 80 percent of the width of the page:

```
<HR SIZE=5 WIDTH=80% ALIGN="left" NOSHADE>
```

Hypermedia Links

The ability to add links to other HTML documents or to entirely different sorts of documents is what makes the HTML-driven readers so powerful. The special sort of highlight that your reader clicks on to traverse a hypermedia link is called an anchor, and all links are created with the anchor tag, **<A>**. The basic format for this tag is:

```
<A HREF="URL"
   NAME="text"
   REL=next|previous|parent|made
   REV=next|previous|parent|made
   TITLE="text">

text</A>
```

Links To Other Documents

While you can define a link to another point within the current page, most links are to other documents. Links to points within a document are very similar to links to other documents, but are slightly more complicated, so we will talk about them later. (See the section *Links to Anchors*.)

Each link has two parts: The visible part, or anchor, which the user clicks on, and the invisible part, which tells the browser where to go. The anchor is the text between the <A> and </A> tags of the <A> tag pair, while the actual link data appears in the <A> tag.

Just as the <IMG> tag has a SRC= parameter that specifies an image file, so does the <A> tag have an HREF= parameter that specifies the hypermedia reference. Thus, <A HREF=SomeFile.Type>click here</A> is a link to *somefile.type* with the visible anchor *click here*.

Browsers will generally use the linked document's filename extension to decide how to display the linked document. For example, HTML or HTM files will be interpreted and displayed as HTML, whether they come from an http server, an FTP server, or a gopher site. Conversely, a link can be to any sort of file—a large bitmap, sound file, or movie.

Images As Hotspots

Since inline images are in many ways just big characters, there's no problem with using an image in an anchor. The anchor can include text on either side of the image, or the image can be an anchor by itself. Most browsers show an image anchor by drawing a blue border around the image (or around the placeholder graphic). The image anchor may be a picture of what is being linked to, or for reasons we'll explain shortly, it may even just point to another copy of itself:

```
<A HREF=image.gif><IMG SRC=image.gif></A>.
```

Thumbnail Images

One sort of *picture of the link* is called a thumbnail image. This is a tiny image, perhaps 100 pixels in the smaller dimension, which is either a condensed version of a larger image or a section of the image. Thumbnail images can be transmitted quickly, even via slow communication lines, leaving it up to the reader to decide which larger images to request. A secondary issue is aesthetic: Large images take up a lot of screen space, smaller images don't.

Linking An Image To Itself

Many people turn off inline images to improve performance over a slow network link. If the inline image is an anchor for itself, these people can then click on the placeholder graphic to see what they missed.

Using Many Anchors In An Image

The <IMG> tag's optional ISMAP parameter allows you to turn rectangular regions of a bitmap image into clickable anchors. Clicking on these parts of the image will activate an appropriate URL. (A default URL is also usually provided for when the user clicks on an area outside of one of the predefined regions.) While forms let you do this a bit more flexibly, the ISMAP approach doesn't require any custom programming—just a simple text file that defines the rectangles and their URLs—and this technique may work with browsers that do not support forms. An example of how to do this can be found on the Web site at:

```
http://wintermute.ncsc.uiuc.edu:8080/map-tutorial/image-maps.html
```

Links To Anchors

When an HREF parameter specifies a filename, the link is to the whole document. If the document is an HTML file, it will replace the current document and the reader will be placed at the top of the new document. Often this is just what you want. But sometimes you'd rather have a link take the reader to a specific section of a document. Doing this requires two anchor tags: one that defines an anchor name for a location, and one that points to that name. These two tags can be in the same document or in different documents.

Defining An Anchor Name

To define an anchor name, you need to use the NAME parameter: <A NAME=AnchorName>. You can attach this name to a phrase, not just a single point, by following the <A> tag with a </A> tag.

Linking To An Anchor In The Current Document

To then use this name, simply insert an <A HREF=...> tag as usual, except that instead of a filename, use a # followed by an anchor name. For example, <A HREF=#AnchorName> refers to the example in the previous paragraph.

Names do not have to be defined before they are used; it's actually fairly common for lengthy documents to have a table of contents with links to names defined later in the document. It's also worth noting that while tag and parameter names are not case sensitive, anchor names are; <A HREF=#anchorname> will not take you to the AnchorName example.

Table A.4　Summary of the <A> tag syntax.

To:	Use:
Link to another document	<A HREF="URL">highlighted anchor text</A>
Name an anchor	<A NAME="Anchor Name">normal text</A>
Link to a named anchor in this document	<A href="#Anchor Name">highlighted anchor text</A>
Link to a named anchor in another document	<A href="URL#Anchor Name">highlighted anchor text</A>

Linking To An Anchor In A Different Document

You can also link to specific places in any other HTML document, anywhere in the world—provided, of course, that it contains named anchors. To do this, you simply add the # and the anchor name after the URL that tells where the document can be found. For example, to plant a link to the anchor named "Section 1" in a file named complex.html in the same directory as the current file, you could use **<A HREF="Complex.html#Section 1">**. Similarly, if the named anchor was in http://www.another.org/Complex.html, you'd use **<A HREF="http://www.another.org/Complex.html#Section 1">**.

Using URLs

Just as a complete DOS file name starts with a drive letter followed by a colon, so a full URL starts with a resource type—HTTP, FTP, GOPHER, and so on—followed by a colon. If the name doesn't have a colon in it, it's assumed to be a local reference, which is a file name on the same file system as the current document. Thus, **<A HREF=Another.html>** refers to the file "Another.html" in the same directory as the current file, while **<A HREF=/html/File.html>** refers to the file "File.html" in the top-level directory *html*. One thing to note here is that a URL always uses "/" (the Unix-style forward slash) as a directory separator, even when the files are on a Windows machine, which would normally use "\", the DOS-style backslash.

Local URLs can be very convenient when you have several HTML files with links to each other, or when you have a large number of inline images. If you

Table A.5	A partial table of URL resource types.	
Resource	**Interpretation**	**Format**
HTTP	Hypertext Transfer Protocol	http://machine-name/file-name
FTP	File Transfer Protocol	ftp://machine-name/file-name
GOPHER	Gopher	gopher://machine-name/file-name
NEWS	Internet News	news:group-name
TELNET	Log on to a remote system	telnet://machine-name
MAILTO	Normal Internet e-mail	mailto:user-name@machine-name

ever have to move them all to another directory, or to another machine, you don't have to change all the URLs.

<BASE> Tag

One drawback of local URLs is that if someone makes a copy of your document, the local URLs will no longer work. Adding the optional **<BASE>** tag to the **<HEAD>** section of your document will help eliminate this problem. While many browsers do not yet support it, the intent of the **<BASE>** tag is precisely to provide a context for local URLs.

The **<BASE>** tag is like the **<IMG>** tag, in that it's a so-called empty tag. It requires an HREF parameter—for example, **<BASE HREF**=http://www.imaginary.org/index.html>—which should contain the URL of the document itself. When a browser that supports the **<BASE>** tag encounters a URL that doesn't contain a protocol and path, it will look for it relative to the base URL, instead of relative to the location from which it actually loaded the document. The format for the **<BASE>** tag is:

```
<BASE HREF="URL">
```

Reading And Constructing URLs

Where a local URL is just a file name, a global URL specifies an instance of one of several resource types, which may be located on any Internet machine in the world. The wide variety of resources is reflected in a complex URL syntax. For example, while most URLs consist of a resource type followed by a colon, two forward slashes, a machine name, another forward slash, and a resource name, others consist only of a resource type, a colon, and the resource name.

The resource-type://machine-name/resource-name URL form is used with centralized resources, where there's a single server that supplies the document to the rest of the net, using a particular protocol. Thus, "http://www.another.org/Complex.html" means "use the Hypertext Transfer Protocol to get file complex.html from the main www directory on the machine www.another.org", while "ftp://foo.bar.net/pub/www/editors/README" means "use the File Transfer Protocol to get the file /pub/www/editors/README from the machine foo.bar.net".

Conversely, many resource types are distributed. We don't all get our news or mail from the same central server, but from the nearest one of many news and mail servers. URLs for distributed resources use the simpler form resource-type:resource-name. For example, "news:comp.infosystems.www.providers" refers to the Usenet newsgroup comp.infosystems.www.providers, which, by the way, is a good place to look for further information about writing HTML.

Using www And Actual Machine Names

In the HTTP domain, you'll often see "machine names" like "www.coriolis.com". This usually does not mean there's a machine named www.coriolis.com that you can FTP or Telnet to; "www" is an alias that a Webmaster can set up when he or she registers the server. Using the www alias makes sense, because machines come and go, but sites (and, we hope, the Web) last for quite a while. If URLs refer to www at the site and not to a specific machine, the server and all the HTML files can be moved to a new machine simply by changing the www alias, without having to update all the URLs.

Using Special Characters

Since < and > have special meanings in HTML, there must be a way to represent characters like these as part of text. While the default character set for the Web is ISO Latin-1, which includes European language characters like _ and § in the range from 128 to 255, it's not uncommon to pass around snippets of HTML in 7-bit email, or to edit them on dumb terminals, so HTML also needs a way to specify high-bit characters using only 7-bit characters.

Two Forms: Numeric And Symbolic

There are two ways to specify an arbitrary character: numeric and symbolic. To include the copyright symbol, ©, which is character number 169, you can use ©. That is, &#, then the number of the character you want to include, and a closing semicolon. The numeric method is very general, but not easy to read.

The symbolic form is much easier to read, but its use is restricted to the four low-bit characters with special meaning in HTML. To use the other symbols in the ISO Latin-1 character set, like ® and the various currency symbols, you have to use the numeric form. The symbolic escape is like the numeric escape, except there's no #. For example, to insert é, you would use é, or &, the character name, and a closing semicolon. You should be aware that symbol names are case sensitive: É is É, not é, while &EAcute; is no character at all, and will show up in your text as &EAcute;!

Preformatted And Other Special Paragraph Types

HTML supports three special "block" formats. Any normal text within a block format is supposed to appear in a distinctive font.

<BLOCKQUOTE> ... </BLOCKQUOTE> Tag

The block quote sets an extended quotation off from normal text. That is, a **<BLOCKQUOTE>** tag pair does not imply indented, single-spaced, and italicized; rather, it's just meant to change the default, plain text font. The format for this tag is:

```
<BLOCKQUOTE>text</BLOCKQUOTE>
```

<PRE> ... </PRE> Tag

Everything in a preformatted block will appear in a monospaced font. The **<PRE>** tag pair is also the only HTML element that pays any attention to the line breaks in the source file; any line break in a preformatted block will be treated just as a **
** elsewhere. Since HTML tags can be used within a preformatted block, you can have anchors as well as bold or italic monospaced text. The format for this tag is:

```
<PRE WIDTH=value>text</PRE>
```

The initial **<PRE>** tag has an optional **WIDTH=** parameter. Browsers won't trim lines to this length; the intent is to allow the browser to select a monospaced font that will allow the maximum line length to fit in the browser window.

<ADDRESS> ... </ADDRESS> Tag

The third block format is the address format: **<ADDRESS>**. This is generally displayed in italics, and is intended for displaying information about a document, such as creation date, revision history, and how to contact the author. Official style guides say that every document should provide an address block. The format for this tag is:

```
<ADDRESS>text</ADDRESS>
```

Many people put a horizontal rule, **<HR>**, between the body of the document and the address block. If you include a link to your home page or to a page that lets the reader send mail to you, you won't have to include a lot of information on each individual page.

Using Tables

Features like lists are great for organizing data; however, sometimes you need a more compact way of grouping related data. Fortunately, some of the newer browsers like Netscape have implemented the proposed HTML 3 specification for tables. Tables can contain a heading and row and column data. Each unit of a table is called a cell and cell data can be text and images.

<TABLE > ... </TABLE> Tag

This tag is used to define a new table. All of the table-specific tags must be placed within the pair **<TABLE>** ... **</TABLE>**, otherwise they will be ignored. The format for the **<TABLE>** tag is:

```
<TABLE BORDER>table text</TABLE>
```

Leaving out the **BORDER** modifier will display the table without a border.

Creating A Table Title

Creating a title or caption for a table is easy with the **<CAPTION>** tag. This tag must be placed within the **<TABLE>** ... **</TABLE>** tags. Here is its general format:

```
<CAPTION ALIGN=top|bottom>caption text</CAPTION>
```

Notice that you can display the caption at the top or bottom of the table. By default, the caption will be displayed at the top of the table.

Creating Table Rows

Every table you create will have one or more rows. (Otherwise it won't be much of a table!) The simple tag for creating a row is:

```
<TR>text</TR>
```

For each row that you want to add, you must place the **<TR>** tag inside the body of the table, between the **<TABLE>** ... **</TABLE>** tags.

Defining Table Data Cells

Within each **<TR>** ... **</TR>** tag pair come one or more **<TD>** tags to define the table cell data. You can think of the cell data as the column definitions for the table. Here is the format for a **<TD>** tag:

```
<TD ALIGN=left|center|right
    VALIGN=top|middle|bottom|baseline
    NOWRAP
    COLSPAN=number
    ROWSPAN=number>
text</TD>
```

The size for each cell is determined by the width or height of the data that is displayed. The **ALIGN** parameter can be used to center or left- or right-justify the data displayed in the cell. The **VALIGN** parameter, on the other hand, specifies how the data will align vertically. If you don't want the text to wrap within the cell, you can include the **NOWRAP** modifier.

When defining a cell, you can manually override the width and height of the cell by using the **COLSPAN** and **ROWSPAN** parameters. **COLSPAN** specifies the number of columns the table cell will span and **ROWSPAN** specifies the number of rows to span. The default setting for each of these parameters is 1.

Defining Headings For Cells

In addition to displaying a table caption, you can include headings for a table's data cells. The tag for defining a heading looks very similar to the <TD> tag:

```
<TH ALIGN=left|center|right
    VALIGN=top|middle|bottom|baseline
    NOWRAP
    COLSPAN=number
    ROWSPAN=number>
text</TH>
```

Using Forms

The HTML features presented so far correspond with traditional publishing practices: You create a hypermedia document, and others read it. With HTML forms, however, you can do much more. You can create a form that lets your readers search a database using any criteria they like. Or you can create a form that lets them critique your Web pages. Or—and this is what excites business people—you can use forms to sell things over the Internet.

Forms are easy to create. However, to use them, you'll need a program that runs on your Web server to process the information that the user's client sends back to you. For simple things like a "comments page," you can probably use an existing program. For anything more complex, you'll probably need a custom program. While we will briefly describe the way form data looks to the receiving program, any discussion of form programming is beyond this book's scope.

<FORM> ... </FORM> Tag

All input widgets—text boxes, check boxes, and radio buttons—must appear within a <FORM> tag pair. When a user clicks on a submit button or an image map, the contents of all the widgets in the form will be sent to the program that you specify in the <FORM> tag. HTML widgets include single- and multi-line text boxes, radio buttons and check boxes, pull-down lists, image maps, a couple of standard buttons, and a hidden widget that might be used to identify the form to a program that can process several forms.

Within your form, you can use any other HTML elements, including headers, images, rules, and lists. This gives you a fair amount of control over your form's appearance, but you should always remember that the user's screen size and font choices will affect the actual appearance of your form.

While you can have more than one form on a page, you cannot nest one form within another.

The basic format for the **<FORM>** tag is as follows:

```
<FORM ACTION="URL"
      METHOD=get|post>
text</FORM>
```

Notice that text can be included as part of the form definition.

Form Action And Method Attributes

Nothing gets sent to your Web server until the user presses a Submit button or clicks on an image map. What happens then depends on the **ACTION**, **METHOD**, and **ENCTYPE** parameters of the **<FORM>** tag.

The ACTION parameter specifies which URL the form data should be sent to for further processing. This is most commonly in the cgi-bin directory of a Web server. If you do not specify an action parameter, the contents will be sent to the current document's URL.

The **METHOD** parameter tells how to send the form's contents. There are two possibilities here: Get and Post. If you do not specify a method, Get will be used. Get and Post both format the form's data identically; they differ only in how they pass the form's data to the program that uses that data.

Get and Post both send the forms contents as a single long text vector consisting of a list of WidgetName=WidgetValue pairs, each separated from its successor by an ampersand. For example:

```
"NAME=Tony Potts&Address=aapotts@coriolis.com"
```

(Any & or = sign in a widget name or value will be quoted using the standard ampersand escape; any bare "&" and any "=" sign can therefore be taken as a separator.) You will not necessarily get a name and value for every widget in the form; while empty text is explicitly sent as a WidgetName= with an empty value, unselected radio buttons and check boxes don't send even their name.

Where Get and Post differ is that the Get method creates a "query URL," which consists of the action URL, a question mark, and the formatted form data. The Post method, on the other hand, sends the formatted form data to the action URL in a special data block. The Web server parses the query URL that a Get method creates and passes the form data to the form processing program as a command line parameter. This creates a limitation on form data length that the Post method does not.

Currently, all form data is sent in plain text. This creates a security problem. The optional **ENCTYPE** parameter offers a possible solution, which only allows you to ratify the plain text default. In the future, however, values may be provided that call for an encrypted transmission.

Widgets

From a users' point of view, there are seven types of Web widgets; all of them are generated by one of three HTML tags. Except for the standard buttons, all widgets must be given a name.

<INPUT> Tag

The **<INPUT>** tag is the most versatile, and the most complex. It can create single-line text boxes, radio buttons, check boxes, image maps, the two standard buttons, and the hidden widget. It's somewhat like the **<IMG>** tag in that it appears by itself, not as part of a tag pair, and has some optional parameters. Of these, the **TYPE=** parameter determines both the widget type and the meaning of the other parameters. If no other parameters are provided, the **<INPUT>** tag generates a text box.

The format for the **<INPUT>** tag is:

```
<INPUT TYPE=
    "text"|"password"|"checkbox"|"radio"|"submit"|"reset"|"hidden"|"image"
    NAME="name"
    VALUE="value"
    SIZE="number"
    MAXLENGTH="number"
    CHECKED>
```

The **TYPE** parameter can be set to one of eight values. We'll look at each of these options shortly. Each input must contain a unique name defined with **NAME**. The **VALUE** parameter specifies the initial value of the input. This value is optional. The **SIZE** parameter defines the size of a text line and **MAXLENGTH** is the maximum size allowed for the returned text.

Text Boxes

If the **TYPE=** parameter is set to text (or no parameter is used), the input widget will be a text box. The password input type is just like the text type, except that the value shows only as a series of asterisks. All text areas must have a name. Text areas always report their value, even if it is empty.

Check Boxes And Radio Buttons

Check boxes and radio buttons are created by an **<INPUT>** tag with a checkbox or radio type. Both must have a name and a value parameter, and may be initially checked. The name parameter is the widget's symbolic name, used in returning a value to your Web server, not its onscreen tag. For that, you use normal HTML text next to the **<INPUT>** tag. Since the display tag is not part of the **<INPUT>**

Table A.6 Syntax of the text and password input types.

Attribute	Required?	Format	Meaning
TYPE	No	TYPE="text" or TYPE="password" will be. Default is "text".	Determines what type of widget this
NAME	Yes	NAME="WidgetName"	Identifies the widget.
VALUE	No	VALUE="Default text"	You supply default value. Cannot contain HTML commands.
SIZE	No	SIZE=Cols	Width (in characters) of a single line text area. Default is 20.
SIZE	No	SIZE=Cols,Rows	Height and width (in characters) of a multi-line text area.
MAXLENGTH	No	MAXLENGTH=Chars	Longest value a single line text area can return. Default unlimited.

Table A.7   Syntax of the checkbox and radio types.

Attribute	Required?	Format	Meaning
TYPE	Yes	TYPE=checkbox or TYPE=radio	Determines what type of widget this will be. Default is "text".
NAME	Yes	NAME="WidgetName"	A unique identifier for a checkbox; a group identifier for radio buttons.
VALUE	Yes	VALUE="WidgetValue"	The value is sent if the widget is checked.
CHECKED	No	CHECKED	If this attribute is present, the widget starts out checked.

tag, Netscape check boxes and radio buttons operate differently from their dialog box kin; you cannot toggle a widget by clicking on its text, you have to click on the widget itself.

Radio buttons are grouped by having identical names. Only one (or none) of the group can be checked at any one time; clicking on a radio button will turn off whichever button in the name group was previously on.

Check boxes and radio buttons return their value only if they are checked.

Image Maps

Image maps are created with the **TYPE**="image" code. They return their name and a pair of numbers that represents the position that the user clicked on; the form handling program is responsible for interpreting this pair of numbers. Since this program can do anything you want with the click position, you are not restricted to rectangular anchors, as with **<IMG ISMAP>**.

Clicking on an image map, like clicking on a Submit button, will send all form data to the Web server.

Table A.8   Syntax of the image type.

Attribute	Required?	Format	Meaning
TYPE	Yes	TYPE=image	Determines what type of widget this will be. Default is "text".
NAME	Yes	NAME="WidgetName"	Identifies the widget.
SRC	Yes	SRC="URL"	The URL of a bitmapped image to display.

Submit/Reset Buttons

The submit and reset types let you create one of the two standard buttons. Clicking on a Submit button, like clicking on an image map, will send all form data to the Web server. Clicking on a Reset button resets all widgets in the form to their default values. These buttons are the only widgets that don't need to have names. By default, they will be labeled Submit and Reset; you can specify the button text by supplying a VALUE parameter.

Hidden Fields

A hidden type creates an invisible widget. This widget won't appear onscreen, but its name and value are included in the form's contents when the user presses the Submit button or clicks on an image map. This feature might be used to identify the form to a program that processes several different forms.

Table A.9   Syntax of the submit and reset types.

Attribute	Required?	Format	Meaning
TYPE	Yes	TYPE=submit or TYPE=reset	Determines what type of widget this will be. Default is "text".
NAME	No	NAME="WidgetName"	The buttons never return their values, so a name will never be used.
VALUE	No	VALUE="WidgetValue"	The button text. Default is Submit or Reset, respectively.

Table A.10 Syntax of the hidden type.

Attribute	Required?	Format	Meaning
TYPE	Yes	TYPE=hidden	Determines what type of widget this will be. Default is "text".
NAME	Yes	NAME="WidgetName"	Identifies the widget.
VALUE	Yes	VALUE="WidgetValue"	Whatever constant data you might want to include with the form.

<TextArea> ... </TextArea> Tag

The <TEXTAREA> tag pair is similar to a multi-line text input widget. The primary difference is that you always use a <TextArea> tag pair and put any default text between the <TEXTAREA> and </TEXTAREA> tags. As with <PRE> blocks, any line breaks in the source file are honored, which lets you include line breaks in the default text. The ability to have a long, multi-line default text is the only functional difference between a **TEXTAREA** and a multi-line input widget.

The format for the <**TEXTAREA**> tag is:

```
<TEXTAREA NAME="name"
          ROWS="rows"
          COLS="cols"> </TEXTAREA>
```

<SELECT> ... </SELECT> Tag

The <SELECT> tag pair allows you to present your users with a set of choices. This is not unlike a set of check boxes, yet it takes less room on the screen.

Table A.11 Syntax of the <TEXTAREA> tag.

Attribute	Required?	Format	Meaning
NAME	Yes	NAME="WidgetName"	Identifies the widget.
ROWS	No	ROWS=Rows	TextArea height, in characters.
COLS	No	COLS=Cols	TextArea width, in characters. Default is 20.

Just as you can use check boxes for 0 to N selections, or radio buttons for 0 or 1 selection, you can specify the cardinality of selection behavior. Normally, select widgets act like a set of radio buttons; your users can only select zero or one of the options. However, if you specify the multiple option, the select widget will act like a set of check boxes, and your users may select any or all of the options.

The format for the **<SELECT>** tag is:

```
<SELECT NAME="name"
        SIZE="rows"
        MULTIPLE>text/option list</SELECT>
```

Within the **<SELECT>** tag pair is a series of **<OPTION>** statements, followed by the option text. These are similar to **<LI>** list items, except that **<OPTION>** text may not include any HTML markup. The **<OPTION>** tag may include an optional selected attribute; more than one option may be selected if and only if the **<SELECT>** tag includes the **MULTIPLE** option.

For example:

```
Which Web browsers do you use?
<SELECT NAME="Web Browsers" MULTIPLE>
<OPTION>Netscape
<OPTION>Lynx
<OPTION>WinWeb
<OPTION>Cello
</SELECT>
```

Table A.12 Syntax of the <SELECT> tag.

Attribute	Required?	Format	Meaning
NAME	Yes	NAME="WidgetName"	Identifies the widget.
SIZE	No	SIZE=Rows	This is the widget height, in character rows. If the size is 1, you get a pull-down list. If the size is greater than 1, you get a scrolling list. Default is 1.
MULTIPLE	No	MULTIPLE	Allows more than one option to be selected.

Online Resources

For more information on creating HTML documents, go to the following World Wide Web sites:

A Beginner's Guide to HTML
http://www.ncsa.uiuc.edu/General/Internet/WWW/HTMLPrimer.html

The HTML Quick Reference Guide
http://kuhttp.cc.ukans.edu/lynx_help/HTML_quick.html

Information on the Different Versions of HTML
http://www.w3.org/hypertext/WWW/MarkUp/MarkUp.html

Composing Good HTML
http://www/willamette.edu/html-composition/strict-html.html

HTML+ Specifications
http://info.cern.ch/hypertext/WWW/MarkUp/HTMLPlus/htmlplus_1.html

HTML Specification Version 3.0
http://www.hpl.hp.co.uk/people/dsr/html3/CoverPage.html

HTML Editors
http://akebono.stanford.edu/yahoo/Computers/World_Wide_Web/HTML_Editors/

Resources for Converting Documents to HTML
http://info.cern.ch/hypertext/WWW/Tools/Filters.html

An Archive of Useful HTML Translators
ftp://src.doc.ic.ac.uk/computing/information-systems/www/tools/translators/

Appendix B
VBScript For Visual Basic Users

VBScript is a subset of the Visual Basic language. That means it has most of Visual Basic's features, but leaves out those that aren't relevant to Web page scripting. Table B.1 summarizes the Visual Basic features left out of VBScript.

Table B.1   Visual Basic language features not in VBScript.

Language Feature	Left Out Of VBScript
Arrays	Option Base: declaring arrays whose first slot is numbered something other than 0
Clipboard	Clipboard object: Clear, GetFormat, GetData, SetData, GetText, SetText
Collection	Add, Count, Item, Remove; access to collection elements with !
Conditional compilation	#const, #if...then...#else
Constants and literals	const; all intrinsic Visual Basic constants; exponent-based real numbers; data type suffixes (e.g., &)
Control structures	DoEvents, GoSub...Return, Goto, On Error Goto, On...GoSub, On...Goto, line numbers and line labels, With...End With
Type conversion	Chr$, Hex$, Oct$, CCur, CVar, CVDate, Format, Format$, Str, Str$, Val
Data types	All data types except Variant (but most types are handled implicitly through subtypes of Variant); user-defined types with Type...End Type
Date and time	Date statement, Time statement, Date$, Time$
Dynamic Data Exchange	LinkExecute, LinkPoke, LinkRequest, LinkSend
Debugging	Debug.Print, End, Stop
Declaration	Declare (for declaring DLLs), Property.Get, Property.Let, Property.Set; keywords Public and Private; ParamArray, Optional, New
Error handling	Erl, Error, Error$, On Error...Resume, Resume...Resume Next

continued

Table B.1 Visual Basic language features not in VBScript (Continued).

Language Feature	Left Out Of VBScript
File I/O	All
Financial functions	All
Graphics	Cls, Circle, Line, Point, PSet, Scale, Print, Space, Tab; TextHeight, TextWidth; LoadPicture, SavePicture; QBColor
Miscellaneous	Environ, Environ$, SendKeys, Command, Command$, AppActivate, Shell, Beep
Object manipulation	Arrange, ZOrder, SetFocus; Drag; Hide, Show, Load, Unload, Move; PrintForm, Refresh
Operators	Like
Options	Def type, Option Base, Option Compare, Option Private Module
Printing	TextHeight, TextWidth, EndDoc, NewPage, PrintForm
Strings	All fixed-length strings; LCase$, UCase$; LSet, RSet; Space$, String$; Format, Format$; Left$, Mid$, Right$; Mid statement; Trim$, LTrim$, RTrim$; StrConv
Using classes	TypeName
Optional arguments	IsMissing

what's on the cd-rom

The CD-ROM included with this book contains all the program projects developed in the book, as well as a ton of utility software and images you can use in creating your own Web pages with VBScript.

There are megabytes of multimedia files, clip art files, movie viewers, and paint and image processing programs. There are HTML utilities and editors, such as HotMetal and Microsoft's HTML Assistant for Word. You'll also find graphics programs, Internet utilities, email and FTP programs, reference documents, and scores of other valuable goodies.

So get started activating your Web pages with VBScript and enhancing them with the tools on this CD-ROM!

(One important note: A few example programs in Chapters 11 and 12 use image, sound, and video files that we couldn't include on the CD-ROM because they're copyrighted. As a result, if you want to run those example programs, you'll need to modify them slightly to work with your own image, sound, and video files.)

INDEX

B

C

Serving the Web

Jam-packed with sample Web documents, useful Internet utilities, and complete working Web server software.

Everything you need to set up and run your own Web server

CD-ROM packed with complete Web server software for Windows, sample Web documents, and hot setup utilities

Learn the Secrets of:
- Common Gateway Interface (CGI)
- Perl Scripts
- Server Security and Firewalls
- Mozilla Extensions
- Client Pull and Server Push

CORIOLIS GROUP BOOKS

Robert Jon Mudry

Only $39.99

Call 800-410-0192

Fax (602) 483-0193

Outside U.S.: 602-483-0192

Learn everything you need to know to set up your own Windows-based Web server the easy way. Mudry will show you not only how the Web works, but what available software is needed to publish on the Web, and how to create Web content in HTML. You'll also find the best reference to the Common Gateway Interface (CGI), and you'll discover the best of the available Web server software.

CORIOLIS GROUP BOOKS

http://www.coriolis.com

Microsoft's Internet Explorer 3.0 has taken the online world by storm. MSIE 3.0 sets new standards in interactivity by introducing technology that has other browsers scrambling to keep up—even Netscape. The *Microsoft Internet Explorer 3.0 FrontRunner* puts you in the driver's seat, so you'll be in control of all the technology MSIE has to offer.

Multimedia, ActiveX, MSIE, And The Web

Not long ago, text-based documents ruled the Net. Today, the Internet is a world of images, sound, animation, three dimensional graphics, and interactive games.

As the Net world rapidly expands into a universe, keeping abreast of new developments can prove difficult. You have to keep your eyes (and ears) open to catch the latest technologies. As Internet technologies evolve, MSIE runs more and more Internet applications automatically—but not all of them. We have to undertake the responsibility ourselves to understand what's available; we have to hunt down the applications we need if MSIE doesn't hand them to us.

This chapter introduces you to some hot Internet tools—tools that will help you get the most out of your Internet explorations and get a jump on today's technologies. Some tools are bundled with MSIE, others you'll have to download. I suggest you download the applications you need now, because a year from now, you'll be on your own (unless, of course, we meet again in the next edition of this book).

1

Let's start this chapter's multimedia discussion slowly, reviewing frames and audio applications first. Then, we can pick up some speed as we check out video and mixed-media applications. After that, I suggest we take an introductory look at Java and ActiveX—programming applications sure to change the way we use the Internet for years to come. Finally, let's close out the chapter with an exploration of the world of virtual reality and 3D programs.

Frames

Before we dive headfirst into the flashing lights and sirens of the Net, we need to address *frames*—one of the newest Internet features. Frame technology allows Web pages to be divided into several panes called *frames*. Each frame displays a different HTML page with a unique URL, so you can view a number of different Web pages at once. Figure 1 shows Microsoft's sample page for using frames. To test the linking capabilities of frames, let's go to the sample page at **http://www.microsoft.com/ie/showcase/howto_3/ volcano3.htm** (*Note:* Microsoft has updated the Volcano Coffee Company site with a later version, but I'm leaving Figure 1 here because it's a good example of how frames and links interact. Microsoft has left past versions of their Volcano Coffee Company sample pages online, so you should be able to access this page as you read this book.)

If you click on the Ancient Art, Gift Packs, or Catalog link, the frame to the right of the links displays the resulting information. As you can see, MSIE supports borderless frames, as well as frames without scroll bars. The elimination of borders and scrollbars on frames allows for a seamless, almost magazine appearance to Web pages.

While frames add a graphic elegance to Web pages, they are also extremely useful. Frames allow Web pages to offer sophisticated layouts that can mix a variety of sounds, video, animation, and background colors and patterns in one place. Plus, with multiple frames, information can be organized more effectively. For example, Figure 1 illustrates how menu links in one frame can display linked information in a separate frame.

Floating Frames

Another frame innovation available with MSIE is the *floating frame*. Floating frames essentially enable you to open a browser within a browser—a window

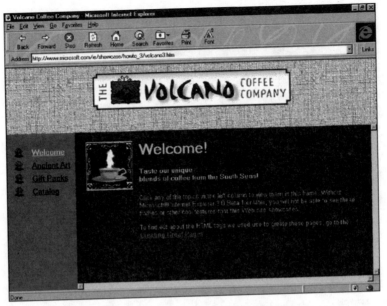

Figure 1   Frames allow you to view multiple Web pages at once.

to the Net within your browser's window. Floating frames can appear anywhere images can appear, and they can be designed to display in any size, with or without borders. Microsoft's example of a floating frame displays in Figure 2 and can be found at **http://www.microsoft.com/ie/htmlext/ samples/fframeex.htm**.

You can click on a hypertext cinema link, as shown in Figure 2. Clicking on a cinema link displays movie times in the floating frame, while leaving the remainder of the page unchanged. In the previous example, I clicked on the Renton Cinema link to display the movie times for that theater. This example is very simplistic, but you get the idea.

Pop-up Frames

Yet another frame feature supported by MSIE is the capability for Web designers to include pop-up menus on Web pages. Microsoft provides an example of pop-up menus in its latest version of the Volcano Coffee Company sample page, as shown in Figure 3.

In Figure 3, clicking on the image of a Volcano Coffee product, such as the coffee cup, results in a pop-up menu that you can use to order the product.

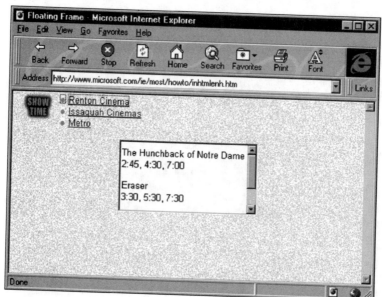

Figure 2 MSIE supports floating frames, which act as a browser within the browser.

The most recent version of the Volcano Coffee Company site is a good place to look for some of the latest frame innovations running today. You

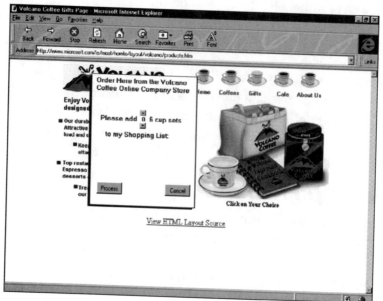

Figure 3 MSIE supports pop-up menu frames, which act as Web site dialog boxes.

can visit the latest Volcano Company site at **http://www.microsoft.com/ ie/most/howto/layout/volcano/Volcano.htm**.

Frame Exploration

Exploring frames is similar to exploring basic Internet pages. You can click on links, refresh, and go backwards and forwards within the frame. Depending on the design of a page, clicking on links within a frame might take you to another page within the same frame, or it might change the display in another frame on your screen. To refresh a particular frame (as opposed to refreshing the entire page), right-click in a frame and select the Refresh command. To go backward or forward within a frame, click in the frame, then press the Backspace key to go backward or press Shift+Backspace to move forward.

Don't worry if you get lost while exploring frames. Over time, you will become comfortable with them. Soon enough, everyone will take frames for granted, but in the meantime, rest assured that frames are a new exploration tool for even the most veteran surfers.

Audio: Surfing With Sound Waves

Before you can listen to audio files, your system has to be the proud owner of a sound card. Most systems sold today come with sound cards, so running audio files shouldn't be a problem. I'm going to introduce you to three types of sound applications: MIDI files, sound clips, and RealAudio.

MIDI Files

Think back to Chapter 5. Remember when we were setting up the MSN start page, and we had the option to play background music? That background music came in the form of a Musical Instrument Digital Interface (MIDI) file. MIDI files are digitized computer music files, usually carrying the file extension .MID. The popularity of MIDI files stems from the fact that the files are fast and small compared to other sound formats. MSIE comes already equipped to play MIDI files. Some MIDI files play automatically when a page opens, others have to be opened or downloaded.

If a MIDI file plays as part of a Web page, you probably won't see a MIDI recorder. However, if you are opening or downloading a MIDI file, you'll probably see a recorder similar to Figure 4.

Saving MIDI files to disk.

If you happen upon a MIDI file that you like, you can save it to disk. After you are finished listening to the recording, open your cache file (C:\Windows\Temporary Internet Files). Your cache file saves a copy of the MIDI file as a cached document, which you can then copy to another directory. From that point, you can rename and manipulate the file to suit your needs.

Basically, the MSIE MIDI recorder consists of a Pause button, a Stop button, and a File Meter (the bar showing how much of the MIDI clip has played). You can adjust the music loudness by adjusting your system or speaker volume controls. There are a couple good sites with lists of links to MIDI files. I'm willing to bet that you can find enough links to meet your MIDI needs at **http://www.flexfx.com**, **http://xraent.uel.ac.uk**, and **http://www.tst-medhat.com/midi**. (Choose to view this last site with frames, and you'll get a nice sampling of frame technology along with your MIDI file exploration.)

Sound Clips

Sound clips are similar to MIDI files in that they are music files, and you might have to download the file before you can listen to it. Usually sound clips carry the extensions .AU, .AIFF, .SND, and .WAV. Samples of sound clips can be found everywhere. Remember in Chapter 12 when we visited the Froggy Page (**http://www.cs.yale.edu/homes/sjl/froggy.html**) and listened to frog noises? Those were AU sound clip files. Sound clips differ from MIDI files because sound clips can be much more than digitally synthesized music.

Figure 4   The MIDI file recorder displays when you open or download a MIDI file.

MSIE recognizes sound clips automatically—you don't need to add any special features to your browser to play a sound clip. Most of the time, MSIE displays a recorder complete with a File Meter and Play, Pause, Stop, and Done buttons when you click on a sound clip, as shown in Figure 5.

As with MIDI files, you can adjust the volume using your system or speaker volume controls. Sound clips are not as compact as MIDI files, so you might have to wait while your computer downloads the files. There are a couple good sites to visit to listen to sound clip samples. For example, check out the WWW TV Theme Songs home page at **http:// ai.eecs.umich.edu/people/kennyp/tv2/tvtemp.html** for a great collection of AU files. And for hundreds more AU audio file samples, check out **http: //sunsite.unc.edu/pub/multimedia/sun-sounds**.

RealAudio

I've saved the most advanced audio system for last—RealAudio. RealAudio enables you to obtain instantaneous feedback from audio files via the Internet. With RealAudio, you can listen to good quality live and recorded music, speeches, newscasts, radio broadcasts, simulcasts, audio greetings, and sound effects. To run RealAudio, you need to have a 14.4 Kbps modem (28.8 Kbps to play music), a 486/33 SX processor or higher, 4 MB of RAM, 2 MB of disk space, and a 16-bit sound card. RealAudio files, which are popping up all over the Net, carry the .RA or .RAM extensions. Fortunately, MSIE already bundles the RealAudio player with your browser. The RealAudio player, shown in Figure 6, appears whenever you click on a RealAudio application.

Figure 5   Listening to a sound clip.

RealAudio Player: nc6y1601.ra

File View Clip Sites Help

> / II ■

Title: All Things Considered - July 16, 1996

Author: National Public Radio

Copyright: 1996

Playing 14.4 network stream 08:21.1 / 51:40.3

Figure 6 **Using the RealAudio Player.**

Notice the RealAudio player is more advanced than the two audio players we viewed previously. When you use RealAudio, you can play, pause, and stop the player; change the volume; view the status bar; and use the menu bar to change your display settings or go to another RealAudio site.

Along with the CNN Interactive page (which we've viewed previously), there are a couple RealAudio sites worth noting. First, you should visit the RealAudio home page at **http://www.realaudio.com**. This page offers links to ABC and NPR news audio sites, as well as directs you to tips and information about using RealAudio. A second must-hear RealAudio page is AudioNet (**http://www.audionet.com**), shown in Figure 7. AudioNet links you to live radio broadcasts from across the nation. Now you can listen to radio news and music while you download files or browse the Web.

There are other audio-streaming technologies out there, but RealAudio is by far the most popular and the easiest to use with MSIE.

Animated Graphics

After audio, but before video and mixed media, comes the animated graphic. The most popular form of animated graphic is the animated GIF file.

Animated GIFs

You're probably familiar with GIFs, because GIF files are common graphic files. *Animated GIFs* are GIF files layered on top of other GIF files to produce the effect of an animation. Animated GIFs are small (averaging around 2 K) and easy to use (you can save and copy them just like graphics). To see

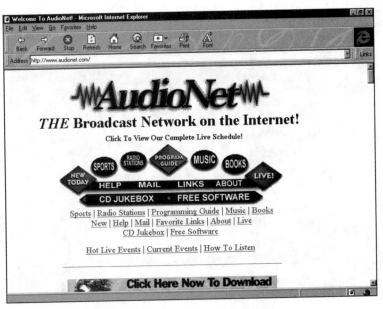

Figure 7   Listening to live radio broadcasts using RealAudio.

some examples of animated GIFs, visit the MMMM Animated Icon Browser Web site at **http://www.teleport.com/~cooler/MMMM/giving index.html**.

To view some of the animated GIFs on the MMMM Animated Icon Browser page, click on a topic button, such as the Misc. button near the bottom-left corner of the page. When icons display in the main window, click on an icon and the animated GIF will display in the top-right frame (disregard MMMM's Netscape comment—MSIE can display animated GIFs as well as the next guy). Figure 8 displays the Misc. page of animated icons after selecting the dancing skeleton icon.

Your cursor in the groove.

If you are interested in animated cursors (which are mostly ANI files and animated GIF files), you should visit Dierk's List of Animated Cursors at http:// ourworld.compuserve.com/homepages/dierk/moreani.htm. Dierk's page lists over 2500 animated cursors, in addition to instructions on how to download, install, and create animated cursors. While you are strolling through Dierk's park, check out his Cool Links—he's listed over 700 cool sites for you to visit!

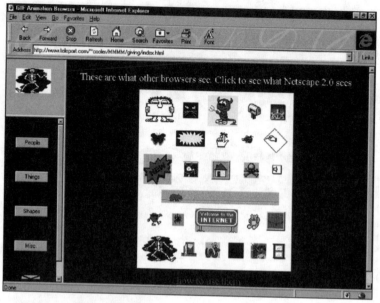

Figure 8   Viewing animated GIF files.

Video And Mixed Media

So far you've experienced frames, sound files, and animated graphics. Now comes true multimedia: video and mixed media. MSIE's incorporation of ActiveX and ActiveMovie means your multimedia experiences are simplified. No more downloading plug-ins if you don't want to (and if you don't know what plug-ins are—don't worry; you won't need to mess with plug-ins as long as you surf the Net using MSIE).

ActiveMovie

As an MSIE user, ActiveMovie will serve many of your video, audio, and multimedia needs. ActiveMovie is Microsoft's innovative approach to incorporating the best of today's multimedia offerings by providing integrated video and audio services. Best of all, ActiveMovie is built into your version of MSIE. Because of Microsoft's new ActiveMovie technology, you can play popular media formats on the Web efficiently, including MPEG audio and video, AVI, QuickTime, AU, WAV, MIDI, and AIFF. In addition, ActiveMovie includes MPEG playback for full-screen, television-quality video on mainstream computer systems; playback and streaming of all popular media types on the Internet; and a flexible, extendible architecture so future technologies can be integrated easily. To find out more about ActiveMovie, check out Microsoft's Interactive Movie Technologies home page at **http://www.microsoft.com/imedia/activemovie/activem.htm** shown in Figure 9.

Shockwave

An extremely popular application, Shockwave enables users to view animation, movies, and other types of multimedia presentations on the Internet. Using Shockwave, designers can deliver rich multimedia Internet experiences to viewers by adding animation, buttons, links, digitized video movies, sound, and more to their Web sites.

Shockwave, brought to you by the folks at Macromedia, works in conjunction with MSIE to bring you the fabulous world of multimedia. To see how your shocked version of MSIE works, visit the Macromedia site (**http://www.macromedia.com/shockwave**), shown in Figure 10. I suggest you go directly to the game page to see the best Shockwave action around.

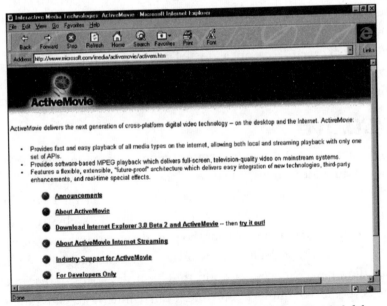

Figure 9 Microsoft's Interactive Movie Technologies page provides helpful information about ActiveMovie.

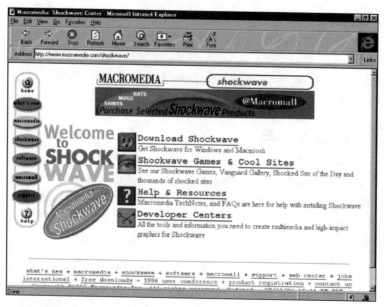

Figure 10   The Macromedia Shockwave page.

QuickTime

QuickTime is another application supported by MSIE's integrated ActiveMovie feature. Quicktime provides full-motion video with digitized sound. QuickTime, from Apple Corporation, enables you to view movies inside Web pages. To try out a QuickTime application, visit the QuickTime home page at **http://quicktime.apple.com/qt/qthome.html**. I suggest you click on the *Samples* icon to view some of the cool sites using QuickTime.

VDOLive

VDOLive offers realtime (streaming) video and audio over the Internet, and, as an added bonus, MSIE can play VDOLive applications without any tweaking on your part. All you have to do is click on a video link—no downloading or configuring plug-ins required. Web sites proffering VDOLive links go beyond static Web page design and advance into Internet video broadcasting. VDOLive is used for a wide range of applications, including news services, vacation tours, music videos, movie premieres, and corporate communications, and it can handle video clips ranging from several seconds to several hours, serving both Internet and intranet users.

VDOLive enables Web site designers to incorporate video into their pages and eliminates lengthy download times for users. To get your fill of information on this new technology, visit the VDOLive home page at **http://www.vdo.net**. Click on the VDOLive Gallery graphic link to view some cool VDOLive sites.

Multimedia Programming Tools

If you've surfed the Net, you've heard the news—multimedia programming is hotter than the streets of Arizona in July. With the advent of Java and ActiveX programming tools, multimedia elements on the Web have become more dynamic and interactive than ever. By this time next year, you'll be wondering how you ever managed without the instant interactivity that is about to descend upon you within the next few months. From the user's perspective, Java and ActiveX give you more, while you do less (sounds too good to be true, but that's the nature of this beast). Java and ActiveX open up a whole new realm of programming tools, enabling programmers and designers to hold a stronger reign over their creative endeavors. Let's take a quick look at Java and ActiveX. Don't expect to become programmers from reading this section—this is strictly an introduction to the terms, so you'll know what people are talking about when they drop some techno-jargon on you.

Java

If you've ever surfed before, you've heard about Java. Java is a new multimedia programming tool that allows you to see and interact with animation built into Web pages. Using Java technology, icons wave at you, game pieces move on your screen, and realtime charts and graphs update automatically (popular with Wall Street stock market sites). Java, created by Sun Microsystems, uses applets, which are mini programs embedded in Web sites. The MSIE browser comes Java enabled, so you don't have to do anything extra to view a Java applet. (In fact, you've probably already seen a lot of applets without even knowing it.) When you go to a site that has Java, MSIE temporarily transfers the applet to your computer for your use. Visit Sun Microsystems (**http://www.javasoft.com**), the creators of Java, for more information.

You can also read about Java in the Java World online magazine, located at **http://www.javaworld.com** and shown in Figure 11.

Finally, the best way to see Java's presence on the Internet is to visit sites sporting Java applets. A great site with a full supply of Java applets is the Gamelan Java directory at **http://www.gamelan.com**, a major source of Java links and information.

Gamelan provides all kinds of links to cool Java applets. You could start your tour by clicking on the Special Features link. Next, and this isn't just a cheap excuse to fool around, I suggest you scroll down the page and click on the Our Favorite Games link. Games provide an excellent illustration of Java capabilities. In addition, I've provided a little more play-and-learn encouragement by listing a couple Java games appearing on the Gamelan site (not all of them are listed on the Our Favorite Games list). Figure 12 displays a recent Pick-of-the-Week game called Iceblox.

Iceblox—Penguins playing with fire
http://www.tdb.uu.se/~karl/java/iceblox.html

Figure 11   Reading up on Java in the Java World online magazine.

Figure 12   Playing Iceblox—a Java-enabled game.

Tetris—The traditional falling blocks game
http://www.lookup.com/Homepages/96457/blocks.html

Flip—A well done version of Othello
http://www.theglobe.com/fungames/flip/flip.html

NetCell—Competition Solitaire on the Net (May be addictive!)
http://www.cd.com/netcell

Crossword—Updated every night at midnight
http://www.starwave.com/people/haynes/xword.html

ActiveX

ActiveX is Microsoft's step beyond Java. ActiveX incorporates Internet interactivity with application interactivity, enabling hassle-free local and Internet access to all types of applications and files. Are you wondering what that just meant? OK, here are some examples of how ActiveX technology might affect you. ActiveX enables you to view QuickTime files (as we just saw) even though you don't have the QuickTime application on your system. ActiveX controls Java applets, so that Java applets—like all

ActiveX components—can be supported by any application, not just MSIE and other Internet browsers. ActiveX allows non-HTML content, such as spreadsheets, to be inserted into HTML files, enabling Internet accessibility to non-HTML documents. It may seem very convoluted right now, but as you see what happens with Internet interactivity, you'll understand the flexibility gained with ActiveX.

Now, back to the techie-side of things. ActiveX is a stripped-down implementation of *OLE (Object Linking and Embedding)* technology designed to run over slow Internet links (a.k.a. telephone modems). OLE allows an editor, such as Word, to "farm out" part of a document to another editor, such as Excel, then reimport it. ActiveX uses the same technology on the Internet level. When ActiveX is fully implemented, you will be able to use your browser to run HTML documents as well as other applications. In addition, you will be able to run Internet files, such as Java and HTML documents, in your desktop applications. You will be able to use your browser to open a spreadsheet on the Web, complete with its own toolbar, or you will be able to browse the Internet from your local spreadsheet application. Fortunately, MSIE enables ActiveX controls to install automatically when you download documents and applications. Once installed, the ActiveX controls run the Web page contents. You will not need to download any additional files or applications.

ActiveX is a dramatic step toward Microsoft's vision of complete interactivity; netizens sit (in front of their monitors) in anticipation of the changes sure to accompany ActiveX. Eventually, Microsoft envisions users moving from desktop, to Internet, to intranet without noticeable transition—sounds good to me! For more information on ActiveX, Microsoft provides a number of sites. You can visit the ActiveX pages offered on the Internet Explorer site at **http://www.microsoft.com/ie/ie3**. Or, you can check out Microsoft's new Site Builder Workshop at **http://www.microsoft.com/workshop**.

Better yet, run a search on ActiveX using SavvySearch or the Microsoft Search engine, and you'll pull up all kinds of information on this hot new technology.

The Future: Surfing in 3D

Beyond interactive application technology lies the possibility of entirely new worlds. You've probably heard of virtual reality. The Internet brings us its version of virtual reality using Virtual Reality Modeling Language (VRML). In turn, MSIE enables you to exist in virtual reality by supporting the full integration of VRML, without opening a separate browser. VRML is the language used to create digitized virtual realities. 3D virtual realities are starting to pop up on the Internet, and no doubt they will be commonplace before long. WorldView and Alpha World are two 3D applications that seem to stand out at the moment (keep in mind, as with most Internet technologies, statements like that can fall apart in a matter of hours). Regardless of the Internet's rapid change, I'm including this short discussion on 3D applications because, whether WorldView or Alpha World specifically makes it, 3D technology is here to stay and will influence future Internet technologies.

WorldView

WorldView is a VRML application that allows you to navigate through virtual reality sites as a standalone application or through Microsoft's Internet Explorer. WorldView is the first browser to incorporate Microsoft's powerful Reality Lab 3D software, which enables realtime manipulation of 3D objects on the Internet. The WorldView home page, shown in Figure 13, is located at **http://www.webmaster.com/vrml**.

Netizens entering the dimension of WorldView experience realtime, full-color, 3D "worlds" over the Internet. WorldView is simple to use and offers fast and accurate rendering for average complexity 3D objects. Other features include:

- Easy navigation through fully rendered, 3D VRML worlds

- Smooth, fully controllable movements

- Easy access to your designated home world

- Controllable image quality

- Variable speed of movement

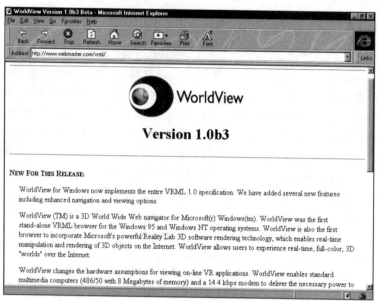

Figure 13   Entering the dimension of WorldView.

- A helpful Information Center

- Controllable lighting

- User-designated background color or texture

- The ability to save different camera views

- A hot list of favorite places

- Animation control

Microsoft recently licensed WorldView technology to be included in the new multimedia toolkit BlackBird. Through this license, WorldView potentially may become the most widely available and used 3D application on the market.

Alpha World

Alpha World, a virtual world on the Web, is the latest project of the people who developed Worlds Chat. Alpha World utilizes VRML to create an interactive world that allows visitors to manipulate it as they wish. Alpha World, displayed in Figure 14, is located at **http://www.worlds. net/alphaworld**.

In Alpha World, residents build their own environments and interact with each other. Residents can acquire and develop property, assume online personas, and interact in and with a living, breathing, multiuser community. Alpha World is not a preprogrammed simulation—it is as unpredictable and unique as the residents who create it. As of this writing, Alpha World isn't completed yet, and it only appears as a beta release. The good news is that membership is free while beta testing continues. Unless you're using a 28.8 Kbps modem, be prepared for long download times and jerky motion.

Chapter In Review

Well, we've come to the end of the chapter. As you've probably learned, the more you play on the Net, the greater your astonishment. Additionally, the more you learn, the more you sense the continual flux of the Internet's evolution. That's okay—in fact, it's good, because that's what makes it all so exciting. Maybe we can talk about it in a virtual world sometime, sipping coffee while we shoot the breeze and watch Net activities march past our virtual window.

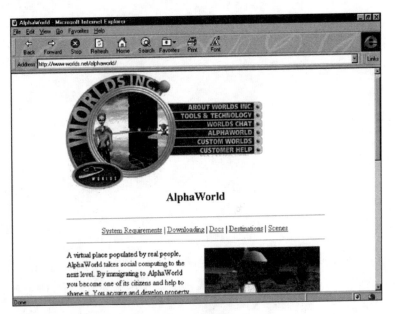

Figure 14   Visiting the residents in Alpha World.

As it is, we've merely caught a glimpse of the Internet's parade (in which the majorettes have barely begun to march). With the rapid advancement of ActiveX and Java technologies, the way you use your computer is about to change. Soon your movement from desktop to disk, to Internet, to local area networks will be so fluid and efficient, that you won't give your file manipulation efforts a second thought. One minute, you'll be viewing a file that's at least a five-hour flight away; the next minute, you'll be copying a file to your desktop from the server down the hall; and to top it off, your email will be running while you're writing a report on your desktop, illustrated with Java applets and links to the Internet. Of course, high-quality videos and realtime sound effects will compliment your seamless explorations throughout the day. And from the sounds of the drums, that day isn't too far away. The best thing you can do now is to grab a good spot on the curb—that way you'll be ready to join the parade when it gets to your block.